The One Year Book of PSALMS

The ONE YEAR® BOOK OF

Devotionals written by

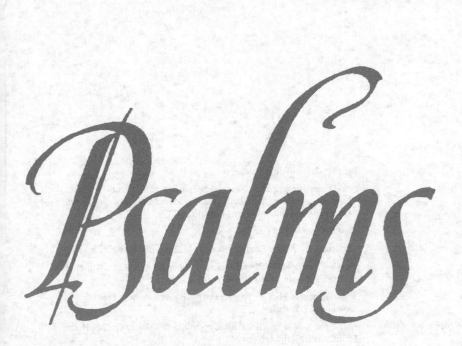

Psalms

William J. Petersen and
Randy Petersen

Tyndale House Publishers
Carol Stream, Illinois

Visit Tyndale online at tyndale.com.

For information about special discounts for bulk purchases, please contact Tyndale House Publishers at csresponse@tyndale.com, or call 1-855-277-9400.

ISBN 978-0-8423-4372-5

Printed in China

28 27 26 25 24 23
10 9   8   7   6   5

PREFACE

For millennia people have been singing, reading, praying, and meditating on the Psalms. Through all ages, believers have rejoiced in the Psalms, repented through them, and found immense comfort in them. In the sixth century B.C., Jews in captivity sang them tearfully in Babylon. Five hundred years later Jesus and his disciples sang them in the upper room. Christians in Rome, meeting in secret, began the day by singing Psalm 73 and closed it by singing Psalm 141.

After the persecution of Christians ceased, one church father remarked, "Of other Scripture, most men know nothing, but the Psalms are learned by heart and are repeated in homes, streets, and shops." In 1512 Martin Luther began his public career with lectures on the Psalms. In 1620 Pilgrims launched the *Mayflower* by singing a psalm and landed in the New World singing another one. One of the first books printed in America was the *Bay Psalm Book*.

The Psalms are exquisite poetry, crisp theology, and stirring history, but they are far more than all that. Most of all, they are intensely personal. The Psalms meet us where we are, and they take us to where we ought to be. You don't have to dress up for the Psalms. Come as you are. The writers were honest, sometimes embarrassingly honest, about their thoughts and feelings. They were often baffled by what was going on, just as we are. They fell short, just as we do. They got discouraged and disheartened—so what else is new? The Psalms mirror life as it really is, presenting the whole drama of humanity in a few pages. And somehow, when you finish, you end up trusting and praising a God who is your protector, your hope, and your friend.

In preparing this book, we tried to capture the diversity of the Psalms. Besides the Scripture portion from the New Living Translation and the daily devotional reading, you will find an appropriate hymn stanza. We have also added other tidbits, quotes, and facts about particular psalms.

We trust that when you finish this *One Year Book of Psalms*, you will say along with Martin Luther, "I love them all."

We join with the psalmist in saying, "How good it is to sing praises to our God," and we thank him for his blessing upon us as we wrote these devotionals. We also want to thank Ardythe Petersen, researcher, collaborator, and organizer; David Barrett, editor; and Warren Wiersbe, encourager and bibliographer.

BOOK ONE (PSALMS 1–41)
PSALM 1

[1] Oh, the joys of those
  who do not follow the advice of the wicked,
  or stand around with sinners,
  or join in with scoffers.

[2] But they delight in doing everything the LORD wants;
  day and night they think about his law.

[3] They are like trees planted along the riverbank,
  bearing fruit each season without fail.
Their leaves never wither,
  and in all they do, they prosper.

[4] But this is not true of the wicked.
  They are like worthless chaff, scattered by the wind.

[5] They will be condemned at the time of judgment.
  Sinners will have no place among the godly.

[6] For the LORD watches over the path of the godly,
  but the path of the wicked leads to destruction.

In A.D.386 the great Bible translator Jerome began his work in the little town of Bethlehem—almost four centuries after Jesus was born there and fourteen centuries after King David was born there. It took Jerome twenty-three years to complete his translation of the Scriptures from Greek and Hebrew into Latin and thereby fulfill his dream "to give my Latin readers the hidden treasures." His translation, the Vulgate, was valued as the authorized Latin version of the Scriptures for centuries.

Jerome loved the entire Bible, but he took special delight in the Psalms. His favorite verse was Psalm 1:2: "They delight in doing everything the Lord wants; day and night they think about his law." Jerome knew, as did the psalmist, that spending time with God's Word is the key to joyful living.

When Joshua stood on the shores of the Jordan ready to lead the Israelites into the Promised Land, he was given a similar message: "Study this Book of the Law continually. Meditate on it day and night. . . . Only then will you succeed" (Joshua 1:8).

If you want to be joyful, if you wish to be truly successful, make it a priority to study God's Word this year. Like Jerome's readers, you will find that God's Word is full of hidden treasures just waiting to be claimed.

> The law of God is my delight,
> That cloud by day, the fire by night,
> Shall be my comfort in distress
> And guide me through life's wilderness.
> JAMES MONTGOMERY

A Word on Words

In Hebrew the word for "think about" carries the sense of someone gently uttering, as though contemplating and repeating words from an enchanting verse.

Notable Quotable

"In the day of his prosperity he sings psalms out of the Word of God, and in the night of his affliction he comforts himself with promises out of the same book."
CHARLES HADDON SPURGEON

PSALM 2:1-6

¹ Why do the nations rage?
   Why do the people waste their time with futile plans?
² The kings of the earth prepare for battle;
   the rulers plot together
against the LORD
   and against his anointed one.
³ "Let us break their chains," they cry,
   "and free ourselves from this slavery."

⁴ But the one who rules in heaven laughs.
   The Lord scoffs at them.
⁵ Then in anger he rebukes them,
   terrifying them with his fierce fury.
⁶ For the LORD declares, "I have placed my chosen king
      on the throne
   in Jerusalem, my holy city."

*I*n its first three hundred years the Christian church endured repeated waves of persecution, but perhaps the worst came while Diocletian was emperor of Rome (A.D.284–305). Convinced that the Christians were conspiring against him, Diocletian sought to annihilate them throughout his empire, and he ordered entire towns to be massacred.

But, as Psalm 2:4 recognizes, the one who rules in heaven is sovereign over the wicked, and he will have the last laugh.

Back home in Diocletian's palace his own wife and daughter were turning to Christ. And after his death a new emperor by the name of Constantine took the throne. Constantine became a Christian, and Christianity eventually became the favored religion of the entire Roman Empire.

Similarly, in the story of the Exodus, Pharaoh thought he had subdued the Israelites when he ordered the drowning of all their baby boys. Little did he realize that his own daughter would give a princely education to one of those babies, Moses, who would eventually lead the Israelites out of Egypt. Again, God had the last laugh.

You may not have to face a Diocletian or a Pharaoh this year, but you will face opposition to your faith. As you look ahead with perhaps some trepidation, remember that the King of kings and Lord of lords is on your side, and he will have the last laugh.

> Our God the Father from his throne
> Laughs at their pride, their rage controls
> He'll vex their hearts with pains unknown
> And speak in thunder to their souls.
> OLD SCOTTISH PSALTER

A Word on Words
In verse 2 the Hebrew word for "anointed one" is messiah. The Greek word for this is christ.

Bible Networking
There are only three places in Scripture where God is depicted as laughing—here as well as in Psalms 37:13 and 59:8.

Notable Quotable
"We should not judge God's drama until the final act."
THOMAS ADAMS

PSALM 2:7-12

⁷ The king proclaims the LORD's decree:
"The LORD said to me, 'You are my son.
Today I have become your Father.
⁸ Only ask, and I will give you the nations as your
inheritance,
the ends of the earth as your possession.
⁹ You will break them with an iron rod
and smash them like clay pots.' "

¹⁰ Now then, you kings, act wisely!
Be warned, you rulers of the earth!
¹¹ Serve the LORD with reverent fear,
and rejoice with trembling.
¹² Submit to God's royal son, or he will become angry,
and you will be destroyed in the midst of your
pursuits—
for his anger can flare up in an instant.
But what joy for all who find protection in him!

*O*ne night in Jerusalem, God gave his prophet Nathan a message to relay to King David. The message was this: "I will be his father, and he will be my son. . . . My unfailing love will not be taken from him" (2 Samuel 7:14-15). Quite a message!

When David received the Lord's message, he was overwhelmed, "Who am I, O Sovereign Lord? . . . Do you deal with everyone this way? . . . You know what I am really like." (2 Samuel 7:18-20). Years earlier, when David was only a shepherd boy, God had anointed him to be king. But now God called him his son. To David, it was a higher honor to be God's son than to be king.

In the New Testament, Jesus is the great fulfillment of this psalm. He is God's Son (see Matthew 3:17; Acts 13:33, Hebrews 1:5; 5:5; and 2 Peter 1:17), and, like David, he has been anointed and appointed by God. Unlike David, however, Jesus is also God (John 1:18).

Amazingly, God says that we, too, can become his sons and daughters. The apostle John writes that all who have believed and accepted Jesus Christ have the right to become God's children (John 1:12). As you read Psalm 2, reflect on the wonderful privilege you have been given to become a child of God through God's unique Son, and give God praise.

> *Praise, my soul, the King of heaven,*
> *To his feet thy tribute bring.*
> *Ransomed, healed, restored, forgiven,*
> *Who like me his praise shall sing?*
> *Alleluia! Alleluia!*
> *Praise the everlasting King!*
> HENRY F. LYTE

Fascinating Fact
"The first psalm is the outer door of practical insight with a prophetic close; the second psalm is the inner door of prophetic insight with a practical close."
JOHN KER

PSALM 3

A psalm of David, regarding the time David fled from his son Absalom.

[1] O LORD, I have so many enemies;
   so many are against me.
[2] So many are saying,
   "God will never rescue him!"   *Interlude*

[3] But you, O LORD, are a shield around me,
   my glory, and the one who lifts my head high.
[4] I cried out to the LORD,
   and he answered me from his holy mountain.
                                          Interlude

[5] I lay down and slept.
   I woke up in safety,
   for the LORD was watching over me.
[6] I am not afraid of ten thousand enemies
   who surround me on every side.

[7] Arise, O LORD!
   Rescue me, my God!
Slap all my enemies in the face!
   Shatter the teeth of the wicked!

[8] Victory comes from you, O LORD.
   May your blessings rest on your people.   *Interlude*

*I*n the sixteenth century the Huguenots of France were known for their psalm singing. They sang when they ate, they sang when they worked, they sang when they worshiped. They even sang when they were persecuted or when they were going into battle. In battle, psalms were chanted whenever sentries took their posts. The chanting of certain psalms signified certain things. Chanting Psalm 3 signaled danger. Whenever a Huguenot heard this psalm, he knew an attack by the enemy was imminent.

That must have been the way David felt when he wrote Psalm 3. His son Absalom was trying to usurp the throne, enemy armies were pursuing him, and he didn't know which friends he could count on. David and his contingent of soldiers had hastily crossed the Jordan River during the night, not knowing what would happen in the hours of darkness (see 2 Samuel 17:22). The situation seemed hopeless. Despite the anxiety, however, David continued to trust in the Lord as his shield, his glory, and the one who lifted his head.

When danger seems imminent, will you trust God as David did? Will you look to the Lord as your shield, your glory, and the one who lifts your head?

> *I cried and from his holy hill*
> *He bowed a listening ear.*
> *I called my Father and my God*
> *And he subdued my fear.*
> ISAAC WATTS

Bible Networking
Read the story of David's flight from Absalom in 2 Samuel 15–17.

Notable Quotable
"Though David had many enemies, the Lord was his shield. Though his enemies were putting him to shame, the Lord was his glory. And though they had publicly humiliated him, the Lord lifted his head high."
MARTIN LUTHER

PSALM 4
For the choir director: A psalm of David, to be accompanied by stringed instruments.

¹ Answer me when I call,
    O God who declares me innocent.
Take away my distress.
    Have mercy on me and hear my prayer.

² How long will you people ruin my reputation?
    How long will you make these groundless
        accusations?
    How long will you pursue lies?   *Interlude*

³ You can be sure of this:
    The LORD has set apart the godly for himself.
    The LORD will answer when I call to him.

⁴ Don't sin by letting anger gain control over you.
    Think about it overnight and remain silent.   *Interlude*
⁵ Offer proper sacrifices,
    and trust in the LORD.

⁶ Many people say, "Who will show us better times?"
    Let the smile of your face shine on us, LORD.
⁷ You have given me greater joy
    than those who have abundant harvests of grain and
        wine.

⁸ I will lie down in peace and sleep,
    for you alone, O LORD, will keep me safe.

*S*ome think David wrote Psalm 4 the evening after he wrote Psalm 3, when Absalom's army was tightening the noose around David and his soldiers. Others believe it was written during a famine that caused the Israelites to consider following other gods (see verses 6-7).

Regardless of which theory is correct, David was in a tight spot (which is what the Hebrew word for "distress" in verse 1 literally means) when he wrote this psalm. Yet, despite his difficulties, David basked in God's smile, and that gave him all the comfort he needed.

About 150 years later Elijah the prophet was in a difficult situation like David's. He, too, was in a tight spot—faced with starvation on the other side of the Jordan River. But Elijah discovered that God can work in mysterious ways to rescue his people. Elijah was fed by ravens, of all things (1 Kings 17:6).

Throughout history God's people have continued to experience his peace time and again. Saint Augustine said Psalm 4 should be sung aloud before the whole world as a testimony of the peace God gives in the midst of both inward and outward trouble. Martin Luther agreed. This psalm was a favorite of his. In fact, he asked a composer to put the final verse of this psalm to music so that it could be sung at his funeral. Luther wanted the world to know that he was basking in the peace and confidence of God's smile.

> *If you will only let God guide you,*
> *And hope in him through all your ways,*
> *Whatever comes, he'll stand beside you,*
> *To bear you through the evil days;*
> *Who trusts in God's unchanging love*
> *Builds on the rock that cannot move.*
> GEORG NEUMARK

Bible Networking
For more on the light of God's smile upon us, see Numbers 6:24-26; Psalm 119:135; and 2 Corinthians 4:6.

Notable Quotable
"It is better to enjoy him without anything else than to enjoy everything else without him."
WILLIAM SECKER

The Psalms are honest, poetic expressions of the experiences, thoughts, and emotions of David and others as they followed God. Many of these spiritual songs are also prayers. Various kinds of psalms were written for different purposes and circumstances, and they can generally be grouped into five categories. These categories are listed below along with an example of each.

◆ *Individual prayers* (often poignant pleas for help)
Have compassion on me, LORD, for I am weak.
  Heal me, LORD, for my body is in agony.
I am sick at heart.
  How long, O LORD, until you restore me?
PSALM 6:2-3

◆ *Instructional psalms*
Come, my children, and listen to me,
  and I will teach you to fear the LORD. . . .
Turn away from evil and do good.
  Work hard at living in peace with others.
PSALM 34:11, 14

◆ *Prayers of the community*
Only by your power can we push back our enemies;
  only in your name can we trample our foes. . . .
But now you have tossed us aside in dishonor.
  You no longer lead our armies to battle.
PSALM 44:5, 9

◆ *Hymns of thanksgiving*
Let the whole world bless our God and sing aloud his praises.
Our lives are in his hands,
  and he keeps our feet from stumbling.
PSALM 66:8-9

◆ *Psalms for special occasions*
Your procession has come into view, O God—

the procession of my God and
    King
as he goes into the sanctuary.
Singers are in front, musicians are
    behind;
    with them are young women
        playing tambourines.
PSALM 68:24-25

In looking at these various kinds of psalms, we see that God wants us to bring our heart before him in every situation. The Psalms teach us to call upon him in our time of need, both individually and corporately; to praise him when he answers us; to acknowledge him on special occasions; and to learn to obey him and live right.

Perhaps it is because the Psalms speak to all of life that they are so popular. They have been able to touch the hearts of many people in all sorts of circumstances. We can relate to the Psalms very personally, and their honesty endears them to us. More than simply teaching us *about* God, the Psalms help us express our inmost feelings *to* God in all of life, reminding us that God has created our emotions as well as our mind and desires that we yield our whole self to him in all things.

The psalmists don't pretend to have all the answers. Instead, they ask genuine questions and often cry out in agony. In other words, the psalmists are quite human—so much so, in fact, that their humanity can almost be embarrassing to us at times. Yet, in spite of all their travail, the psalmists almost always end up praising God because they know he is bigger than their problems and wiser than their questions.

In short, the Psalms are songs to be sung, laments to be cried, prayers to be prayed, and praises to be lifted on high. Let the Psalms speak to your heart this year, whatever you may be feeling. Learn to give God your whole self—heart, mind, and soul—and discover what he desires to teach you in all your circumstances.

∾

Let us before his presence come
With praise and thankful voice;
Let us sing psalms to him with grace
And make a joyful noise.
OLD SCOTTISH PSALTER

∾

"Elsewhere in the Bible God speaks to us; in the Psalms He helps us speak to Him."
J. C. GREY

∾

Consider the way you feel today. Which of the five types of psalms would you use to express your thoughts and feelings? Try writing a psalm of your own—an honest expression of your emotions before God.

Selah

PSALM 5:1-6
For the choir director: A psalm of David, to be accompanied by the flute.

1 O LORD, hear me as I pray;
    pay attention to my groaning.
2 Listen to my cry for help, my King and my God,
    for I will never pray to anyone but you.
3 Listen to my voice in the morning, LORD.
    Each morning I bring my requests to you and wait
        expectantly.

4 O God, you take no pleasure in wickedness;
    you cannot tolerate the slightest sin.
5 Therefore, the proud will not be allowed to stand in
        your presence,
    for you hate all who do evil.
6 You will destroy those who tell lies.
    The LORD detests murderers and deceivers.

*I*n World War I, Field Marshal Foch, the Allied commander in chief, could not be found when a military conference was about to start. An officer friend said, "I think I know where he might be." Foch was found praying nearby at a bombed-out chapel.

Abraham Lincoln once said, "I would be the greatest fool on earth if I did not realize that I could never satisfy the demands of the high office without the help of One who is greater and stronger than I am."

David realized this truth, too. Although he was a powerful king, he daily acknowledged his dependence on someone far greater and stronger than he was.

Not only did David begin each day depending on the Lord, but he waited expectantly throughout the day to see how God would work on his behalf. When you live each day looking upward, God often sends delightful surprises.

You are probably not a field marshal, a president, or a king, but your daily needs are important to the Lord, too. And he is just as eager to assist you as he was to assist Marshal Foch, President Lincoln, or even King David. Depend on him today, and await his surprises.

> *When we don't pray, we quit the fight.*
> *Prayer keeps the Christian's armor bright.*
> *And Satan trembles when he sees*
> *The weakest saint upon his knees.*
> WILLIAM COWPER

Fascinating Fact
The little word my *appears nearly 450 times in the psalms. The psalmist refers to the Lord as "my King," "my God," "my Shepherd," and "my Rock," to name a few.*

Notable Quotable
"Let not our prayers and praises be the flashes of a hot and hasty brain, but the steady burning of a well-kindled fire."
CHARLES HADDON SPURGEON

PSALM 5:7-12

⁷ Because of your unfailing love, I can enter your house;
with deepest awe I will worship at your Temple.

⁸ Lead me in the right path, O LORD,
or my enemies will conquer me.
Tell me clearly what to do,
and show me which way to turn.

⁹ My enemies cannot speak one truthful word.
Their deepest desire is to destroy others.
Their talk is foul, like the stench from an open grave.
Their speech is filled with flattery.

¹⁰ O God, declare them guilty.
Let them be caught in their own traps.
Drive them away because of their many sins,
for they rebel against you.

¹¹ But let all who take refuge in you rejoice;
let them sing joyful praises forever.
Protect them,
so all who love your name may be filled with joy.

¹² For you bless the godly, O LORD,
surrounding them with your shield of love.

*T*hings didn't look good for Martin Luther when he was summoned to Augsburg in late October 1518. He was being charged with heresy. Up to this point Frederick the Wise, elector of Saxony, had protected Luther from the church authorities, but now the prince was under pressure to withdraw his protection. It seemed only a matter of time before he would.

In Augsburg, Luther was asked, "If the elector of Saxony abandons you, where will you find shelter?"

The Reformer responded, "Under the shelter of heaven."

In this last part of Psalm 5, we find that David, like Luther, trusted in the Lord to rescue him from his enemies. He took comfort in the fact that God had shown him unfailing love, allowing him to enter the Temple to worship. And it was in this context of worship that David asked for divine guidance.

Did the psalmist escape from the trap? We don't know, but the psalm closes with "joyful praises," because David knew that he was now surrounded by God's protection (see also Psalm 91:4). Like Martin Luther, he found refuge under the shelter of heaven.

> *Under his wings, O what precious enjoyment!*
> *There will I hide till life's trials are o'er.*
> *Sheltered, protected, no evil can harm me;*
> *Resting in Jesus I'm safe evermore.*
> WILLIAM O. CUSHING

A Word on Words

Five different Hebrew words are used in the Old Testament for "shield," ranging from a small shield on the arm to a large body shield. Verse 12 refers to the largest shield, the kind that Goliath's armor bearer held (see 1 Samuel 17:7). It protected the whole body.

Bible Networking

Look up Romans 3:13 to see how Paul quotes Psalm 5:9.

PSALM 6

For the choir director: A psalm of David, to be accompanied by an eight-stringed instrument.

1 O LORD, do not rebuke me in your anger
    or discipline me in your rage.
2 Have compassion on me, LORD, for I am weak.
    Heal me, LORD, for my body is in agony.
3 I am sick at heart.
    How long, O LORD, until you restore me?

4 Return, O LORD, and rescue me.
    Save me because of your unfailing love.
5 For in death, who remembers you?
    Who can praise you from the grave?

6 I am worn out from sobbing.
    Every night tears drench my bed;
    my pillow is wet from weeping.
7 My vision is blurred by grief;
    my eyes are worn out because of all my enemies.

8 Go away, all you who do evil,
    for the LORD has heard my crying.
9 The LORD has heard my plea;
    the LORD will answer my prayer.
10 May all my enemies be disgraced and terrified.
    May they suddenly turn back in shame.

*W*henever he was in a no-win situation, the noted reformer John Calvin quoted verse 3 of this psalm. But a no-win situation to us is not necessarily a no-win situation to God. Early in his ministry John Calvin was driven out of the city of Geneva, Switzerland, and he left feeling that the city was hopeless.

Years later God brought him back to Geneva, almost against his will, and Geneva became the center of his greatest triumphs. All the while Calvin learned to focus more and more on the Lord and less and less on his daily successes.

Obviously the writer of this psalm was feeling lousy. He was sick—both in soul and body. He was troubled by his heart within and by enemies without. He seemed to believe that his miserable condition was a judgment from God, and he called out for mercy.

When we are ill, our suffering often seems to affect us in both physical and spiritual ways. Because we feel bad spiritually, our health suffers, which makes us even more susceptible to spiritual attack. Soon things begin to spiral quickly downward. Illness also tends to bring our focus to ourself and our own troubles, just as it did for David in the first seven verses. But, as David shows us in verse 8, when we look to God in faith, our burdens begin to lift.

> *Lord, I am sick of soul.*
> *I know you see my tears.*
> *Oh, save me for your mercies' sake*
> *And drive away my fears.*
> OLD SCOTTISH PSALTER, Adapted

Bible Networking
This is one of seven penitential psalms. The others are 32, 38, 51, 102, 130, and 143.

Notable Quotable
"However low I may sink, there is not a depth but grace goes deeper."
ALFRED EDERSHEIM

PSALM 7:1-9

A psalm of David, which he sang to the LORD concerning Cush of the tribe of Benjamin.

¹ I come to you for protection, O LORD my God.
Save me from my persecutors—rescue me!
² If you don't, they will maul me like a lion,
tearing me to pieces with no one to rescue me.

³ O LORD my God, if I have done wrong
or am guilty of injustice,
⁴ if I have betrayed a friend
or plundered my enemy without cause,
⁵ then let my enemies capture me.
Let them trample me into the ground.
Let my honor be left in the dust.   *Interlude*

⁶ Arise, O LORD, in anger!
Stand up against the fury of my enemies!
Wake up, my God, and bring justice!
⁷ Gather the nations before you.
Sit on your throne high above them.
⁸ The LORD passes judgment on the nations.
Declare me righteous, O LORD,
for I am innocent, O Most High!
⁹ End the wickedness of the ungodly,
but help all those who obey you.
For you look deep within the mind and heart,
O righteous God.

Often gigantic problems are created by seemingly small causes. Sometimes it is precisely because the causes go unnoticed that the problems become so huge.

Benjamin, the smallest of the Israelite tribes, caused David some of his biggest problems. To start with, Saul, Israel's first king, was a Benjaminite, and he pursued David up and down the Judean wilderness trying to kill him. After David became king, the tribe of Benjamin resisted his rule. Years later a Benjaminite named Shimei cursed King David, and still later another Benjaminite, Sheba, revolted against him.

The superscription to Psalm 7 says it was written concerning a Benjaminite named Cush. No one knows for sure who Cush was, but the psalm seems to suggest that he was persecuting David unjustly. So David, helpless to resolve the issue himself, calls on the Lord to act as judge and jury to his persecutors and declare him innocent.

We, too, can allow seemingly small problems to grow into big ones if we do not take care of them. Call upon the Lord for help, for no problem is too insignificant to bring before him, and we need not be embarrassed that we are struggling with such things. The Lord desires to help us overcome our struggles and live triumphantly for him.

> He is a Judge who is fair;
> He is a Shield that is sure.
> His mighty power is everywhere,
> And His Word will e'er endure.
> OLD SCOTTISH PSALTER, Adapted

PSALM 7:10-17

[10] God is my shield,
saving those whose hearts are true and right.

[11] God is a judge who is perfectly fair.
He is angry with the wicked every day.

[12] If a person does not repent,
God will sharpen his sword;
he will bend and string his bow.

[13] He will prepare his deadly weapons
and ignite his flaming arrows.

[14] The wicked conceive evil;
they are pregnant with trouble
and give birth to lies.

[15] They dig a pit to trap others
and then fall into it themselves.

[16] They make trouble,
but it backfires on them.
They plan violence for others,
but it falls on their own heads.

[17] I will thank the LORD because he is just;
I will sing praise to the name of the LORD Most High.

*I*n football, referees tell you whether a catch was made in bounds or not. In tennis, linesmen render instant judgment calls on whether a ball landed in or out. In baseball, umpires signal fair or foul.

But in life it often seems as though the game isn't being played fairly and that no one is around to call foul. Flagrant violations of the rules go unnoticed, and so many people are playing out-of-bounds and getting away with it.

David seemed to feel this way in Psalm 7. When he called upon the Lord to save those whose hearts were true and right, it wasn't because he believed he had never missed the mark. He knew he had. But his opponent was consistently out-of-bounds and never seemed to be penalized. Was there no justice?

Sometimes we do see the harmful effects of playing out-of-bounds (see verse 15 of this psalm or Numbers 32:23). But other times the Lord's ruling extends farther than our mortal eye can see. Paul told the Athenians that God "has set a day for judging the world with justice" (Acts 17:31), so we can trust that he will one day set everything right, although we may not see his ruling in our lifetime.

David knew this, too, and that's why he concluded this psalm as he did, thanking and praising the Lord for his ultimate justice. Let us thank God that he is the just Judge over all the earth.

> *Fatherlike he tends and spares us;*
> *Well our feeble frame he knows.*
> *In his hands he gently bears us,*
> *Rescues us from all our foes.*
> CAROLINA SANDELL BERG

Bible Networking
Regarding verse 16, see Esther 7:10 and Daniel 6:24 to learn about two troublemakers whose plans for violence backfired on them.

Notable Quotable
"Every sin is a lie."
SAINT AUGUSTINE

January 12

PSALM 8:1-4
For the choir director: A psalm of David, to be accompanied by a stringed instrument.

¹ O LORD, our Lord, the majesty of your name fills the
    earth!
  Your glory is higher than the heavens.

² You have taught children and nursing infants
    to give you praise.
  They silence your enemies
    who were seeking revenge.

³ When I look at the night sky and see the work of your
    fingers—
  the moon and the stars you have set in place—
⁴ what are mortals that you should think of us,
    mere humans that you should care for us?

On a clear Judean night David could probably see five thousand stars. Today with a four-inch telescope a person can see more than 2 million stars. Even more amazing than that, using the two-hundred-inch mirror on Mount Palomar, California, astronomers can see more than a billion stars! We have dispatched the Voyager II spacecraft to send back photographs of our solar system. It sent back photos of Neptune at the speed of light, and they still took four hours to reach us! Our galaxy, the Milky Way, is merely one of 100 billion or more galaxies, each between a million and 10 million light-years across.

David didn't know all those facts, but he still marveled as he gazed at the sky. Like David, when we get a glimpse of the vastness of God's creation, it overwhelms us! All this wonder at the greatness of God, however, did not cause David to speak of God's remoteness from us but of his great care for us. The universe is indeed vast, but God is near. He thinks of us and cares for us, and this should cause us to marvel all the more. In Isaiah the Lord told his people, "I set all the stars in space and established the earth. I am the one who says to Israel, 'You are mine!' " (Isaiah 51:16).

Let us give praise to the God who has created such a magnificent universe and who still cares for us.

> Lord, what is worthless man
> That you should love him so.
> Next to the angels he is placed
> And lord of all below.
> ISAAC WATTS

A Word on Words

The words translated "LORD" and "Lord" in verse 1 are different in Hebrew. The first is Yahweh, the sacred, personal name of God that is often associated with his covenant with his people. The second is Adonai, which means Sovereign or Master, emphasizing his dominion.

PSALM 8:5-9

5 For you made us only a little lower than God,
   and you crowned us with glory and honor.
6 You put us in charge of everything you made,
   giving us authority over all things—
7 the sheep and the cattle
   and all the wild animals,
8 the birds in the sky, the fish in the sea,
   and everything that swims the ocean currents.

9 O LORD, our Lord, the majesty of your name fills the
   earth!

*T*wo men looked out into space. One said, "Astronomically speaking, man is insignificant." The other said, "Astronomically speaking, man is the astronomer."

Both were correct. The first half of Psalm 8 emphasizes the greatness of the Creator and the wonder that he cares for us, who seem insignificant by comparison. The second half puts the spotlight on us as "astronomers," that is, as those who watch over God's creation.

If we look closely at Psalm 8, we will notice that we are not the subject; God is. He has bestowed authority on us, placing us in charge of creation to care for it (see Genesis 1:26; 2:15). God is the creator of this planet; we are the caretakers. Just as God cares for us, so we have the privilege of caring for the other wonders he has crafted. What an honor to be God's representative on earth!

> *This is my Father's world:*
> *I rest me in the thought*
> *Of rocks and trees, of skies and seas—*
> *His hand the wonders wrought.*
> MALTBIE BABCOCK

A Word on Words

Verse 5 may throw you if you are used to the King James Version, which reads that God made us "a little lower than the angels." The Hebrew word here is elohim, which can refer to either heavenly beings or God himself.

Bible Networking

God has placed us in charge of all God's creation, but see James 3:7-8 for one thing we all have trouble controlling.

Notable Quotable

"The age of the telescope was the age of the microscope. There are as many worlds of wonder which are too minute for our vision as there are too great for our understanding."
F. B. MEYER

As you read the psalms, you may notice that many verses seem redundant. What is written on one line is repeated to some extent on the next. This repetition might be a bit puzzling to us. After all, poetry is supposed to rhyme, isn't it?

Despite its unfamiliar form, Hebrew poetry does follow a set of conventions or rules. One of these rules is parallelism. Instead of rhyming sounds, like English poetry often does (e.g., "Jack and Jill / Went up the hill"), Hebrew poetry rhymes ideas, and we call this parallelism. Hebrew parallelism takes three primary forms: synonymous, antithetical, and synthetic.

SYNONYMOUS PARALLELISM

Synonymous parallelism consists of two lines that say virtually the same thing. An example of this form is Psalm 5:1:

O LORD, hear me as I pray;
    pay attention to my groaning.

Here the psalmist uses two imperatives to exhort God to listen to him. The first imperative is "hear," the second "pay attention." Although the words used are different, the idea is the same: Listen to what I have to say. The repetition of the idea adds emphasis to it.

ANTITHETICAL PARALLELISM

Some Hebrew poetry uses antithetical parallelism. This consists of two lines that contain opposite ideas. Psalm 1:6 uses this form:

For the LORD watches over the path
    of the godly,
        but the path of the wicked leads
        to destruction.

In this case, by using antithetical parallelism, the author can clearly contrast the consequences of two types of people—the godly and the wicked. This "two ways" approach to life and morality is a favorite of the Hebrew writers.

SYNTHETIC PARALLELISM

Sometimes two lines of Hebrew poetry build on each other. Psalm 14:2 exhibits such synthetic parallelism:

The LORD looks down from heaven
    on the entire human race;
he looks to see if there is even one
        with real understanding,
    one who seeks for God.

In this case, "on the entire human race" certainly isn't parallel with the idea of the Lord looking down from heaven, nor is it an opposite idea. Instead, this second line completes the thought begun in the first line. The same is true for "one who seeks for God." Sometimes it's hard to know if two lines mean the same thing or whether the second line is adding to the first. Examine a few psalms, and you will see that it can be a challenge to figure it out.

There are other variations on these three types of parallelism. It is not necessary for you to learn all the forms intimately in order to enjoy the Psalms. Nevertheless, gaining a basic understanding of parallelism in Hebrew poetry will help you gain a greater appreciation for the Psalms and the skill with which the authors composed them.

∞

Let fields rejoice, and everything
That springs up from the earth;
Then woods and every tree shall sing
With gladness and with mirth.
OLD SCOTTISH PSALTER

∞

"The Book of Psalms is a theatre, in which God allows us to behold both Himself and His works; a most pleasant green field; a vast garden where we see all manner of flowers."
PAULUS GERHARDT

∞

When you think of the greatness of God, is there any better way to describe him than poetically? Compose a psalm that expresses your thoughts about God, and consider using some of the devices of the Hebrew poets.

Selah

PSALM 9:1-10

For the choir director: A psalm of David, to be sung to the tune "Death of the Son."

¹ I will thank you, LORD, with all my heart;
    I will tell of all the marvelous things you have done.
² I will be filled with joy because of you.
    I will sing praises to your name, O Most High.

³ My enemies turn away in retreat;
    they are overthrown and destroyed before you.
⁴ For you have judged in my favor;
    from your throne, you have judged with fairness.

⁵ You have rebuked the nations and destroyed the
      wicked;
    you have wiped out their names forever.
⁶ My enemies have met their doom;
    their cities are perpetual ruins.
    Even the memory of their uprooted cities is lost.

⁷ But the LORD reigns forever,
    executing judgment from his throne.
⁸ He will judge the world with justice
    and rule the nations with fairness.

⁹ The LORD is a shelter for the oppressed,
    a refuge in times of trouble.
¹⁰ Those who know your name trust in you,
    for you, O LORD, have never abandoned anyone who
      searches for you.

*I*n our day conquering heroes are greeted with ticker-tape parades. But when King David returned home from a triumphant battle, he wrote a psalm praising God for his successes.

In verse 2 of this psalm, David extols God as *Elyon*, "O Most High."

In the Bible, God is often called Most High when other nations or peoples are involved. Melchizedek, king of Salem, blessed Abraham in the name of God Most High (Genesis 14:20). Balaam prophesied to the Moabite king in the name of the Most High (Numbers 24:16). Daniel in Babylon worshiped God as the Most High (Daniel 4:24).

Other nations claimed to have their gods, but David and others recognized that the God of Israel is *Elyon*, the Most High above all others. That's why this God can give victory. That's why he is worthy of praise. That's why those who know his name—not just know it in their heads, but know it by experience in their hearts—put their trust in him.

As you face the world today, put your trust in *Elyon*, the Most High above all gods. He reigns forever and is a refuge in times of trouble.

> *The God of Abraham praise, who reigns enthroned above,*
> *Ancient of everlasting days, and God of love.*
> *Jehovah, great I AM, by earth and heaven confessed:*
> *We bow and bless the sacred name forever blessed.*
> THOMAS OLIVERS

Fascinating Fact
This psalm, when combined with Psalm 10, is the first of the acrostic psalms (see the devotional for April 14, "The Acrostic Psalms"). That is, each verse of these psalms begins with the succeeding letter of the Hebrew alphabet.

Bible Networking
Contrast the "I wills" of verses 1 and 2 in this psalm with the "I wills" of Isaiah 14:12-14.

PSALM 9:11-20

¹¹ Sing praises to the Lord who reigns in Jerusalem.
   Tell the world about his unforgettable deeds.
¹² For he who avenges murder cares for the helpless.
   He does not ignore those who cry to him for help.

¹³ Lord, have mercy on me.
   See how I suffer at the hands of those who hate me.
   Snatch me back from the jaws of death.
¹⁴ Save me, so I can praise you publicly at Jerusalem's
      gates,
   so I can rejoice that you have rescued me.

¹⁵ The nations have fallen into the pit they dug for others.
   They have been caught in their own trap.
¹⁶ The Lord is known for his justice.
   The wicked have trapped themselves in their own
      snares.   *Quiet Interlude*

¹⁷ The wicked will go down to the grave.
   This is the fate of all the nations who ignore God.
¹⁸ For the needy will not be forgotten forever;
   the hopes of the poor will not always be crushed.

¹⁹ Arise, O Lord!
   Do not let mere mortals defy you!
   Let the nations be judged in your presence!
²⁰ Make them tremble in fear, O Lord.
   Let them know they are merely human.   *Interlude*

*A*lthough he was a king and a powerful warrior, David maintained a concern for the poor and needy. The story of his dealings with the crippled Mephibosheth is a beautiful example of his concern (2 Samuel 9). The fact that this story follows immediately after a chapter chronicling David's military successes underscores David's clear focus in this area.

In this psalm David rejoices that the Lord defends the poor and helpless as well. It is clear from the rest of Scripture that God holds a special concern for the poor and needy, just as David did (see Deuteronomy 15:11; Isaiah 58:7; Amos 2:7; and Luke 6:20). He is attentive to their cries and will bring them justice.

When troubles begin to press in around us, it is easy to think we are powerless to do anything about them. But David knew, and we should know, too, that we serve a powerful God who defends the helpless. We can call upon him to rescue us and trust that he will answer. This power that we find in God is a far greater power than any mortals can ever possess.

> O Lord, you are a shelter
> For all who are oppressed;
> A refuge and a hiding place
> For those who are distressed.
> ISAAC WATTS

A Word on Words

Enosh is the Hebrew word used to refer to humanity when the emphasis is on frailty and mortality. It is used in Psalm 8:4 and in verses 19-20 of this chapter.

Notable Quotable

"Prayer is a haven to the shipwrecked, a staff to limbs that totter, a mine of jewels to the poor, a healer of disease, and a guardian of health." SAINT JOHN CHRYSOSTOM

PSALM 10:1-11

1 O LORD, why do you stand so far away?
    Why do you hide when I need you the most?
2 Proud and wicked people viciously oppress the poor.
    Let them be caught in the evil they plan for others.
3 For they brag about their evil desires;
    they praise the greedy and curse the LORD.
4 These wicked people are too proud to seek God.
    They seem to think that God is dead.
5 Yet they succeed in everything they do.
    They do not see your punishment awaiting them.
    They pour scorn on all their enemies.
6 They say to themselves, "Nothing bad will ever happen
        to us!
    We will be free of trouble forever!"

7 Their mouths are full of cursing, lies, and threats.
    Trouble and evil are on the tips of their tongues.
8 They lurk in dark alleys,
    murdering the innocent who pass by.

    They are always searching
    for some helpless victim.
9 Like lions they crouch silently,
    waiting to pounce on the helpless.
Like hunters they capture their victims
    and drag them away in nets.
10 The helpless are overwhelmed and collapse;
    they fall beneath the strength of the wicked.
11 The wicked say to themselves, "God isn't watching!
    He will never notice!"

*I*n 1805 Henry Martyn had one arm around his sweetheart as he read Psalm 10:1. This twenty-four-year-old felt sure that God wanted him to go to India as a missionary. But the girl he loved, Lydia Grenfell, was too frail to handle India's climate. As they read this psalm together, their hearts were heavy, for in a few hours they would be separated, never to see each other again.

Why, God, why? Why did God allow them to fall in love if he wanted Henry to go to India? We don't know that Henry ever got an explanation. We do know that God had great plans for young Henry and that Henry didn't have much time to fulfill them, for it was just seven years later that he died. In that brief time, however, he translated the New Testament into Hindustani and both the New Testament and his beloved Psalms into Persian. Because he followed God's plans for him, millions of people could read the Scriptures in their own languages.

Twice in the first verse of Psalm 10 the psalmist asks God *why*—a question the psalmists will cry out again and again throughout the Psalms. We may never find an answer to this question, but we can take great comfort in the answer to a much more important question: Who? This is what the psalmist does at the end of this psalm. Once we catch a glimpse of who God is, we can learn to trust him while his specific purposes remain hidden from us.

> I am not skilled to understand
> What God has willed, what God has planned;
> I only know at his right hand
> Stands one who is my Savior.
> DORA GREENWELL

Fascinating Fact
The three books in the Old Testament that ask the question why most often are Job, Jeremiah, and Psalms. The entire book of Job is about the main character's struggle to answer this question. In the end the Lord answers Job's question not with a what but a who.

Notable Quotable
"It is not until the flower has fallen off that the fruit begins to ripen."
J. C. GREY

PSALM 10:12-18

¹² Arise, O Lord!
> Punish the wicked, O God!
> Do not forget the helpless!

¹³ Why do the wicked get away with cursing God?
> How can they think, "God will never call us to
>> account"?

¹⁴ But you do see the trouble and grief they cause.
> You take note of it and punish them.
The helpless put their trust in you.
> You are the defender of orphans.

¹⁵ Break the arms of these wicked, evil people!
> Go after them until the last one is destroyed!

¹⁶ The Lord is king forever and ever!
> Let those who worship other gods be swept from the
>> land.

¹⁷ Lord, you know the hopes of the helpless.
> Surely you will listen to their cries and comfort them.

¹⁸ You will bring justice to the orphans and the oppressed,
> so people can no longer terrify them.

*T*he old spiritual says, "Nobody knows the trouble I've seen; nobody knows but Jesus." And that, in a nutshell, is the message of this psalm.

The psalmist is speaking on behalf of the needy, the helpless, the orphans, and the oppressed. These people have every reason to feel ignored by the rest of society, because all too often they are. But the Lord knows what they're going through.

But what about those who oppress these poor ones? They may say, "God will never call us to account" (verse 13), or they may think that God is dead (verse 4). But this psalm spells out the truth of the matter: God does see what happens (verse 14). He knows the hopes of the helpless and listens to their cries (verse 17). He will comfort them (verse 17) and bring justice to them (verse 18).

So does this mean we can stop here and let God take care of the helpless and the oppressed? Not at all! Maybe "nobody [truly] knows but Jesus," but Christians are still called to carry out God's work on earth. All too often we just pass by on the other side (see Luke 10:31-32), ignoring others' needs and suffering.

When you hear the cries of the helpless, what do you do? Are you like the uncaring Levite, who passes by on the other side, or more like the Lord, who hears and knows and cares?

> *He who reigns above the sky*
> *Once became as poor as I.*
> *Poor and needy, though I be*
> *God, my Maker, cares for me.*
> OLD SCOTTISH PSALTER, Adapted

A Word on Words
By asking the Lord to "break the arms" of wicked people (verse 15) the psalmist is calling upon the Lord to break their power.

Bible Networking
For more on God's concern for the poor, read Amos 5:10–6:8.

PSALM 11

For the choir director: A psalm of David.

¹ I trust in the LORD for protection.
So why do you say to me,
"Fly to the mountains for safety!
² The wicked are stringing their bows
and setting their arrows in the bowstrings.
They shoot from the shadows at those who do right.
³ The foundations of law and order have collapsed.
What can the righteous do?"

⁴ But the LORD is in his holy Temple;
the LORD still rules from heaven.
He watches everything closely,
examining everyone on earth.
⁵ The LORD examines both the righteous and the wicked.
He hates everyone who loves violence.
⁶ He rains down blazing coals on the wicked,
punishing them with burning sulfur and scorching
winds.
⁷ For the LORD is righteous, and he loves justice.
Those who do what is right will see his face.

The year was 1606. The Scottish Covenanters had been hoping and praying that the new king of England would give them more religious freedom. Instead, King James VI took away what freedom they had. The foundations of law and order were being shaken and on the verge of collapse.

In October of that year, the new regime had thrown John Welsh and his small group of Covenanters into prison. After being summoned to a nighttime trial, the prisoners marched to the courtroom singing Psalm 11 from the Scottish Psalter, beginning with the words, "I trust in God."

Young David also knew about hostile kings. When King Saul tried to kill him, David fled to the city of Nob, where he received food from a priest there. When Saul heard of this, he massacred the entire town of Nob—all the men, women, children, and even animals (1 Samuel 21:1–22:19). It seemed as if the foundations of law and order had collapsed. But David maintained his trust in God. Eventually Saul was killed, and David was crowned king in his place.

What do you do when it seems that the foundations of law and order are collapsing? When you sense the nation drifting from its moorings, your church faltering in its priorities, or even your family falling apart—how do you respond? Do you "fly to the mountains"? David encourages us to put our trust in the Lord, for "those who do what is right will see his face" (verse 7).

> *All my trust on Thee is stayed,*
> *All my help from Thee I bring;*
> *Cover my defenseless head*
> *With the shadow of Thy wing.*
> CHARLES WESLEY

Bible Networking

The blazing coals and burning sulfur in verse 6 allude to the destruction of Sodom and Gomorrah (see Genesis 19:24).

Notable Quotable

"To the psalmist the surrounding circumstances were not foundations. He saw God, enthroned, watching, acting. To him this was the one foundation."
G. CAMPBELL MORGAN

PSALM 12

For the choir director: A psalm of David, to be accompanied by an eight-stringed instrument.

¹ Help, O LORD, for the godly are fast disappearing!
  The faithful have vanished from the earth!
² Neighbors lie to each other,
  speaking with flattering lips and insincere hearts.
³ May the LORD bring their flattery to an end
  and silence their proud tongues.
⁴ They say, "We will lie to our hearts' content.
  Our lips are our own—who can stop us?"

⁵ The LORD replies, "I have seen violence done to the
    helpless,
  and I have heard the groans of the poor.
  Now I will rise up to rescue them,
  as they have longed for me to do."
⁶ The LORD's promises are pure,
  like silver refined in a furnace,
  purified seven times over.

⁷ Therefore, LORD, we know you will protect the
    oppressed,
  preserving them forever from this lying generation,
⁸ even though the wicked strut about,
  and evil is praised throughout the land.

*H*ave you ever felt the way the psalmist felt in these opening verses? After years of eluding the clutches of King Saul, David got news that the Philistines were plundering the border town of Keilah. With his men he hurried to Keilah's rescue, routing the Philistines and bringing back all the plunder to its rightful owners (1 Samuel 23:1-12). David and his men were heroes.

But when King Saul heard that David was at Keilah, he sent his entire army to capture David. David learned of Saul's plan and asked God for guidance. Would the people of Keilah betray him if he stayed in Keilah?

"Yes," God responded, "they will betray you"—despite all David had done for them.

Betrayal is a stab in the back—whether you're talking about friends who have not kept their promises, about allies who have proved faithless, or about associates who have said one thing but really believed the opposite.

Paul warned Timothy that in the last days, some will turn away from the faith (1 Timothy 4:1) despite all the Lord has done for them. And if you can't even count on those who claim to know Christ, who can you trust?

In verse 6 of this psalm David assures us that we can trust in the Lord's promises. His promises are perfectly pure, so we need not fear when we are surrounded by wicked liars.

> *Your Word like silver seven times tried*
> *Through ages shall endure.*
> *All those who in your truth confide*
> *Shall find the promise sure.*
> OLD SCOTTISH PSALTER

A Word on Words

"Flattering lips" (verse 2) is literally "smooth talk," and "insincere hearts" is literally "a heart and a heart," referring to someone whose loyalties are divided.

Bible Networking

To learn more about the wickedness of those who lie, read 1 Timothy 4:1-2 and 2 Timothy 3:1-9.

About three-fourths of all psalms have a superscription. In other words, at the beginning of a psalm there are comments, often about who wrote it, under what circumstances it was written, and how it is to be sung. According to the superscriptions, the following people are credited with various psalms:

- *David:* 73 psalms (nearly half of them)

- *The sons of Korah:* 10 psalms

- *Asaph:* 12 psalms

- *Solomon:* 2 psalms

- *Heman the Ezrahite:* 1 psalm

- *Ethan the Ezrahite, who may be the same as Jeduthun:* 1 psalm

- *Moses:* 1 psalm

It is difficult to be certain, however, whether the superscriptions are truly speaking of authorship or whether they are indicating some other information about the psalm. This is because it is difficult to know exactly how to interpret the phrase "a psalm of." It could be translated "a psalm concerning," "a psalm in the style of," or a few other ways. These other interpretations are supported by the fact that some of the psalms attributed to David in the latter half of the book seem to have been written after David's time.

Some of these superscriptions seem to have been written after the psalms themselves, while others may have been written along with the psalms they describe. The translators of the Septuagint (the Greek translation of the Old Testament com-

pleted around 200 B.C.)
included these superscriptions,
so they had to have been written before then. Some of these
superscriptions may be quite
old, since the translators of the
Septuagint apparently didn't
understand all the technical
musical words and left them in
Hebrew.

Probably the best way to
understand the superscriptions
is to see them as ancient
Hebrew tradition, an understanding of how the psalms
were written and how they were
meant to be used. Thus, the
superscription should be
viewed as an aid to our appreciation of the psalm but not
necessarily authoritative.

Although these superscriptions may not be authoritative,
we can learn a great deal from
them. These superscriptions
show that the psalms have been
associated with many different
people, from kings to Temple
singers. The psalms reflect the
thoughts and feelings of people
in all sorts of positions and circumstances, and these same
psalms still speak to us today in
all our situations. Wherever you
are today, know that there are
others who have gone before
you and have found great peace
in trusting the Lord in all
things.

∞
How precious is the Book divine
By inspiration given
Bright as a lamp its doctrines shine
To guide our souls to heaven.
JOHN FAWCETT

Selah

PSALM 13
For the choir director: A psalm of David.

¹ O Lord, how long will you forget me? Forever?
  How long will you look the other way?
² How long must I struggle with anguish in my soul,
  with sorrow in my heart every day?
  How long will my enemy have the upper hand?

³ Turn and answer me, O Lord my God!
  Restore the light to my eyes, or I will die.
⁴ Don't let my enemies gloat, saying, "We have defeated
    him!"
  Don't let them rejoice at my downfall.

⁵ But I trust in your unfailing love.
  I will rejoice because you have rescued me.
⁶ I will sing to the Lord
  because he has been so good to me.

About a hundred years ago the great Bible teacher F. B. Meyer preached a sermon aimed at people who "dwell in the dust." Such people express feelings as David did in this psalm: "Lord, how long will you forget me? Forever?"

Meyer said five kinds of people dwell in the dust: (1) those who feel forsaken by God; (2) those who feel their prayers are going nowhere; (3) those who are discouraged with life's possibilities; (4) those who are going through difficult financial or physical stresses; and (5) those who are stuck in a job or family situation they can't get out of. A person's problems are compounded when he or she falls into three or four of the above classifications at the same time.

If you feel this way, take special note of this psalm. In the first two verses David is complaining; in the next two he is praying; in the last two he is trusting and rejoicing. By the end of the psalm David's eyes are no longer on himself; he is trusting in the Lord. No longer is he dwelling in the dust; he recognizes that God has been good to him. Paul spoke similarly about how God has raised us from our lowly estate and seated us with Christ in the heavenly realms (Ephesians 2:6-7). Don't let yourself remain in the "how longs" of verses 1-2. Look to the Lord and trust in him, and he will bring you to the point of rejoicing once again.

> Whate'er my fears or foes suggest,
> You are my hope, my joy, my rest.
> My heart shall feel your love and raise
> My cheerful voice to sing your praise.
> ISAAC WATTS

Bible Networking
Four times in the first two verses the psalmist asks, "How long?" Check out a few other biblical "how longs": Job 8:2; Psalms 79:5; 89:46; 119:84; Isaiah 6:11; Habakkuk 1:2; John 10:24; Revelation 6:10.

Notable Quotable
"Let me be one of the upward and outward lookers, not one of the downward and inward lookers."
ALFRED EDERSHEIM

PSALM 14
For the choir director: A psalm of David.

¹ Only fools say in their hearts,
  "There is no God."
They are corrupt, and their actions are evil;
  no one does good!

² The LORD looks down from heaven
    on the entire human race;
he looks to see if there is even one with real
      understanding,
  one who seeks for God.
³ But no, all have turned away from God;
  all have become corrupt.
No one does good,
  not even one!

⁴ Will those who do evil never learn?
  They eat up my people like bread;
    they wouldn't think of praying to the LORD.
⁵ Terror will grip them,
  for God is with those who obey him.
⁶ The wicked frustrate the plans of the oppressed,
  but the LORD will protect his people.

⁷ Oh, that salvation would come from Mount Zion to
      rescue Israel!
  For when the LORD restores his people,
  Jacob will shout with joy, and Israel will rejoice.

Young John Newton called himself an atheist, and his life demonstrated his lack of belief in God. Even the coarsest sailors aboard his slave-trading ship could not stand his filthy speech. He brutalized the male slaves and sexually abused the women, and he prodded other sailors to do the same. The ship's captain finally put him ashore on the coast of Africa, and there he became a servant of slavers.

Finally rescued by another merchant ship, Newton once again fouled the ship with his presence. In a drunken stupor he almost plunged overboard, and the captain wished that he had. Then, amazingly in the midst of a vicious ocean storm in 1748, God touched his heart. Years after his remarkable conversion, Newton commented, "I see no reason why the Lord singled me out for mercy . . . unless it was to show that with him nothing is impossible."

The fool who had said in his heart that there was no God was now transformed. He became famous throughout England, both as a preacher and a writer of hymns. Without a doubt, the best-known hymn of this former atheist is the following:

> Amazing grace! how sweet the sound
> That saved a wretch like me!
> I once was lost but now am found,
> Was blind but now I see.
> JOHN NEWTON

A Word on Words
In Hebrew the word for "fool" is nabal. To read about a fool who bore the name Nabal, see 1 Samuel 25:25, and then read the entire chapter.

Fascinating Fact
In his essay "On Atheism," Francis Bacon commented that when the fool says in his heart that there is no God, he says it "by rote" in an attempt to convince himself.

Bible Networking
Compare Psalm 14 with Psalm 53. What differences do you find?

PSALM 15
A psalm of David.

¹ Who may worship in your sanctuary, LORD?
   Who may enter your presence on your holy hill?

² Those who lead blameless lives
   and do what is right,
   speaking the truth from sincere hearts.
³ Those who refuse to slander others
   or harm their neighbors
   or speak evil of their friends.
⁴ Those who despise persistent sinners,
   and honor the faithful followers of the LORD
   and keep their promises even when it hurts.
⁵ Those who do not charge interest on the money they
      lend,
   and who refuse to accept bribes to testify against the
      innocent.

   Such people will stand firm forever.

*T*o gain entrance to the White House or the palace of a foreign ruler, you must get past the guards. It's their job to screen all visitors. Their mere presence asks: What right do you have to enter this special place?

In the ancient world priests stood outside their sanctuaries to make sure that only those who were qualified might enter. So Psalm 15 begins with that question: Who may enter? The customary answer would be, "Anyone who has a sacrifice to offer," or "People who have fulfilled the ritual requirements." But the psalmist's answer is not about ritual correctness, it's about lifestyle. It's not about what you have brought with you, but how you have lived.

Are you a person of integrity? What you say must match who you are.

Is your speech restrained? Do you refuse to get involved with gossip?

Do you honor your friendships and keep your promises?

Are you honorable in your business dealings?

Interesting, isn't it, that this psalm appears directly after the one with the verse, "No one does good, not even one."

Who then can enter God's presence?

We enter, not because of our righteousness, but because we know the King's Son, and he has replaced our filthy garments of sin with his clean garments.

> For nothing good have I whereby thy grace to claim—
> I'll wash my garments white in the blood of Calvary's Lamb.
> And when before the throne, I stand in him complete,
> "Jesus died my soul to save," my lips shall still repeat.
> ELVINA M. HALL

Bible Networking
Compare Psalm 15 with these other question-and-answer sessions: Psalm 24:3-6 and Isaiah 33:14-17.

Notable Quotable
Regarding Psalm 15:3, St. Augustine had this quote over his table, "If you love to gnaw on men in their absence, this table does not like your presence."

PSALM 16:1-6
A psalm of David.

¹ Keep me safe, O God,
  for I have come to you for refuge.

² I said to the LORD, "You are my Master!
  All the good things I have are from you."
³ The godly people in the land
  are my true heroes!
  I take pleasure in them!
⁴ Those who chase after other gods will be filled with
      sorrow.
  I will not take part in their sacrifices
  or even speak the names of their gods.

⁵ LORD, you alone are my inheritance, my cup of blessing.
  You guard all that is mine.
⁶ The land you have given me is a pleasant land.
  What a wonderful inheritance!

One day a wealthy estate owner took a friend to the third floor of his palatial manor to show him the extent of his landholdings. Gesturing out the window to the west, he said, "All that you can see is mine."

The guest said nothing.

Then the owner added, "Can you see that farmhouse at a distance? That belongs to me, too." They walked to the east side and once again the owner pointed out the window. "Can you see that valley down there? I own that, too."

Finally the guest spoke up. "Just beyond that valley is a little village, and I know a woman in that village who lives in a small cottage. But she can say more than that."

"Oh, what can she say?" asked the owner.

The guest responded, "She can say, 'Christ is mine.'"

What a wonderful inheritance!

Paul wrote to the Romans, "Since we are his children, we will share his treasures—for everything God gives to his Son, Christ, is ours, too" (Romans 8:17). And to the Ephesians he wrote, "Because of Christ, we have received an inheritance from God" (Ephesians 1:11).

Since God has given us this wonderful inheritance in Christ, we, too, can rejoice with David in this psalm.

> I'm an heir of the king, Hallelujah;
> He safeguards my treasures each day.
> He gives me the joy of his presence
> And leads me along the right way.
> OLD SCOTTISH PSALTER, Adapted

A Word on Words
In verse 5 "my cup" signifies that God is the satisfying drink that refreshes and invigorates the soul. This idea is developed more fully by Jesus in John 4:10-14.

Bible Networking
The tribe of Levi was allotted no portion of land in the Promised Land of Canaan. Why not? (See Numbers 18:20.)

PSALM 16:7-11

7 I will bless the LORD who guides me;
    even at night my heart instructs me.
8 I know the LORD is always with me.
    I will not be shaken, for he is right beside me.

9 No wonder my heart is filled with joy,
    and my mouth shouts his praises!
    My body rests in safety.
10 For you will not leave my soul among the dead
    or allow your godly one to rot in the grave.
11 You will show me the way of life,
    granting me the joy of your presence
    and the pleasures of living with you forever.

*I*t was probably the last week of May A.D. 30. A rugged-looking Galilean stood tall in the courtyard of the Jerusalem Temple, remembering what had happened in early April. It had been the lowest point of his entire life. After denying that he even knew the man, he had watched Jesus of Nazareth being hauled off to be executed.

Now, only seven weeks later, Peter stood in front of thousands. "Listen carefully, all of you," he shouted, and then he explained what had happened just seven weeks earlier. Jesus, who had done many miracles, had been crucified, but amazingly God "raised him back to life again" (Acts 2:14-36).

Then he quoted Scripture: "King David said this about him," and he began reciting four verses from Psalm 16, which seem to refer to a resurrection. But whose resurrection? David's? No, obviously not, for David was still dead. This prophecy was speaking of Jesus (Acts 2:25-31).

That combination of Peter's personal testimony and Scripture was used by the Holy Spirit to bring three thousand people into the Kingdom of God that day, which is called Pentecost. If early April had been Peter's lowest point, can you imagine how different he felt on the Day of Pentecost?

Take a moment to rejoice in the wonderful news that Jesus has risen from the dead, conquering death for us, just as David foretold in this psalm.

Though the clouds from sight received him
When the forty days were o'er,
Shall our hearts forget His promise,
I am with you evermore.
AUTHOR UNKNOWN

A Word on Words

The literal wording of the end of verse 8 reads, "We are at his right hand." The end of verse 11 reads literally, "In his right hand are joys forever." In ancient Israel the right hand carried a great deal of significance, and we can see that we gain security at God's right hand and pleasure because of what he holds in his right hand.

Notable Quotable

"To have Him is to enjoy not only guidance (verse 7) and stability (verse 8), but resurrection (verse 9ff.) and endless bliss (verse 11)."
DEREK KIDNER

PSALM 17:1-8
A prayer of David.

1 O LORD, hear my plea for justice.
    Listen to my cry for help.
Pay attention to my prayer,
    for it comes from an honest heart.
2 Declare me innocent,
    for you know those who do right.

3 You have tested my thoughts and examined my heart in
        the night.
    You have scrutinized me and found nothing amiss,
    for I am determined not to sin in what I say.
4 I have followed your commands,
    which have kept me from going along with cruel and
        evil people.
5 My steps have stayed on your path;
    I have not wavered from following you.

6 I am praying to you because I know you will answer,
        O God.
    Bend down and listen as I pray.
7 Show me your unfailing love in wonderful ways.
    You save with your strength
    those who seek refuge from their enemies.
8 Guard me as the apple of your eye.
    Hide me in the shadow of your wings.

*W*e cannot be sure when this psalm was written, but some relate it to 1 Samuel 23:24-28, when David was being pursued by King Saul in the wilderness of Maon. In that story David was on one side of the mountain and Saul on the other. David had no idea what Saul was doing on the other side of the mountain—and he probably wasn't sure what God was up to, either.

Just as Saul and his men were about to close in on David, Saul got a message about a Philistine raid, and so he "quit the chase." God had saved David again.

Often we fear what is happening on the other side of the "mountains" of our life. People are making decisions about us or events are changing our life, and we have no control over them. We worry about what may happen to us.

But God promises to watch over us always, though we don't always know exactly how he will take care of us. Still, we can trust him. We are the apple of his eye, and we can call on him to hide us in the shadow of his wings. So there is no need to fear what is on the other side of the mountain.

> Praise to the Lord, who o'er all things so wondrously reigneth;
> Shelters thee under his wings, yea, so gently sustaineth!
> Hast thou not seen how thy desires e'er have been Granted in what he ordaineth?
>
> JOACHIM NEANDER

A Word on Words

The "apple of your eye" (verse 8) is literally the "daughter" of the eye—that which is dearest and most precious. See also Deuteronomy 32:10; Proverbs 7:2; and Zechariah 2:8.

Psalm at a Glance

If you want a simple outline for this prayer psalm, it is (1) heard, (2) held, and (3) hidden. As W. Graham Scroggie says, he who is heard, held, and hidden by the Lord need not fear the fiercest foe.

PSALM 17:9-15

⁹ Protect me from wicked people who attack me,
    from murderous enemies who surround me.

¹⁰ They are without pity.
    Listen to their boasting.
¹¹ They track me down, surround me,
    and throw me to the ground.
¹² They are like hungry lions, eager to tear me apart—
    like young lions in hiding, waiting for their chance.

¹³ Arise, O Lord!
    Stand against them and bring them to their knees!
    Rescue me from the wicked with your sword!
¹⁴ Save me by your mighty hand, O Lord,
    from those whose only concern is earthly gain.
    May they have their punishment in full.
    May their children inherit more of the same,
        and may the judgment continue to their children's
        children.

¹⁵ But because I have done what is right, I will see you.
    When I awake, I will be fully satisfied,
    for I will see you face to face.

*I*n England John Howard is known as the father of prison reform. As an eighteenth-century county sheriff, he was appalled by the conditions of British prisons and resolved to make changes wherever he could. He traveled across England and then to Europe, to France's Bastille, to the prisons of the Spanish Inquisition, and even to the lazarettos of Turkey. He found cells infested with rats and prisoners confined to live among the bodies of dead inmates. Smallpox, tuberculosis, and dysentery threatened his own life, but still Howard pressed on. "Trusting in divine providence," he said, "and believing myself in the way of my duty, I visit the most noxious cells, and fear no evil."

The verse that prodded him onward was Psalm 17:5: "My steps have stayed on your path; I have not wavered from following you."

Howard became seriously ill at the age of fifty-two and wrote to a friend, "Every refuge but Christ is a refuge of lies. My soul, stay thou upon the Rock." Later he wrote that he would like a short inscription over his grave: "My hope is in Christ."

Because of John Howard, prisons began to be reformed, not only in England, but also throughout Europe. His death finally came as he was preparing to visit many of the plague centers of Europe. As he had requested, his funeral sermon was based on the last verse of Psalm 17: "When I awake, I will be fully satisfied."

> *What others value, I resign,*
> *Lord, 'tis enough that thou are mine.*
> *I shall behold thy blessed face*
> *And stand complete in righteousness.*
> ISAAC WATTS

Bible Networking
If you want to read more about seeing the Lord face-to-face, check out 1 John 3:2.

EXODUS 15:19-21 (Miriam's Song)

¹⁹When Pharaoh's horses, chariots, and charioteers rushed into the sea, the LORD brought the water crashing down on them. But the people of Israel had walked through on dry land!

²⁰Then Miriam the prophet, Aaron's sister, took a tambourine and led all the women in rhythm and dance. ²¹And Miriam sang this song:

"I will sing to the LORD, for he has triumphed gloriously;

he has thrown both horse and rider into the sea."

Psalm Link
PSALM 30:11-12

¹¹ You have turned my mourning into joyful dancing.

You have taken away my clothes of mourning and clothed me with joy,

¹² that I might sing praises to you and not be silent.

O LORD my God, I will give you thanks forever!

*L*ike most of us, Miriam had moments of greatness and, well, moments of less than greatness.

Moment 1: When Pharaoh's daughter retrieved Miriam's brother, Moses, from a basket floating in the Nile river, Miriam suggested that she get a Hebrew nurse for the baby. Then she ran home and called her mother (Exodus 2:1-8). That was a moment of greatness.

Moment 2: It looked as if the Egyptian army would overtake the Israelites and slaughter them. But the Lord parted the Red Sea, allowing the Israelites to escape while the pursuing Egyptians drowned. Miriam seized upon this opportunity to lead the women in a jubilant song of praise to the Lord. The Scriptures even call her a prophet, for she spoke God's truths to his people (Exodus 15:19-21). That, too, was a moment of greatness.

Moment 3: Later, Miriam and Aaron criticized their brother, Moses, for his marriage to a Cushite woman. This was fueled by their jealousy of their brother's leadership role. God became angry with them and struck Miriam with leprosy (Numbers 12:1-12). That was a moment of smallness.

We all have moments of greatness, but we are also capable of acts of smallness. With this in mind, be careful to call upon God each day to lead you where he desires.

> Leave no unguarded place, no weakness of the soul;
> Take every virtue, every grace, and fortify the whole.
> That having all things done, and all your conflicts past,
> You may overcome through Christ alone, and stand complete at last.
> CHARLES WESLEY

Notable Quotable
"As the first of the sweet singers of Israel, Miriam sang for God, using her gift for the elevation of human souls into a higher life."
HERBERT LOCKYER

PSALM 18:1-6

For the choir director: A psalm of David, the servant of the LORD. He sang this song to the LORD on the day the LORD rescued him from all his enemies and from Saul.

¹ I love you, LORD; you are my strength.
² The LORD is my rock, my fortress, and my savior;
   my God is my rock, in whom I find protection.
   He is my shield, the strength of my salvation, and my
      stronghold.
³ I will call on the LORD, who is worthy of praise,
   for he saves me from my enemies.

⁴ The ropes of death surrounded me;
   the floods of destruction swept over me.
⁵ The grave wrapped its ropes around me;
   death itself stared me in the face.
⁶ But in my distress I cried out to the LORD;
   yes, I prayed to my God for help.
He heard me from his sanctuary;
   my cry reached his ears.

*W*hat is God to you? Is your understanding of him today any different than it was ten years ago? Are you growing in your personal experience with God?

To David, God was "my strength," "my rock," "my fortress," "my savior," "my shield," "the strength of my salvation," and "my stronghold." Nine times in the first two verses he uses the pronoun *my*. This shows that David had personally come to know God in many different ways.

Twice he refers to God as "my rock." It's quite possible this imagery came from David's extended time in the wilderness, which was strewn with rocks. There he probably learned that rocks serve many valuable purposes.

The superscription of this psalm, which is repeated almost word for word in 2 Samuel 22, indicates that it was written after David was no longer threatened by Saul. It was also probably written before the problems with his family erupted. If he had written this psalm toward the end of his life, would he have addressed God in some additional ways?

Think of what God meant to you ten years ago. In what new ways can you appreciate God today? What new names might you ascribe to him?

> Frail children of dust, and feeble as frail,
> In thee do we trust, nor find thee to fail;
> Thy mercies how tender, how firm to the end,
> Our Maker, Defender, Redeemer and Friend.
> ROBERT GRANT

Bible Networking

How many differences do you find between 2 Samuel 22:1-7 and Psalm 18:1-6 (including the superscription)?

Notable Quotable

"What a comfort would it be to you to read how good your God was to your father or grandfather. So would your children and grandchildren rejoice in the Lord upon the reading of his goodness to you."
RICHARD STEELE

PSALM 18:7-19

⁷ Then the earth quaked and trembled;
  the foundations of the mountains shook;
  they quaked because of his anger.

⁸ Smoke poured from his nostrils;
  fierce flames leaped from his mouth;
  glowing coals flamed forth from him.

⁹ He opened the heavens and came down;
  dark storm clouds were beneath his feet.

¹⁰ Mounted on a mighty angel, he flew,
  soaring on the wings of the wind.

¹¹ He shrouded himself in darkness,
  veiling his approach with dense rain clouds.

¹² The brilliance of his presence broke through the clouds,
  raining down hail and burning coals.

¹³ The LORD thundered from heaven;
  the Most High gave a mighty shout.

¹⁴ He shot his arrows and scattered his enemies;
  his lightning flashed, and they were greatly confused.

¹⁵ Then at your command, O LORD,
  at the blast of your breath,
  the bottom of the sea could be seen,
  and the foundations of the earth were laid bare.

¹⁶ He reached down from heaven and rescued me;
  he drew me out of deep waters.

¹⁷ He delivered me from my powerful enemies,
  from those who hated me and were too strong for me.

¹⁸ They attacked me at a moment when I was weakest,
  but the LORD upheld me.

¹⁹ He led me to a place of safety;
  he rescued me because he delights in me.

*H*ow powerful is your God? In theology we use big, four-syllable words like *omnipresent, omnipotent,* and *everlasting* to describe him, and often those words don't really help people understand very well. But David describes God in language we can grasp. In stark, strong images, David paints the picture of God shooting arrows and flashing lightning. He speaks of smoke pouring from God's nostrils and flames leaping from his mouth. He sees God stepping down from heaven and soaring on the wings of the wind, veiled in darkness until he brilliantly breaks through the clouds.

A majestic picture indeed. But why is God doing this? Go back to verse 6. God is doing all this in answer to a shepherd boy's prayer.

No doubt David was recalling how God had rescued the people of Israel over and over again, and he was also recalling how God had rescued *him.*

As you look back on your life, you, too, will realize that these magnificent verses are not simply for David or the Israelites. They are your verses as well because you, too, have a magnificent God.

> *How Thou canst think so well of me*
> *And be the God Thou art*
> *Is darkness to my intellect*
> *But sunshine to my heart.*
> FREDERICK W. FABER

A Word on Words

In verse 19 the "place of safety" is literally a broad, open space. By contrast, "distress" in verse 6 is literally a narrow place, a "tight spot." Perhaps David is thinking back to times when he was hiding from Saul in a cave and longed to be free to come out into a broad, safe place.

Notable Quotable

Making his way through the rubble after an earthquake devastated San Francisco, a newsboy said, "It took a long time to put all this stuff up, but God tumbled it over in a minute."

PSALM 18:20-30

²⁰ The LORD rewarded me for doing right;
    he compensated me because of my innocence.
²¹ For I have kept the ways of the LORD;
    I have not turned from my God to follow evil.
²² For all his laws are constantly before me;
    I have never abandoned his principles.
²³ I am blameless before God;
    I have kept myself from sin.
²⁴ The LORD rewarded me for doing right,
    because of the innocence of my hands in his sight.

²⁵ To the faithful you show yourself faithful;
    to those with integrity you show integrity.
²⁶ To the pure you show yourself pure,
    but to the wicked you show yourself hostile.
²⁷ You rescue those who are humble,
    but you humiliate the proud.
²⁸ LORD, you have brought light to my life;
    my God, you light up my darkness.
²⁹ In your strength I can crush an army;
    with my God I can scale any wall.

³⁰ As for God, his way is perfect.
    All the LORD's promises prove true.
    He is a shield for all who look to him for protection.

*S*top your bragging, David! That's our first reaction as we read verses 20-24. But this is the same David who says to God, "Compared to you, no one is perfect" (Psalm 143:2), and "I was born a sinner" (Psalm 51:5). So David knows better than to think that he has never sinned. Perhaps this psalm can be read in the same light as Paul's remarks, "I obeyed the Jewish law so carefully that I was never accused of any fault" (Philippians 3:6).

David treasured the covenant that God had made with Moses on Mount Sinai. David wanted to live according to God's laws, in keeping with this covenant. But David also received another covenant from the Lord—a covenant that required nothing on David's part. This was a covenant of gracious blessing upon David and his descendants, and his humble response was "Who am I, O Sovereign Lord, and what is my family? . . . You know what I am really like" (2 Samuel 7:18, 20).

The Lord has established a new covenant with us as well, and it requires nothing on our part except to receive it. Jesus Christ has sealed this new covenant in his blood and made us God's people (Luke 22:20). Like David, let us always respond in humble gratitude for God's mercy and then affirm, "We will do everything the Lord has said."

> Take time to be holy, speak oft with thy Lord;
> Abide in him always, and feed on his Word.
> Make friends of God's children; help those who are weak,
> Forgetting in nothing his blessing to seek.
> WILLIAM D. LONGSTAFF

Bible Networking

In this psalm David is speaking from the context of the old Mosaic covenant. To read about God's new covenant, see Jeremiah 31:31-34; Hebrews 9:15; and 2 Corinthians 3:6.

Notable Quotable

"God first gives us holiness and then rewards us for it. The prize is awarded to the flower at the flower show, but the gardener raised it." CHARLES HADDON SPURGEON

PSALM 18:30-36

30 As for God, his way is perfect.
    All the LORD's promises prove true.
    He is a shield for all who look to him for protection.

31 For who is God except the LORD?
    Who but our God is a solid rock?

32 God arms me with strength;
    he has made my way safe.

33 He makes me as surefooted as a deer,
    leading me safely along the mountain heights.

34 He prepares me for battle;
    he strengthens me to draw a bow of bronze.

35 You have given me the shield of your salvation.
    Your right hand supports me;
    your gentleness has made me great.

36 You have made a wide path for my feet
    to keep them from slipping.

*D*avid was a great soldier and an excellent general. Everybody knew it, especially the Philistines. But in these verses David gives all the credit to God. It was God who prepared, strengthened, and supported him.

In the New Testament we are reminded that we are in a battle with the powers of darkness, "the evil rulers and authorities of the unseen world" (Ephesians 6:12). How do we prepare ourselves for such spiritual warfare? As Martin Luther wrote, "Did we in our own strength confide, our striving would be losing." We must allow God to put his armor on us. Then we can be victorious, too.

Note also in verse 35 that, amid all the military language, David says, "Your gentleness has made me great." Ultimately, it's not superior weaponry and strategic plans that win the battle but God's gentleness toward us. He compassionately stoops down to lift us up and save us.

Ask God today to help you put on the armor he has offered us. Then we can be confident that the Lord will help us fend off any attack from the enemy.

> Stand then in His great might, with all His strength endued,
> And take to arm you for the fight the panoply of God;
> That having all things done, and all your conflicts passed,
> You may o'ercome through Christ alone and stand entire at last.
> CHARLES WESLEY

A Word on Words
The bow of bronze in verse 34 was probably a wooden bow strengthened with metal.

Bible Networking
David used the imagery of armor to describe how the Lord protects him. Read Ephesians 6:10-18 and compare Paul's use of armor imagery with David's.

PSALM 18:37-50

[37] I chased my enemies and caught them;
    I did not stop until they were conquered.
[38] I struck them down so they could not get up;
    they fell beneath my feet.
[39] You have armed me with strength for the battle;
    you have subdued my enemies under my feet.
[40] You made them turn and run;
    I have destroyed all who hated me.
[41] They called for help, but no one came to rescue them.
    They cried to the LORD, but he refused to answer them.
[42] I ground them as fine as dust carried by the wind.
    I swept them into the gutter like dirt.
[43] You gave me victory over my accusers.
    You appointed me as the ruler over nations;
    people I don't even know now serve me.
[44] As soon as they hear of me, they submit;
    foreigners cringe before me.
[45] They all lose their courage
    and come trembling from their strongholds.
[46] The LORD lives! Blessed be my rock!
    May the God of my salvation be exalted!
[47] He is the God who pays back those who harm me;
    he subdues the nations under me
[48] and rescues me from my enemies.
    You hold me safe beyond the reach of my enemies;
    you save me from violent opponents.
[49] For this, O LORD, I will praise you among the nations;
    I will sing joyfully to your name.
[50] You give great victories to your king;
    you show unfailing love to your anointed,
    to David and all his descendants forever.

Rocks are cold, hard, and lifeless. So why on earth does David say, "The Lord lives! Blessed be my rock!" (verse 46)? It's a strange image. We would think that David would pick some other object to convey the living power of the Lord.

But David knew rocks a lot better than we do. No doubt in the wilderness he found that rocks could protect him from the scorching sun, from the driving sand and wind storms, and from enemies who outnumbered him. David also knew that a rock could serve as a strong, unmoving foundation for anything that was meant to be permanent. Sands constantly shifted, but rocks stood firm. Rocks could be depended on. No wonder David thought of God as a rock.

But our question still stands: Why would David declare that the Lord *lives* and then portray him as a rock?

Maybe the answer is that David was trying to show that the Lord possesses all the strengths of a rock, yet he also lives. In other words, instead of the two concepts being synonymous, they are meant to complement each other.

So the Lord is a living rock. He offers strength and certainty for his people, and he acts on our behalf. As you face today's challenges, count on God as your living rock.

> O safe to the Rock that is higher than I,
> My soul in its conflicts and sorrows would fly;
> So sinful, so weary, thine, thine would I be;
> Thou blest "Rock of Ages," I'm hiding in thee.
> WILLIAM O. CUSHING

Bible Networking
For other instances where the Lord is referred to as a rock, look up Deuteronomy 32:4 and Isaiah 32:2.

Notable Quotable
"Where the desert touches an oasis, life is continuously under attack from the wind-driven infiltrating sand . . . but set a rock in the sand. After brief rains, life springs up on its leeward side and in time becomes a garden. The boulder has stayed the drift."
GEORGE ADAM SMITH

JUDGES 5:1-9 (Deborah's Song, Part 1)

² "When Israel's leaders take charge,
  and the people gladly follow—
bless the LORD!
³ "Listen, you kings!
  Pay attention, you mighty rulers!
For I will sing to the LORD.
  I will lift up my song to the LORD, the God of Israel.
⁴ "LORD, when you set out from Seir
  and marched across the fields of Edom,
the earth trembled
  and the cloudy skies poured down rain.
⁵ The mountains quaked at the coming of the LORD.
  Even Mount Sinai shook in the presence of the LORD,
    the God of Israel.
⁶ "In the days of Shamgar son of Anath, and in the days
    of Jael,
  people avoided the main roads,
  and travelers stayed on crooked side paths.
⁷ There were few people left in the villages of Israel—
  until Deborah arose as a mother for Israel.
⁸ When Israel chose new gods,
  war erupted at the city gates.
Yet not a shield or spear could be seen
  among forty thousand warriors in Israel!
⁹ My heart goes out to Israel's leaders,
  and to those who gladly followed.
  Bless the LORD!"

Psalm Link
PSALM 18:39-40

³⁹ You have armed me with strength for the battle;
  you have subdued my enemies under my feet.
⁴⁰ You made them turn and run;
  I have destroyed all who hated me.

*H*ave you ever experienced frustration in trying to get a group of people to do something? Many mothers can relate to this frustration. They have to constantly prod everyone to get ready to go, for if they don't, nothing seems to get done. At times they probably feel like shouting, "Doesn't anyone else care? Am I the only one who is doing anything about this?"

It was something like that in the days of Deborah. The Israelites were being oppressed by the Canaanites, but the Israelites had no weapons (Judges 5:8). The Canaanites, on the other hand, had nine hundred chariots! So nobody did anything about the situation.

Deborah wore three hats: a judge, a prophet, and "a mother for Israel" (Judges 5:7). Israel desperately needed all three right then. They needed a judge to bring law to a land that was falling apart. They needed a prophet to bring them God's message when they thought God had forgotten them. And they needed a mother to call everyone together and get them moving.

Because of Deborah's actions, Israel was rescued from the Canaanites. Just as the Lord used Deborah to accomplish his purposes for his people, he can use you as well. All you need to do is submit yourself to his leading.

> Lead on, O King Eternal, we follow, not with fears;
> For gladness breaks like morning where'er thy face appears;
> Your cross is lifted o'er us; we journey in its light;
> The crown awaits the conquest: lead on, O God of might.
> ERNEST W. SHURTLEFF

Bible Networking
Israel often celebrated national victories with songs. See Exodus 15:1-18; Numbers 21:27-30; and 1 Samuel 18:7.

Notable Quotable
"Let us adore the God before whom the unconscious earth and sky act as if they recognized their Maker and were moved with a tremor of reverence."
CHARLES HADDON SPURGEON

PSALM 19:1-6
For the choir director: A psalm of David.

¹ The heavens tell of the glory of God.
 The skies display his marvelous craftsmanship.
² Day after day they continue to speak;
 night after night they make him known.
³ They speak without a sound or a word;
 their voice is silent in the skies;
⁴ yet their message has gone out to all the earth,
 and their words to all the world.

 The sun lives in the heavens
 where God placed it.
⁵ It bursts forth like a radiant bridegroom
 after his wedding.
 It rejoices like a great athlete
 eager to run the race.
⁶ The sun rises at one end of the heavens
 and follows its course to the other end.
 Nothing can hide from its heat.

A student stood on the crest of a hill silently admiring the sunset. As the colors came to a brilliant crescendo, he suddenly shouted, "Way to go, God. Fantastic!" Then he raised his hand in praise to the Creator.

Dr. Carl Sagan marveled that a single human chromosome contains 20 billion bits of information. This corresponds to four thousand 500-page books—and that's only one chromosome! Yet Dr. Sagan never professed any belief in God.

When it comes to praising God for his incredible work in creation, some of us are more like Dr. Sagan than the student. We are quick to condemn those who deny that God created the universe, yet we, too, often forget to praise him for all that he has made.

The first six verses of this psalm remind us that all of nature testifies of the glory of God. The apostle Paul reiterated this truth when he wrote, "From the time the world was created, people have seen the earth and sky and all that God made. . . . So they have no excuse whatsoever for not knowing God" (Romans 1:20).

We praise God for salvation but forget to praise him for creation. Whether we look at the grandeur of the heavens or the intricacies of a chromosome, we should stand in awe of our Creator. Praise him today for his masterful work.

The unwearied sun, from day to day
Does His Creator's power display,
And publishes to every land
The work of an Almighty hand.
JOSEPH ADDISON

Bible Networking
It is a good thing to see God as the creator of the heavens, but the Bible warns against worshiping the stars themselves. See Job 31:26-28 and 2 Kings 23:5.

Notable Quotable
One of the leaders of the French Revolution, Jean Bon St. Andre, said to a peasant, "I will have all your steeples pulled down, so you will not be reminded any more of your old religion." The peasant replied, "But you cannot help leaving us the stars."

PSALM 19:7-14

⁷ The law of the LORD is perfect,
  reviving the soul.
The decrees of the LORD are trustworthy,
  making wise the simple.
⁸ The commandments of the LORD are right,
  bringing joy to the heart.
The commands of the LORD are clear,
  giving insight to life.
⁹ Reverence for the LORD is pure,
  lasting forever.
The laws of the LORD are true;
  each one is fair.
¹⁰ They are more desirable than gold,
  even the finest gold.
They are sweeter than honey,
  even honey dripping from the comb.
¹¹ They are a warning to those who hear them;
  there is great reward for those who obey them.

¹² How can I know all the sins lurking in my heart?
  Cleanse me from these hidden faults.
¹³ Keep me from deliberate sins!
  Don't let them control me.
Then I will be free of guilt
  and innocent of great sin.

¹⁴ May the words of my mouth and the thoughts of my
    heart
    be pleasing to you,
    O LORD, my rock and my redeemer.

John Bunyan, who wrote the classic *The Pilgrim's Progress*, had been a godless youth with "a great desire to take [his] fill of sin, still studying what sin was yet to be committed, that [he] might taste the sweetness of it." However, while still in his twenties, Bunyan was convicted by the Holy Spirit of his sinfulness and his need for a Redeemer.

After this Bunyan's conscience became so tender that he feared he was committing sins that would not be forgiven. Bunyan spent time studying Scripture, at times finding comfort and at other times being weighed down by guilt. "No one knows the terror of those days but myself," he wrote.

Looking back on those turbulent days in his life, Bunyan recognized he had made some big mistakes. Although he had prayed for cleansing (verse 12), he had not prayed to be kept from future sin (verse 13). In addition, he was not standing firmly on the rock of his salvation (verse 14), even though he had asked Christ to be his Redeemer.

Perhaps you have trusted Christ to save you, but you still experience spiritual defeat. This is not unusual, but you do need to address the problem. Each new day ask God to help you follow him more closely. But do not be afraid, for, as Bunyan later wrote, our "righteousness is Jesus Christ himself, the same yesterday, today, and forever."

> I lay my sins on Jesus, the spotless Lamb of God;
> He bears them all and frees us from the accursed load.
> I bring my guilt to Jesus, to wash my crimson stains,
> White in His blood most precious, till not a spot remains.
>
> HORATIUS BONAR

A Word on Words

In verses 7-10 David uses six nouns, six adjectives, and six verbs to describe the laws and commands of the Lord. What are they?

Notable Quotable

"If our Rock were not our Redeemer, we would be without hope. If our Redeemer were not our Rock, we might be afraid. Let us never forget that our redemption has in it the strength of the Mighty One."
G. CAMPBELL MORGAN

PSALM 20
For the choir director: A psalm of David.

¹ In times of trouble, may the LORD respond to your cry.
　　May the God of Israel keep you safe from all harm.
² May he send you help from his sanctuary
　　and strengthen you from Jerusalem.
³ May he remember all your gifts
　　and look favorably on your burnt offerings.　*Interlude*

⁴ May he grant your heart's desire
　　and fulfill all your plans.
⁵ May we shout for joy when we hear of your victory,
　　flying banners to honor our God.
May the LORD answer all your prayers.

⁶ Now I know that the LORD saves his anointed king.
　　He will answer him from his holy heaven
　　and rescue him by his great power.
⁷ Some nations boast of their armies and weapons,
　　but we boast in the LORD our God.
⁸ Those nations will fall down and collapse,
　　but we will rise up and stand firm.

⁹ Give victory to our king, O LORD!
　　Respond to our cry for help.

On March 8, 1839, the sides of a coal mine in Musselburg, Scotland, collapsed. The coal shaft quickly filled with dirt, imprisoning thirteen miners. They desperately tried to escape. At first they thought an abandoned shaft might be an exit route, but as the avalanche of dirt and coal dust continued to cascade upon them, they found themselves trapped in an 18-by-24-foot area that was only 3 feet high.

In this space they prepared for what seemed inevitable—meeting their Maker. They prayed together, and then they sang Psalm 20 as they had memorized it from the Scottish Psalter.

This psalm speaks of hope, but what was its application to the miners in this seemingly hopeless situation? People on the surface were frantically digging, but how would they ever find the tiny space where these men were trapped? Would God grant them their hearts' desire (verse 4)? Would he rescue them by his great power (verse 6)? And when everything was falling down and collapsing all around them (verse 8), would they be able to rise up? The miners' oxygen supply was rapidly diminishing, but still they prayed and sang psalms.

Miraculously, rescuers managed to find the area in which the miners were buried, and all thirteen were brought out alive with Psalm 20 still on their lips. The last verse in the psalter reads:

> Now save us, Lord, from slavish fear;
> Now let our hope be firm and strong,
> Till thy salvation shall appear
> And joy and triumph raise the song.
> OLD SCOTTISH PSALTER

Fascinating Fact
In Old Testament times, horses were used mainly for warfare. Thus, the words translated "armies and weapons" in verse 7 are literally "chariots and horses."

Bible Networking
See how banners (verse 5) were used elsewhere in Scripture (Numbers 2:2; Psalm 60:4; Isaiah 11:10; and Song of Songs 6:4, 10).

PSALM 21:1-7
For the choir director: A psalm of David.

¹ How the king rejoices in your strength, O Lord!
He shouts with joy because of your victory.
² For you have given him his heart's desire;
you have held back nothing that he requested.

Interlude

³ You welcomed him back with success and prosperity.
You placed a crown of finest gold on his head.
⁴ He asked you to preserve his life,
and you have granted his request.
The days of his life stretch on forever.
⁵ Your victory brings him great honor,
and you have clothed him with splendor and
majesty.
⁶ You have endowed him with eternal blessings.
You have given him the joy of being in your
presence.
⁷ For the king trusts in the Lord.
The unfailing love of the Most High will keep him
from stumbling.

*H*enry IV of France (Henry of Navarre) had been imprisoned in Paris because of his Protestant beliefs. Eventually he managed to escape and find refuge with the Huguenots, who were being persecuted throughout the country. At a Huguenot service, he heard the worshipers singing Psalm 21. Learning that it was about God's blessing upon a king, Henry assumed it was chosen to honor his arrival. When he was told that Psalm 21 was simply the next one to be sung, he was sure that God had prearranged it and was in awe of God's providential leading.

In the King James Version, verse 3 reads: "For thou preventest him with the blessings of goodness." Commentaries explain that the word *prevent* has changed its meaning in the last four hundred years. It used to mean "to go before." Therefore, when theologians speak of "prevenient grace," they mean that God's grace paves the way for our salvation.

That was what amazed Henry IV: God had gone before him. This is what amazed King David: God was there already, welcoming him back with great celebration.

As we move toward God, we discover that he has already moved toward us. Whether we are a king, a peasant, or someone in between, God has paved the way for our salvation. All we need to do is surrender ourselves to him.

> *For the love of God is broader*
> *Than the measure of man's mind,*
> *And the heart of the Eternal*
> *Is most wonderfully kind.*
> FREDERICK W. FABER

Fascinating Fact

The Targum (an ancient Aramaic translation/interpretation of the Old Testament) interpreted this psalm as relating to the Messiah. It rendered verse 1 as "The King Messiah rejoices."

Psalm at a Glance

Psalm 20 and Psalm 21 correspond to each other. They both speak about the king. The first is a psalm of intercession, perhaps as the king goes out to battle. The second is a psalm of thanksgiving, perhaps for the king's triumphant return.

PSALM 21:8-13

8 You will capture all your enemies.
  Your strong right hand will seize all those who hate
    you.
9 You will destroy them as in a flaming furnace
  when you appear.
The Lord will consume them in his anger;
  fire will devour them.
10 You will wipe their children from the face of the earth;
  they will never have descendants.
11 Although they plot against you,
  their evil schemes will never succeed.
12 For they will turn and run
  when they see your arrows aimed at them.

13 We praise you, Lord, for all your glorious power.
  With music and singing we celebrate your mighty
    acts.

*T*he experienced hiker pointed to a distant peak. "That's where we're headed. It should take us four days, if we're lucky."
"Four days!" a younger, novice hiker responded. "We can take this hill by supper time!"

The older one just shook his head and smiled. "It's farther than you think."

They climbed the wooded trail all day, with the young hiker pressing hard to reach the peak by the end of the day. Sure enough, as the sun began to dip below the horizon, the hill leveled off and they reached a clearing. "See," crowed the young hiker. "We made it to the top."

The veteran hiker smiled again and pointed to the next hill, which loomed even larger ahead of them. "No, that's where we're headed."

Psalm 21 is like that. On the surface this psalm is about David. But a closer look will reveal a deeper meaning beyond this. Verse 4 says: "The days of his life stretch on forever." Verse 9 says: "You will destroy them as in a flaming furnace when you appear," reminding us of Jesus in Revelation 6:16. Indeed, many Jewish scholars considered this psalm to be speaking of the Messiah.

As you read this psalm, praise God for his justice, righteousness, and sovereignty. But don't stop there. Lift your eyes and look for the hill beyond—the coming future king whose "life [and reign] stretch on forever."

> *Yea, Amen! let all adore Thee,*
> *High on Thine eternal throne;*
> *Savior, take the power and glory,*
> *Claim the Kingdom for Thine own:*
> *O come quickly, O come quickly,*
> *Hallelujah! Come, Lord, come.*
> JOHN CENNICK

PSALM 22:1-10

For the choir director: A psalm of David, to be sung to the tune "Doe of the Dawn."

¹ My God, my God! Why have you forsaken me?
    Why do you remain so distant?
    Why do you ignore my cries for help?
² Every day I call to you, my God, but you do not answer.
    Every night you hear my voice, but I find no relief.

³ Yet you are holy.
    The praises of Israel surround your throne.
⁴ Our ancestors trusted in you,
    and you rescued them.
⁵ You heard their cries for help and saved them.
    They put their trust in you and were never
        disappointed.

⁶ But I am a worm and not a man.
    I am scorned and despised by all!
⁷ Everyone who sees me mocks me.
    They sneer and shake their heads, saying,
⁸ "Is this the one who relies on the LORD?
    Then let the LORD save him!
If the LORD loves him so much,
    let the LORD rescue him!"

⁹ Yet you brought me safely from my mother's womb
    and led me to trust you when I was a nursing infant.
¹⁰ I was thrust upon you at my birth.
    You have been my God from the moment I was
        born.

Lancelot Andrewes, an Anglican clergyman who helped translate the King James Version of the Bible, once preached a sermon on the first part of verse 6, "But I am a worm and not a man."

He said a fisherman knows that fish will never bite unless there is a worm on the hook. Similarly, Andrewes said that when Jesus came for our redemption, he hid "his godhead within the worm of his human nature. The great water serpent, the Devil, thinking to swallow the worm of his humanity, was caught upon the hook of his divinity. . . . By thinking to destroy Christ, he destroyed his own kingdom and lost his own power."

Psalm 22 describes a man in deep depression, feeling forsaken by everyone, including God. The entire psalm is similar to the account of Jesus' crucifixion, so it's no wonder that Jesus quoted verse 1 from the cross. There, bearing the world's sin, he felt utterly forsaken by his heavenly Father, who had called him his "beloved Son" (Matthew 3:17). But, as Andrewes reminds us, the Father had not completely abandoned his Son. He was working out a greater, eternal purpose—the salvation of humanity.

> What thou, my Lord, hast suffered was all for
>   sinners' gain;
> Mine, mine was the transgression, but thine the
>   deadly pain.
> Lo, here I fall, my Savior! 'Tis I deserve thy place;
> Look on me with thy favor, and grant to me thy
>   grace.
> BERNARD OF CLAIRVAUX

Bible Networking

Compare how the sufferings of this character resemble those described in Isaiah 52:13–53:12 and with Matthew 27:41-46.

Notable Quotable

"Here is comfort to 'deserted' souls. Christ himself was deserted. You may be beloved of God and not feel it. Christ was."
JOHN ROW

PSALM 22:11-21

¹¹ Do not stay so far from me,
for trouble is near,
and no one else can help me.
¹² My enemies surround me like a herd of bulls;
fierce bulls of Bashan have hemmed me in!
¹³ Like roaring lions attacking their prey,
they come at me with open mouths.
¹⁴ My life is poured out like water,
and all my bones are out of joint.
My heart is like wax,
melting within me.
¹⁵ My strength has dried up like sunbaked clay.
My tongue sticks to the roof of my mouth.
You have laid me in the dust and left me for dead.

¹⁶ My enemies surround me like a pack of dogs;
an evil gang closes in on me.
They have pierced my hands and feet.
¹⁷ I can count every bone in my body.
My enemies stare at me and gloat.
¹⁸ They divide my clothes among themselves
and throw dice for my garments.

¹⁹ O LORD, do not stay away!
You are my strength; come quickly to my aid!
²⁰ Rescue me from a violent death;
spare my precious life from these dogs.
²¹ Snatch me from the lions' jaws,
and from the horns of these wild oxen.

The New Testament writers recognized that this psalm speaks of Jesus' suffering on the cross (Mark 15:34; John 19:24). But how could the psalmist have so accurately described something that happened hundreds of years later? Crucifixion had not even been invented when this psalm was written.

The superscription calls it a psalm of David, but when was David in such dire straits? Some say it sounds more like Jeremiah, who did face persecution. Whoever he was, he was inspired by God to describe some very personal torment that mirrored Jesus' crucifixion hundreds of years later.

The first eleven verses alternate between descriptions of suffering and prayers for relief—two or three verses about suffering and then two or three verses about relief. But these middle verses paint all the gruesome details. Besides all the pain, we see a picture of utter humiliation.

"You have laid me in the dust," it says (verse 15). Who has done this? Not the "fierce bulls," the "roaring lions," the "pack of dogs," or the "evil gang," but rather "My God, my God" (verse 1). As Isaiah 53:10 says: "It was the Lord's good plan to crush him." And Isaiah tells us why: "He was wounded and crushed for our sins. He was beaten that we might have peace. He was whipped, and we were healed!" (Isaiah 53:5).

In light of Jesus' willingness to suffer all this for us, let us cry, "Hallelujah, what a Savior!"

> Bearing shame and scoffing rude,
> In my place condemned he stood;
> Sealed my pardon with his blood:
> Hallelujah! what a Savior!
> PHILIP P. BLISS

A Word on Words

What were "bulls of Bashan" (verse 12)? Bashan was an area east of the Sea of Galilee. It had great grassy plains, so the livestock there were well fed and strong. See Deuteronomy 32:14 and Ezekiel 39:18.

Notable Quotable

"Christ submitted to suffer nakedness [verse 18] that we might be covered with righteousness and glory and walk with him in white forever." GEORGE HUTCHESON

PSALM 22:22-31

22 Then I will declare the wonder of your name to my
　　　brothers and sisters.
　　I will praise you among all your people.
23 Praise the LORD, all you who fear him!
　　　Honor him, all you descendants of Jacob!
　　　Show him reverence, all you descendants of Israel!
24 For he has not ignored the suffering of the needy.
　　　He has not turned and walked away.
　　　He has listened to their cries for help.

25 I will praise you among all the people;
　　　I will fulfill my vows in the presence of those who
　　　　worship you.
26 The poor will eat and be satisfied.
　　　All who seek the LORD will praise him.
　　　Their hearts will rejoice with everlasting joy.
27 The whole earth will acknowledge the LORD and return
　　　to him.
　　People from every nation will bow down before him.
28 For the LORD is king!
　　　He rules all the nations.

29 Let the rich of the earth feast and worship.
　　　Let all mortals—those born to die—bow down in
　　　　his presence.
30 Future generations will also serve him.
　　　Our children will hear about the wonders of the
　　　　Lord.
31 His righteous acts will be told to those yet unborn.
　　　They will hear about everything he has done.

*S*omething wonderful must have happened between the desperation of verse 21 and the exaltation of verse 22 in this psalm. In yesterday's reading the psalmist was facing a "violent death" (verse 20) at the hands of his enemies. In fact, all of Psalm 22 to this point has been a cry for help and a graphic description of suffering. But suddenly the psalmist is praising the Lord and inviting everyone to do the same. There are other psalms that start out in the pits and end with praise, but none of them catapult from such deep suffering into such lofty joy.

We have already seen how the description of suffering in Psalm 22 is uncannily appropriate to Jesus' crucifixion. Well, today's passage can't help but remind us of the book of Acts, as people "declare the wonder" (verse 22) of God's name throughout the whole world.

Contributing to the joyous theme of the second half of Psalm 22 is a description of a feast (verses 25-29), perhaps alluding to the peace offering in Leviticus 7. As far as the New Testament goes, it may refer to the feast Jesus spoke of where the poor, crippled, lame, and blind will be invited (Luke 14:15-24). The book of Revelation describes the feast to end all feasts—the wedding supper of the Lamb (19:9).

Let us praise God that we can feast like the last half of Psalm 22, since Jesus has endured the agony of the first half of Psalm 22.

> From earth's wide bounds, from ocean's farthest
>   coast,
> Through gates of pearl stream in the countless host,
> Singing to Father, Son, and Holy Ghost:
> Alleluia! Alleluia!
> WILLIAM W. HOW

Bible Networking

How is the celebration of the Lord's Supper (1 Corinthians 11:23-26) like this invitation to "eat and be satisfied" (verse 26)?

Notable Quotable

"It is possible to die of starvation at the door of a granary. By the act of faith in Jesus Christ, partake of the food. See that it becomes yours by your own taking of it into the very depths of your heart."
ALEXANDER MACLAREN

PSALM 23
A psalm of David.

1 **The LORD is my shepherd;
    I have everything I need.**
2 He lets me rest in green meadows;
    he leads me beside peaceful streams.
3   He renews my strength.
He guides me along right paths,
    bringing honor to his name.

4 Even when I walk
    through the dark valley of death,
I will not be afraid,
    for you are close beside me.
Your rod and your staff
    protect and comfort me.

5 You prepare a feast for me
    in the presence of my enemies.
You welcome me as a guest,
    anointing my head with oil.
    My cup overflows with blessings.
6 Surely your goodness and unfailing love will pursue me
    all the days of my life,
and I will live in the house of the LORD
    forever.

*A*ll you need for eternity is packed into the first five words of Psalm 23:1:

The—He is the only God, as the first commandment says. He isn't a Lord; he is the Lord.

Lord—This name emphasizes his amazing grace, love, and faithfulness to us.

Is—This present tense verb shows that God lives. He is the same today as he was yesterday.

My—God is not an abstract power. He wants to be your personal shepherd.

Shepherd—And what a shepherd! He loves and cares for his sheep, even dying for them.

A pastor visited a very sick child once and took him word by word through Psalm 23:1 to try and comfort him. With each word the child was taught to grasp a different finger, concluding with his thumb, which represented the word *shepherd*. The pastor didn't really know at the time how much the child understood.

Shortly after the little boy died, the mother spoke to the pastor and said, "Just before he died, he held very tightly to his index finger, and he seemed to want to tell me something."

The pastor knew that the boy had understood. He had been clutching his "my" finger. He knew that the Lord was his personal shepherd to guide him "through the dark valley of death."

> *The king of love my Shepherd is,*
> *Whose goodness faileth never;*
> *I nothing lack if I am his*
> *And he is mine forever.*
> HENRY W. BAKER

Bible Networking
For more about the Lord as a shepherd, read John 10:14-16.

Notable Quotable
"When this is said, all is said. Whatever may be added is only to help us understand the fullness of this great truth. . . . If we wander, we are not abandoned. In the darkest hours he is still with us. In our conflicts he upholds us."
G. CAMPBELL MORGAN

PSALM 23
A psalm of David

[1] The LORD is my shepherd;
I have everything I need.
[2] **He lets me rest in green meadows;**
he leads me beside peaceful streams.
[3] He renews my strength.
He guides me along right paths,
bringing honor to his name.

[4] Even when I walk
through the dark valley of death,
I will not be afraid,
for you are close beside me.
Your rod and your staff
protect and comfort me.

[5] You prepare a feast for me
in the presence of my enemies.
You welcome me as a guest,
anointing my head with oil.
My cup overflows with blessings.
[6] Surely your goodness and unfailing love will pursue me
all the days of my life,
and I will live in the house of the LORD
forever.

In *A Shepherd Looks at Psalm 23*, Philip Keller shares his experiences in raising sheep. He discovered rather quickly that "sheep do not just take care of themselves. . . . They require, more than any other class of livestock, endless attention and meticulous care."

He also found that sheep do not rest or lie down unless they are free from fear, free from tension with other sheep, free of flies or other pests, and free from hunger. Keller then points out how the Lord delivers us from fear (2 Timothy 1:7), tensions (Philippians 4:6-7), irritations of daily life (John 14:27), and spiritual hunger (John 6:35).

Regarding peaceful streams, Keller says there are three ways sheep quench their thirst: (1) licking up the morning dew; (2) drinking water drawn from deep wells; or (3) drinking from flowing streams. Once again there are parallels to the Christian life. The morning dew reminds us of our need for spiritual drink as we start each day; the deep wells remind us of what God supplies to deepen our spiritual life; and the flowing streams remind us of the work of the Holy Spirit (see John 7:39) to lead us into truth.

Let us look to our great Shepherd to provide for us and lead us where we need to go.

> *Drop thy still dews of quietness,*
> *Till all our strivings cease;*
> *Take from our souls the strain and stress,*
> *And let our ordered lives confess*
> *The beauty of thy peace.*
> JOHN GREENLEAF WHITTIER

Bible Networking
For another look at the Lord as a shepherd, read Ezekiel 34:11-24.

Notable Quotable
"The green pastures were a seasonal phenomenon. The fields, even parts of the desert, would 'green' during the winter and spring. But in summer and fall the sheep would be led to many places to search for food. God's care is not seasonal, but constant and abundant."
WILLEM VAN DEMEREN

PSALM 23
A psalm of David.

¹ The LORD is my shepherd;
  I have everything I need.
² He lets me rest in green meadows;
  he leads me beside peaceful streams.
³ **He renews my strength.**
He guides me along right paths,
  bringing honor to his name.

⁴ Even when I walk
  through the dark valley of death,
I will not be afraid,
  for you are close beside me.
Your rod and your staff
  protect and comfort me.

⁵ You prepare a feast for me
  in the presence of my enemies.
You welcome me as a guest,
  anointing my head with oil.
  My cup overflows with blessings.
⁶ Surely your goodness and unfailing love will pursue me
  all the days of my life,
and I will live in the house of the LORD
  forever.

*I*n George Macdonald's *The Marquis of Lossie*, a hunchback child moans constantly, "I dinna ken whaur I cam frae, and I dinna ken whaur I'm gaein' till!" (I don't know where I came from. I don't know where I'm going to.")

Omar Khayyam echoed the same sentiment when he said, "I come like water, and like wind I go! . . . I know not whither, willy-nilly blowing."

The German philosopher Immanuel Kant devoted himself to resolving three questions: (1) What am I? (2) Whence came I? (3) Whither go I? But after a long life of research and analysis, the three questions remained unanswered for Kant.

Sadly, most people today don't know where they are going either. They follow whatever seems right to them at the time. Some enjoy their journey and never question their final destination. Others change directions constantly but never find the "right paths."

Fortunately, we do not need to wander in the wilderness. Instead, God gives direction to those who seek him, guiding us along right paths (verse 3).

As you travel physical paths today, take time to thank and praise God for guiding you spiritually and for helping you make wise decisions that bring "honor to his name" (verse 3).

> All the way my Savior leads me;
> What have I to ask beside?
> Can I doubt his tender mercy,
> Who through life has been my guide?
> Heavenly peace, divinest comfort, here by faith in
>   him to dwell,
> For I know, whate'er befall me, Jesus doeth all
>   things well.
> FANNY J. CROSBY

Bible Networking
Read Proverbs 2:12-15; 5:3-6; and 10:9 and see the difference between right paths and crooked paths.

Notable Quotable
"Just as sheep will blindly, habitually, stupidly follow one another along the same little trails until they become ruts that erode into gigantic gullies, so we humans cling to the same habits that we have seen ruin other lives."
PHILIP KELLER

PSALM 23
A psalm of David.

¹ The LORD is my shepherd;
  I have everything I need.
² He lets me rest in green meadows;
    he leads me beside peaceful streams.
³   He renews my strength.
  He guides me along right paths,
    bringing honor to his name.

⁴ **Even when I walk**
    through the dark valley of death,
  I will not be afraid,
    for you are close beside me.
  Your rod and your staff
    protect and comfort me.

⁵ You prepare a feast for me
    in the presence of my enemies.
  You welcome me as a guest,
    anointing my head with oil.
  My cup overflows with blessings.
⁶ Surely your goodness and unfailing love will pursue me
    all the days of my life,
  and I will live in the house of the LORD
    forever.

Joseph Addison was one of the finest English essayists of the eighteenth century. He dabbled in politics, but because he was shy and embarrassingly clumsy, he never went any farther than being a cabinet member. Once he tried to speak before Parliament, but he stuttered, stammered, blushed, coughed, apologized, sat down, and never tried it again.

F. S. Boreham notes that there were two things Addison was passionately fond of. He loved the fields and streams of his home county, and he loved Psalm 23. In fact, Addison wrote paraphrases of both Psalm 23 and Psalm 19, which were published in *The Spectator Magazine* in 1712.

Addison had learned Psalm 23 at his mother's knee. As a writer he always treasured its exquisite writing, and as a Christian he revered its message. Lord Thomas Macauley eulogized Addison in this way: "He loved the psalm which represents the Ruler of all things under the endearing image of a shepherd, whose crook guides the flock through gloomy and desolate glens to meadows well watered and rich in herbage."

As Addison lay dying at the age of forty-seven, he clung to the promise of Psalm 23:4: "I will not be afraid, for you are close beside me." Knowing his death was imminent, he sent for his son-in-law, the earl of Warwick, who was a sheep gone astray. When the earl arrived, Addison said, "See in what peace a Christian can die."

Sometimes mid scenes of deepest gloom,
Sometimes where Eden's bowers bloom,
By waters still, o'er troubled sea,
Still 'tis his hand that leadeth me.
JOSEPH H. GILMORE

A Word on Words
Notice the pronouns he *and* his, *which are used five times in verses 2-3. Notice in the last three verses that the pronouns are* you *and* your.

Fascinating Fact
The rod was used to club down wild animals that threatened the sheep (1 Samuel 17:35, 43). The staff was used to keep the sheep under control.

PSALM 23
A psalm of David.

¹ The LORD is my shepherd;
 I have everything I need.
² He lets me rest in green meadows;
 he leads me beside peaceful streams.
³ He renews my strength.
He guides me along right paths,
 bringing honor to his name.

⁴ Even when I walk
 through the dark valley of death,
I will not be afraid,
 for you are close beside me.
Your rod and your staff
 protect and comfort me.

⁵ You prepare a feast for me
 in the presence of my enemies.
You welcome me as a guest,
 anointing my head with oil.
 My cup overflows with blessings.
⁶ Surely your goodness and unfailing love will pursue me
 all the days of my life,
and I will live in the house of the LORD
 forever.

*I*n this verse, the imagery of Psalm 23 shifts. No longer is the psalmist a sheep grazing on a verdant hillside. Now he is a guest of honor at a sumptuous feast.

Feasts are a frequent theme in Scripture. Matthew threw a banquet for Jesus and his disciples, with enemies (the Pharisees) standing outside. The Pharisees' said to the disciples, "Why does he eat with such scum?" (Mark 2:16).

Later in the Gospels a Pharisee invites Jesus to a banquet (Luke 7:36) but neglects to anoint his head with oil. Instead an immoral woman comes and anoints Jesus' feet (Luke 7:36-50).

Another banquet is mentioned in the Song of Songs. Here the young woman says, "He brings me to the banquet hall, so everyone can see how much he loves me" (Song of Songs 2:4).

In Psalm 23 the Good Shepherd invites us "scum" to his banquet to show how much he loves us, and instead of us anointing *his* head with oil, he anoints *ours!* If we look at the requirements for entering God's presence in Psalm 15, we may think that we are excluded—and we would be if it were up to us. But what a joy it is to know that God has invited us to his banquet and made us honored guests! Our cup truly overflows with blessings!

> *In the midst of affliction my table is spread*
> *With blessings unmeasured my cup runneth o'er;*
> *With perfume and oil thou anointest my head,*
> *Oh, what shall I ask of thy providence more?*
> JAMES MONTGOMERY

Bible Networking
Check out the feast in Isaiah 25:6-8. How does that feast compare with the one described in Psalm 23:5?

Notable Quotable
"Sin finds its master in grace. The big thing can be buried in the bigger thing. And divine grace is the only bigger thing that can ever be found."
JAMES AND EDWARD HASTINGS

PSALM 23
A psalm of David.

¹ The Lord is my shepherd;
    I have everything I need.
² He lets me rest in green meadows;
    he leads me beside peaceful streams.
³   He renews my strength.
He guides me along right paths,
    bringing honor to his name.

⁴ Even when I walk
    through the dark valley of death,
I will not be afraid,
    for you are close beside me.
Your rod and your staff
    protect and comfort me.

⁵ You prepare a feast for me
    in the presence of my enemies.
You welcome me as a guest,
    anointing my head with oil.
My cup overflows with blessings.
⁶ **Surely your goodness and unfailing love will pursue me**
    all the days of my life,
and I will live in the house of the LORD
    forever.

*S*ome people think of "goodness and un-failing love" (verse 6) as God's watch-dogs. The Good Shepherd is leading up ahead, and the dogs are keeping us moving from behind.

This imagery brings to mind a poem by Francis Thompson entitled "The Hound of Heaven." The opening lines read:

I fled Him, down the nights and down the days;
* I fled Him, down the arches of the years;*
I fled Him, down the labyrinthine ways
* Of my own mind . . .*
From those strong Feet that followed, followed after.

People run from God and his love all the time. Even those who say they follow God occasionally run from him. Exactly why people run from God is somewhat of a mystery. Regarding his own time of running from God the Elizabethan poet George Herbert explained, "Love bade me welcome: yet my soul drew back, Guilty of dust and sin." Fortunately, as Francis Thompson has noted, "Love is a better pursuer than Fear is an evader." When we run from God, he is able to catch us with his goodness and unfailing love, escorting us back into his green pastures.

> *Green pastures are before me, which yet I have not*
> * seen;*
> *Bright skies will soon be o'er me where darkest*
> * clouds have been;*
> *My hope I cannot measure, my path to life is free;*
> *My Savior has my treasure, and he will walk with me.*
> ANNA L. WARING

Fascinating Fact
In pain after a long and arduous trip, John Wesley was unable to stand up, so he preached a sermon on Psalm 23 from his knees.

Notable Quotable
"One soon tires of being 'on the go.' Man looks for some place he can with finality call home."
NORMAN KELLOW

PSALM 24
A psalm of David.

¹ The earth is the LORD's, and everything in it.
  The world and all its people belong to him.
² For he laid the earth's foundation on the seas
  and built it on the ocean depths.

³ Who may climb the mountain of the LORD?
  Who may stand in his holy place?
⁴ Only those whose hands and hearts are pure,
  who do not worship idols
  and never tell lies.
⁵ They will receive the LORD's blessing
  and have right standing with God their savior.
⁶ They alone may enter God's presence
  and worship the God of Israel.   *Interlude*

⁷ Open up, ancient gates!
  Open up, ancient doors,
  and let the King of glory enter.
⁸ Who is the King of glory?
  The LORD, strong and mighty,
  the LORD, invincible in battle.
⁹ Open up, ancient gates!
  Open up, ancient doors,
  and let the King of glory enter.
¹⁰ Who is the King of glory?
  The LORD Almighty—
  he is the King of glory.   *Interlude*

This psalm may have been written in honor of the Ark coming at last to Mount Zion (1 Chronicles 13:8), but that's only part of the story.

For the Israelite, the excitement as well as the pageantry must have been overwhelming, far greater than any opening ceremony of the Olympic Games (see 1 Chronicles 15–16). Ever since the Ark had been built soon after the Exodus it had been in temporary quarters. Now in Jerusalem it would have a permanent home at last.

As it approached the city, the gates were commanded to open. The Ark came in, and King David came in, but the King of glory was still to come.

A thousand years later the King of glory came to this world as a lowly baby in Bethlehem, where David had been born. Jesus grew up and entered the ancient gates of Jerusalem on Palm Sunday. A week later he was crucified and buried, but he rose again and "ascended higher than all the heavens, so that his rule might fill the entire universe" (Ephesians 4:10).

David called for the ancient doors to open and let the King of glory enter. Jesus wants us to open the doors to our heart and let him enter, for he is knocking (Revelation 3:20). Will you open the gate to him today?

The king of glory! Who can tell
The wonders of his might?
He rules the nations; but to dwell
With saints is his delight.
ISAAC WATTS

Psalm at a Glance

Psalms 22, 23, and 24 fit well together. Psalm 22 speaks of the Savior who suffered for us. Psalm 23 speaks of the Shepherd who guides us day by day. Psalm 24 speaks of the Sovereign Lord in glory. These psalms show us Jesus yesterday, today, and forever. In them we see the Cross, the Crook, and the Crown.

Notable Quotable

"If the earth is the Lord's (verses 1-2), and he is holy (verses 3-6), the challenge to the ancient doors is a battle cry for the church [see 2 Corinthians 10:5-8]."
DEREK KIDNER

Most people think of David as a shepherd, a giant-killer, a king of Israel, and a writer of psalms. But David was also the founder of organized professional choirs for the Tabernacle and Temple.

Here are some verses you might not have noticed before about singing in the Temple:

♦ "David assigned the following men to lead the music at the house of the LORD after he put the Ark there. They ministered with music there at the Tabernacle until Solomon built the Temple of the LORD in Jerusalem. Then they carried on their work there, following all the regulations handed down to them." (1 Chronicles 6:31-32)

♦ "They transported the Ark of God from the house of Abinadab. . . . David and all Israel were celebrating before God with all their might, singing and playing all kinds of musical instruments—lyres, harps, tambourines, cymbals, and trumpets." (1 Chronicles 13:7-8)

♦ "They and their families were all trained in making music before the LORD, and each of them—288 in all—was an accomplished musician. The musicians were appointed to their particular term of service by means of sacred lots, without regard to whether they were young or old, teacher or student." (1 Chronicles 25:7-8)

♦ "As the burnt offering was presented, songs of praise to the LORD were begun, accompanied by the trumpets and other instruments of David, king of Israel. The entire assembly worshiped the LORD as the singers sang and the trumpets blew, until all the burnt offerings were finished." (2 Chronicles 29:27-28)

♦ "The two choirs that were giving thanks then proceeded to the Temple of God, where they took their places. . . . We went together with the trumpet-playing priests . . . and the singers. . . . They played and sang loudly and clearly under the direction of Jezrahiah the choir director." (Nehemiah 12:40-42)

It has been argued that David's most significant contribution to Israelite worship practices was the formation of professional musical divisions. He organized three music guilds that had the responsibility of composing and directing songs of praise and thanksgiving that were used in Temple celebrations and worship services. In fact, many of the psalms between Psalm 42 and 91 were written by leaders of these guilds.

The book we now call Psalms was started by David and developed and shaped by his music directors and their descendants. It became the Jewish hymnal. An entire chapter of Scripture (1 Chronicles 25) spells out the duties of the musicians. Four thousand priests were organized into minstrel groups and choirs. These musicians not only sang but also played a variety of musical instruments. In Hebrew worship singing was not only done by an individual or the entire congregation but often by choirs.

The apostle Paul speaks of the early church singing "psalms and hymns and spiritual songs," exhorting Christians to make music to the Lord "in your hearts" (Ephesians 5:19). Whether it's the "joyous shout" of Psalm 95:1 that might be accompanied by cymbals and drums, or whether it is the "in your hearts" music that Paul describes, we have much to sing about, and the Psalms can help us express our joy. What will you sing about today?

∾

Saints below, with heart and voice,
Still in songs of praise rejoice;
Learning here, by faith and love,
Songs of praise to sing above.
JAMES MONTGOMERY

Selah

PSALM 25:1-6
A psalm of David.

¹ To you, O Lord, I lift up my soul.
²   I trust in you, my God!
    Do not let me be disgraced,
      or let my enemies rejoice in my defeat.
³ No one who trusts in you will ever be disgraced,
      but disgrace comes to those who try to deceive
        others.

⁴ Show me the path where I should walk, O Lord;
      point out the right road for me to follow.
⁵ Lead me by your truth and teach me,
      for you are the God who saves me.
      All day long I put my hope in you.

⁶ Remember, O Lord, your unfailing love and
        compassion,
      which you have shown from long ages past.

I n the middle of his second missionary journey, the apostle Paul wasn't sure where to go. He had split up with his mentor, Barnabas, and was the leader of his own team, which included Silas and young Timothy. Paul planned to go one way, but the Holy Spirit didn't let him. Then he turned to go another way, and once again the door was closed to him. How frustrating it must have been! God had called Paul to travel through Asia Minor spreading the word about Jesus, and he had been faithful to that calling. Was God now going to leave him stranded?

No doubt Paul and his friends called upon God with the same requests that David did in Psalm 25: "Show me the path . . . point out the right road . . . lead me by your truth."

And the very next night God did give them direction. Paul had a vision of a man beckoning him to enter Europe (Acts 16:9). Paul heeded this message from the Lord, and, as a result, the evangelization of a whole new continent was begun.

In every age Christians long to hear God's clear direction: "This is the way; turn around and walk here" (Isaiah 30:21). This is where we must truly recognize that the Lord is indeed our Shepherd and trust him to show us the way.

Whatever problem you are facing today, call upon God, and in his perfect timing he will guide you.

> Lead, kindly Light, amid the encircling gloom;
> Lead thou me on.
> The night is dark, and I am far from home;
> Lead thou me on.
> Keep thou my feet; I do not ask to see
> The distant scene—one step enough for me.
> JOHN H. NEWMAN

Fascinating Fact
This is an acrostic psalm, with each verse beginning with the next letter of the Hebrew alphabet (with a few exceptions). This was probably a psalm that parents taught their children, since its alphabetical arrangement would make it easier to memorize and it calls for the Lord to "teach," "show," and "lead."

Notable Quotable
"Do what you know to be your present duty, and God will acquaint you with your future duty."
SAMUEL ANNESLEY

PSALM 25:7-13

⁷ Forgive the rebellious sins of my youth;
  look instead through the eyes of your unfailing love,
  for you are merciful, O LORD.

⁸ The LORD is good and does what is right;
  he shows the proper path to those who go astray.
⁹ He leads the humble in what is right,
  teaching them his way.
¹⁰ The LORD leads with unfailing love and faithfulness
  all those who keep his covenant and obey his
    decrees.

¹¹ For the honor of your name, O LORD,
  forgive my many, many sins.
¹² Who are those who fear the LORD?
  He will show them the path they should choose.
¹³ They will live in prosperity,
  and their children will inherit the Promised Land.

*T*he date will not be forgotten. On July 5, 1800, a schoolboy found himself locked inside Westminster Abbey in London. In the night he made his way to the hallowed Coronation Chair, where English kings and queens are crowned. In that chair he fell asleep. In the morning when he awoke, he took out his pocket knife and carved the following inscription into the solid oak seat of the chair: "F Abbot slept in this chair July 5, 1800."

No doubt other youths have committed more heinous crimes, but few have so indelibly etched a record of their sin as did F. Abbot.

In this psalm the major theme is divine guidance, but a secondary theme is a plea for forgiveness from the sins of one's past (verses 7, 11, 18). David knows that in order to walk in right paths, he must seek to put away his sinful ways. And we can see from this psalm that he knows that God will forgive his sins if he asks him to.

We, too, need to be forgiven of our sins, which have been etched upon our heart like the sin of F. Abbot. Through Christ comes forgiveness for all who are ashamed of their sins. "If we confess our sins to him, he is faithful and just to forgive us and to cleanse us from every wrong" (1 John 1:9).

> *Your many sins are all forgiven;*
> *Oh, hear the voice of Jesus;*
> *Go on your way in peace to heaven*
> *And wear a crown with Jesus.*
> WILLIAM HUNTER

Bible Networking
God's honor and reputation were a concern to many in the Old Testament. See also Joshua 7:9; Isaiah 63:14, 16; and Ezekiel 36:22-23.

PSALM 25:14-22

¹⁴ Friendship with the LORD is reserved for those who fear
  him.
    With them he shares the secrets of his covenant.
¹⁵ My eyes are always looking to the LORD for help,
    for he alone can rescue me from the traps of my
      enemies.

¹⁶ Turn to me and have mercy on me,
    for I am alone and in deep distress.
¹⁷ My problems go from bad to worse.
    Oh, save me from them all!
¹⁸ Feel my pain and see my trouble.
    Forgive all my sins.
¹⁹ See how many enemies I have,
    and how viciously they hate me!
²⁰ Protect me! Rescue my life from them!
    Do not let me be disgraced, for I trust in you.
²¹ May integrity and honesty protect me,
    for I put my hope in you.

²² O God, ransom Israel
    from all its troubles.

*W*illiam Edwards was a magistrate in the Rohilkhund district of India when the Indian Mutiny erupted in 1857. For more than two months he was a fugitive, living first in a cow house, then in a hut on a small barren island. Separated from his wife and children, he heard of massacres but could not find out whether his loved ones were safe or not. In the distance he could hear gunfire, and he was gripped with anxiety.

During this time Edwards lived in the Psalms. On August 5, 1857, he wrote in his diary: "There is not a day on which we do not find something that appears as if written especially for persons in our unhappy circumstances, to meet the feelings and wants of the day. This morning, for instance, I derived unspeakable comfort from the fourteenth and seventeenth verses of the Twenty-fifth Psalm."

Then he began a trek of 150 miles along the river through enemy territory and got out safely.

If you know you are a friend of God, you can endure a great deal of distress. That is what strengthened David through his darkest times, and that is what can strengthen you. At times we may not understand all that God is doing, so we pray as David did in these verses. Yet it provides great comfort to know that God feels our pain and loves us very much.

> I've found a Friend, oh, such a Friend
> So kind and true and tender;
> So wise a Counselor and Guide,
> So mighty a Defender.
> JAMES G. SMALL

Bible Networking
To find out who has been called a friend of the Lord, read Exodus 33:11; Isaiah 41:8; Matthew 11:19; and John 15:15.

Notable Quotable
"Jesus' home was the road along which he walked with his friends in search of new friends."
GIOVANNI PAPINI

PSALM 26:1-5
A psalm of David.

¹ Declare me innocent, O LORD,
    for I have acted with integrity;
    I have trusted in the LORD without wavering.
² Put me on trial, LORD, and cross-examine me.
    Test my motives and affections.
³ For I am constantly aware of your unfailing love,
    and I have lived according to your truth.

⁴ I do not spend time with liars
    or go along with hypocrites.
⁵ I hate the gatherings of those who do evil,
    and I refuse to join in with the wicked.

George Whitefield, newly ordained to the ministry and only twenty-five years old, was hauled before a clerical tribunal for the grievous offense of preaching the gospel outdoors. He had preached to a group of about two hundred coal miners in a field. The young Oxford-trained cleric was also charged with being an "enthusiast" and a Methodist.

To these charges Whitefield replied, "Every Christian must be an 'enthusiast' [which means 'to have God in you']. You think that I am going to make you methodically mad. So you may breathe out your invectives against me, yet Christ knows all; he takes notice of it, and I shall leave it to him to plead my cause." Whitefield must have felt like David did in this psalm (verses 1-2).

We should note that this psalm seems to connect with the previous psalm, where David prays for integrity and declares his trust in the Lord. Here David declares his integrity (verse 1) and acknowledges God's unfailing love (verse 3). So the psalmist recognized that his integrity was dependent upon God's mercy.

The same is true for us. When our trust in the Lord is solid, our integrity is also solid. Failing to trust in the Lord will only lead us to take ethical shortcuts to achieve our goals.

Check the areas where you might be tempted to take some ethical shortcuts. Then ask the Lord to help you trust him in those circumstances.

> Search me, O God, and know my heart today;
> Try me, O Savior, know my thoughts, I pray.
> See if there be some wicked way in me;
> Cleanse me from every sin and set me free.
> J. EDWIN ORR

Bible Networking

For a further description of the people described in verse 4, read Proverbs 6:12-14. For more on the psalmist's relationship with such people, see Psalm 1:1.

Notable Quotable

"Two things will always be found together—love of God and recoil from sin. There cannot be attachment without detachment."
W. GRAHAM SCROGGIE

PSALM 26:6-12

6 I wash my hands to declare my innocence.
  I come to your altar, O LORD,
7 singing a song of thanksgiving
  and telling of all your miracles.
8 I love your sanctuary, LORD,
  the place where your glory shines.

9 Don't let me suffer the fate of sinners.
  Don't condemn me along with murderers.
10 Their hands are dirty with wicked schemes,
  and they constantly take bribes.

11 But I am not like that; I do what is right.
  So in your mercy, save me.
12 I have taken a stand,
  and I will publicly praise the LORD.

*W*e may have read God's Word many times before, but how often do we truly think about what it says and praise him for what he has given us? We often take God and his Word for granted. The story of a women's Bible study group in ancient Rome should both humble us and inspire us in this regard.

In A.D. 380 a group of educated, cultured women met regularly on Rome's Aventine Mount in the palatial home of Marcella, a young and wealthy widow. These women studied God's Word seriously. They wanted to sing the Psalms in their original language, so they learned Hebrew. Daily they sang the psalms, pledging to learn them all by heart.

One of the women was Paula, who traced her ancestry to the famous rulers of Sparta and Mycenae. When Paula died in A.D. 404, she had just finished memorizing Psalm 26:8 in Hebrew: "I love your sanctuary, Lord, the place where your glory shines." For three days after her death, this small community sang the psalms in four languages—Greek, Hebrew, Latin, and Syriac—to celebrate her life.

These women were following David's example in verses 6-7: "I come to your altar, O Lord, singing a song of thanksgiving and telling of all your miracles." How do you plan to publicly declare your love for God and tell of all he has done for you?

> I love thy Church, O God! Her walls before thee stand,
> Dear as the apple of thine eye, and graven on thy hand.
> For her my tears shall fall, for her my prayers ascend;
> To her my cares and toils be given, till toils and
>   cares shall end.

TIMOTHY DWIGHT

Bible Networking

In the wilderness the glory of God was visible over the Tabernacle (Exodus 40:34-38). Look up John 1:14 to see how the glory of God was made visible in New Testament times.

Notable Quotable

An elderly woman who could not hear the loudest of sounds was asked in writing why she was so faithful to attend church. She replied: "I come to God's house because I love it, because I like the company, and because I am not satisfied with serving God in private."

PSALM 27:1-6
A psalm of David.

¹ The LORD is my light and my salvation—
  so why should I be afraid?
The LORD protects me from danger—
  so why should I tremble?

² When evil people come to destroy me,
  when my enemies and foes attack me,
  they will stumble and fall.
³ Though a mighty army surrounds me,
  my heart will know no fear.
Even if they attack me,
  I remain confident.

⁴ The one thing I ask of the LORD—
  the thing I seek most—
is to live in the house of the LORD all the days of my life,
  delighting in the LORD's perfections
  and meditating in his Temple.
⁵ For he will conceal me there when troubles come;
  he will hide me in his sanctuary.
He will place me out of reach on a high rock.
⁶ Then I will hold my head high,
  above my enemies who surround me.
At his Tabernacle I will offer sacrifices with shouts of
    joy,
  singing and praising the LORD with music.

*L*ight was a precious commodity in ancient societies. At nighttime or in dark caves, where David sometimes hid from his enemies, everything was dark as pitch. Even in houses, whether a peasant's or prince's, the lighting was from a smoky pine torch or a tiny oil-fed stone lamp. In our world of light-bulbs and neon signs, we have less appreciation for the value of light.

From the opening words of Genesis to the closing words of Revelation, the theme of the Lord being light recurs again and again in Scripture. David said, "The Lord is my light" (Psalm 27:1). Jesus said, "I am the light of the world" (John 9:5). John wrote, "God is light" (1 John 1:5). And Paul wrote, "For God, who said, 'Let there be light in the darkness,' has made us understand that this light is the brightness of the glory of God that is seen in the face of Jesus Christ" (2 Corinthians 4:6).

But spiritually the world is as dark as it has ever been. Jesus tells us, "You are the light of the world" (Matthew 5:14) and Paul says that we are living "in a dark world full of crooked and perverse people," so we must "let [our] lives shine brightly before them" (Philippians 2:15). The world desperately needs to see God's light shining through us, so consider how you can bring light to those around you today.

> The Lord of glory is my light
> And my salvation, too.
> God is my strength, nor will I fear
> What all my foes can do.
> ISAAC WATTS

Bible Networking
David asked the Lord for "one thing" (verse 4). The apostle Paul also desired one thing (Philippians 3:13-14). What is the one thing that you desire today?

Notable Quotable
"Adorable Sun, enlighten my steps. Be thou the true noonday of my soul; exterminate its darkness, disperse its clouds; burn, dry up and consume all its filth and impurities. Divine Sun, rise upon my mind and never set."
JEAN BAPTISTE AVRILLON

PSALM 27:7-14

⁷ Listen to my pleading, O LORD.
   Be merciful and answer me!

⁸ My heart has heard you say, "Come and talk with me."
   And my heart responds, "LORD, I am coming."

⁹ Do not hide yourself from me.
   Do not reject your servant in anger.
   You have always been my helper.
   Don't leave me now; don't abandon me,
   O God of my salvation!

¹⁰ Even if my father and mother abandon me,
    the LORD will hold me close.

¹¹ Teach me how to live, O LORD.
    Lead me along the path of honesty,
    for my enemies are waiting for me to fall.

¹² Do not let me fall into their hands.
    For they accuse me of things I've never done
    and breathe out violence against me.

¹³ Yet I am confident that I will see the LORD's goodness
    while I am here in the land of the living.

¹⁴ Wait patiently for the LORD.
    Be brave and courageous.
    Yes, wait patiently for the LORD.

*F*ew hurts are as grievous as the loss of your parents. You are left feeling alone, abandoned.

Perhaps this is how David felt in 1 Samuel 22:3-4. Still a young man, David had just escaped from King Saul, who was determined to kill him. David ran and hid in a cave along with his brothers and other relatives. But what about his parents, who were now elderly and unable to seek refuge in the cave?

David left his parents in the care of the king of Moab. This was a risky move because he could not be certain that the king would not harm his parents. No doubt David wondered if he would ever see his parents alive again.

According to Jewish rabbinic tradition, the king of Moab betrayed David's trust and killed his parents. If so, that would account for the revenge David took on Moab in 2 Samuel 8:2. It could also account for verse 10 in this psalm.

Sometimes you may feel abandoned by those close to you as well. This may be due to a death, to divorce, or to some other situation that causes you to distrust someone. This may even lead you to distrust God. Yet, at the same time, you may also feel a deep need for a close relationship.

David found great comfort in the truth that, though his own parents might abandon him, the Lord would hold him close (verse 10). This holds true for you as well.

> Nearer, still nearer, nothing I bring,
> Naught as an offering to Jesus my King;
> Only my sinful, now contrite heart,
> Grant me the cleansing Thy blood doth impart.
> LELIA N. MORRIS

Bible Networking
Will God ever forget you? Will he abandon you? Read Isaiah 49:13-16.

Notable Quotable
"*Man's best plea is always an echo of God's promise [see verse 9]. He who has bidden his servants to seek will not hide his face when they obey him.*"
A. B. DAVISON

Here are some poignant words of David found in 2 Samuel:

- Regarding his friend Jonathan after he died: "How I weep for you, my brother Jonathan! Oh, how much I loved you! And your love for me was deep, deeper than the love of women!" (2 Samuel 1:26)

- Regarding David's adultery with Bathsheba: "Then Nathan said to David, 'You are that man!' . . . Then David confessed to Nathan, 'I have sinned against the LORD.'" (2 Samuel 12:7, 13)

- When David heard about Absalom's death, he cried: "O my son Absalom! My son, my son Absalom! If only I could have died instead of you! O Absalom, my son, my son." (2 Samuel 18:33)

When most people think about David, they think of him first as a shepherd boy, lolling in the pastures, and then as a king, garbed in a royal robe. In other words, it seems to have been an idyllic life, perfectly suited to playing the harp and writing a few psalms.

But as you read the life of David, you see that life was seldom serene. In his youth he fought with at least one lion and one bear; his brothers seemed to resent him; and King Saul, jealous of David's popularity, tried repeatedly to kill him. Finally, David fled to live with the Philistines, the arch-enemies of Israel, where he headed a band of outlaws. Living sometimes in caves, sometimes in enemy territory, and once pretending insanity, David kept eluding Saul's troops as if he were in a TV rerun of *The Fugitive*.

When King Saul died in battle, David's claim to the throne was recognized by only one of twelve tribes. It took seven years before the entire nation united under his reign. Militarily, David extended the borders of the country and subjugated the nearby enemies. He made Jerusalem the center of worship as well as the capital of government.

But personal problems dogged David's reign. His adultery with Bathsheba and murder of her husband were followed by devastating dysfunction in his children. One of his sons raped his own sister and then was murdered by his brother Absalom. Later, Absalom tried to wrest the throne from his father, David.

There's more, but that's enough to give you the idea that the sweet singer of Israel had a life filled with pain, sorrow, and heartache. Yet this shows that often the sweetest music comes from those who have gone through the greatest difficulties.

∾

Though clouds may gather in the sky
  and billows round me roll,
However dark the world may be,
  there's sunlight in my soul.
Since the Savior found me, took away
  my sin,
I have had the sunlight of his love
  within.
JUDSON W. VAN DEVENTER

Selah

PSALM 28
A psalm of David.

¹ O LORD, you are my rock of safety.
　　Please help me; don't refuse to answer me.
　For if you are silent,
　　I might as well give up and die.
² Listen to my prayer for mercy
　　as I cry out to you for help,
　　as I lift my hands toward your holy sanctuary.

³ Don't drag me away with the wicked—
　　with those who do evil—
　those who speak friendly words to their neighbors
　　while planning evil in their hearts.
⁴ Give them the punishment they so richly deserve!
　　Measure it out in proportion to their wickedness.
　Pay them back for all their evil deeds!
　　Give them a taste of what they have done to others.
⁵ They care nothing for what the LORD has done
　　or for what his hands have made.
　So he will tear them down like old buildings,
　　and they will never be rebuilt!

⁶ Praise the LORD!
　　For he has heard my cry for mercy.
⁷ The LORD is my strength, my shield from every danger.
　　I trust in him with all my heart.
　He helps me, and my heart is filled with joy.
　　I burst out in songs of thanksgiving.

⁸ The LORD protects his people
　　and gives victory to his anointed king.

[9] Save your people!

Bless Israel, your special possession!

Lead them like a shepherd,

and carry them forever in your arms.

*T*he book of Genesis describes a battle with four kings swooping down from the north to battle five kings in the Dead Sea area (Genesis 14–15). Abraham did not take sides in this battle, but when the four kings won, they looted the city of Sodom and kidnapped Abraham's nephew Lot. Abraham gathered his men and attacked the four kings at night.

Abraham recovered Lot, but he made an enemy of a powerful army. He had no assurance that the four kings would not return and attack him. But God assured Abraham (or Abram), "Do not be afraid, Abram, for I will protect you [literally, 'I will be your shield' (Genesis 15:1)]."

Abraham believed God, and God declared him righteous because of his faith (Genesis 15:6). David also knew the Lord as "my strength, my shield from every danger" and said, "I trust him with all my heart" (verse 7). Paul responded similarly when he was up against the strategies of the Devil. He took faith as his shield (Ephesians 6:16).

How will you respond today? Will you too take up the shield of faith?

> *Strong in the Lord of Hosts,*
> *And in his mighty power,*
> *Who in the strength of Jesus trusts*
> *Is more than conqueror.*
> CHARLES WESLEY

Bible Networking
Verse 9 is a tender verse, speaking of the Lord as a shepherd (see Psalm 23) and of Israel as God's special possession (see Deuteronomy 9:29 and Isaiah 19:25). We are called God's very own possession as well in 1 Peter 2:9.

Notable Quotable
"Faith substantiates things that are not yet seen. It changes the tenses; it puts the future into the present tense."
JOHN TRAPP

PSALM 29
A psalm of David.

1 Give honor to the LORD, you angels;
   give honor to the LORD for his glory and strength.
2 Give honor to the LORD for the glory of his name.
   Worship the LORD in the splendor of his holiness.

3 The voice of the LORD echoes above the sea.
   The God of glory thunders.
   The LORD thunders over the mighty sea.
4 The voice of the LORD is powerful;
   the voice of the LORD is full of majesty.
5 The voice of the LORD splits the mighty cedars;
   the LORD shatters the cedars of Lebanon.
6 He makes Lebanon's mountains skip like a calf
   and Mount Hermon to leap like a young bull.
7 The voice of the LORD strikes with lightning bolts.
8 The voice of the LORD makes the desert quake;
   the LORD shakes the desert of Kadesh.
9 The voice of the LORD twists mighty oaks
   and strips the forests bare.
   In his Temple everyone shouts, "Glory!"

10 The LORD rules over the floodwaters.
   The LORD reigns as king forever.
11 The LORD gives his people strength.
   The LORD blesses them with peace.

In the past the Psalms were arranged according to the months of the year. This psalm was relegated to July, the month of thunderstorms, because it graphically depicts the voice of the Lord causing a mighty thunderstorm.

As David describes the storm, he is no TV weatherman. He looks beyond the high-pressure fronts and air masses to see God at work. He tracks the storm entering from the Lebanon coast and ravaging the mighty forests of Mount Hermon. David watches it sweep across the nation to the southern desert outpost of Kadesh. But through it all, he sees God's power displayed, and he hears the roaring thunder of God's voice. Lightning and thunder strike panic into the hearts of many, but not for David. Not only does the storm remind him of God's power; it also reminds him of God's holiness, so he worships (verse 2).

When the storm passes by, all becomes quiet once again, and David speaks of the Lord giving his people peace.

Our God is a mighty God, an awesome God, no question about that, and a thunderstorm speaks of his immense power. The next time you hear thunder and watch the trees twist in the fierce wind, praise God for his greatness and rejoice that he blesses you with peace.

> From every stormy wind that blows,
> From every swelling tide of woes,
> There is a calm, a sure retreat:
> 'Tis found beneath the mercy seat.
> HUGH STOWELL

Fascinating Fact
Augustus Caesar was so terrified of thunderstorms that he wrapped himself in sealskin and hid in a corner. Another Roman emperor, Caligula, often hid under a bed when a thunderstorm struck.

Bible Networking
Elijah looked for God in a storm as well. Read 1 Kings 19:11-13.

March 3

PSALM 30:1-7
A psalm of David, sung at the dedication of the Temple.

¹ I will praise you, LORD, for you have rescued me.
    You refused to let my enemies triumph over me.
² O LORD my God, I cried out to you for help,
    and you restored my health.
³ You brought me up from the grave, O LORD.
    You kept me from falling into the pit of death.

⁴ Sing to the LORD, all you godly ones!
    Praise his holy name.
⁵ His anger lasts for a moment,
    but his favor lasts a lifetime!
Weeping may go on all night,
    but joy comes with the morning.

⁶ When I was prosperous I said,
    "Nothing can stop me now!"
⁷ Your favor, O LORD, made me as secure as a mountain.
    Then you turned away from me, and I was shattered.

*T*his psalm may have been written shortly after David made the mistake of ordering a census. God had blessed him greatly. Perhaps it was that prosperity that caused him to say, "Nothing can stop me now!" (verse 6).

We all have times like that. Then comes a shattered marriage, a tragic death in the family, a severe illness, a financial disaster, a church split, or the loss of a job. Often the catastrophe hits us in the area we felt the strongest. Then we feel cut off from God and fall into depression and grief.

That's the way David felt, as the story is told in 2 Samuel 24 and 1 Chronicles 21. David counted his troops, as if to say that with enough manpower he no longer needed to depend on God for help. But God sent a plague that killed seventy thousand of David's people. David prayed to God: "I am the one who has sinned. . . . These people are innocent. . . . Let your anger fall against me and my family" (2 Samuel 24:17).

David then bought land for an altar (which later became the location for the Temple), and there he made sacrifices to God. And God answered his prayer. Verse 5 may describe the joy that David felt after this.

When you experience difficult times as David did, take comfort in David's words. Know that the night is a vanquished foe. Daybreak is coming, and joy will come, for God answers prayer.

> All through the night I wept full sore,
> But morning brought relief.
> That hand, which broke my bones before,
> Then broke my bonds of grief.
> CHARLES HADDON SPURGEON

Bible Networking
For the full story of the Temple dedication, read 1 Kings 8 and 2 Chronicles 6–7. For some New Testament stories of nighttime weeping and morning joy, read chapters 12 and 16 of Acts.

Notable Quotable
"At nightfall Weeping comes as a guest to tarry; but in the morning Joy comes to stay."
W. GRAHAM SCROGGIE

PSALM 30:8-12

8 I cried out to you, O LORD.
   I begged the Lord for mercy, saying,
9 "What will you gain if I die,
   if I sink down into the grave?
Can my dust praise you from the grave?
   Can it tell the world of your faithfulness?
10 Hear me, LORD, and have mercy on me.
   Help me, O LORD."

11 You have turned my mourning into joyful dancing.
   You have taken away my clothes of mourning and
      clothed me with joy,
12 that I might sing praises to you and not be silent.
   O LORD my God, I will give you thanks forever!

*S*hortly after hearing of two missionaries martyred in East Africa, Oxford-trained James Hannington resigned his church and volunteered to be a replacement. The year was 1882, less than a decade after David Livingstone had died there.

After arriving in Africa, Hannington was beset with fever after fever and was forced to return to England to recover. A year later Hannington headed back to Africa.

Though it was riskier, he chose the shortest route to the interior. Trekking through Masai country, Hannington survived many threats. Each morning he would repeat his "Traveling Psalm" (Psalm 121) and then continue on his way. But then he was unexpectedly seized, stripped, beaten, and imprisoned in a filthy grass hut. Drunken guards surrounded him. There he read the Psalms and wrote brief notes in his diary.

On the morning of the day he died, Hannington read Psalm 30 and wrote, "If this is the last chapter of my earthly history, then the next will be the first page of the heavenly—with no blots and smudges, and no incoherence." James Hannington, aged thirty-eight, was murdered October 27, 1885.

England was so stirred by Hannington's ultimate sacrifice that scores of volunteers enlisted to take his place, and within five years twelve thousand East Africans had become Christians. Truly Hannington's dust continued to tell the world of God's faithfulness.

> *Walk in the light, and e'en the tomb*
> *No fearful shade shall wear.*
> *Glory shall chase away its gloom,*
> *For Christ hath conquered there.*
> BERNARD BARTON

Bible Networking
Compare Psalm 30:11 with Isaiah 61:10 and see what a wonderful clothier God is.

Notable Quotable
"What is praise? The rent we owe to God. And the larger the farm, the greater the rent should be."
G. S. BOWES

PSALM 31:1-5
For the choir director: A psalm of David.

¹ O LORD, I have come to you for protection;
    don't let me be put to shame.
    Rescue me, for you always do what is right.
² Bend down and listen to me;
    rescue me quickly.
    Be for me a great rock of safety,
        a fortress where my enemies cannot reach me.

³ You are my rock and my fortress.
    For the honor of your name, lead me out of this
        peril.
⁴ Pull me from the trap my enemies set for me,
    for I find protection in you alone.
⁵ I entrust my spirit into your hand.
    Rescue me, LORD, for you are a faithful God.

*T*he dying words of many saints have often been those of verses 1 and 5 of this psalm.

As Charles V, the Holy Roman Emperor at the time of Martin Luther, neared the last years of his life, he retired to a convent, carrying with him a commentary on Psalm 31:1. He passed his time there transacting official business, studying the Psalms, listening to the choir, and tending his garden. As the time of his death drew near, he asked that the Psalms be read to him. Then he received the Sacrament and said a few words, repeating verse 5 of this psalm. Early the next morning he died.

The great Catholic missionary Francis Xavier also loved Psalm 31. He had planted Christianity in India, Indonesia, and Japan, but his ultimate goal was to bring the gospel to China. Although foreigners entering that country were threatened with death, when he landed on Chinese shores, it was fever that struck him down, not humans. Xavier spent his last hours alone, far from home, and without a human friend. As he lay on his bed, Xavier thought he saw Christ standing and welcoming him with outstretched arms, and he quoted Psalm 31:1.

Like these believers who have gone before us, make this psalm your words to live by.

Fascinating Fact
Jesus and Stephen weren't the only ones who quoted Psalm 31:5 as they were dying; others included Charlemagne, Thomas à Becket, John Hus, Jerome of Prague, Martin Luther, Philipp Melanchthon, Christopher Columbus, Thomas Cromwell, Lady Jane Grey, Mary Queen of Scots, George Herbert, and John Knox.

Bible Networking
The first half of verse 5 was quoted by Christ on the cross (Luke 23:46) and by Stephen as he was stoned to death (Acts 7:59).

> My God! I love you, not to gain the bliss of your
>   eternal reign,
> Nor to escape the fiery lot reserved for those who
>   love you not.
> But you, my Jesus, on the tree did in your arms
>   encompass me.
> Most loving Jesus, God and King, you are my
>   Source of everything.

ATTRIBUTED TO FRANCIS XAVIER

PSALM 31:6-13

⁶ I hate those who worship worthless idols.
  I trust in the LORD.
⁷ I am overcome with joy because of your unfailing love,
  for you have seen my troubles,
  and you care about the anguish of my soul.
⁸ You have not handed me over to my enemy
  but have set me in a safe place.

⁹ Have mercy on me, LORD, for I am in distress.
  My sight is blurred because of my tears.
  My body and soul are withering away.
¹⁰ I am dying from grief;
  my years are shortened by sadness.
  Misery has drained my strength;
  I am wasting away from within.
¹¹ I am scorned by all my enemies
  and despised by my neighbors—
  even my friends are afraid to come near me.
  When they see me on the street,
  they turn the other way.
¹² I have been ignored as if I were dead,
  as if I were a broken pot.
¹³ I have heard the many rumors about me,
  and I am surrounded by terror.
  My enemies conspire against me,
  plotting to take my life.

The ups and downs of life are common for all of us, and the only surprising thing is how quickly the downs follow the ups. This was true for David as well.

But for the Old Testament prophet Jeremiah, there seldom seemed to be any ups. "Surrounded by terror" (verse 13) could have been his motto. He spoke about it so much that he was given the nickname "The Man Who Lives in Terror" (Jeremiah 20:10). He was terrified, however, because he foresaw what his fellow citizens could not see: the city of Jerusalem surrounded by the attacking Babylonians. Jeremiah said that everyone else, not he, was surrounded by terror.

Life was always difficult for Jeremiah: in the stocks, in the pit, in the prison. Yet even in his darkest times, he knew two overarching truths: "The Lord stands beside me like a great warrior" (Jeremiah 20:11) and "Great is his faithfulness; his mercies begin afresh each day" (Lamentations 3:23).

In an old inn, the Chesa Veglia at St. Moritz in the Swiss Alps, is an inscription that reads: "When you think everything is hopeless, a little ray of light comes from somewhere." Or as Jeremiah might say, "When you are surrounded by terror, remember that the Lord stands beside you like a great warrior."

> Whate'er your sacred will ordains
> Oh, give me strength to bear.
> Let me but know my Father reigns
> And trust his tender care.
> ANNE STEELE

Psalm at a Glance

Many psalms start on a low note and end on a high note. This psalm does it twice. The psalmist begins with a prayer for help in the early verses, and by verse 7 he is "overcome with joy." But then in verse 9, he begins all over again as if he is in deep distress. It is as if David is on an emotional roller coaster.

Bible Networking

David wasn't the only one who felt deserted by his friends. Check out how Job felt in Job 19:13-19.

PSALM 31:14-18

¹⁴ But I am trusting you, O Lord,
saying, "You are my God!"

¹⁵ My future is in your hands.
Rescue me from those who hunt me down
relentlessly.

¹⁶ Let your favor shine on your servant.
In your unfailing love, save me.

¹⁷ Don't let me be disgraced, O Lord,
for I call out to you for help.
Let the wicked be disgraced;
let them lie silent in the grave.

¹⁸ May their lying lips be silenced—
those proud and arrogant lips that accuse the godly.

*D*an Crawford was only nineteen years old in 1889 when he ventured into central Africa for the first time. He served as a missionary for more than three decades and translated the Bible into Luba-Sanga. When Crawford died in 1926, the Old Testament had just been printed, and the national Christians put a copy of the translation under his head when they buried him.

Psalm 31:15 had been a particularly difficult challenge for Crawford to translate. Finally it was decided that the best way to put it into the language of the people would be like this: "All my life's *whys* and *whens* and *wheres* and *wherefores* are in God's hands." They were releasing all the questions of life to God's control.

We place the past in God's hands when we turn to him in faith and accept his gift of salvation. We receive his forgiveness, and our sin is placed on the one who died for us. Our present is placed in the hands of the Shepherd of Psalm 23. But our future should be committed to him as well. God knows the future far better than we do. Often we worry about the next week, the next month, or the next year. But we don't need to. If we are in God's hands, we need not fear anything, for ultimately he will take care of us.

> *Let good or ill befall;*
> *It must be good for me,*
> *Secure of having Thee in all*
> *And having all in Thee.*
> HENRY F. LYTE

PSALM 31:19-24

¹⁹ Your goodness is so great!

    You have stored up great blessings for those who
        honor you.

    You have done so much for those who come to you for
        protection,

    blessing them before the watching world.

²⁰ You hide them in the shelter of your presence,

    safe from those who conspire against them.

You shelter them in your presence,

    far from accusing tongues.

²¹ Praise the LORD,

    for he has shown me his unfailing love.

    He kept me safe when my city was under attack.

²² In sudden fear I had cried out,

    "I have been cut off from the LORD!"

But you heard my cry for mercy

    and answered my call for help.

²³ Love the LORD, all you faithful ones!

    For the LORD protects those who are loyal to him,

    but he harshly punishes all who are arrogant.

²⁴ So be strong and take courage,

    all you who put your hope in the LORD!

*I*t is not clear what David was facing when he wrote Psalm 31. Some scholars believe the psalm relates to 1 Samuel 23 or 27 when he was hiding in enemy cities. Though David was being hunted by King Saul deep within enemy territory, he was preserved by the Lord. Even when the city was under attack, God kept him safe.

The prophet Jonah knew this psalm. He quoted part of it when he was in the belly of the great fish (compare Jonah 2:4 and Psalm 31:22). Like David, Jonah prayed for God to rescue him, and God mercifully did so. Jonah vowed to make sacrifices to God with songs of praise after his rescue, but there is no record that Jonah did. Instead, Jonah complained because God was blessing others more than they deserved.

Because of this, Jonah probably missed out on blessings that God had stored up for him (verse 19). Tragic, isn't it, that a person could know Scripture so well and not follow through on it?

Often we use pieces of God's Word to comfort us in tough times, but, like Jonah, we conveniently forget God's challenges when the coast is clear. God wants us to rest in perfect safety in his hands, but don't make Jonah's mistake and forget to praise and thank God for it.

> *Oh, what blessings will attend*
> *Those who make the Lord their friend.*
> *Lord, may this my portion be.*
> *Seek it, all you saints with me.*
> HENRY F. LYTE

Psalm at a Glance
The final six verses of this psalm are thanksgiving verses, but they are not all the same. Verses 19 and 20 thank God for his goodness to his people in general. Verses 21 and 22 thank God for his goodness to the psalmist in particular. Verses 23 and 24 call upon God's children to love him and confidently wait for him to answer, since our future is in God's hands (see verse 15).

Notable Quotable
"All of our visible blessings are but pale shadows of the real wealth that we can have if we live in continual communion with God. He does not put his best gifts in the store windows. He keeps those in the inner chambers. The best good is not the good that we can touch, taste, and handle and that men can see."
ALEXANDER MACLAREN

PSALM 32:1-5
A psalm of David.

¹ Oh, what joy for those
     whose rebellion is forgiven,
     whose sin is put out of sight!
² Yes, what joy for those
     whose record the LORD has cleared of sin,
     whose lives are lived in complete honesty!

³ When I refused to confess my sin,
     I was weak and miserable,
     and I groaned all day long.
⁴ Day and night your hand of discipline was heavy on
          me.
     My strength evaporated like water in the summer
          heat.   *Interlude*

⁵ Finally, I confessed all my sins to you
     and stopped trying to hide them.
     I said to myself, "I will confess my rebellion to the
          LORD."
     And you forgave me! All my guilt is gone.   *Interlude*

Y ou may recall the story: King sees woman. King takes woman. King has woman's husband killed. This plot could have been played out in any ancient culture, but this was Israel, where the king answered to a higher authority.

When the prophet Nathan charged David with his sin of adultery and murder, David openly confessed his sin, writing the deeply personal Psalm 51. Talk about airing your dirty laundry! David's *mea culpa* became a part of the nation's hymnbook, so that future generations could read of David's repentance and confession.

Psalm 32 seems to be the sequel to Psalm 51. After David confesses his sin, he receives God's forgiveness. In Psalm 51 David says that he wants to teach God's ways to other sinners, leading them to repentance, and in Psalm 32 David is teaching God's forgiveness to other sinners.

When Martin Luther was asked which psalm was the best psalm, he replied, "The psalms of Paul." His questioners knew that the apostle Paul didn't write any of the psalms, so they asked him what he meant. He answered that he was referring to Psalms 32, 51, 130, and 143. "They all teach," Luther said, "that the forgiveness of sin comes, without the law and without works, to the man who believes. This is just what Paul says, and that is why I call them the psalms of Paul."

Like David, confess your sins to God, and experience the joy of his forgiveness.

> *My sin—oh, the bliss of this glorious thought,*
> *My sin—not in part but the whole,*
> *Is nailed to the cross and I bear it no more:*
> *Praise the Lord, praise the Lord, O my soul!*
> HORATIO G. SPAFFORD

A Word on Words

Three different Hebrew words for sin are used in verses 1 and 2, along with different phrases for forgiveness, underscoring the completeness of God's forgiveness.

Bible Networking

Check out how Paul used these verses in Romans 4:6-8. Do you think John had verse 5 in mind when he wrote 1 John 1:9?

PSALM 32:6-11

⁶ Therefore, let all the godly confess their rebellion to you
while there is time,

that they may not drown in the floodwaters of
judgment.

⁷ For you are my hiding place;

you protect me from trouble.

You surround me with songs of victory.   *Interlude*

⁸ The LORD says, "I will guide you along the best pathway
for your life.

I will advise you and watch over you.

⁹ Do not be like a senseless horse or mule

that needs a bit and bridle to keep it under control."

¹⁰ Many sorrows come to the wicked,

but unfailing love surrounds those who trust the
LORD.

¹¹ So rejoice in the LORD and be glad, all you who obey
him!

Shout for joy, all you whose hearts are pure!

*S*aint Augustine, the fourth century theologian, had always loved the Psalms. In his classic, *Confessions*, he alludes to the Psalms on almost every page. He spent countless hours studying the Psalms and wrote two commentaries on them.

Augustine especially loved Psalm 32, which was inscribed above his bed so that he would be reminded of it as soon as he awoke each morning. He said he liked it because "the beginning of knowledge is to know oneself a sinner."

But it wasn't until later in life that Augustine fully appreciated the statement in verse 7: "You are my hiding place." In those later years Augustine witnessed the collapse of the Roman Empire, and just before his death, the Vandals besieged his hometown of Hippo in North Africa. No doubt Augustine learned to find refuge in God rather than in the earthly powers around him, just as David learned to do as he fled from Saul.

What makes a good hiding place? It must be free and accessible so that we can get there when we need it; it must be large and able to sustain us for as long as we remain there; and it must be impregnable to all our enemies.

God is our hiding place, and Jesus Christ is the way, the door, the truth that leads us to him.

> Hide me, O my Savior, hide,
> Till the storm of life is past;
> Safe into the haven guide;
> O receive my soul at last!
> CHARLES WESLEY

Bible Networking
Compare Psalm 32:8 with Proverbs 3:17 and see how God's pathway is the scenic route.

Notable Quotable
"If you are willing to know, he will make you know somehow. If not one way, then another."
F. B. MEYER

1 SAMUEL 2:1-7 (Hannah's Song, Part 1)

1 "My heart rejoices in the LORD!
  Oh, how the LORD has blessed me!
Now I have an answer for my enemies,
  as I delight in your deliverance.

2 No one is holy like the LORD!
  There is no one besides you;
  there is no Rock like our God.

3 "Stop acting so proud and haughty!
  Don't speak with such arrogance!
The LORD is a God who knows your deeds;
  and he will judge you for what you have done.

4 Those who were mighty are mighty no more;
  and those who were weak are now strong.

5 Those who were well fed are now starving;
  and those who were starving are now full.
The barren woman now has seven children;
  but the woman with many children will have no
    more.

6 The LORD brings both death and life;
  he brings some down to the grave but raises others
    up.

7 The LORD makes one poor and another rich;
  he brings one down and lifts another up."

Psalm Link
PSALM 126:5
Those who plant in tears
  will harvest with shouts of joy.

A young man from Ontario, Canada, went to Chicago to make a fortune. He started with sixty dollars, with which he purchased a cheese wagon and a horse named Paddy. He bought cheese on credit from a wholesale merchant and tried to sell it. Although he woke up at three in the morning and worked hard all day, he ended his first year three thousand dollars in debt and with no credit left.

He thought the only one he could talk to was his horse, and so he discussed the problem with Paddy. To his surprise he seemed to hear a voice saying, "You're trying to work without God." The young man looked around, saw no one, and then said, "Paddy, get up. If God can do any better with this cheese business than we've done, we'll let him."

So young James Kraft entered a partnership with God, and for the rest of his life he continually asked God's guidance. When he discovered a way to preserve cheese, his business grew fantastically, and Kraft cheese became a household name.

Before Hannah composed her song of praise to God, she, too, experienced great struggles. But finally, when she was at her lowest and her self-esteem was all but gone because of her childlessness, Hannah prayed to the Lord, and he granted her request for a son. That's what Hannah's song is all about.

In what ways can you sing Hannah's song today?

> Just when I am disheartened, just when with cares oppressed,
> Just when my way is darkest, just when I am distressed,
> Then is my Savior near me, He knows my every care;
> Jesus will never leave me; He helps my burden to bear.
> J. BRUCE EVANS

Bible Networking
Read Luke 1:46-55 and note the similarities between Hannah's song and Mary's Magnificat.

Notable Quotable
"What we win by prayer, we may wear with comfort, and must wear with praise."
MATTHEW HENRY

PSALM 33:1-9

¹ Let the godly sing with joy to the LORD,
   for it is fitting to praise him.
² Praise the LORD with melodies on the lyre;
   make music for him on the ten-stringed harp.
³ Sing new songs of praise to him;
   play skillfully on the harp and sing with joy.

⁴ For the word of the LORD holds true,
   and everything he does is worthy of our trust.
⁵ He loves whatever is just and good,
   and his unfailing love fills the earth.

⁶ The LORD merely spoke,
   and the heavens were created.
 He breathed the word,
   and all the stars were born.
⁷ He gave the sea its boundaries
   and locked the oceans in vast reservoirs.

⁸ Let everyone in the world fear the LORD,
   and let everyone stand in awe of him.
⁹ For when he spoke, the world began!
   It appeared at his command.

Do you see something missing from this psalm?

Every psalm since Psalm 2 has had a superscription, except for Psalm 10—and that one seems to be an extension of Psalm 9. But why is a superscription missing from Psalm 33?

Perhaps the answer is to be found by comparing the first verse of Psalm 33 with the last verse of Psalm 32. Since these two verses are similar, many scholars feel that Psalm 33 is an addendum to Psalm 32. Psalm 32 is very personal, and this psalm may have been written for the entire congregation to sing. After thinking about forgiveness and restoration in Psalm 32, how can you do anything else but rejoice and praise the Lord, as Psalm 33 calls people to do?

What kind of praise does Psalm 33 call us to give? Praise that is fresh, joyful, and skillfully presented (verse 3). Because God's mercies are new every morning, our praise to him should be fresh; because the gospel is good news, our praise should be joyful; and because our God is a great God who has done great things for us, he deserves our very best praise.

In the grand scheme of things it matters little why this psalm is missing a superscription. But it is great cause for concern when we are missing fresh, joyful, and skillful praise.

> Then let our songs abound,
> And every tear be dry;
> We're marching through Emmanuel's ground
> To fairer worlds on high.
> ISAAC WATTS

A Word on Words

Many kinds of instruments—brass, percussion, and stringed—were used in worship, but stringed instruments (verse 2) had a special place in the Temple. Because they are frequently referred to in parallel phrases, many scholars believe they were very similar, perhaps differing only in the number of strings.

Notable Quotable

"Put off oldness. . . . A new man, a new testament, a new song. A new song does not belong to the old man; none learn it but new men, renewed through grace from oldness, and belonging now to the new testament."
SAINT AUGUSTINE

PSALM 33:10-22

¹⁰ The LORD shatters the plans of the nations
and thwarts all their schemes.
¹¹ But the LORD's plans stand firm forever;
his intentions can never be shaken.

¹² What joy for the nation whose God is the LORD,
whose people he has chosen for his own.

¹³ The LORD looks down from heaven
and sees the whole human race.
¹⁴ From his throne he observes
all who live on the earth.
¹⁵ He made their hearts,
so he understands everything they do.
¹⁶ The best-equipped army cannot save a king,
nor is great strength enough to save a warrior.
¹⁷ Don't count on your warhorse to give you victory—
for all its strength, it cannot save you.

¹⁸ But the LORD watches over those who fear him,
those who rely on his unfailing love.
¹⁹ He rescues them from death
and keeps them alive in times of famine.

²⁰ We depend on the LORD alone to save us.
Only he can help us, protecting us like a shield.
²¹ In him our hearts rejoice,
for we are trusting in his holy name.
²² Let your unfailing love surround us, LORD,
for our hope is in you alone.

On November 6, 1627, the French army encircled the town of Rochelle. For nearly thirty years the Huguenots, a minority group of Protestant Christians, had lived there. But Cardinal Richelieu ordered a complete blockade of Rochelle. Soon all provisions within the city were scarce. All animals were killed for food, and bones, plaster, leather gloves, and saddles were devoured.

A widow named Prosni, however, shared whatever she owned with those who were starving. Her sister-in-law chided her, saying, "What will you do when your own supplies run out?"

Widow Prosni responded, "The Lord will provide." Then she quoted Psalm 33:18-19, closing with "[He] keeps them alive in times of famine."

The siege continued, and the widow and her four children ran out of food. Her sister-in-law scoffed at her and refused to help her.

The widow returned home, resolving to trust in the Lord even if it meant death. When she got to her house, her children were dancing with joy. In her absence a stranger had dropped off a sack of wheat. The provision was enough to support her family until the siege was lifted the following June.

God does not always choose to rescue his people in such concrete ways, but he does promise to take care of our true needs. Like this faithful widow, let us trust in our great God, who "watches over those who fear him" (verse 18).

> Praise the Lord! for he is glorious;
> Never shall his promise fail.
> God hath made his saints victorious;
> Sin and death shall not prevail.
> FOUNDLING HOSPITAL COLLECTION

Notable Quotable
"The wheels in a clock move contrary to each other, some one way, some another, yet all serve the intent of the watchmaker, to show the time. So in the world the providence of God may seem to run contrary to his promises; one man takes this way, another runs that way, yet all in conclusion center in the purpose of God the great Creator."
RICHARD SIBBES

Following are some verses that show that God's people have always been encouraged to sing praises to the Lord:

◆ Psalm 33:3

◆ Acts 16:25

◆ 1 Corinthians 14:26

◆ Ephesians 5:19-20

◆ Colossians 3:16

Governor Pliny was having a hard time. The number of Christians in his province of Bithynia was increasing daily. He had put a few of them to death, but this didn't seem to have any effect on the growing sect. Finally, Pliny wrote to Emperor Trajan in Rome asking for advice. He explained that he had been trying hard to find something to accuse them of, but he couldn't find anything—except that they refused to offer sacrifices to the emperor. Oh, yes, there was one other thing that was a bit peculiar: "They meet at dawn to sing a hymn to Christ as God"—a rather generous "criticism" that has gone down in history as one of our earliest outside descriptions of Christian worship.

Sing psalms, hymns, and spiritual songs, Paul told the Colossians. The psalms were from the Old Testament, but they found new meaning in Jesus Christ. The hymns were early Christian compositions of praise to God that had come to be accepted by the church as a whole. We will be looking at some of these throughout the year. Spiritual songs were probably more spontaneous expressions by members of the congregation.

And notice the accompaniment that Paul speaks of in Ephesians 5:19. The actual instruments used are not as important as the joyous sound of thankful hearts and harmony among the believers. If the voices blend musically—all the better! But what God desires most is the blending of our hearts.

∾

How sweet and heavenly is the sight
When those who love the Lord,
In one another's peace delight
And so fulfill his Word.
R. G. SWAIN

∾

"The early church was a singing church; it had a happiness that made men sing."
WILLIAM BARCLAY

Selah

PSALM 34:1-10

A psalm of David, regarding the time he pretended to be insane in front of Abimelech, who sent him away.

¹ I will praise the LORD at all times.
   I will constantly speak his praises.
² I will boast only in the LORD;
   let all who are discouraged take heart.
³ Come, let us tell of the LORD's greatness;
   let us exalt his name together.

⁴ I prayed to the LORD, and he answered me,
   freeing me from all my fears.
⁵ Those who look to him for help will be radiant with
      joy;
   no shadow of shame will darken their faces.
⁶ I cried out to the LORD in my suffering, and he heard
      me.
   He set me free from all my fears.
⁷ For the angel of the LORD guards all who fear him,
   and he rescues them.

⁸ Taste and see that the LORD is good.
   Oh, the joys of those who trust in him!
⁹ Let the LORD's people show him reverence,
   for those who honor him will have all they need.
¹⁰ Even strong young lions sometimes go hungry,
   but those who trust in the LORD will never lack any
      good thing.

Born into an aristocratic family in India, Sadhu Sundar Singh was trained by his mother to become a Sikh holy man. But after a conversion like that of the apostle Paul, Sundar began to travel throughout India, Afghanistan, and Tibet as a Christian evangelist. His family forsook him, and people persecuted him, but he continued on with his mission.

Once Sundar was lost in a jungle, and night was falling. He could hear the jungle predators on the prowl. Fortunately he came to a river and realized that he would be safe if he could cross it. But as he stepped into the water, he discovered that the current was too swift for him. What could he do?

Sundar prayed for God's help. Then he saw a man across the river calling to him, "I am coming to help you." The man plunged into the river and swam to Sundar. He told him to get on his back, and then they swam to the other side. Shortly after this, Sundar looked for the man, but he was gone. Perhaps Sundar had just experienced the reality of Psalm 34:7.

This psalm tells us much about fear and trust and why we are safe in God's keeping. Whether we see those angels or not, we can trust God that they are there watching over us.

> O magnify the Lord with me; with me exalt His
>   name;
> When in distress to him I called, He to my rescue came.
> The Hosts of God encamp around the dwellings of
>   the just;
> Deliverance he affords to all who in his goodness
>   trust.
> NAHUM TATE

Bible Networking
See 2 Kings 6:13-17 for a further commentary on Psalm 34:7.

Notable Quotable
"It is far better to be delivered from all our fears than from all our troubles. The wicked may be free from trouble, but can they be free from fear? No. The enjoyment, not only of tranquility, but security, is a privilege only of the godly."
RICHARD BAKER

PSALM 34:11-22

¹¹ Come, my children, and listen to me,
    and I will teach you to fear the LORD.
¹² Do any of you want to live
    a life that is long and good?
¹³ Then watch your tongue!
    Keep your lips from telling lies!
¹⁴ Turn away from evil and do good.
    Work hard at living in peace with others.

¹⁵ The eyes of the LORD watch over those who do right;
    his ears are open to their cries for help.
¹⁶ But the LORD turns his face against those who do evil;
    he will erase their memory from the earth.

¹⁷ The LORD hears his people when they call to him for
        help.
    He rescues them from all their troubles.
¹⁸ The LORD is close to the brokenhearted;
    he rescues those who are crushed in spirit.

¹⁹ The righteous face many troubles,
    but the LORD rescues them from each and every one.
²⁰ For the LORD protects them from harm—
    not one of their bones will be broken!

²¹ Calamity will surely overtake the wicked,
    and those who hate the righteous will be punished.
²² But the LORD will redeem those who serve him.
    Everyone who trusts in him will be freely pardoned.

The date was June 6, 597. Columba, the pioneer missionary to Scotland, was translating the Psalms into the local dialect. When he completed the tenth verse of Psalm 34, he said, "Here I must stop. Let Baithene [his successor] write what follows." Early the next day the seventy-seven-year-old Columba died.

A controversial and sometimes irascible Irishman, Columba loved the Psalms, people, and animals (in that order). In fact, it may have been a controversy over a copy of the Psalms that caused him to leave his beloved Donegal in Ireland and establish a base on the little isle of Iona to evangelize Scotland and northern England. With a group of twelve monks, who copied Scripture and then brought it to the people, he confronted the druids and converted the kings.

The second half of Psalm 34, which seeks to teach "children" several lessons, was particularly appropriate for Columba's successor, for he spent much of his energies instructing new converts in the Scriptures.

What were the lessons the "children" were to learn? (1) Fear the Lord; (2) watch your tongue; (3) turn from evil; and (4) work for peace. Which of those lessons has been the hardest for you to learn?

> Teach me, my God and King,
> In all things thee to see.
> And what I do in anything
> To do it as for thee.
> GEORGE HERBERT

Fascinating Fact
This is another acrostic psalm, with each verse beginning with the next letter of the Hebrew alphabet.

Bible Networking
For more on controlling the tongue (verse 13), check out Proverbs 4:24; 13:3; and James 3:2-12.

PSALM 35:1-10
A psalm of David.

1 O Lord, oppose those who oppose me.
   Declare war on those who are attacking me.
2 Put on your armor, and take up your shield.
   Prepare for battle, and come to my aid.
3 Lift up your spear and javelin
   and block the way of my enemies.
   Let me hear you say,
      "I am your salvation!"

4 Humiliate and disgrace those trying to kill me;
   turn them back in confusion.
5 Blow them away like chaff in the wind—
   a wind sent by the angel of the Lord.
6 Make their path dark and slippery,
   with the angel of the Lord pursuing them.
7 Although I did them no wrong,
   they laid a trap for me.
   Although I did them no wrong,
   they dug a pit for me.
8 So let sudden ruin overtake them!
   Let them be caught in the snare they set for me!
   Let them fall to destruction in the pit they dug for me.

9 Then I will rejoice in the Lord.
   I will be glad because he rescues me.
10 I will praise him from the bottom of my heart:
   "Lord, who can compare with you?
   Who else rescues the weak and helpless from the strong?
      Who else protects the poor and needy from those
         who want to rob them?"

*P*salm 35:3 marked a turning point in the life of a young Dutch boy named Thomas Hemerken (later called à Kempis after his birthplace). In 1392 Thomas had been sent by his parents to join the Brothers of the Common Life, a devout group of believers whose message was "Turn away from sin, live like Jesus, and read God's Word."

Thomas thought that the Brotherhood would bring him salvation, but soon he learned that it didn't do any good just to copy a pattern of good works. He loved the Psalms, and, like the psalmists, he struggled with his own sinfulness and the perplexities of life. Thomas wrote a book, *The Soliloquy of the Soul,* in which he drew on one psalm after another in his search for peace and salvation. Then he came to verses 3 and 10 of Psalm 35 and others like them. He realized he had to trust in Christ alone—and he did. Thomas's better-known book, *On the Imitation of Christ,* interlaces Thomas's meditations with more than a thousand Scripture references, including Psalm 35:3: "I am your salvation!"

The Lord is our salvation, and three things continue to testify that he has indeed saved us: the Holy Spirit (Galatians 4:6), our love for other believers (1 John 3:14), and God's promises (John 1:12). What a difference that made for young Thomas, and what a difference it should make for you!

A Word on Words
"The bottom of my heart" (verse 10) is literally "all my bones." A similar expression might be "I know it in my bones."

Bible Networking
Note similarities and differences between this and the previous psalm. Angels are mentioned in both, and both refer to deliverance. But the mood is quite different.

'Tis everlasting peace! Sure as Jehovah's name.
'Tis stable as his steadfast throne for evermore the same.
I change, he changes not; for Christ can never die;
His love, not mine, the resting place; his truth,
    not mine, the tie.
HORATIUS BONAR

PSALM 35:11-18

[11] Malicious witnesses testify against me.
They accuse me of things I don't even know about.
[12] They repay me with evil for the good I do.
I am sick with despair.
[13] Yet when they were ill,
I grieved for them.
I even fasted and prayed for them,
but my prayers returned unanswered.
[14] I was sad, as though they were my friends or family,
as if I were grieving for my own mother.

[15] But they are glad now that I am in trouble;
they gleefully join together against me.
I am attacked by people I don't even know;
they hurl slander at me continually.
[16] They mock me with the worst kind of profanity,
and they snarl at me.

[17] How long, O Lord, will you look on and do nothing?
Rescue me from their fierce attacks.
Protect my life from these lions!
[18] Then I will thank you in front of the entire
congregation.
I will praise you before all the people.

*I*f you've ever been double-crossed or betrayed, then you can understand how David must have felt when he wrote this psalm.

And David knew betrayal. When David became king, instead of killing or exiling the entire household of the previous dynasty, he showed them kindness (2 Samuel 9). But Saul's servant Ziba held a grudge and later tried to deceive David. How's that for gratitude?

On another occasion David sent emissaries to express his sympathy regarding the death of a neighboring king's father, but the king openly humiliated the ambassadors (2 Samuel 10). Later, David's own son Absalom and trusted adviser Ahithophel rebelled against him (2 Samuel 14–15). As the rebellion continued, many of David's friends and allies turned against him.

David had to feel stung by these betrayals. How do you feel when your trusted friends stab you in the back? You may find it difficult to trust anyone again. You may want to pay them back for what they have done to you.

But Scripture tells us: "If your enemies are hungry, feed them. . . . Don't let evil get the best of you, but conquer evil by doing good" (Romans 12:20-21). These words are hard to follow, but God will give us the strength to do whatever he asks.

> Discouraged in the work of life,
> Disheartened by its load,
> Shamed by its failures or its fears,
> I sink beside the road.
> But let me only think of Thee
> And then new heart springs up in me.
> SAMUEL LONGFELLOW

Psalm at a Glance

Three times the psalmist launches into lamentation and prayers of desperation (verses 1, 11, 19), but in spite of the seeming hopelessness of his situation, each section of this psalm concludes with praise (verses 9, 18, 27). Even our prayers of desperation should end up in praise.

PSALM 35:19-28

¹⁹ Don't let my treacherous enemies
    rejoice over my defeat.
Don't let those who hate me without cause
    gloat over my sorrow.
²⁰ They don't talk of peace;
    they plot against innocent people
    who are minding their own business.
²¹ They shout that they have seen me doing wrong.
    "Aha," they say. "Aha!
    With our own eyes we saw him do it!"

²² O LORD, you know all about this.
    Do not stay silent.
    Don't abandon me now, O Lord.
²³ Wake up! Rise to my defense!
    Take up my case, my God and my Lord.
²⁴ Declare me "not guilty," O LORD my God, for you give
    justice.
    Don't let my enemies laugh about me in my
    troubles.
²⁵ Don't let them say, "Look! We have what we wanted!
    Now we will eat him alive!"

²⁶ May those who rejoice at my troubles
    be humiliated and disgraced.
May those who triumph over me
    be covered with shame and dishonor.

²⁷ But give great joy to those
    who have stood with me in my defense.
Let them continually say, "Great is the LORD,
    who enjoys helping his servant."
²⁸ Then I will tell everyone of your justice and goodness,
    and I will praise you all day long.

*T*ake up my case, my God and my Lord. Declare me 'not guilty,'" pleads David in verses 23-24.

What a great way to conclude the psalm. In the first ten verses the images are all military. We read of war, armor, shield, spear, and javelin. In the next section it seems as if we are in a civil trial, and we hear the legal terms "testify," "accuse," and "slander."

In the upper room, it was the once-doubting Thomas who gasped, "My Lord and my God!" as the risen Jesus stood before him (John 20:28). In that moment he seemed to realize that his nail-scarred Lord would take up his case, guaranteeing God's not-guilty verdict. When God becomes "my Lord," the Judge becomes our defense attorney.

"Not guilty" is the verdict that God declares in the New Testament. According to Romans 8:1, there is no condemnation for those who are in Christ Jesus. In 2 Corinthians 5:21 we read that "God made Christ, who never sinned, to be the offering for our sin, so that we could be made right [declared 'not guilty'] with God through Christ."

At times in our desperation we may feel as distant from the Lord as the psalmist (or Thomas) did. But, just as the Lord said to Thomas in the upper room, he says to us, "Don't be faithless any longer. Believe!" If we trust in Jesus Christ for our salvation, we can be confident that God has declared us "not guilty."

> *O for a faith that will not shrink*
> *Though pressed by many a foe,*
> *That will not tremble on the brink*
> *Of any earthly woe.*
> WILLIAM H. BATHURST

Bible Networking
See how Jesus referred to verse 19 in John 15:24-25.

Notable Quotable
"Whatever you do, do well, and you praise God. Do you transact business? Do no wrong, and you have praised God. Do you till your field? Raise no strife, and you praise God. In the innocence of your works, prepare to praise God all the day long."
SAINT AUGUSTINE

PSALM 36:1-7
For the choir director: A psalm of David, the servant of the LORD.

¹ Sin whispers to the wicked, deep within their hearts.
  They have no fear of God to restrain them.
² In their blind conceit,
  they cannot see how wicked they really are.
³ Everything they say is crooked and deceitful.
  They refuse to act wisely or do what is good.
⁴ They lie awake at night, hatching sinful plots.
  Their course of action is never good.
  They make no attempt to turn from evil.

⁵ Your unfailing love, O LORD, is as vast as the heavens;
  your faithfulness reaches beyond the clouds.
⁶ Your righteousness is like the mighty mountains,
  your justice like the ocean depths.
You care for people and animals alike, O LORD.
⁷   How precious is your unfailing love, O God!

J H. Jowett tells of crossing the Atlantic and passing over the spot where the Titanic went down:

> And I thought of all that life and wreckage beyond the power of man to recover and redeem. . . . And then I thought of all the human wreckage engulfed and sunk in oceanic depths of nameless sin. Too far down. But there is no human wreckage lying in the ooze of the deepest sea of iniquity that His deep love cannot reach and redeem.

Psalm 36 describes a "sinking ship"—humanity apart from God. But, after following the wicked down their slippery slope into pitch darkness, the psalmist talks about God's love, faithfulness, righteousness, and justice in terms of the heavens, clouds, mountains, and ocean depths.

In Romans 3 the apostle Paul has a similar contrast. After using a barrage of Old Testament references (ending with Psalm 36:1) to convey human wickedness, he adds, "Now God has shown us a different way," which is Jesus Christ (verse 21).

Modern engineering may raise the treasures of the Titanic, but only God can salvage twisted and fallen people, transforming them into trophies of his grace.

> There's a wideness in God's mercy, like the wideness of the sea;
> There's a kindness in his justice which is more than liberty.
> For the love of God is broader than the measure of our mind;
> And the heart of the Eternal is most wonderfully kind.
>
> FREDERICK W. FABER

Bible Networking

In Romans 3:9-18 Paul quotes seven Old Testament passages as he makes his case that all people have sinned. Six of these are from the Psalms (14:1-3; 53:1-3; 5:9; 140:3; 10:7; and 36:1; the other is Isaiah 59:7-8). How does the progression of sin in Romans 3 differ from what we see here in Psalm 36?

Notable Quotable

"It is only man's world that is cramping. Human fickleness makes a drooping contrast to God's towering covenant love and faithfulness; human standards, where all is relative, are a marshland beside the exacting, exhilarating mountains of His righteousness."
DEREK KIDNER

PSALM 36:7-12

7 All humanity finds shelter
   in the shadow of your wings.
8 You feed them from the abundance of your own house,
   letting them drink from your rivers of delight.
9 For you are the fountain of life,
   the light by which we see.

10 Pour out your unfailing love on those who love you;
   give justice to those with honest hearts.
11 Don't let the proud trample me;
   don't let the wicked push me around.
12 Look! They have fallen!
   They have been thrown down, never to rise again.

*W*e often take water for granted, but in the arid Middle East it is associated with delight and pleasure, and in the book of Revelation it is one of the blessings of heaven.

As Saint Augustine was writing a commentary on Psalm 36:8, he began thinking of heaven. Augustine imagined asking the noted bible scholar Jerome, some questions about heaven.

Jerome responded that he would be happy to answer Augustine's questions. "But first let me ask you this question: Can you put all the waters of the sea in a little pot? Can you measure the waters in your fist? Can you weigh the mountains on a scale? If not, then it would be impossible for your understanding to comprehend the least of the joys of heaven."

We can't measure the joys of heaven, but we can enjoy some of God's rivers of delight even now. In verse 9 David said, "You are the fountain of life," and in the New Testament Jesus shouted to the crowds in Jerusalem, "If you are thirsty, come to me!" (John 7:37). To the Samaritan woman, Jesus said, "The water I give them takes away thirst altogether. It becomes a perpetual spring within them, giving them eternal life" (John 4:14).

Don't wait for heaven to enjoy God's delights; delight in him now.

> I heard the voice of Jesus say, "Behold I freely give
> The living water; thirsty one, stoop down, and
>   drink, and live."
> I came to Jesus and I drank of that life-giving stream;
> My thirst was quenched, my soul revived, and
>   now I live in him.
> HORATIUS BONAR

A Word on Words
The word for "delight" in verse 8 is translated from the plural form of the Hebrew word for "Eden."

Bible Networking
Compare Psalm 36:9 with John 1:3-5. What are the similarities? What are the differences?

One of the first books printed in America was *The New England Primer*. Schoolchildren learned their ABC's from it for more than a hundred years. It began, "In Adam's fall, we sinned all," and continued, "This Book attend, thy life to mend." For D it had "A Dog will bite a thief at night" and it closed the alphabet with "Zaccheus he did climb a tree his Lord to see."

But twenty-five hundred years before New England schoolmasters were teaching their youngsters the ABC's with poetry, teachers in the Temple in Jerusalem were doing the same thing. We can still read some of these poems in the book of Psalms.

Eight or nine of the Psalms were written in acrostic form, meaning that each line of the psalm begins with a successive letter of the Hebrew alphabet. This format helped youngsters learn their ABC's, and it helped parents memorize the Psalms.

◆ *Psalms 9–10:* When taken together, these two psalms appear to have been an acrostic, although an incomplete one.

◆ *Psalms 25, 34, and 145:* Each line begins with a successive letter of the Hebrew alphabet.

◆ *Psalms 111 and 112:* Each half line begins with a successive Hebrew letter.

◆ *Psalm 37:* Every other line begins with a successive Hebrew letter.

◆ *Psalm 119:* The stellar example of acrostic poems. It has twenty-four stanzas of eight verses each. Each verse in the first stanza begins with the first Hebrew letter, then the next eight verses begin with the second Hebrew letter, and so on.

Try piecing together an English acrostic based on verses in the Psalms.
Here's a start:

∾
As the deer pants for streams of
    water,
  so I long for you, O God
    (42:1).
But may all who search for you
  be filled with joy and glad-
    ness (40:16).
Come with great power, O God,
  and rescue me!
  Defend me with your might
    (54:1). . . .

∾
Divine Instructor, gracious Lord,
Be thou forever near;
Teach me to love thy sacred Word
And see my Savior there.
ANNE STEELE

Selah

PSALM 37:1-11
A psalm of David.

1 Don't worry about the wicked.
   Don't envy those who do wrong.
2 For like grass, they soon fade away.
   Like springtime flowers, they soon wither.

3 Trust in the LORD and do good.
   Then you will live safely in the land and prosper.
4 Take delight in the LORD,
   and he will give you your heart's desires.

5 Commit everything you do to the LORD.
   Trust him, and he will help you.
6 He will make your innocence as clear as the dawn,
   and the justice of your cause will shine like the
      noonday sun.

7 Be still in the presence of the LORD,
   and wait patiently for him to act.
   Don't worry about evil people who prosper
   or fret about their wicked schemes.

8 Stop your anger!
   Turn from your rage!
   Do not envy others—
   it only leads to harm.
9 For the wicked will be destroyed,
   but those who trust in the LORD will possess the land.

10 In a little while, the wicked will disappear.
   Though you look for them, they will be gone.
11 Those who are gentle and lowly will possess the land;
   they will live in prosperous security.

*I*t is not easy to "wait patiently" for the Lord to act (verse 7). Early in his missionary explorations in Africa, David Livingstone was barred by a local chieftain from crossing through his territory. After several days of futile bantering back and forth, Livingstone whipped out a revolver and demanded to go through. It was a move Livingstone always regretted, for it was not in keeping with Psalm 37, which was a favorite of his.

Livingstone often quoted Psalm 37:5. When he gave a friend a Bible, he inscribed it with Psalm 37:5 in the Sechuana language and then translated it to English. Good advice for a new Christian.

Livingstone regretted that he had not spent time with his children when they were growing up, but he tried to counsel them in their teenage years after their mother had died. To his son Thomas he wrote: "Whatever you feel yourself best fitted for, one ought to endeavor to devote the peculiarities of his nature to his Redeemer's service," and then he quoted Psalm 37:5. Good advice for a teenager.

During Livingstone's final days in Africa, as he was menaced by savage tribesmen, prostrated by fear, gnawed by hunger, and near death, he kept quoting Psalm 37:5. This was the verse that sustained him throughout his explorations in Africa. Good advice for anyone in any circumstance and in any location.

> *Thy way, not mine, O Lord*
> *However dark it be;*
> *O lead me by thine own right hand,*
> *Choose out the path for me.*
> HORATIUS BONAR

A Word on Words

The Hebrew word for "commit" (verse 5) is literally "roll." You are to roll your burdens off your shoulders and onto the shoulders of the Lord.

Notable Quotable

"Note your part and God's part in verse 4. If you delight, he will give."
CHARLES HADDON SPURGEON

PSALM 37:12-22

¹² The wicked plot against the godly;
  they snarl at them in defiance.
¹³ But the Lord just laughs,
  for he sees their day of judgment coming.

¹⁴ The wicked draw their swords
   and string their bows
  to kill the poor and the oppressed,
   to slaughter those who do right.
¹⁵ But they will be stabbed through the heart with their
    own swords,
   and their bows will be broken.

¹⁶ It is better to be godly and have little
   than to be evil and possess much.
¹⁷ For the strength of the wicked will be shattered,
   but the LORD takes care of the godly.

¹⁸ Day by day the LORD takes care of the innocent,
   and they will receive a reward that lasts forever.
¹⁹ They will survive through hard times;
   even in famine they will have more than enough.

²⁰ But the wicked will perish.
   The LORD's enemies are like flowers in a field—
   they will disappear like smoke.

²¹ The wicked borrow and never repay,
   but the godly are generous givers.
²² Those blessed by the LORD will inherit the land,
   but those cursed by him will die.

*I*n the seventeenth century Paul Gerhardt and his family had to flee Berlin because of his religious convictions. As they fled, they stopped at an inn and tried to understand why God was allowing this to happen to them. Gerhardt's wife was especially concerned about what might lie ahead for their young children.

Gerhardt read Psalm 37 to his family that night. You can imagine him slowing down around verse 16 and emphasizing these verses: "It is better to be godly and have little than to be evil and possess much.... The Lord takes care of the godly.... They will survive through hard times."

Apparently the psalm struck a chord with Mr. Gerhardt himself, because the next day, sitting underneath an apple tree, he wrote a hymn based on this same theme of trusting God in hard times. That evening two messengers came to Gerhardt and offered him refuge and a church position in nearby Merseberg.

The hymn Gerhardt wrote, "Give to the Winds Your Fears," became popular in Germany, second only in fame to Luther's "A Mighty Fortress Is Our God." School children sang it as a graduation hymn, and in the United States, when the first Lutheran church was opened in Philadelphia in 1743, Gerhardt's hymn was the first to be sung. Translations into English were made by John Wesley and others. It remains a solid testimony to God's gracious provision in tough times.

> *Through waves and clouds and storms*
> *His power will clear your way;*
> *Wait for his time; the darkest night*
> *Shall end in brightest day.*
> PAUL GERHARDT

Bible Networking
Check out other advice that the Bible gives for surviving through hard times (verse 19). See Psalm 73:26; Habakkuk 3:17-18; 2 Corinthians 6:10; and Philippians 4:12-13.

Notable Quotable
"A little blessed is better than a great deal cursed; a black crust blessed is better than a feast cursed; a drop of mercy blessed is better than a sea of mercy cursed; a chimney corner with a blessing is better than a stately palace with a cursing."
THOMAS BROOKS

PSALM 37:23-29

²³ The steps of the godly are directed by the LORD.
   He delights in every detail of their lives.
²⁴ Though they stumble, they will not fall,
   for the LORD holds them by the hand.

²⁵ Once I was young, and now I am old.
   Yet I have never seen the godly forsaken,
      nor seen their children begging for bread.
²⁶ The godly always give generous loans to others,
   and their children are a blessing.

²⁷ Turn from evil and do good,
   and you will live in the land forever.
²⁸ For the LORD loves justice,
   and he will never abandon the godly.

   He will keep them safe forever,
   but the children of the wicked will perish.
²⁹ The godly will inherit the land
   and will live there forever.

Through Charles Dickens's famous novel *Oliver Twist* many people have read about the problems of orphans in England. But George Müller of Bristol, England, was a man who did something about the problem.

Müller was an amazing man of faith. When he felt God was directing him to do something, he did it without arguing. In 1836, by faith, he opened an orphanage for twenty-six girls. Through prayer and faith and no money of his own, he opened more and more such houses, until in 1875 he was feeding and housing thousands of orphans. By the time of his death, more than ten thousand orphans had been cared for in his orphanages.

Müller never asked for money. He simply fell on his knees and prayed, and miraculously the provision arrived, sometimes in the nick of time.

There was no doubt that he valued Psalm 37:23. A stickler for details, George found comfort in the fact that God took delight in all the details of his life. And Müller had no doubt that the steps of the godly were ordered by the Lord.

But it is interesting to learn that Müller added two words to this verse in his Bible. His rendition read, "The steps *and stops* of the godly . . ." It may have seemed that there were no "stops," or closed doors, in George Müller's life, but he knew better. He knew that he could trust the one who ordered the stops as well as the steps.

> *Though they lead o'er the cold, dark mountains,*
> *seeking His sheep;*
> *Or along by Siloam's fountains, helping the weak.*
> *Footprints of Jesus that make the pathway glow;*
> *We will follow the steps of Jesus where'er they go.*
> MARY SLADE

Bible Networking
Trace the steps of Joseph in Genesis 39–50 or the steps of the apostle Paul in Acts 16–18.

Notable Quotable
"The godly man is not left in the trackless forest without a guide, or doomed to struggle in the darkness without a kindly light; he is not orphaned in the world without a loving hand to aid. His Father, unseen but not unknown, has prepared the path and somehow guides the steps of those who commit their way to him."
JAMES AND EDWARD HASTINGS

PSALM 37:30-40

³⁰ The godly offer good counsel;
  they know what is right from wrong.
³¹ They fill their hearts with God's law,
  so they will never slip from his path.

³² Those who are evil spy on the godly,
  waiting for an excuse to kill them.
³³ But the LORD will not let the wicked succeed
  or let the godly be condemned when they are
    brought before the judge.

³⁴ Don't be impatient for the LORD to act!
  Travel steadily along his path.
He will honor you, giving you the land.
  You will see the wicked destroyed.

³⁵ I myself have seen it happen—
  proud and evil people thriving like mighty trees.
³⁶ But when I looked again, they were gone!
  Though I searched for them, I could not find them!

³⁷ Look at those who are honest and good,
  for a wonderful future lies before those who love peace.
³⁸ But the wicked will be destroyed;
  they have no future.

³⁹ The LORD saves the godly;
  he is their fortress in times of trouble.
⁴⁰ The LORD helps them,
  rescuing them from the wicked.
He saves them,
  and they find shelter in him.

*I*n the great Christian classic *The Practice of the Presence of God*, Brother Lawrence explains how believers can practice the presence of God not only while reading Scripture, praying, or meditating but also while peeling potatoes in the kitchen.

For David, the challenge was to practice the presence of God in the midst of the wicked. Throughout this psalm we go back and forth between instruction about how to regard the wicked and advice on how we should trust, wait patiently, and obey.

It's not easy to put all this together. We are to practice the presence of God—to have a right attitude—even when we are peeling potatoes and getting impatient with the drudgery of the task.

Brother Lawrence said, "The time of busyness does not differ from the time of prayer, and in the noise and clatter of my kitchen, while several persons are at the same time calling for different things, I possess God in as great tranquility as if I were upon my knees."

Brother Lawrence admits this was a challenge, but he began each day by asking God to be with him, to help him apply his mind to his tasks, and to receive what he did as an offering to God. No matter how the ungodly may seem to be prospering and whatever the din and clatter around you, you, too, can learn to practice the presence of God.

> *Wait on the Lord, you trembling saints!*
> *And keep your courage up;*
> *He'll raise your spirit when it faints,*
> *And far exceed your hope.*
> ISAAC WATTS

Notable Quotable
"He who truly trusts in God will wait in God's time, use God's means, and walk in God's way, even though it may seem round about."
DAVID CLARKSON

PSALM 38:1-12

A psalm of David, to bring us to the LORD's remembrance.

¹ O LORD, don't rebuke me in your anger!
　　Don't discipline me in your rage!
² Your arrows have struck deep,
　　and your blows are crushing me.

³ Because of your anger, my whole body is sick;
　　my health is broken because of my sins.
⁴ My guilt overwhelms me—
　　it is a burden too heavy to bear.
⁵ My wounds fester and stink
　　because of my foolish sins.
⁶ I am bent over and racked with pain.
　　My days are filled with grief.
⁷ A raging fever burns within me,
　　and my health is broken.
⁸ I am exhausted and completely crushed.
　　My groans come from an anguished heart.

⁹ You know what I long for, Lord;
　　you hear my every sigh.
¹⁰ My heart beats wildly, my strength fails,
　　and I am going blind.
¹¹ My loved ones and friends stay away, fearing my
　　disease.
　　Even my own family stands at a distance.
¹² Meanwhile, my enemies lay traps for me;
　　they make plans to ruin me.
　　They think up treacherous deeds all day long.

*S*ome scholars think David wrote this psalm shortly after his sin with Bathsheba. Others say he must have written it later when he was in ill health. Whenever it was that David wrote the psalm, he knew that he was sick and that he had sinned.

John Bunyan, author of *The Pilgrim's Progress*, records a similar time of anguish. Bunyan had just become a Christian when he succumbed to temptation. Spiritual, mental, emotional, and physical disturbances knotted him up. He wrote: "I struck into a very great trembling, insomuch that sometime I could, for whole days together, feel my very body, as well as my mind, to shake and totter under the sense of the dreadful judgment of God. . . . I felt also such a clogging and heat at my stomach, by reason of this my terror, that I was, especially at some times, as if my breast bone would have split in sunder. . . . Thus did I wind, and twine, and shrink, under the burden that was upon me, which burden did so oppress me that I could neither stand, nor go, nor lie, either at rest or quiet."

God has made us in such a way that our spiritual well-being is closely connected with our physical well-being. When we are plagued by guilt, all is anguish, fear, and loneliness. Is there any way out? Yes! We find it in 1 John 1:9: "If we confess our sins to him, he is faithful and just to forgive us and to cleanse us from every wrong."

> O my offended Lord,
> Restore my inward peace.
> I know you can; pronounce the word,
> And bid the tempest cease.
> CHARLES WESLEY

Bible Networking

Learn about a godly person who experienced similar trials as David in this psalm. Read Job 2:3-8 and 13:23.

Notable Quotable

"David was being punished for a serious transgression. Not all sickness is punishment, however; most is not. It is important to say this, because physical suffering often depresses us mentally and in such depressions we are inclined to see connections between our past sins and our present sickness that do not necessarily exist. We need to remember Job, who was a righteous man and yet suffered."
JAMES MONTGOMERY BOICE

PSALM 38:13-22

¹³ But I am deaf to all their threats.
  I am silent before them as one who cannot speak.
¹⁴ I choose to hear nothing,
  and I make no reply.

¹⁵ For I am waiting for you, O LORD.
  You must answer for me, O Lord my God.
¹⁶ I prayed, "Don't let my enemies gloat over me
  or rejoice at my downfall."
¹⁷ I am on the verge of collapse,
  facing constant pain.
¹⁸ But I confess my sins;
  I am deeply sorry for what I have done.
¹⁹ My enemies are many;
  they hate me though I have done nothing against
    them.
²⁰ They repay me evil for good
  and oppose me because I stand for the right.

²¹ Do not abandon me, LORD.
  Do not stand at a distance, my God.
²² Come quickly to help me, O Lord my savior.

*G*eorge Herbert, an Elizabethan poet and contemporary of William Shakespeare, came from a Welsh family famous for its statesmen and soldiers. But in his thirties, Herbert felt God calling him to the ministry, so he gave up wealth, glory, and position to become a parish priest.

"Why, George, why?" came the question. To his friends and relatives, his call to the ministry didn't make sense. Finally he turned to Psalm 38:15: "You must answer for me, O Lord my God," and he wrote a poem called "The Quip":

> Yet when the hour of Thy design
> To answer these fine things shall come,
> Speak not at large; say, I am Thine,
> And then they have their answer home.

Unlike Herbert's problem, David's problem was complicated by his own sin, and he admitted this. His enemies were accusing him falsely, but if he protested, it would seem as though he were claiming to be sinless. So he turned to the Lord and said, "You must answer for me, O Lord my God."

Though their situations were somewhat different, both Herbert and David knew that the best answer oftentimes is simply no answer—at least on our part. Like Jesus before Pilate, we can trust that the Lord knows our heart and that he will one day see that we are vindicated.

> Be still, my soul! The Lord is on thy side;
> Bear patiently the cross of grief or pain;
> Leave to thy God to order and provide;
> In every change, he faithful will remain.
> Be still, my soul! Thy best, thy heavenly Friend
> Through thorny ways leads to a joyful end.
> KATHARINA VON SCHLEGEL

Bible Networking
See how Christ responded to the charges against him. Read Isaiah 53:7 and 1 Peter 2:23.

Notable Quotable
"When we answer back, we may win a battle and lose the campaign; but when we are silent we may lose a battle but shall win the campaign. It is well to sacrifice a passing victory for the sake of the final triumph."
W. GRAHAM SCROGGIE

PSALM 39:1-7
For Jeduthun, the choir director: A psalm of David.

¹ I said to myself, "I will watch what I do
and not sin in what I say.
I will curb my tongue
when the ungodly are around me."
² But as I stood there in silence—
not even speaking of good things—
the turmoil within me grew to the bursting point.
³ My thoughts grew hot within me
and began to burn,
igniting a fire of words:
⁴ "LORD, remind me how brief my time on earth will be.
Remind me that my days are numbered,
and that my life is fleeing away.
⁵ My life is no longer than the width of my hand.
An entire lifetime is just a moment to you;
human existence is but a breath." *Interlude*

⁶ We are merely moving shadows,
and all our busy rushing ends in nothing.
We heap up wealth for someone else to spend.

⁷ And so, Lord, where do I put my hope?
My only hope is in you.

*T*wo kings spoke of the brevity of life and mulled over its meaning. In some ways the statements may sound quite similar, but in other ways they are very different.

One of them was King Macbeth, the subject of Shakespeare's great tragedy. In the drama, which is loosely based upon the story of a real king who lived in Scotland in the eleventh century, Macbeth murders his rivals to the throne. His wife, driven mad by her conscience, commits suicide. "Out, out, brief candle!" Macbeth broods. "Life's but a walking shadow, a poor player, that struts and frets his hour upon the stage, and then is heard no more. It is a tale told by an idiot, full of sound and fury, signifying nothing."

And then there was King David. He, too, talked about people as "moving shadows, and all our busy rushing ends in nothing" (verse 6).

But what a difference! David began his soliloquy with the words "Lord, remind me," and closed by asking, "And so, Lord, where do I put my hope?"

Without God, life is meaningless, as Macbeth discovered. With God, life has purpose, as David discovered.

However, even Christians live some days more in tune with Macbeth's outlook than with David's. How are you living your life today?

> I take your promise, Lord, in all its length,
> And breadth, and fullness, as my daily strength,
> Into life's future fearless I may gaze,
> For Jesus, you are with me all my days.
> HENRY DECK

Bible Networking
Compare Psalm 39:7 with some New Testament verses about hope. Read Romans 15:13; 2 Thessalonians 2:16; and 1 Timothy 4:10.

Notable Quotable
"Sweet it is that our hope should rest in him who is never shaken, should abide in him who never changes, should bind us to him who alone is the full contentment of the soul, should enter into him, since in him is our being."
E. B. PUSEY

PSALM 39:8-13

⁸ Rescue me from my rebellion,
for even fools mock me when I rebel.

⁹ I am silent before you; I won't say a word.
For my punishment is from you.

¹⁰ Please, don't punish me anymore!
I am exhausted by the blows from your hand.

¹¹ When you discipline people for their sins,
their lives can be crushed like the life of a moth.
Human existence is as frail as breath.   *Interlude*

¹² Hear my prayer, O LORD!
Listen to my cries for help!
Don't ignore my tears.
For I am your guest—
a traveler passing through,
as my ancestors were before me.

¹³ Spare me so I can smile again
before I am gone and exist no more.

David may have been thinking of Abraham when he wrote verse 12. Abraham was a stranger in a foreign land when he came to Canaan. Or perhaps David was thinking of someone like Ittai, one of his generals.

Ittai, a Philistine from the city of Gath, commanded a contingent of six hundred Gittites in David's army. When David was fleeing from Absalom and everything was in disarray, David told Ittai to go back. "You are a guest in Israel, a foreigner in exile. . . . I don't even know where we will go. Go on back."

But Ittai responded, "I will go wherever you go, no matter what happens—whether it means life or death" (2 Samuel 15:19-21).

Or maybe instead of Ittai, David was thinking of his great-grandmother, Ruth, a Moabite, who had chosen to live as a foreigner in the land of Canaan. She told her mother-in-law, "Your people will be my people, and your God will be my God" (Ruth 1:16).

"My only hope is in you," David confessed earlier in this psalm (verse 7). Now, recognizing his sinfulness, David pleads for God's mercy. He knew he had no rightful claim on God's favor. But God had established laws to protect the guests and travelers in the land, and David was coming as Abraham, Ittai, and Ruth had come. He knew that whenever people came as outcasts—requesting, not demanding, and trusting in God's goodness—God always proved merciful.

> I once was an outcast stranger on earth,
> A sinner by choice, and an alien by birth;
> But I've been adopted, my name's written down,
> An heir to a mansion, a robe, and a crown.
> HARRIET E. BUELL

A Word on Words

Regarding verse 11:
"The moths of the East are very large and beautiful, but short lived. After a few showers these splendid insects may be seen fluttering in every breeze, but the dry weather, and their numerous enemies, soon consign them to a common lot."
JOHN KITTO

Bible Networking

For some of the regulations that God had established to safeguard the rights of aliens and guests in the land, see Exodus 12:48-49; 22:21; Leviticus 19:33-34; Deuteronomy 10:18-19.

Many verses throughout the Psalms conclude with the single word *selah* (which is simply a transliteration of the Hebrew word) or *interlude*, depending on the translation you are reading. Here is a sampling of verses that contain this word:

◆ *Psalm 3:4*
I cried out to the LORD,
　and he answered me from his
　　holy mountain. *Interlude*

◆ *Psalm 24:10*
Who is the King of glory?
　The LORD Almighty—
　　he is the King of glory.
　　　　　　　Interlude

◆ *Psalm 39:5*
My life is no longer than the
　　width of my hand.
An entire lifetime is just a
　　moment to you;
human existence is but a
　　breath. *Interlude*

◆ *Psalm 59:5*
O LORD God Almighty, the God
　of Israel,
rise up to punish hostile
　nations.
Show no mercy to wicked
　traitors. *Interlude*

◆ *Psalm 82:2*
"How long will you judges
　hand down unjust deci-
　sions?
How long will you shower
　special favors on the
　wicked?" *Interlude*

◆ *Psalm 143:6*
I reach out for you.
　I thirst for you as parched
　　land thirsts for rain.
　　　　　　　Interlude

Selah is one of those words like *hallelujah* that translators of the King James Version never bothered to translate into English. The difference, however, is that they knew *hallelujah* meant "Praise the Lord," but they didn't seem to be sure what *selah* meant.

Four hundred years later scholars still scratch their heads about the meaning of *selah*, but at least a few of them have made some educated guesses.

One of the possible meanings for *selah* may be inferred from its similarity to a Hebrew word meaning "to lift up." If this theory is correct, the word carries the sense of "interlude," and several contemporary translations have chosen to render the word in this way. The word would have indicated that those singing were to pause, perhaps to allow for a musical interlude so that the people could pray individually or apply the words to their own lives.

We all need interludes in our life. We need to let the music go on without us. We need to take breaks from the routine in order to meditate on what God has for us this day.

∾

*Jesus, I am resting, resting, in the joy
  of what thou art,
I am finding out the greatness of thy
  loving heart. . . .*

*Yes, I rest in thee, Lord Jesus, for I
  know what grace is thine.
And I trust in what you've promised,
  and have made it mine.*
JEAN S. PIGOTT

∾

The Hebrew word *selah* (or *interlude*) occurs seventy-four times in the Bible, and seventy-one of those times in the Psalms. The other three instances are in the small book of Habakkuk.

selah

PSALM 40:1-10
For the choir director: A psalm of David.

[1] I waited patiently for the LORD to help me,
  and he turned to me and heard my cry.
[2] He lifted me out of the pit of despair,
  out of the mud and the mire.
He set my feet on solid ground
  and steadied me as I walked along.
[3] He has given me a new song to sing,
  a hymn of praise to our God.
Many will see what he has done and be astounded.
  They will put their trust in the LORD.

[4] Oh, the joys of those who trust the LORD,
  who have no confidence in the proud,
  or in those who worship idols.
[5] O LORD my God, you have done many miracles for us.
  Your plans for us are too numerous to list.
If I tried to recite all your wonderful deeds,
  I would never come to the end of them.

[6] You take no delight in sacrifices or offerings.
  Now that you have made me listen, I finally
    understand—
  you don't require burnt offerings or sin offerings.
[7] Then I said, "Look, I have come.
  And this has been written about me in your scroll:
[8] I take joy in doing your will, my God,
  for your law is written on my heart."

[9] I have told all your people about your justice.
  I have not been afraid to speak out,
  as you, O LORD, well know.

¹⁰ I have not kept this good news hidden in my heart;
   I have talked about your faithfulness and saving power.
I have told everyone in the great assembly
   of your unfailing love and faithfulness.

*P*salm 40:6 says something about ears that might make you raise your eyebrows. David is talking about sacrifices, and then he says (literally) that God has dug ears for him. What is he talking about?

Quoting from the Greek translation of the Old Testament, the New Testament quotes this passage as, "You have given me a body" (Hebrews 10:5). Such a translation makes the messianic meaning of verses 7 and 8 even more obvious, so we can clearly see that Jesus is its ultimate fulfillment.

But what about the meaning for David's time? Some scholars think this passage is referring to the custom of piercing the ear of a servant who pledges lifelong servitude to his master (Exodus 21:6). But the problem with this is that the servant had only one ear pierced, not two.

Most likely the correct reading is that God has opened up (dug) David's ears so that he hears, understands, and obeys.

Like David, allow your ears to be "dug" every day so that you might hear and obey God's word.

> *Open, Lord, my inward ear, and bid my heart*
>   *rejoice;*
> *Bid my quiet spirit hear your comforting voice.*
> *From the world of sin and noise and hurry I*
>   *withdraw;*
> *For the small and inward voice I wait with*
>   *humble awe.*
> CHARLES WESLEY

Notable Quotable
"There is no pit so deep, either within you, or around you, that it can stop the ear of God when he inclines to listen. Be thy pit then ever so horrible, and ever so deep, only you cry like David, and you will sooner or later share David's deliverance. As long as you have the knowledge and the feeling of the horrible pit that is in your heart you are in no real danger."
ROBERT BRUCE

PSALM 40:11-17

[11] LORD, don't hold back your tender mercies from me.
  My only hope is in your unfailing love and
    faithfulness.
[12] For troubles surround me—
  too many to count!
They pile up so high
  I can't see my way out.
They are more numerous than the hairs on my head.
  I have lost all my courage.

[13] Please, LORD, rescue me!
  Come quickly, LORD, and help me.
[14] May those who try to destroy me
  be humiliated and put to shame.
May those who take delight in my trouble
  be turned back in disgrace.
[15] Let them be horrified by their shame,
  for they said, "Aha! We've got him now!"

[16] But may all who search for you
  be filled with joy and gladness.
May those who love your salvation
  repeatedly shout, "The LORD is great!"

[17] As for me, I am poor and needy,
  but the Lord is thinking about me right now.
You are my helper and my savior.
  Do not delay, O my God.

Every day millions of people play the lottery, hoping for a big payoff. If they win, they figure they can quit working, buy a mansion, and live it up. Their biggest worry will be how to count all that money.

It was the church of Laodicea that boasted, "I am rich. I have everything I want. I don't need a thing!" (Revelation 3:17). Apparently they had already won their lottery. But that was a church in deep, deep trouble. When you bask in your own riches, you stop looking to God to meet your needs.

In this section of Psalm 40, David has more troubles than he can count. They are piled up so high around him that he can't see his way out. Maybe you know that feeling.

What's the answer? The lottery? No way. David looks to another treasure trove that he has already mentioned in verse 5: God's many miracles, plans, and wonderful deeds for his people. David exclaims that he could never even count all of God's wonderful deeds—and this outweighs all of David's innumerable troubles. God's care for us is always greater than our troubles.

Although he is king of Israel, David acknowledges that he is "poor and needy" (verse 17). That's a confession the self-satisfied church of Laodicea refused to make. But it is when we admit our need that God begins to meet it.

> Just as I am, poor, wretched, blind,
> Sight, riches, healing of the mind,
> Yea, all I need in thee I find,
> O Lamb of God, I come! I come!
> CHARLOTTE ELLIOTT

Bible Networking
Psalm 40:13-17 is almost identical to Psalm 70. What are the differences? Why might these differences exist?

Notable Quotable
"To compare what 'I am' with what 'You are' (verse 17) is a steadying thing, but to pray for God's glory (see verse 16) is a liberation, the way of victory and the way of Christ himself."
DEREK KIDNER

PSALM 41
For the choir director: A psalm of David.

1 Oh, the joys of those who are kind to the poor.
  The Lord rescues them in times of trouble.
2 The Lord protects them
  and keeps them alive.
  He gives them prosperity
  and rescues them from their enemies.
3 The Lord nurses them when they are sick
  and eases their pain and discomfort.

4 "O Lord," I prayed, "have mercy on me.
  Heal me, for I have sinned against you."
5 But my enemies say nothing but evil about me.
  "How soon will he die and be forgotten?" they ask.
6 They visit me as if they are my friends,
  but all the while they gather gossip,
  and when they leave, they spread it everywhere.
7 All who hate me whisper about me,
  imagining the worst for me.
8 "Whatever he has, it is fatal," they say.
  "He will never get out of that bed!"
9 Even my best friend, the one I trusted completely,
  the one who shared my food,
  has turned against me.

10 Lord, have mercy on me.
   Make me well again, so I can pay them back!
11 I know that you are pleased with me,
   for you have not let my enemy triumph over me.
12 You have preserved my life because I am innocent;
   you have brought me into your presence forever.

[13] Bless the LORD, the God of Israel,
who lives forever from eternal ages past.
Amen and amen!

A century ago a minister related a story to his congregation about a sick friend who told him that he was resting on the three pillows of God's infinite power, love, and wisdom. Several months later a young woman in the congregation said she had recently gone through a major operation. When the surgeon took away the pillow she had been clutching, she responded that she still had the three pillows of God's infinite love, power, and wisdom, which the surgeon couldn't take away.

David knew of the comforting power of God as well. In Psalm 23 David refers to the Lord as a caring shepherd, and in Psalm 103 God is a loving parent showing compassion for his children. In this psalm David describes God as one who nurses the poor back to health (verse 3).

David wrote this psalm as he was feeling the effects of some sin he had committed. His friends visited him but thought he would never get well. Even David's best friend (Ahithophel?) had turned against him. Yet in all of this, David rejoices in God's protection and calls for everyone to bless the Lord.

When you are sick, call upon God, for he is powerful and compassionate, stooping down to tend to your most basic needs.

> O Love Divine, that stooped to share
> Our sharpest pang, our bitterest tear;
> On you we cast each earth-born care,
> We smile at pain when you are near.
> OLIVER W. HOLMES

Bible Networking
In verse 9 David may have been referring to his trusted counselor Ahithophel (2 Samuel 16:23). See how Jesus read it as a messianic prophecy in John 13:18.

Notable Quotable
"Into what minuteness of exquisite and touching tenderness does the Lord condescend to enter [verse 3]! One feels almost as we may suppose Peter felt when the Lord came to him and would have washed his feet. Here the Lord, the great God of heaven, does indeed take upon him the form of a servant, fulfilling all the loving and tender offices of an assiduous nurse." BARTON BOUCHIER

Many people won't believe you if you say there are five books of Psalms. They will look at the contents page in their Bibles and say, "I see one; where are the other four?" But all you have to do is turn to Psalm 42, Psalm 73, Psalm 90, and Psalm 107 and look at what it says immediately above the psalm. You will find the same in any version you inspect.

Here is a short summary of each of the books:

♦ *Book One*—Psalms 1–41

- The superscriptions identify most of these psalms with David.

- These psalms are mostly personal.

- God is almost always identified as Yahweh (the LORD).

- Key verse—Psalm 23:1: "The Lord is my shepherd; I have everything I need."

♦ *Book Two*—Psalms 42–72

- Among these psalms, eighteen of them are identified with David and seven with Korah and his descendants.

- These psalms are mostly national.

- God is usually identified as Elohim (God).

- Key verse—Psalm 51:17: "A broken and repentant heart, O God, you will not despise."

♦ *Book Three*—Psalms 73–89

- Most of these psalms are attributed to Asaph, David's choirmaster, and some are attributed to Korah and his descendants.

- These psalms are mostly national.

- God is often identified as Elohim (God).

- Key verse—Psalm 80:3: "Turn us again to yourself, O God. Make your face shine down upon us."

♦ *Book Four*—Psalms 90–106

- Aside from one psalm attributed to Moses and two to David, the others have no superscriptions.

- These psalms are mostly for worship.

- God is usually identified as Yahweh (the LORD).

- Key verse—Psalm 98:6: "Make a joyful symphony before the LORD, the King!"

◆ *Book Five*—Psalms 107–150

- Fifteen of these psalms are attributed to David.

- These psalms are mostly for worship and contain many *hallel*, or praise psalms.

- God is often identified as Yahweh (the LORD).

- Key verse—Psalm 125:1: "Those who trust in the LORD are as secure as Mount Zion."

By the way, as you look up where each book starts, notice how the previous chapter closes. The last verse in each of the five books of Psalms closes with a doxology.

Frankly, no one knows who divided the Psalms into five smaller books, when the divisions were made, or exactly why the Psalms were put in a particular order. Ancient Jewish commentators compared the five books of the Psalms to the first five books of the Old Testament. They said, "As Moses gave five books of laws to Israel, so David gave five books of Psalms to Israel."

Another theory is that the Psalms were divided up for the purpose of reading them in public worship along with the books of the Law. In ancient times Jews customarily read through the five books of the Law in three-year reading cycles for public worship. They spent forty-one Sabbaths reading Genesis along with the first book of Psalms (which has forty-one psalms), thirty-one reading Exodus along with the second book of Psalms (which has thirty-one), and so on.

However the books came to be divided up, the Psalms are now grouped much like hymns in a modern hymnal. Modern hymnals are a collection of all sorts of hymns and gospel songs, and they are usually grouped according to different subjects. Sometimes it's obvious why one hymn follows another; sometimes it isn't. So it is with the Psalms.

The resulting variety of moods and styles throughout the books of the Psalms makes reading them an adventure. There is hardly a mood or feeling you can experience that isn't touched upon by one psalm or another.

∾

Thy Word is like a garden, Lord, with
 flowers bright and fair;
And everyone who seeks may pluck a lovely
 cluster there.
Thy Word is like a deep, deep mine; and
 jewels rich and rare
Are hidden in its mighty depths for every
 searcher there.
EDWIN HODDER

April 5

BOOK TWO (PSALMS 42–72)
PSALM 42:1-6a
For the choir director: A psalm of the descendants of Korah.

¹ As the deer pants for streams of water,
    so I long for you, O God.
² I thirst for God, the living God.
    When can I come and stand before him?
³ Day and night, I have only tears for food,
    while my enemies continually taunt me, saying,
    "Where is this God of yours?"

⁴ My heart is breaking
    as I remember how it used to be:
I walked among the crowds of worshipers,
    leading a great procession to the house of God,
singing for joy and giving thanks—
    it was the sound of a great celebration!

⁵ Why am I discouraged?
    Why so sad?
I will put my hope in God!
    I will praise him again—
    my Savior and ⁶my God!

*K*ing David's son rebelled against his father and "stole the hearts" of the Israelites. As Absalom gathered political and military power, he forced David to flee from Jerusalem (2 Samuel 15).

Imagine how David must have felt. While Psalm 42 was not written by David, it certainly presents emotions that fit this situation—and any situation in which we find ourself betrayed and hopeless.

Heading into exile, David wasn't just leaving his capital city; he was barred from worshiping God before the Ark. "When can I go and meet with God?" was surely a question David was asking at this time.

As David crossed the Mount of Olives, he was "weeping as he went" and taunted by those who opposed him (2 Samuel 15:30–16:8), just as the psalmist was. Absalom was claiming to be God's newly appointed ruler. Where was God in this time of hardship? Why was this happening? After all his battles, maybe David really was a "man of blood" and was simply receiving his just desserts.

No doubt David remembered his joyous times of worship before the Ark and longed to return to the Tabernacle. Would he ever know that joy again? Like the psalmist, David could only hope.

Do you have similar questions, similar hardships? Put your trust in God, just as the psalmist did in verse 5. Someday the clouds will lift, and you'll be able to praise your Savior and God once more.

> *Jesus, the very thought of thee*
> *With sweetness fills my breast;*
> *But sweeter far thy face to see,*
> *And in thy presence rest.*
> BERNARD OF CLAIRVAUX

Fascinating Fact
The thirsty deer was a symbol used by the early church, denoting a Christian's passion for God.

Notable Quotable
"[In verse 1] the psalmist's craving is directly associated to his worship of God in his sanctuary. Those people, then or now, who are lackadaisical about attendance at church have never known what it really means to worship God."
NORMAN SNAITH

April 6

PSALM 42:6b-11

6 Now I am deeply discouraged,
    but I will remember your kindness—
from Mount Hermon, the source of the Jordan,
    from the land of Mount Mizar.
7 I hear the tumult of the raging seas
    as your waves and surging tides sweep over me.

8 Through each day the LORD pours his unfailing love
        upon me,
    and through each night I sing his songs,
    praying to God who gives me life.

9 "O God my rock," I cry,
    "Why have you forsaken me?
Why must I wander in darkness,
    oppressed by my enemies?"
10 Their taunts pierce me like a fatal wound.
    They scoff, "Where is this God of yours?"

11 Why am I discouraged?
    Why so sad?
I will put my hope in God!
    I will praise him again—
    my Savior and my God!

"Why go to church? I can worship God on a mountain or by the sea." You may have heard those words from "freelance" Christians, who want to do their own thing apart from other believers. The problem is, they're half right. You can worship God on a mountain or by the sea, as Psalm 42 shows us, but there's more to it than this.

You can picture the psalmist on a Galilean hillside, with Mount Hermon towering in the north and the sea churning below him. With those visual aids, he understands God's kindness and power in a new way. Reviewing the taunts of his enemies—"Where is this God of yours?"—perhaps he needs the reassurance of God's presence in nature. God is here. The mountains and seas declare his glory. The seasons teach us about how God works. The beauty of God's creation refreshes our soul.

But if you stay on the mountain, you may begin to worship the mountain rather than the God who made it. The mountain will not lift you above your troubles. The sea will not sweep them away. Only God can deliver you. So let the wonders of creation bring you back to God, and put your trust and hope in him. And then, by all means, join the rest of us—needy people who are sometimes struggling, sometimes doubtful, sometimes depressed—join us in singing praises to our God, who refreshes our soul.

> Why restless, why cast down, my soul?
> Trust God, and thou shalt sing
> His praise again, and find him still
> Thy health's eternal spring.
>
> NAHUM TATE AND NICHOLAS BRADY

A Word on Words

Mount Mizar (which literally means "little") was apparently a small mountain near Mount Hermon, although some scholars think it is a reference to Mount Zion.

Notable Quotable

"Sorrow is always a sense of lack. The ultimate sorrow is the sense of the lack of God."
G. CAMPBELL MORGAN

PSALM 43

1 O God, take up my cause!
   Defend me against these ungodly people.
   Rescue me from these unjust liars.
2 For you are God, my only safe haven.
   Why have you tossed me aside?
Why must I wander around in darkness,
   oppressed by my enemies?

3 Send out your light and your truth;
   let them guide me.
Let them lead me to your holy mountain,
   to the place where you live.
4 There I will go to the altar of God,
   to God—the source of all my joy.
I will praise you with my harp,
   O God, my God!

5 Why am I discouraged?
   Why so sad?
I will put my hope in God!
   I will praise him again—
   my Savior and my God!

*P*erhaps this psalm was on Elijah's heart as he was climbing Mount Carmel to challenge the prophets of Baal (1 Kings 18–19). The surrounding nations honored Baal as the mighty sky god, who crashed the thunder and sent rain, and now Israel, led by the weak-willed King Ahab and his idolatrous queen, Jezebel, had plunged headlong into the worship of Baal as well.

"O God, take up my cause!" you can almost hear Elijah praying as he anticipated his match with the Baal priests. No doubt he felt very alone in his efforts to call the sinful Israelites back to their God, back to a life of holiness and faithfulness to the Lord.

And God did take up Elijah's cause by sending fire to consume his sacrifice. But even that victory didn't eliminate Elijah's loneliness. A chapter later we find him at Mount Sinai with a downcast soul. Yes, depression dies hard, but there is hope. The Lord assures Elijah that there are seven thousand others who have remained faithful to him, and he gives Elijah instructions to replace the wicked King Ahab.

We, too, serve such a God, so even in our darkest times we can echo the psalmist's refrain: "I will praise him again—my Savior and my God!"

> Oh, send thy light to guide my feet,
> And bid thy truth appear;
> Conduct me to thy holy hill
> To taste thy mercies there.
> C. D. BARLOW

Bible Networking
To read more about rejoicing in the Lord (verse 4), turn to Psalm 71:23; Isaiah 61:10; Habakkuk 3:17-18; and Romans 5:11.

Notable Quotable
"What oxygen is to the lungs, such is hope for the meaning of life."
EMIL BRÜNNER

PSALM 44:1-8

For the choir director: A psalm of the descendants of Korah.

¹ O God, we have heard it with our own ears—
    our ancestors have told us
of all you did in other days,
    in days long ago:
² You drove out the pagan nations
    and gave all the land to our ancestors;
you crushed their enemies,
    setting our ancestors free.
³ They did not conquer the land with their swords;
    it was not their own strength that gave them victory.
It was by your mighty power that they succeeded;
    it was because you favored them and smiled on
        them.

⁴ You are my King and my God.
    You command victories for your people.
⁵ Only by your power can we push back our enemies;
    only in your name can we trample our foes.
⁶ I do not trust my bow;
    I do not count on my sword to save me.
⁷ It is you who gives us victory over our enemies;
    it is you who humbles those who hate us.
⁸ O God, we give glory to you all day long
    and constantly praise your name.   *Interlude*

Y ou probably know the story of young David slaying the mighty Goliath (1 Samuel 17), but there's a detail in the story that's both comical and instructive.

The giant had been challenging the Israelites to send out some warrior to fight him, and King Saul's best soldiers were quaking in their sandals. David, on a supply run to feed his brothers, shocked everybody by volunteering for the job. He was convinced that God would give him the victory. When Saul finally agreed to let the boy fight, he tried to dress young David in his own royal armor.

This had to be a funny scene. Remember that Saul was a head taller than anyone else in Israel, and so his armor would have been way too big for David, who probably wasn't fully grown yet. So there's David, fully outfitted in the oversized pieces of armor, clanking around the camp. Fortunately, David concluded, "I can't go in these," and took the armor off.

Instead of trusting in human strength and armor, David chose to place his trust in the Lord. Armed only with a slingshot and five smooth stones plucked from a streambed—and the power of the living God—David felled the giant.

Like David, we must not place our trust solely in our own devices to win victories. "It is [God] who gives us victory over our enemies" (verse 7).

> I am trusting thee to guide me—
> Thou alone shalt lead,
> Every day and hour supplying
> All my need.
> FRANCES R. HAVERGAL

Bible Networking
For more about the Lord fighting for his people, see Deuteronomy 20:4; Joshua 1:8-9; and Isaiah 41:10; 50:7-9.

Notable Quotable
"The link with the past [in verses 1-3] is all the stronger for the fact that the fathers' exploits were not their own but God's."
DEREK KIDNER

PSALM 44:9-19

⁹ But now you have tossed us aside in dishonor.
  You no longer lead our armies to battle.
¹⁰ You make us retreat from our enemies
  and allow them to plunder our land.
¹¹ You have treated us like sheep waiting to be
    slaughtered;
  you have scattered us among the nations.
¹² You sold us—your precious people—for a pittance.
  You valued us at nothing at all.

¹³ You have caused all our neighbors to mock us.
  We are an object of scorn and derision to the nations
    around us.
¹⁴ You have made us the butt of their jokes;
  we are scorned by the whole world.
¹⁵ We can't escape the constant humiliation;
  shame is written across our faces.
¹⁶ All we hear are the taunts of our mockers.
  All we see are our vengeful enemies.

¹⁷ All this has happened despite our loyalty to you.
  We have not violated your covenant.
¹⁸ Our hearts have not deserted you.
  We have not strayed from your path.
¹⁹ Yet you have crushed us in the desert.
  You have covered us with darkness and death.

When the Israelites finally crossed the Jordan River into the Promised Land, they immediately encountered a major obstacle—the walled city of Jericho. Their battle plan was certainly a bit weird, marching around the city thirteen times in all. But Jericho's walls crumbled, and God's people had a foothold in their new land. Their victory was a mighty testimony to God's power.

Battle number two didn't go as well. The little town of Ai was hardly a bump on a hillside, but the Israelites failed in their first attempt to capture it. Unbeknownst to most of the Israelites, one of them had stolen something from Jericho, disobeying God's explicit commands, so the whole nation suffered this humiliating defeat. You can imagine Joshua's complaint to God in the words of Psalm 44: "Now you have tossed us aside in dishonor."

Life with God has its ups and downs. We have some incredible victories, but sometimes we also suffer puzzling defeats. If you're scratching your head, wondering why life is so tough lately, you're not alone. Here and in other psalms, the psalmist seems to say, "God, what on earth are you doing?" But God always knows what he is doing. He gave the Israelites another opportunity to take Ai, and they emerged victorious.

As we'll see tomorrow, this psalm ends with an appeal to God's "unfailing love." When it seems that God has forgotten you, know that he loves you and that you can call out to him.

> Redeem us from perpetual shame,
> Our Savior and our God!
> We plead the honors of thy name,
> The mercies of thy blood.
> ISAAC WATTS

Bible Networking
For more on the Lord's selling of his people (verse 12), look up Judges 2:14. Then look up Isaiah 52:3.

Notable Quotable
"Sometimes God takes away all sensible enjoyment and encouragement to see whether we still cling to Him for Himself."
F. B. MEYER

PSALM 44:20-26

[20] If we had turned away from worshiping our God
   or spread our hands in prayer to foreign gods,
[21] God would surely have known it,
   for he knows the secrets of every heart.
[22] For your sake we are killed every day;
   we are being slaughtered like sheep.

[23] Wake up, O Lord! Why do you sleep?
   Get up! Do not reject us forever.
[24] Why do you look the other way?
   Why do you ignore our suffering and oppression?
[25] We collapse in the dust,
   lying face down in the dirt.
[26] Rise up! Come and help us!
   Save us because of your unfailing love.

*T*his psalm asks some hard questions: Where is God in our suffering? Why isn't he doing anything? Doesn't he care about us anymore?

This psalm no doubt echoes the thoughts of other Old Testament figures such as Job, who innocently endured terrible suffering, or Joseph, who was repeatedly wronged even though he honored God. It also expresses the sentiments of Jeremiah, who was nearly killed as he prophesied truth to a rebellious nation. And certainly it captures the feelings of millions of believers through the centuries. The truth is, sometimes it's downright dangerous to trust in God.

But the apostle Paul helps put things in perspective: "What we suffer now is nothing compared to the glory he will give us later" (Romans 8:18). It's not over till it's over. Bad things happen to good people, but through it all "God causes everything to work together for the good of those who love God" (Romans 8:28). It may not always seem that way. In fact, later in Romans 8, Paul quotes Psalm 44:22: "We are being slaughtered like sheep" (verse 36). But ultimately our enemies can never take away our most valuable possession—God's love for us.

So if bad things are happening to you, it doesn't mean God has stopped loving you. On the contrary, "God blesses those who are persecuted because they live for God, for the Kingdom of Heaven is theirs" (Matthew 5:10).

> God His own doth tend and nourish;
> In His holy courts they flourish.
> From all evil things He spares them;
> In His mighty arms He bears them.

CAROLINA SANDELL BERG

Fascinating Fact
One of the great pioneers of hymn singing in the early church, Bishop Ambrose, was working on a commentary on Psalm 44 when he died. Just as he reached verse 23, exhorting God to wake up, Ambrose "fell asleep" and awoke on the other side of eternity.

Notable Quotable
"It is mercy to us, that when God might punish us for our sin, he doth make our correction honorable, and our troubles to be for a good cause—'For thy sake.'"
DAVID DICKSON

When we think of the Psalms, often we think of praising God and giving him thanks. Praise certainly is a major theme, but it may surprise you to learn that more than fifty psalms are called "laments."

There are seven ingredients that are typically found in a psalm of lament, although it is unusual for any one psalm to contain all seven ingredients.

◆ Addressing God with a cry for help

Listen to my prayer, O God.
Do not ignore my cry for help!
PSALM 55:1

◆ Referring to God's blessings in the past or to his character

O Lord, you are so good, so ready to forgive,
so full of unfailing love for all who ask your aid.
PSALM 86:5

◆ Describing the cause of distress

They are always twisting what I say;
they spend their days plotting ways to harm me.
PSALM 56:5

◆ Confessing trust and confidence

You are my strength; I wait for you to rescue me,
for you, O God, are my place of safety.
PSALM 59:9

◆ Asking God to hear and deliver

Please, LORD, rescue me!
Come quickly, LORD, and help me.
PSALM 40:13

◆ Further questioning and petitioning

Please, don't punish me any-
    more!
I am exhausted by the blows
    from your hand.
PSALM 39:10

♦ Praising God for his answer or
  promising to praise and worship in the future
I will praise you forever, O God,
    for what you have done.
PSALM 52:9

What is a "lament"? It is a
psalm in which the psalmist is
troubled and seeking deliverance. He is going through a
time of physical, spiritual, or
emotional distress, which may
be caused by something within
him or by something outside of
him, such as an attacking
enemy. As he cries to God for
help, however, he displays his
confidence that God will hear
and answer him, providing protection, forgiveness, or whatever
else he needs. Often the psalmist offers praise for what the
Lord will do, even though there
is no indication of what will
happen.

There are many different
kinds of problems that the
psalmist could have been expe-
riencing as he wrote his
laments. In Psalm 51, for
instance, the problem is his
own sin; in Psalm 54, he needs
physical deliverance; in Psalm

55, the psalmist is suffering
from emotional distress.

Like the psalmists in ancient
times, we encounter difficulties
and struggles and need God's
help. Sometimes our problems
are brought about by our own
sin. Other times our problems
are physical in nature. Still
other times our problems stem
from some emotional difficulty. Whatever the case, the
psalmists have shown us that
we can cry out to God and
express our distress. We can do
so with confidence that God is
listening and will reach out to
us.

∾

Jesus knows all about our struggles,
He will guide till the day is done;
There's not a friend like the lowly
    Jesus,
No, not one! no, not one!
JOHNSON OATMAN

Selah

April 12

PSALM 45:1-9

For the choir director: A psalm of the descendants of Korah, to be sung to the tune "Lilies." A love song.

1 My heart overflows with a beautiful thought!
    I will recite a lovely poem to the king,
        for my tongue is like the pen of a skillful poet.

2 You are the most handsome of all.
    Gracious words stream from your lips.
    God himself has blessed you forever.

3 Put on your sword, O mighty warrior!
    You are so glorious, so majestic!

4 In your majesty, ride out to victory,
        defending truth, humility, and justice.
    Go forth to perform awe-inspiring deeds!

5 Your arrows are sharp,
        piercing your enemies' hearts.
    The nations fall before you,
        lying down beneath your feet.

6 Your throne, O God, endures forever and ever.
    Your royal power is expressed in justice.

7 You love what is right and hate what is wrong.
    Therefore God, your God, has anointed you,
        pouring out the oil of joy on you more than on
            anyone else.

8 Your robes are perfumed with myrrh, aloes, and cassia.
    In palaces decorated with ivory,
        you are entertained by the music of harps.

9 Kings' daughters are among your concubines.
    At your right side stands the queen,
        wearing jewelry of finest gold from Ophir!

*I*f you were alive and conscious in 1981, you heard at least some news about Great Britain's royal wedding. Prince Charles, heir to the royal throne, was marrying Lady Diana. It was a gloriously ornate event. Saint Paul's Cathedral was packed with nobles in their finest finery. The bridal gown alone cost eight thousand dollars and had a twenty-five-foot train.

This is the sort of celebration we read about in Psalm 45. In this first section, the author (perhaps the king's poet laureate) is praising the king, who is about to take a bride. Some scholars believe this was Solomon marrying Pharaoh's daughter (1 Kings 3:1) or some other foreign princess. Imagine the glamour of that event!

But this psalm changes direction in verse 6. After flattering the "handsome" ruler and extolling his military victories, the poet starts to focus on the divine King, the coming Messiah. The rest of the psalm reads in two dimensions: the human king's royal wedding and the Messiah's connection with his people.

The glory of Britain's royal wedding didn't last, nor did the glory of Solomon's wedding. Charles and Diana's romance soured, and Solomon married hundreds of other women. But the Lord's commitment to his people will never end.

> I shall see the King in His beauty in the land that
>   is far away,
> When the shadows at length have lifted, and the
>   darkness has turned into day.
> And to none will the King be a stranger of the
>   throngs who surround His seat.
> For the hearts of the saved will know Him by the
>   prints of the nails in His feet.
> A. B. SIMPSON

A Word on Words

Myrrh and aloes (verse 8) were some of the ingredients of the choicest perfumes, which were used as holy anointing oil (Exodus 30:23-33). The Israelites were forbidden to use these perfumes for their personal desires.

Notable Quotable

[Regarding verse 2], "Certainly never were such words of love, sweetness, and tenderness spoken here upon this earth as those last words of [Christ's] which were uttered a little before his sufferings recorded in the thirteenth through seventeenth chapters of John."
JOHN ROW

PSALM 45:10-17

¹⁰ Listen to me, O royal daughter; take to heart what I say.
   Forget your people and your homeland far away.

¹¹ For your royal husband delights in your beauty;
   honor him, for he is your lord.

¹² The princes of Tyre will shower you with gifts.
   People of great wealth will entreat your favor.

¹³ The bride, a princess, waits within her chamber,
   dressed in a gown woven with gold.

¹⁴ In her beautiful robes, she is led to the king,
   accompanied by her bridesmaids.

¹⁵ What a joyful, enthusiastic procession
   as they enter the king's palace!

¹⁶ Your sons will become kings like their father.
   You will make them rulers over many lands.

¹⁷ I will bring honor to your name in every generation.
   Therefore, the nations will praise you forever and ever.

*P*salm 45, as we learned yesterday, is a wedding psalm. Imagine the first nine verses being sung to the king as he leads the procession to claim his bride. Verses 10-13 show us the bride, waiting in her own home. Then she is "led to the king" and they go to the palace in a "joyful, enthusiastic procession."

As we catch the psalm's double meaning (groom as king and Messiah), we see ourself in the bride's role. And we can grab two nuggets of wisdom for our own relationship with our King.

"Forget your people and your homeland far away." When we commit ourself to God, it's like a marriage. We need to forsake all others. Whatever previous attachments we have had, they must take second place. Make the Lord the center of your attention and loyalty.

"For your royal husband delights in your beauty." On a human level this is normal, but when we're talking about the divine King, it's breathtaking. God delights in us! When we truly accept this wonderful truth, there is no room for fear or insecurity.

> *The Bride eyes, not her garment,*
> *but her dear Bridegroom's face;*
> *I will not gaze at glory*
> *but on my King of grace,*
> *Not at the crown He giveth,*
> *but on His pierced hand;*
> *The Lamb is all the glory of Immanuel's land.*
> ANNE ROSS COUSIN

Bible Networking
For more on brides preparing to marry their husbands, read Isaiah 61:10 and Song of Songs.

Notable Quotable
"Nowhere in Old Testament writings do we find a nearer approach to the disclosure of the secret of the Church than in this psalm."
G. CAMPBELL MORGAN

April 14

PSALM 46:1-7
For the choir director: A psalm of the descendants of Korah, to be sung by soprano voices. A song.

¹ God is our refuge and strength,
    always ready to help in times of trouble.
² So we will not fear, even if earthquakes come
    and the mountains crumble into the sea.
³ Let the oceans roar and foam.
    Let the mountains tremble as the waters surge!

Interlude

⁴ A river brings joy to the city of our God,
    the sacred home of the Most High.
⁵ God himself lives in that city; it cannot be destroyed.
    God will protect it at the break of day.
⁶ The nations are in an uproar,
    and kingdoms crumble!
God thunders,
    and the earth melts!

⁷ The LORD Almighty is here among us;
    the God of Israel is our fortress.   *Interlude*

Martin Luther was a brash, bold bear of a man. He knew about power, but he also knew about fear. Terrified by the power of God displayed in a fierce thunderstorm, young Martin vowed to serve the Lord as a monk. He tore into his monastic duties with a vengeance, fearing that he would displease God if he didn't do every good deed possible.

But God was slowly softening Luther's heart, assuring him of love and not simply judgment. From the Scriptures, Luther learned that the righteous would find eternal life by trusting Christ and that they couldn't earn it with good deeds. He realized that God was not a demanding tyrant but a refuge, a comfort, a help.

The rest is history. Luther's doctrine of "salvation by faith" sparked the Protestant Reformation, transforming the way millions of people would understand God. He wrote many books and essays, but Luther's most famous work is a hymn, "A Mighty Fortress Is Our God," based on Psalm 46. There are few texts that portray faith in God as powerfully as this song.

Luther's life wasn't easy. He was arrested, tried, excommunicated, hunted, hidden, and betrayed. But Luther knew that he need not fear the "ancient foe" and all his attacks, for God was his refuge, "a bulwark never failing."

> A mighty fortress is our God, a bulwark never failing;
> Our helper he amid the flood of mortal ills prevailing.
> For still our ancient foe doth seek to work us woe;
> His craft and power are great, and armed with cruel hate,
> On earth is not his equal.
>
> MARTIN LUTHER

Fascinating Fact
Tradition holds that the translators of the King James Version used this psalm to pay homage to their fellow wordsmith William Shakespeare on his forty-sixth birthday. The forty-sixth word in Psalm 46 is shake, and the forty-sixth word from the end is spear.

Notable Quotable
"The double prop on which our faith rests: the infinite power whereby he can subdue the universe unto himself and the fatherly love which he has revealed in his Word."
JOHN CALVIN

PSALM 46:8-11

8 Come, see the glorious works of the LORD:
  See how he brings destruction upon the world
9 and causes wars to end throughout the earth.
  He breaks the bow and snaps the spear in two;
  he burns the shields with fire.

10 "Be silent, and know that I am God!
   I will be honored by every nation.
   I will be honored throughout the world."

11 The LORD Almighty is here among us;
   the God of Israel is our fortress.   *Interlude*

*T*he fourteenth century was not a good time to be Russian. The Mongol hordes, led by Genghis Khan, had invaded a century earlier and still dominated Russia. The people chafed under "the Mongol yoke."

But there was a quiet Christian renewal going on. Seeking new intimacy with God, a man named Sergius had established a monastic community outside of Moscow. The spiritual fervor of these monks caught on in the surrounding communities as nobles and peasants alike sought to know God better. It also inspired an artistic explosion, as new religious icons were created in many churches in the area.

During this time twelve-year-old Dmitry became Grand Prince of Russia. Living in Moscow, he learned a great deal from this Christian leader, Sergius. When Dmitry later gathered Russian forces to fight the Mongols, he encouraged his outnumbered troops with the words of Psalm 46: "The Lord Almighty is here among us; the God of Israel is our fortress." Emboldened by these words, Dmitry won an important battle against the Mongols.

Now we must be careful not to conclude that God will reward us with victory simply because we claim Psalm 46 as our battle cry. We can see from verse 9 that God ultimately desires peace, and eventually he will cause all wars to end. But we can be certain that God is our fortress, and we can look to him for our refuge from those who seek to harm us.

> Be still, my soul:
> Thy best, thy heavenly Friend
> Through thorny ways
> Leads to a joyful end.
> KATHARINA VON SCHLEGEL

Fascinating Fact
On his deathbed, John Wesley found peace in the reading of this psalm.

Notable Quotable
Verse 10 "resembles the command to another raging sea: 'Peace be still!' and the end in view is stated in terms not of man's hopes but of God's glory."
DEREK KIDNER

JOB 38:8-18 (God's Poem)

[8] "Who defined the boundaries of the sea
   as it burst from the womb,
[9] and as I clothed it with clouds
   and thick darkness?
[10] For I locked it behind barred gates,
   limiting its shores.
[11] I said, 'Thus far and no farther will you come.
   Here your proud waves must stop!'

[12] "Have you ever commanded the morning to appear
   and caused the dawn to rise in the east?
[13] Have you ever told the daylight to spread to the ends of
   the earth,
   to bring an end to the night's wickedness?
[14] For the features of the earth take shape as the light
   approaches,
   and the dawn is robed in red.

[15] The light disturbs the haunts of the wicked,
   and it stops the arm that is raised in violence.

[16] "Have you explored the springs from which the seas
   come?
   Have you walked about and explored their depths?
[17] Do you know where the gates of death are located?
   Have you seen the gates of utter gloom?
[18] Do you realize the extent of the earth?
   Tell me about it if you know!

Psalm Link
PSALM 46:10
"Be silent, and know that I am God!"

*A*s all parents know, every child's favorite question is *why*: "Why do I have to go to bed now?" "Why do I have to eat my vegetables?" "Why do I have to turn off the TV?" We may think that this is simply a stage the child will grow out of, but the truth is, their *why* questions will continue throughout life.

In fact, even as adults, they will keep on asking *why*. When a relative is killed in a fatal accident, when their parent is afflicted with Alzheimer's, or when their own children are plagued with problems, they will ask the same question.

Apparently *why* was Job's favorite question, too. The German philosopher Friedrich Nietzsche once wrote: "He who knows the why can bear with any how." That seems to be what Job thought, and that's what we often mistakenly think as well.

But in all forty-two chapters of Job, God never answers the *why* question. Instead, he shows Job that knowing *who* is far more important than knowing *why*. If you get to know the *who*, any *why* will be OK. Like a parent who has come to the end of a child's string of *why* questions and answers, "Because I said so," God often must tell us, "Trust me, even when you don't get answers." We are to live by faith—not just with the first step of our journey but with every step.

> When mystery clouds my darkened path,
> I'll check my dread, my doubts reprove;
> In this my soul sweet comfort has,
> That God is love, God is love.
> And though I cannot trace his way,
> I am resolved to always say
> That God is love, God is love.
> ANONYMOUS

Bible Networking
This passage in Job gives us a glimpse of the greatness of our Creator. For another glimpse of our Creator's greatness, read Psalm 148:5-6.

Notable Quotable
"God answered none of Job's questions; they were the wrong questions. Instead, he involved Job in the experience of knowing him through his creative activity. Job's questions about the ways of God could not be answered apart from the knowing of God himself."
WILLIAM E. HULME

April 17

PSALM 47
For the choir director: A psalm of the descendants of Korah.

¹ Come, everyone, and clap your hands for joy!
  Shout to God with joyful praise!
² For the LORD Most High is awesome.
  He is the great King of all the earth.
³ He subdues the nations before us,
  putting our enemies beneath our feet.
⁴ He chose the Promised Land as our inheritance,
  the proud possession of Jacob's descendants, whom
    he loves. *Interlude*

⁵ God has ascended with a mighty shout.
  The LORD has ascended with trumpets blaring.
⁶ Sing praise to God, sing praises;
  sing praise to our King, sing praises!

⁷ For God is the King over all the earth.
  Praise him with a psalm!
⁸ God reigns above the nations,
  sitting on his holy throne.
⁹ The rulers of the world have gathered together.
  They join us in praising the God of Abraham.
  For all the kings of the earth belong to God.
  He is highly honored everywhere.

*T*here's a controversy brewing in some churches these days: To clap or not to clap—that is the question.

If a soloist does a great job with "O Holy Night," or the choir really nails "How Great Thou Art," many church members feel it's only right to applaud them. Great job! Others feel that applause breaks the mood of worship, turning the church into a nightclub. Where's the reverence?

Today's psalm makes it clear that there's nothing wrong with clapping in itself. This form of worship was obviously used by devout Israelites. But notice that God is the recipient of these praises, not Asaph the harpist. Where's the reverence? It's all over the place. See verse 2: "The Lord Most High is awesome."

So clap or don't clap in church—but make sure your heart is full of the joy of the Lord, and let your voice and body act accordingly.

> *O worship the King, all glorious above,*
> *O gratefully sing his power and his love;*
> *Our Shield and Defender, the Ancient of Days,*
> *Pavilioned in splendor and girded with praise.*
> ROBERT GRANT

Notable Quotable
In verse 5, God has come down from heaven in power and great might to deliver his people and is returning to his throne—W. O. E. Osterley describes it as "the culminating act of the eschatological drama."

PSALM 48:1-8
A psalm of the descendants of Korah. A song.

¹ How great is the LORD,
　　and how much we should praise him
in the city of our God,
　　which is on his holy mountain!
² It is magnificent in elevation—
　　the whole earth rejoices to see it!
Mount Zion, the holy mountain,
　　is the city of the great King!
³ God himself is in Jerusalem's towers.
　　He reveals himself as her defender.

⁴ The kings of the earth joined forces
　　and advanced against the city.
⁵ But when they saw it, they were stunned;
　　they were terrified and ran away.
⁶ They were gripped with terror,
　　like a woman writhing in the pain of childbirth
⁷ or like the mighty ships of Tarshish
　　being shattered by a powerful east wind.

⁸ We had heard of the city's glory,
　　but now we have seen it ourselves—
　　the city of the LORD Almighty.
It is the city of our God;
　　he will make it safe forever.　　　　　　　*Interlude*

*J*erusalem is a glorious city. It is set on four hills, and in David's time it was fed by an internal spring. Once Solomon built the Temple and the city walls, Jerusalem gained even more character. Ironically, today the the shining domes of Muslim shrines give us a hint of how brilliant the Temple must have once looked, set against the backdrop of this holy city.

Psalm 48 speaks of Jerusalem's enemies as being so "stunned" and "terrified" that they abandon their attacks on the city. While Jerusalem has had several assaults made on it that might fit this description, the psalmist might also be speaking of a heavenly Jerusalem. Jerusalem has always been regarded as more than merely another fortified capital city. It is where God lives. Because of this, this psalm could be understood as referring to our eternal home with God, "a heavenly city" that has been prepared for those who trust him (Hebrews 11:16).

Sadly, the earthly Jerusalem has been conquered by various foes. Even today there are bombings in markets and bus stations. The city is not yet "safe forever" (verse 8), but we are. God has ensured for us a home with him eternally, and no spiritual foe will ever destroy that.

> *Glorious things of thee are spoken,*
> *Zion, city of our God;*
> *He whose word cannot be broken*
> *Formed thee for his own abode.*
> JOHN NEWTON

Bible Networking
The Bible mentions another time when a ship of Tarshish was battered by a storm. Read Jonah 1:1-16. Solomon also had ships of Tarshish, or trading ships. Read 1 Kings 10:22. Some scholars identify Tarshish as the coast of Spain.

Notable Quotable
"Zion is only beautiful and glad because the temple is there, and in that temple the God of heaven made his earthly sanctuary."
ROBERT ALLEN

PSALM 48:9-14

⁹ O God, we meditate on your unfailing love
    as we worship in your Temple.
¹⁰ As your name deserves, O God,
    you will be praised to the ends of the earth.
    Your strong right hand is filled with victory.
¹¹ Let the people on Mount Zion rejoice.
    Let the towns of Judah be glad,
    for your judgments are just.

¹² Go, inspect the city of Jerusalem.
    Walk around and count the many towers.
¹³ Take note of the fortified walls,
    and tour all the citadels,
  that you may describe them
    to future generations.
¹⁴ For that is what God is like.
    He is our God forever and ever,
    and he will be our guide until we die.

*I*f you go to Jerusalem as a tourist, you will probably find a tour guide who will take you around the city and point out the many historical sites: the Wailing Wall, the Temple Mount, Hezekiah's Tunnel, the Pool of Siloam, the Damascus Gate. You would be doing exactly what verse 12 is talking about—inspecting the city, walking around and counting its many towers. And your tour guide would be doing exactly what verse 13 is talking about—describing these sites to future generations.

It's fascinating when you think about it, that this psalm assumes the towers won't last. The psalmist knew these massive stone structures would fall someday. Why else would anyone need to "describe them to future generations"? And that's exactly what you see in Jerusalem today—ruins of structures that stood strong long ago.

But there's no note of dismay in this psalm. On the contrary! People should rejoice and be glad because they trust in God, not in earthly fortresses. Sure, they worship in a Temple that will crumble someday, but they also "meditate on [God's] unfailing love." God's love will never crumble. "He will be our guide until we die" and even afterward.

> Let strangers walk around the city where we dwell;
> Compass and view thy holy ground, and mark the building well;
> The order of thy house, the worship of thy court,
> The cheerful songs, the solemn vows, and make a fair report.
> ISAAC WATTS

Notable Quotable
"I praise God because he not only guides my directions but overrules my mistakes."
H. NORMAN PELL

PSALM 49:1-9
For the choir director: A psalm of the descendants of Korah.

¹ Listen to this, all you people!
    Pay attention, everyone in the world!
² High and low,
    rich and poor—listen!
³ For my words are wise,
    and my thoughts are filled with insight.
⁴ I listen carefully to many proverbs
    and solve riddles with inspiration from a harp.

⁵ There is no need to fear when times of trouble come,
    when enemies are surrounding me.
⁶ They trust in their wealth
    and boast of great riches.
⁷ Yet they cannot redeem themselves from death
    by paying a ransom to God.
⁸ Redemption does not come so easily,
    for no one can ever pay enough
⁹ to live forever
    and never see the grave.

France is one of the least religious nations on earth today. Though the country is officially 90 percent Catholic, few of those 90 percent regularly participate in any sort of organized religious activity. One of the people who contributed to the demise of religious fervor in France is Voltaire. This eighteenth-century French philosopher waged a written war against "superstitions" like believing in God. Voltaire did contribute some valuable ideas to the study of science and history, and the church of his day certainly deserved some criticism, but he helped to set a tone of disbelief that permanently affected his country and the entire Western world.

Voltaire's writings, such as the satire *Candide*, were extremely popular in his day, making him a very wealthy man. Yet a story is told about Voltaire on his deathbed. Reportedly he told his doctor, "I will give you half of all I have if you will give me six months more to live."

Of course, the doctor couldn't do that. Even today, while the rich may buy the latest medical technology to keep their bodies going a bit longer, they can't cheat death forever. When God says it's quitting time, your life on earth is done. And, as Psalm 49:7 tells us, all the money in the world can't bribe God. So don't place your trust in riches. Place it in God himself, who offers us life through his Son.

> From David's lips this word did roll,
> 'Tis true and living yet:
> No man can save his brother's soul,
> Nor pay his brother's debt.
> MATTHEW ARNOLD, BASED ON PSALM 49:7

PSALM 49:10-20

[10] Those who are wise must finally die,
    just like the foolish and senseless,
    leaving all their wealth behind.

[11] The grave is their eternal home,
    where they will stay forever.
They may name their estates after themselves,
    but they leave their wealth to others.

[12] They will not last long despite their riches—
    they will die like the animals.

[13] This is the fate of fools,
    though they will be remembered as being so wise.

Interlude

[14] Like sheep, they are led to the grave,
    where death will be their shepherd.
In the morning the godly will rule over them.
    Their bodies will rot in the grave,
    far from their grand estates.

[15] But as for me, God will redeem my life.
    He will snatch me from the power of death.   *Interlude*

[16] So don't be dismayed when the wicked grow rich,
    and their homes become ever more splendid.

[17] For when they die, they carry nothing with them.
    Their wealth will not follow them into the grave.

[18] In this life they consider themselves fortunate,
    and the world loudly applauds their success.

[19] But they will die like all others before them
    and never again see the light of day.

[20] People who boast of their wealth don't understand
    that they will die like the animals.

J esus told a story of a rich man who was far too concerned with his wealth (Luke 12:16-21). He had more grain than his barns could handle, so he decided that he would tear down the barns and build bigger ones. (Why didn't he just build more barns? That's part of Jesus' mockery of the wastefulness of wealth.) This man figured that once he did this he would be set for life. He could sit back and "eat, drink, and be merry."

But God had a different plan. The man would die that very night, leaving all his great wealth for others to take. "Yes, a person is a fool to store up earthly wealth but not have a rich relationship with God," Jesus concluded.

In this world people measure things in money, but God has a far different yardstick. As the old adage goes, you can't take it with you. The only thing you can take with you is your "rich relationship with God." So, in the psalmist's words, "Don't be dismayed when the wicked grow rich." Just take a moment to think about where your true treasure lies.

> Let us labor for the Master from the dawn till setting sun,
> Let us talk of all his wondrous love and care;
> Then when all of life is over, and our work on earth is done,
> And the roll is called up yonder, I'll be there.
> JAMES M. BLACK

Notable Quotable
"It is foolish as well as dangerous to put one's trust in something which is even less stable than man himself."
JOHN I. DURHAM

April 22

PSALM 50:1-14
A psalm of Asaph.

¹ The mighty God, the LORD, has spoken;
   he has summoned all humanity from east to west!
² From Mount Zion, the perfection of beauty,
   God shines in glorious radiance.
³ Our God approaches with the noise of thunder.
   Fire devours everything in his way,
   and a great storm rages around him.
⁴ Heaven and earth will be his witnesses
   as he judges his people:
⁵ "Bring my faithful people to me—
   those who made a covenant with me by giving
     sacrifices."
⁶ Then let the heavens proclaim his justice,
   for God himself will be the judge.   *Interlude*

⁷ "O my people, listen as I speak.
   Here are my charges against you, O Israel:
   I am God, your God!
⁸ I have no complaint about your sacrifices
   or the burnt offerings you constantly bring to my altar.
⁹ But I want no more bulls from your barns;
   I want no more goats from your pens.
¹⁰ For all the animals of the forest are mine,
   and I own the cattle on a thousand hills.
¹¹ Every bird of the mountains
   and all the animals of the field belong to me.
¹² If I were hungry, I would not mention it to you,
   for all the world is mine and everything in it.
¹³ I don't need the bulls you sacrifice;
   I don't need the blood of goats.
¹⁴ What I want instead is your true thanks to God;
   I want you to fulfill your vows to the Most High."

*W*here was Samuel? That's what King Saul and his troops were wondering as they prepared to fight the Philistines. The old priest was late, and he had to perform the customary sacrifice before the army went into battle. The sun was rising in the sky, and with every hour more frightened Israelite soldiers deserted camp.

Finally Saul felt he could delay no longer. Taking matters into his own hands, he stepped into the priestly role and prepared the burnt offering himself. As he was finishing the ritual, Samuel showed up.

The priest was not happy. "What is this you have done?" he barked. Saul muttered his excuses, but Samuel wanted none of it. Saul had disobeyed God's command, and as a result the kingdom would be taken from him.

What was Saul's mistake? He was putting his trust in the sacrifice rather than in God. He assumed the ritual alone would give him victory over the Philistines, but he forgot that a personal God was the source of his power.

Today's psalm pictures God at the center of the world, judging his people. "Thanks for all your sacrifices," he says, "but I don't need any more bulls and goats. I need your honest thanks and your obedience." It's a lesson Saul should have learned and one the rest of us can learn as well.

> Not all the blood of beasts on Jewish altars slain
> Could give the guilty conscience peace or wash
>   away the stain.
> But Christ, the heavenly Lamb, takes all our sins
> away;
> A sacrifice of nobler name and richer blood
> ISAAC WATTS

Bible Networking
Follow the leading of verse 14 and celebrate Thanksgiving all year round. See Psalm 69:30; 2 Corinthians 9:11; and Ephesians 5:20.

Notable Quotable
"Our most heinous sin is not the act of wrong done, but the fact that such wrong incapacitates us from fulfilling our highest function of glorifying God."
G. CAMPBELL MORGAN

PSALM 50:15-23

15 "Trust me in your times of trouble,
    and I will rescue you,
    and you will give me glory."

16 But God says to the wicked:
    "Recite my laws no longer,
    and don't pretend that you obey me.

17 For you refuse my discipline
    and treat my laws like trash.

18 When you see a thief, you help him,
    and you spend your time with adulterers.

19 Your mouths are filled with wickedness,
    and your tongues are full of lies.

20 You sit around and slander a brother—
    your own mother's son.

21 While you did all this, I remained silent,
    and you thought I didn't care.
    But now I will rebuke you,
    listing all my charges against you.

22 Repent, all of you who ignore me,
    or I will tear you apart,
    and no one will help you.

23 But giving thanks is a sacrifice that truly honors me.
    If you keep to my path,
    I will reveal to you the salvation of God."

Origen (185–253) was a great Christian in a difficult time. He was the son of a Christian martyr, and he himself aspired to martyrdom. He wrote great works of theology that helped to anchor the young church.

But during another wave of persecution even Origen stumbled. At this time anyone who was brought before the Roman authorities was required to offer a pinch of incense as a sacrifice to the emperor and hail him as a god. Many Christians refused and were executed. Origen, too, was tested in this way. Threatened with death, the great teacher offered the incense.

Origen later traveled to various cities, doing some private teaching and writing. People were amazed at his wisdom. Once in Jerusalem he was asked to preach in a church service. He took the book of Psalms, prayed, and opened it to Psalm 50:16: "Recite my laws no longer, and don't pretend that you obey me." Stricken with remorse over the incense he had offered, Origen shut the book, sat down speechless, and burst into tears. Eventually he said, "The prophet David himself shut the door of my lips."

This section of Psalm 50 is targeted toward wicked people who pretend to be righteous. Origen was convinced that he fell into that category. Maybe we do, too. God's message is: "Stop the act! Repent! Get back on track, and I will show you salvation!"

> With broken heart and contrite sigh,
> A trembling sinner, Lord, I cry;
> Thy pardoning grace is rich and free:
> O God, be merciful to me!
> CORNELIUS ELVEN

Bible Networking
"Repent" (verse 22), or turning from our evil ways, is a New Testament concept, too. See Matthew 11:20; Luke 13:3, 5; 15:7, 10; and Acts 2:38.

Notable Quotable
"It is still easier to offer a bull, sacrifice a goat, make a special gift, or do a job than to grapple with the hard realities of honest faith."
JOHN I. DURHAM

PSALM 51:1-12

*For the choir director: A psalm of David, regarding the time Nathan the prophet
came to him after David had committed adultery with Bathsheba.*

¹ Have mercy on me, O God,
because of your unfailing love.
Because of your great compassion,
blot out the stain of my sins.
² Wash me clean from my guilt.
Purify me from my sin.

³ For I recognize my shameful deeds—
they haunt me day and night.
⁴ Against you, and you alone, have I sinned;
I have done what is evil in your sight.
You will be proved right in what you say,
and your judgment against me is just.

⁵ For I was born a sinner—
yes, from the moment my mother conceived me.
⁶ But you desire honesty from the heart,
so you can teach me to be wise in my inmost being.

⁷ Purify me from my sins, and I will be clean;
wash me, and I will be whiter than snow.
⁸ Oh, give me back my joy again;
you have broken me—
now let me rejoice.
⁹ Don't keep looking at my sins.
Remove the stain of my guilt.
¹⁰ Create in me a clean heart, O God.
Renew a right spirit within me.
¹¹ Do not banish me from your presence,
and don't take your Holy spirit from me.
¹² Restore to me again the joy of your salvation,
and make me willling to obey you.

King David had seen a woman and wanted her. What the king wanted he got, even though she was the wife of another man, a loyal soldier in David's army. When she became pregnant, David feared scandal and tried to cover up the affair. But David's tricks didn't work, and finally he arranged for the husband to be killed in battle. Then he took the dead hero's wife as his own.

He almost got away with it.

Then the prophet Nathan showed up with a story to tell. A poor man had one little lamb he loved dearly, but the rich man next door wanted that lamb. Although he could buy any beast in town, the rich man coveted what the poor man loved, and so he stole the lamb and killed it.

Outrageous, David thought. "Who is that rich man?" he demanded. "I'll see that justice is done!"

"You are the man," Nathan answered. And suddenly David saw his own sin. His attempts at a cover-up had only made matters worse. Now it was time to confess his sin before the nation. This psalm is that confession.

Throughout the ages people of faith have used David's words to bemoan their own failings. We throw ourself on the mercy of our loving God, praying that he will blot out our terrible transgressions. And we can be confident that he does hear us and remove our sins, making us white as snow.

> *Lord Jesus, you see that I patiently wait;*
> *Come now, and within me a new heart create;*
> *To those who have sought you, you never said, "No."*
> *Now wash me, and I shall be whiter than snow.*
> JAMES NICHOLSON

Fascinating Fact
It may be the northernmost grave on earth, belonging to a member of an early Arctic expedition. There on a hill overlooking acres of ice upon ice is a gravestone with a plaque that says simply, "Wash me, and I shall be whiter than snow."

Notable Quotable
"This kind of prayer requires a certain kind of God. No man will go to God just because he knows how poor he is in sin, unless he knows how rich God is in mercy."
DAVID REDDING

PSALM 51:13-19

¹³ Then I will teach your ways to sinners,
    and they will return to you.

¹⁴ Forgive me for shedding blood, O God who saves;
    then I will joyfully sing of your forgiveness.

¹⁵ Unseal my lips, O Lord,
    that I may praise you.

¹⁶ You would not be pleased with sacrifices,
    or I would bring them.
  If I brought you a burnt offering,
    you would not accept it.

¹⁷ The sacrifice you want is a broken spirit.
    A broken and repentant heart, O God,
    you will not despise.

¹⁸ Look with favor on Zion and help her;
    rebuild the walls of Jerusalem.

¹⁹ Then you will be pleased with worthy sacrifices
    and with our whole burnt offerings;
    and bulls will again be sacrificed on your altar.

About the time that Columbus was poking around the New World, a monk named Savonarola was leading a revival in Florence, Italy. Speaking courageously against the corruption and greed of the city's ruling families and church officials as well, Savonarola gained popular support. The reforms he was pushing for actually happened for a while, but then his enemies rallied their forces and took power again.

Savonarola was excommunicated from the church and convicted of treason and heresy. In prison he was cruelly tortured. His left arm was dislocated and broken, but his jailers left his right arm uninjured, so he could write a confession, admitting that he was a fraud. Instead, he used his right arm to write a meditation on Psalm 51. It was a confession, but not the kind they wanted. He could confess his sins to God, but he kept reminding the leaders of society that they, like David of old, needed to confess their sins, too.

Witnesses say he slept soundly the night before his execution, with a sweet smile on his lips. No doubt he knew God had cleansed his heart. And appropriately, when a Florentine artist named Michelangelo created his famous painting of this reformer, he found its motto in Psalm 51:13: "Then I will teach your ways to sinners, and they will return to you." That was the story of Savonarola's life.

> Lord, I confess to you, sadly, my sin;
> All I am, I tell to you, All I have been;
> Purge all my sin away, Wash clean my soul this day;
> Lord, make me clean.
> HORATIUS BONAR

Fascinating Fact
In Shakespeare's Hamlet, the murderous King Claudius wails:
What if this cursed hand
Were thicker than itself with brother's blood,
Is there not rain enough in the sweet heavens
To wash it white as snow?

Notable Quotable
"God is looking for the heart that knows how little it deserves, how much it owes."
DEREK KIDNER

PSALM 52

For the choir director: A psalm of David, regarding the time Doeg the Edomite told Saul that Ahimelech had given refuge to David.

1 You call yourself a hero, do you?
    Why boast about this crime of yours,
    you who have disgraced God's people?
2 All day long you plot destruction.
    Your tongue cuts like a sharp razor;
    you're an expert at telling lies.
3 You love evil more than good
    and lies more than truth.   *Interlude*

4 You love to say things that harm others,
    you liar!
5 But God will strike you down once and for all.
    He will pull you from your home
    and drag you from the land of the living.   *Interlude*

6 The righteous will see it and be amazed.
    They will laugh and say,
7 "Look what happens to mighty warriors
    who do not trust in God.
 They trust their wealth instead
    and grow more and more bold in their wickedness."

8 But I am like an olive tree,
    thriving in the house of God.
 I trust in God's unfailing love
    forever and ever.
9 I will praise you forever, O God,
    for what you have done.
 I will wait for your mercies
    in the presence of your people.

*D*avid was a loyal servant in the royal court. He often played the harp to soothe King Saul's spirit. But Saul decided that David was a threat and wanted to kill him. Warned by Saul's son Jonathan, who was also David's close friend, David fled. Along the way, David stopped at Nob and convinced a priest to give him some holy bread and the sword of Goliath.

Unfortunately, one of Saul's herdsman named Doeg happened to be there. He informed Saul that Ahimelech the priest had helped David escape. The paranoid king summoned the priest for interrogation. Ahimelech protested that he was not trying to hurt the king but only to help his friend David, but Saul wanted none of it. He ordered Doeg to kill the priest along with all the other priests who lived in the city of Nob—which Doeg gladly did.

Later David was plagued by guilt over this incident. He should have known that Doeg would squeal to the king. This psalm is David's comeback, berating Doeg for his wickedness. David asserts that the Lord will pay back the wicked for their deeds.

> Why should the mighty make their boast
> And heavenly grace despise?
> In their own arm they put their trust
> And fill their mouth with lies.
> C. D. BARLOW

A Word on Words

It is thought by some that Nob, where this took place, was situated on the Mount of Olives. Compare with Psalm 1:3.

Bible Networking

Olive trees are often mentioned in Scripture. To whom do they refer? Read Psalm 1:3; Romans 11:17, 24; and Zechariah 4:3, 11-14.

PSALM 53
For the choir director: A meditation of David.

1 Only fools say in their hearts,
    "There is no God."
They are corrupt, and their actions are evil;
    no one does good!

2 God looks down from heaven
    on the entire human race;
he looks to see if there is even one with real
        understanding,
    one who seeks for God.
3 But no, all have turned away from God;
    all have become corrupt.
No one does good,
    not even one!

4 Will those who do evil never learn?
    They eat up my people like bread;
    they wouldn't think of praying to God.
5 But then terror will grip them,
    terror like they have never known before.
God will scatter the bones of your enemies.
    You will put them to shame, for God has rejected
        them.

6 Oh, that salvation would come from Mount Zion to
        rescue Israel!
    For when God restores his people,
    Jacob will shout with joy, and Israel will rejoice.

Jan Huss was ordained a priest in the first year of the fifteenth century—not an easy time to be a devout Christian. The church at the time was riddled with corruption. Huss was a university professor and preacher, and he became known as someone who would not hesitate to speak his mind. For a while he worked for the archbishop investigating miracle claims, but sadly he determined that most of the reported events were fraudulent get-rich-quick schemes. Could anyone be trusted?

Everything was political in those days, with Huss's homeland of Bohemia walking a tightrope of independence between the church and the Holy Roman Empire. For a while there were two popes, then three, with all of them excommunicating one another. Huss tried to stay neutral, focusing on the authority of Scripture rather than any pope. Finally Huss was called before a church council, and the authorities claimed that his teachings were heretical. Given a chance to renounce his words, Huss replied, "I would not, for a chapel full of gold, recede from the truth." So Jan Huss was burned at the stake in 1415. Shortly before his death, he recited Psalm 53, an appropriate text for a good man in the midst of a corrupt generation.

Are you facing a difficult situation in which you must stand for what is right in the midst of corruption? Like Jan Huss, take confidence in Psalm 53, and know that God is watching over you and will strengthen you.

> Are all the foes of Zion fools,
> Who thus devour her saints?
> Do they not know her Savior rules
> And pities her complaints?
> ISAAC WATTS

Fascinating Fact
This psalm is almost identical to Psalm 14.

Bible Networking
Find out what a "fool" is according to these passages: Psalm 92:5-6; Proverbs 14:7-9; and Luke 12:20-21.

Notable Quotable
"The fear of God is either an impelling motive, leading in the ways of life; or it becomes a compelling terror, issuing in destruction."
G. CAMPBELL MORGAN

PSALM 54

For the choir director: A meditation of David, regarding the time the Ziphites came and said to Saul, "We know where David is hiding." To be accompanied by stringed instruments.

¹ Come with great power, O God, and rescue me!
Defend me with your might.
² O God, listen to my prayer.
Pay attention to my plea.

³ For strangers are attacking me;
violent men are trying to kill me.
They care nothing for God.   *Interlude*

⁴ But God is my helper.
The Lord is the one who keeps me alive!
⁵ May my enemies' plans for evil be turned against them.
Do as you promised and put an end to them.

⁶ I will sacrifice a voluntary offering to you;
I will praise your name, O LORD,
for it is good.
⁷ For you will rescue me from my troubles
and help me to triumph over my enemies.

*O*n the run from King Saul, David certainly had to deal with some weasels. He was camping out with his men in the hill country of Ziph when some local residents went running to the king, saying, "We know where David is hiding. . . . we will catch him and hand him over to you" (1 Samuel 23:19-20).

Fortunately, David had some spies of his own, who informed him that Saul was on his way. Earlier, Jonathan, David's best friend and Saul's son, had hurried out to the hill country of Ziph to find David. "Don't be afraid," Jonathan reassured him. "My father will never find you!" (1 Samuel 23:17).

But King Saul nearly did find David, steadily closing in on David's forces until only one mountain separated the troops. And then came an urgent message for the king: "The Philistines are attacking Israel again!" So David was saved as the king's army hurried off to fight the Philistines.

This psalm expresses David's call for God to rescue him from Saul and his trust that God will do so.

When we are in a difficult situation, we, like David, can call out to God and know that he is our helper, the one who keeps us alive.

> Holy God, we praise your name,
> Lord of all, we bow before you;
> All on earth your scepter claim,
> All in heaven above adore you;
> Infinite your vast domain, everlasting is your
>   reign.

IGNACE FRANZ

Bible Networking

In verse 6 we see a reference to a "voluntary offering." Find other references to this in Leviticus 22:18, 21, where it is called a "freewill offering." What kind of an offering must it be?

Notable Quotable

"What faith is here [in verse 4]! Hardly had the prayer ascended than the soul is aware of the gracious answer. Note the present tense, 'God is my helper.'"
F. B. MEYER

PSALM 55:1-8

For the choir director: A psalm of David, to be accompanied by stringed instruments.

1. Listen to my prayer, O God.
   Do not ignore my cry for help!
2. Please listen and answer me,
   for I am overwhelmed by my troubles.
3. My enemies shout at me,
   making loud and wicked threats.
   They bring trouble on me,
   hunting me down in their anger.

4. My heart is in anguish.
   The terror of death overpowers me.
5. Fear and trembling overwhelm me.
   I can't stop shaking.
6. Oh, how I wish I had wings like a dove;
   then I would fly away and rest!
7. I would fly far away
   to the quiet of the wilderness.   *Interlude*
8. How quickly I would escape—
   far away from this wild storm of hatred.

Jerome was a busy man. It seems he was always teaching people the Bible, making some pilgrimage, or running some charitable operation, but he really just wanted to hole up somewhere and study the Bible.

It was the end of the fourth century, and Christianity was still finding its feet after enduring more than two centuries of persecution. Christians were in charge now, but they had a host of issues to tackle—both theological and practical. Jerome had opinions on every one. For a time he worked in Rome as right-hand man to Pope Damasus, where he began work on the project that made him famous: translating the Bible into Latin. But when the pope died, Jerome was disappointed that he wasn't selected to replace him. What's more, Jerome's enemies started criticizing him more freely. Where could he go to find some peace?

He ended up in Bethlehem, where he spent the last thirty-five years of his life writing. It seems he finally found the hideaway he always wanted. In Bethlehem, Jerome finished his Bible translation, the Vulgate, and produced many other commentaries and essays.

It should come as no surprise that Psalm 55 was one of his favorites, especially verses 6 and 7: "Oh, how I wish I had wings like a dove; then I would fly away and rest! I would fly far away to the quiet of the wilderness."

> Oh, were I a feathered dove,
> And innocence had wings.
> I'd fly and with the God I love,
> Leave all these restless things.
> ISAAC WATTS

A Word on Words

Anguish in verse 4 literally means "trembling with pain." In certain forms, the word is sometimes used to describe a woman's pain in childbirth.

Notable Quotable

"The net is not pitched for ravenous birds, as are the hawk and the kite, but for poor harmless birds that never meditate mischief."
JOHN RAWLINSON

PSALM 55:9-23

⁹ Destroy them, Lord, and confuse their speech,
    for I see violence and strife in the city.

¹⁰ Its walls are patrolled day and night against invaders,
    but the real danger is wickedness within the city.

¹¹ Murder and robbery are everywhere there;
    threats and cheating are rampant in the streets.

¹² It is not an enemy who taunts me—
    I could bear that.
It is not my foes who so arrogantly insult me—
    I could have hidden from them.

¹³ Instead, it is you—my equal,
    my companion and close friend.

¹⁴ What good fellowship we enjoyed
    as we walked together to the house of God.

¹⁵ Let death seize my enemies by surprise;
    let the grave swallow them alive,
    for evil makes its home within them.

¹⁶ But I will call on God,
    and the LORD will rescue me.

¹⁷ Morning, noon, and night
    I plead aloud in my distress,
    and the LORD hears my voice.

¹⁸ He rescues me and keeps me safe
    from the battle waged against me,
    even though many still oppose me.

¹⁹ God, who is king forever,
    will hear me and will humble them.   *Interlude*
For my enemies refuse to change their ways;
    they do not fear God.

²⁰ As for this friend of mine, he betrayed me;
    he broke his promises.

²¹ His words are as smooth as cream,
    but in his heart is war.
His words are as soothing as lotion,
    but underneath are daggers!

²² Give your burdens to the LORD,
    and he will take care of you.
He will not permit the godly to slip and fall.

²³ But you, O God, will send the wicked
    down to the pit of destruction.
Murderers and liars will die young,

Can you imagine the scene at the Last Supper when Jesus looked around the room and said, "One of you will betray me" (Mark 14:18)? They had to wonder how any of them could betray him.

Eventually Judas Iscariot slipped out quietly, but probably no one thought anything of it since he was the treasurer. Most of the others were probably shocked a few hours later when Judas showed up with a battalion of soldiers.

We assume that Jesus knew all along that Judas would turn on him, but does that lessen the pain of the situation? No doubt he felt deeply the words of Psalm 55, which bemoan the betrayal of a close, trusted friend.

If you have experienced betrayal by a close friend, you can still "give your burdens to the Lord, and he will take care of you" (verse 22).

> *Cast thy burden upon the Lord,*
> *Only lean upon his Word;*
> *Thou wilt soon have cause to bless*
> *His unchanging faithfulness.*
> ANONYMOUS

Notable Quotable
"*Cast your burden on him [verse 22] in the same way that the ship in a storm casts her burden upon the anchor, which holds on to its sure fixing place.*"
J. M. NEALE

PSALM 56:1-7

For the choir director: A psalm of David, regarding the time the Philistines seized him in Gath. To be sung to the tune "Dove on Distant Oaks."

¹ O God, have mercy on me.

　The enemy troops press in on me.

　My foes attack me all day long.

² My slanderers hound me constantly,

　and many are boldly attacking me.

³ But when I am afraid,

　I put my trust in you.

⁴ O God, I praise your word.

　I trust in God, so why should I be afraid?

　What can mere mortals do to me?

⁵ They are always twisting what I say;

　they spend their days plotting ways to harm me.

⁶ They come together to spy on me—

　watching my every step, eager to kill me.

⁷ Don't let them get away with their wickedness;

　in your anger, O God, throw them to the ground.

Things looked bleak for King Hezekiah and the people of Jerusalem. The northern kingdom of Israel had fallen to the Assyrians, and now the representative of the Assyrian king was standing outside the walls of Jerusalem, inviting Hezekiah to surrender. Clinging to his faith in God, Hezekiah refused.

"What are you trusting in that makes you so confident?" the Assyrian taunted. "Do you think that mere words can substitute for military skill and strength?" Then he wondered if Hezekiah was waiting for the Egyptians to save him. "If you lean on Egypt," he warned, "you will find it to be a stick that breaks beneath your weight and pierces your hand" (2 Kings 18:19-21). The representative then shouted to the people to surrender and threatened a siege if they refused. Finally he suggested that God wanted them to surrender.

But Hezekiah stayed firm in his faith. Instead of responding directly to the Assyrian threat, he prayed. God promised deliverance, and the next night 185,000 of the Assyrian troops died in their sleep. The surviving soldiers hurried home.

Hezekiah responded in this situation much like David did in his. Maybe he even consulted Psalm 56 for courage. What was Hezekiah leaning on? Not on a stick that would break but on a God who would guide. We can call for the same guidance in our troubles.

> When I'm afraid, I'll trust in thee;
> In God I'll praise his Word,
> I will not fear what flesh can do,
> My trust is in the Lord.
> OLD SCOTTISH PSALTER

Bible Networking
Verse 4 puts the power of David's enemies in perspective, as does Isaiah 31:3 and Hebrews 13:6. How can the psalmist say, "What can mere mortals do to me?"

Notable Quotable
"It is possible for fear and faith to occupy the mind at the same moment [verse 3]. To be reliant upon God when occasions for alarm are abundant—is the conquering faith of God's elect."
CHARLES HADDON SPURGEON

PSALM 56:8-13

8 You keep track of all my sorrows.

    You have collected all my tears in your bottle.

    You have recorded each one in your book.

9 On the very day I call to you for help,

    my enemies will retreat.

    This I know: God is on my side.

10 O God, I praise your word.

    Yes, Lord, I praise your word.

11 I trust in God, so why should I be afraid?

    What can mere mortals do to me?

12 I will fulfill my vows to you, O God,

    and offer a sacrifice of thanks for your help.

13 For you have rescued me from death;

    you have kept my feet from slipping.

So now I can walk in your presence, O God,

    in your life-giving light.

O n the run from King Saul, David fled to a place where his pursuers definitely would not look for him—the Philistine city of Gath. Saul had fought against the Philistines and was hated by them, but then again, so had David. You may remember the story about David killing Goliath. Do you also recall what town Goliath was from? You guessed it—Gath.

So David left his soldiers behind and walked alone into a city that hated him. He would have to be crazy to do that! Well, that was the idea. David pretended to be stark raving mad, scratching on doors and drooling. The Philistines watched him like a hawk, but his loony act probably convinced them he was pretty harmless. So for a while they gave him asylum, so to speak, and then he was released unharmed to find another place to hide from King Saul (1 Samuel 21:10–22:1).

Psalm 56 comes from David's Gath experience. You can sense the tension all around; he has to keep up the act. But he puts his trust in the Lord, and that gives him confidence. God knows what David's going through. Every tear is stored in God's bottle. With God watching over him, David mused, "What can mere mortals do to me?" (verse 11).

Ultimately, David's enemies retreated, and he was rescued from death. God had again been faithful, and David could walk freely in God's life-giving light.

> My wand'rings, all what they have been
> Thou know'st their number took;
> Into thy bottle put my tears;
> Are they not in thy book?
> OLD SCOTTISH PSALTER

Bible Networking
Light (verse 13) is often associated with guidance and is seen as giving life. See Job 33:30; John 8:12; and 12:35-36.

Notable Quotable
"It was precious ointment wherewith the woman in the Pharisee's house [probably Mary Magdalene] anointed the feet of Christ; but her tears wherewith she washed them, were worth more than her spikenard."
ABRAHAM WRIGHT

PSALM 57:1-5

For the choir director: A psalm of David, regarding the time he fled from Saul and went into the cave. To be sung to the tune "Do Not Destroy!"

¹ Have mercy on me, O God, have mercy!
  I look to you for protection.
I will hide beneath the shadow of your wings
  until this violent storm is past.

² I cry out to God Most High,
  to God who will fulfill his purpose for me.
³ He will send help from heaven to save me,
  rescuing me from those who are out to get me.

Interlude

My God will send forth his unfailing love and
  faithfulness.

⁴ I am surrounded by fierce lions
  who greedily devour human prey—
whose teeth pierce like spears and arrows,
  and whose tongues cut like swords.

⁵ Be exalted, O God, above the highest heavens!
  May your glory shine over all the earth.

*W*hen we last left our hero David, he was getting kicked out of Gath, which proved to be a short-lived but effective hiding place (see previous devotional). Now David had to find another refuge from the violent paranoia of King Saul. Eventually David came upon a cave in the foothills of Judah (1 Samuel 22:1).

Imagine him settling into that cave, all alone in the world, deciding to make it his home for a while. Psalm 57 expresses some of his feelings at the time. He would hide in God's mercy until the "violent storm" of Saul's wrath had passed. Somehow God would "send help from heaven"—but how?

Then people started to show up—old friends, soldiers, relatives. He had grown up not far from here, so he may have known some of the local people. And people continued to come—homeless people, debtors, those in trouble with the law. This wasn't the toast of society, by any means, but they flocked to David like sheep. Soon this lonely man had an army of four hundred. God had provided a security force.

From David's experience we can learn a few quick lessons: (1) Yes, God does "fulfill his purpose" (Psalm 57:2); (2) he often uses other people to do so; but (3) they aren't always the people we would choose to help us. Important things to remember when you find yourself hiding out in a cave.

> *My God! in whom are all the springs*
> *Of boundless love and grace known,*
> *Hide me beneath thy spreading wings,*
> *Till the dark cloud be over-blown.*
> ISAAC WATTS

Bible Networking
For more about finding shelter under the Lord's "wings" (verse 1), read Ruth 2:12, where Boaz is speaking to Ruth, and Matthew 23:37, where Jesus is speaking to Jerusalem.

Notable Quotable
"When we cannot see the sunshine of God's face, it is blessed to cower down beneath the shadow of his wings."
CHARLES HADDON SPURGEON

PSALM 57:6-11

⁶ My enemies have set a trap for me.
   I am weary from distress.
They have dug a deep pit in my path,
   but they themselves have fallen into it.   *Interlude*

⁷ My heart is confident in you, O God;
   no wonder I can sing your praises!
⁸ Wake up, my soul!
   Wake up, O harp and lyre!
   I will waken the dawn with my song.
⁹ I will thank you, Lord, in front of all the people.
   I will sing your praises among the nations.
¹⁰ For your unfailing love is as high as the heavens.
   Your faithfulness reaches to the clouds.

¹¹ Be exalted, O God, above the highest heavens.
   May your glory shine over all the earth.

*P*rime Minister Haman wanted everyone to bow as he passed. He demanded to be the center of attention. After all, he was the main man in Persia, second only to King Xerxes.

Mordecai refused to bow when Haman walked by, and this outraged the prime minister. When Haman learned that Mordecai was Jewish, he decided to take vengeance, not only on Mordecai, but on his whole race. He planned a massive extermination, and he built a special platform for Mordecai's execution. But Esther, Mordecai's cousin and adopted daughter, had become the queen that year, and she boldly approached King Xerxes and told him of the plot against her people. As a result, Haman was arrested and hanged on the same gallows he had built for Mordecai. You can read the whole story for yourself in the book of Esther.

People dig pits for God's people all the time (see verse 6), but often they themselves fall into them. They may plot and scheme against the righteous, but eventually their evil will roll back on them (see Proverbs 26:27). Sometimes we see that happen in this life, but if not, we can be certain that it will happen in the next. So we need not be concerned that we always get justice in this life. Instead, we can focus on overcoming evil with good, just as the Lord has commanded us (Romans 12:17-21).

> *My heart is fixed on thee, my God!*
> *I rest my hope on thee alone,*
> *I'll spread thy sacred truths abroad,*
> *To all mankind thy love made known.*
> WRANGHAM

Fascinating Fact
In his poem "L'Allegro," John Milton used the same imagery as verse 8 as he spoke of listening to something "cheerly rouse the slumbering morn."

Bible Networking
For more on waking the dawn with a song (verse 8), read Psalm 108:1-3.

Notable Quotable
"Evil is a stream which one day flows back to its source."
CHARLES HADDON SPURGEON

The New Testament writers quoted the Psalms more than any other Old Testament book—ninety-three times, by one scholar's count! Here are ten of the more interesting New Testament references to the Psalms.

◆ Jesus quoted Psalm 110:1 as he disputed with the Pharisees (Matthew 22:43-44).

◆ Jesus quoted Psalm 78:2 to explain his use of parables (Matthew 13:35).

◆ Jesus cited Psalm 118:22-23 regarding his rejection (Matthew 21:42).

◆ On the cross Jesus quoted Psalm 22:1 (Matthew 27:46).

◆ Jesus referred to the Psalms as prophetic (Luke 24:44).

◆ In his sermon at Pentecost, Peter quoted Psalm 16:8-11 (Acts 2:25-28; 34-35).

◆ Jesus' disciples recalled Psalm 69:9 as they witnessed him cleansing the Temple (John 2:17).

◆ Paul cited Psalm 4:4 in teaching about anger (Ephesians 4:26).

◆ The writer of Hebrews quotes Psalm 110:4 to show that Jesus is a priest in the order of Melchizedek (Hebrews 5:6).

◆ Paul encouraged believers to sing psalms (Ephesians 5:19).

Admit it! Some psalms disturb us. We feel a bit uncomfortable with them. Of course we love the Twenty-third Psalm, but some of the other psalms don't sound very, well, Christian. All this talk about knocking your enemy's teeth out—it's hard to mesh that with New Testament thinking.

Yet when Paul writes, "All Scripture is inspired by God and is useful to teach us what is true and to make us realize what is wrong in our lives" (2 Timothy 3:16), he was talking about all the Psalms. In fact, the New Testament writers loved to quote the Psalms on all sorts of subjects—and not just the "nice" parts.

For instance, Psalm 22 is a pretty grisly account of a man who feels forsaken by God as he is being tortured by his enemies. New Testament Christians saw this psalm as an amazingly prophetic portrait of Jesus' suffering. Psalm 69 is another text that bewails the sufferings of the righteous and calls for revenge. But John finds in it a picture of Jesus' passion for God's house as he drove out the money changers.

Sometimes the New Testament also uses the Psalms for inspiration and teaching doctrine. But many psalms deal with emotions, so they are often used in the New Testament to undergird, illustrate, or guide emotional responses. Psalm 4, for example, runs a gamut of feelings from desperation to anger to gratitude to peace. No wonder, then, that Paul found this psalm appropriate for encouraging believers to avoid "letting anger gain control over you" (Ephesians 4:26).

The Psalms are inspired by God, so they can teach us. And because they express emotions that flow out of the psalmists' relationship with God, they can help us in our emotions as well. The Psalms teach us to bring all our concerns to the Lord, whether our emotions are the "right" ones or not. God wants a dialogue with us, not a monologue.

And the New Testament affirms this as well, urging believers to "sing psalms and hymns and spiritual songs to God with thankful hearts" (Colossians 3:16).

∾

O Thou, by whom we come to God,
The Life, the Truth, the Way,
The path of prayer Thyself hast trod;
Lord, teach us how to pray.
JAMES MONTGOMERY

Selah

PSALM 58

For the choir director: A psalm of David, to be sung to the tune "Do Not Destroy!"

¹ Justice—do you rulers know the meaning of the word?
    Do you judge the people fairly?
² No, all your dealings are crooked;
    you hand out violence instead of justice.
³ These wicked people are born sinners;
    even from birth they have lied and gone their own
        way.
⁴ They spit poison like deadly snakes;
    they are like cobras that refuse to listen,
⁵ ignoring the tunes of the snake charmers,
    no matter how skillfully they play.

⁶ Break off their fangs, O God!
    Smash the jaws of these lions, O LORD!
⁷ May they disappear like water into thirsty ground.
    Make their weapons useless in their hands.
⁸ May they be like snails that dissolve into slime,
    like a stillborn child who will never see the sun.
⁹ God will sweep them away, both young and old,
    faster than a pot heats on an open flame.

¹⁰ The godly will rejoice when they see injustice avenged.
    They will wash their feet in the blood of the wicked.
¹¹ Then at last everyone will say,
    "There truly is a reward for those who live for God;
    surely there is a God who judges justly here on
        earth."

*T*he prophet Jeremiah knew all about corruption in high places. His messages angered the leaders of Jerusalem, so four government officials complained to the king, who told them, "Do as you like. I will do nothing to stop you" (Jeremiah 38:5). So they lowered Jeremiah by ropes into a cistern. There was no water in it, and he sank down into the mud at the bottom.

We don't know whether Jeremiah was meditating on Psalm 58 at the time, but it certainly would have been appropriate. This psalm denounces the injustice of the very people who are supposed to rule with justice. David calls for them to "disappear like water into thirsty ground!" (verse 7). No doubt Jeremiah was afraid he would disappear into the thirsty ground, too.

There's an interesting pun in the Hebrew of Psalm 58:1. The word translated "rulers" can also be read as "silent ones." Perhaps that was the problem—the rulers remained silent as injustice swept over the nation. That was why Jeremiah was suffering. The king had turned a blind eye to the actions of the four officials.

Fortunately for the prophet, one government official would not stay silent. Ebed-melech, an Ethiopian, ran to the king and told him that he had to get Jeremiah out of there or else he would die. When this one man spoke up for justice, Jeremiah was saved. We, too, need to stand up for what's right whenever we see injustice occurring in our society.

> Satan tells us we're weak; our hope is in vain.
> The good that we seek we'll never obtain.
> But he can't take from us (though often he's tried)
> The heart-cheering promise—The Lord will provide.
> JOHN NEWTON

Bible Networking
After rereading verses 10-11, see how the New Testament speaks of the day of reckoning in Revelation 14:19 and 19:11.

Notable Quotable
"The principles of the wicked are even worse than their practices; premeditated violence is doubly guilty."
GEORGE ROGERS

PSALM 59:1-10

For the choir director: A psalm of David, regarding the time Saul sent soldiers to watch David's house in order to kill him. To be sung to the tune "Do Not Destroy!"

¹ Rescue me from my enemies, O God.
   Protect me from those who have come to destroy me.
² Rescue me from these criminals;
   save me from these murderers.

³ They have set an ambush for me.
   Fierce enemies are out there waiting,
   though I have done them no wrong, O LORD.
⁴ Despite my innocence, they prepare to kill me.
   Rise up and help me! Look on my plight!
⁵ O LORD God Almighty, the God of Israel,
   rise up to punish hostile nations.
   Show no mercy to wicked traitors.   *Interlude*

⁶ They come at night,
   snarling like vicious dogs
   as they prowl the streets.
⁷ Listen to the filth that comes from their mouths,
   the piercing swords that fly from their lips.
   "Who can hurt us?" they sneer.

⁸ But LORD, you laugh at them.
   You scoff at all the hostile nations.
⁹ You are my strength; I wait for you to rescue me,
   for you, O God, are my place of safety.
¹⁰ In his unfailing love, my God will come and help me.
   He will let me look down in triumph on all my
      enemies.

*H*e was just doing his job, playing his harp for King Saul, when— *thwack!*— a spear went flying past and stuck in the wall behind him! That's when David knew he needed to get out of there! It wasn't just a wrong note Saul was upset about; the king was jealous of David's military success and was determined to kill him.

That night Saul sent troops to watch David's house and ambush him on his way out the next morning. Fortunately, David's wife was Michal, the king's daughter. She warned David of Saul's plans. Psalm 59 is based on this experience. Although David probably didn't put pen to paper right then, he surely remembered his feelings about being betrayed by the king he had loyally served and hunted down by soldiers he had fought beside (1 Samuel 19:8-17).

But the story gets better. David climbed out a window and escaped, and Michal bought him some time the next morning by explaining to the soldiers outside that David was sick in bed. She had even placed a statue in bed under the covers and put a wig on it.

Looking back on this and many other situations, David could say with confidence that God was his place of safety and that he would come and help him (verses 9-10). Praise God that we, too, can trust in him to help us.

> Do thou deliver me from them
> That work iniquity;
> And give me safety from the men
> Of bloody cruelty.
> PRESBYTERIAN CHURCH OF ENGLAND PSALTER

Bible Networking
In Mark 4:38 the disciples' cries to the sleeping Jesus sound a lot like Psalm 59:4. It sometimes seems as if God is asleep to our concerns—but he neither slumbers nor sleeps (Psalm 121:4).

Notable Quotable
"David ridicules the vain boasting of his enemies, who thought no undertaking too great to be accomplished by their numbers."
JOHN CALVIN

PSALM 59:11-17

¹¹ Don't kill them, for my people soon forget such
lessons;
stagger them with your power, and bring them to
their knees,
O Lord our shield.

¹² Because of the sinful things they say,
because of the evil that is on their lips,
let them be captured by their pride,
their curses, and their lies.

¹³ Destroy them in your anger!
Wipe them out completely!
Then the whole world will know
that God reigns in Israel.   *Interlude*

¹⁴ My enemies come out at night,
snarling like vicious dogs
as they prowl the streets.

¹⁵ They scavenge for food
but go to sleep unsatisfied.

¹⁶ But as for me, I will sing about your power.
I will shout with joy each morning because of your
unfailing love.
For you have been my refuge,
a place of safety in the day of distress.

¹⁷ O my Strength, to you I sing praises,
for you, O God, are my refuge,
the God who shows me unfailing love.

*I*n the original Hebrew poetry of Psalm 59, verse 17 starts the same as verse 9, except for a couple of letters. The word for "wait" and the word for "sing" differ by only one letter in their spelling. So verse 9 says: "My strength, I wait for you," and verse 17 says: "My strength, I sing to you." Maybe there's not all that much difference.

When you think of David cooped up in his house, soldiers camped on the doorstep, you don't expect him to burst into song. But why not? He decides to wait for God to display his strength in the situation. And what else are you going to do while you wait? If you're convinced that God will help you, it makes perfect sense to sing!

Paul and Silas were arrested in a strange city for freeing a girl from a demon (Acts 16). Tossed into a dungeon, they sang hymns as they confidently trusted that God was watching over them. Then God sent an earthquake to free them, which led to the conversion of the jailer himself!

What sort of prison do you find yourself in? Are you convinced that God is watching over you and has the power to free you? Then wait for him to act—and as you wait, sing his praises!

> The long, long night is past, the morning breaks
>   at last,
> And hushed the dreadful wail and fury of the blast,
> As o'er the golden hills the day advances fast!
> The Comforter has come!
> FRANK BOTTOME

Notable Quotable
"The greater our present trials, the louder will our future songs be, and the more intense our joyful gratitude."
CHARLES HADDON SPURGEON

PSALM 60

For the choir director: A psalm of David useful for teaching, regarding the time David fought Aram-naharaim and Aram-zobah, and Joab returned and killed twelve thousand Edomites in the Valley of Salt. To be sung to the tune "Lily of the Testimony."

¹ You have rejected us, O God, and broken our defenses.
> You have been angry with us; now restore us to your
>> favor.
² You have shaken our land and split it open.
> Seal the cracks before it completely collapses.
³ You have been very hard on us,
> making us drink wine that sent us reeling.
⁴ But you have raised a banner for those who honor you—
> a rallying point in the face of attack.   *Interlude*

⁵ Use your strong right arm to save us,
> and rescue your beloved people.
⁶ God has promised this by his holiness:
> "I will divide up Shechem with joy.
> I will measure out the valley of Succoth.
⁷ Gilead is mine,
> and Manasseh is mine.
Ephraim will produce my warriors,
> and Judah will produce my kings.
⁸ Moab will become my lowly servant,
> and Edom will be my slave.
> I will shout in triumph over the Philistines."

⁹ But who will bring me into the fortified city?
> Who will bring me victory over Edom?
¹⁰ Have you rejected us, O God?
> Will you no longer march with our armies?
¹¹ Oh, please help us against our enemies,
> for all human help is useless.
¹² With God's help we will do mighty things,
> for he will trample down our foes.

*W*hen David finally came to power, he had a lot of work to do. On all sides enemies chipped away at Israelite territory. In the west Saul had tried to fight the Philistines, but he was badly distracted by his obsession with David. In fact, Saul died in a losing battle against those Philistines. Meanwhile, the land of Israel was threatened by the Moabites, the Arameans, and the Edomites. Assuming the throne, David quickly mobilized his forces against the nation's enemies, waging successful campaigns on all sides.

Was David a master military strategist? Maybe. But he had another secret, as he expresses in Psalm 60. When Israel acts in a way that pleases God, things go well; but when the nation turns away from God, things fall apart. This psalm serves as a national confession. It doesn't name Saul, but it seems to refer to the struggles the nation had during his reign, when he was straying from God's desires. Now, however, the army was victorious. Apparently God was smiling on them once again.

Be careful about this. Good fortune doesn't always mean that you're living well, nor does bad fortune automatically mean you're sinning. Other Scriptures, such as the book of Job and even other psalms, confirm this. But we can be certain that sin ultimately takes a toll on us and that right living will bring blessings, even if we don't experience those blessings until eternity.

> Give us now relief from pain
> Human aid is all in vain;
> We, through God, shall yet prevail,
> HATFIELD

Bible Networking

If you are looking for help (verse 11), see Psalms 108:12; 124:1-3; 140:1-3.

Notable Quotable

"So long as sight and reason find footing in matters, there is no place for faith and hope; the abundance of human help puts not grace to proof, but the strength of faith is in the absence of them all."
WILLIAM STRUTHER

PSALM 61

For the choir director: A psalm of David, to be accompanied by stringed instruments.

¹ O God, listen to my cry!
   Hear my prayer!
² From the ends of the earth,
   I will cry to you for help,
   for my heart is overwhelmed.
   Lead me to the towering rock of safety,
³   for you are my safe refuge,
   a fortress where my enemies cannot reach me.
⁴ Let me live forever in your sanctuary,
   safe beneath the shelter of your wings!   *Interlude*
⁵ For you have heard my vows, O God.
   You have given me an inheritance reserved for those
      who fear your name.

⁶ Add many years to the life of the king!
   May his years span the generations!
⁷ May he reign under God's protection forever.
   Appoint your unfailing love and faithfulness to
      watch over him.

⁸ Then I will always sing praises to your name
   as I fulfill my vows day after day.

For more than twenty years William O. Cushing pastored small churches in New York. It wasn't easy, and it certainly wasn't prosperous, but he and his wife loved it, and their congregations loved them. Then suddenly his wife died, and Cushing went into depression. Soon a creeping paralysis of his vocal cords came upon him, and he could no longer preach. At the age of forty-seven, he felt all alone in a wilderness.

What could he do?

Then he remembered how a few years earlier he had written a hymn for his Sunday school children, "When He Cometh." God had used that little song in great ways. Maybe God could use other things he wrote.

About this time he received a letter from Ira Sankey, who was the song leader for famous preacher Dwight L. Moody. Sankey asked Cushing to supply a new hymn for Moody. Cushing prayed, and then the words of "Hiding in Thee" seemed to come to him. Cushing later said, "It was the outgrowth of many tears, many heart conflicts and yearnings of which the world could know nothing." Over the next thirty years, Cushing wrote more than three hundred gospel hymns.

Like David, William Cushing had learned the blessing of hiding in God's towering rock of safety (verse 2). God offers this same rock of safety to us as well.

How oft in the conflict, when pressed by the foe,
I have fled to my Refuge and breathed out my woe;
How often when trials like sea billows roll,
Have I hidden in Thee, O Thou Rock of my soul.
Hiding in Thee, hiding in Thee,
Thou blest Rock of Ages, I'm hiding in Thee.
WILLIAM O. CUSHING

Notable Quotable
"The rock that is higher than he [verse 2, KJV] must be higher than any man; for David was a mighty monarch. It must therefore be divine."
FOUNTAIN ELWIN

PSALM 62:1-7
For Jeduthun, the choir director: A psalm of David.

¹ I wait quietly before God,
    for my salvation comes from him.
² He alone is my rock and my salvation,
    my fortress where I will never be shaken.

³ So many enemies against one man—
    all of them trying to kill me.
To them I'm just a broken-down wall
    or a tottering fence.
⁴ They plan to topple me from my high position.
    They delight in telling lies about me.
They are friendly to my face,
    but they curse me in their hearts.   *Interlude*

⁵ I wait quietly before God,
    for my hope is in him.
⁶ He alone is my rock and my salvation,
    my fortress where I will not be shaken.
⁷ My salvation and my honor come from God alone.
    He is my refuge, a rock where no enemy can reach
        me.

salm 62 credits David as its writer and Jeduthun as its director. Jeduthun has his name attached to two other psalms, and apparently he was one of the leading musicians in David's court. He had six sons who followed in his profession (1 Chronicles 25:3).

Now imagine you're one of Jeduthun's sons, and you're conducting the Temple singers for the first time. Maybe you've even been given this psalm to direct. How nervous would you be with your father looking on and the whole crowd waiting to hear your choir? Would you be worrying about other trainees vying for your position, perhaps even your own brothers? Would they be sniping at you, picking apart every mistake?

Certainly David felt this way as he advanced to the throne, but you may feel the same way in whatever you do. Are there people trying to topple you? Do they flatter you to your face and then rip your back to shreds? How can you handle that? "Wait quietly before God." He is your refuge, and you should look to him for your salvation and honor (verse 7).

> Little flock, to joy then yield thee!
> Jacob's God will ever shield thee;
> Rest secure with this Defender,
> At His will all foes surrender.
> CAROLINA SANDELL BERG

Bible Networking
God is often compared to a rock (verse 6). See also Deuteronomy 32:18; 32:31; Isaiah 44:8; and Habakkuk 1:12.

Notable Quotable
"Let him that walks in ingloriousness and contempt of the world contemplate God, as God is glory [see verse 7]."
ABRAHAM WRIGHT

PSALM 62:8-12

8 O my people, trust in him at all times.
   Pour out your heart to him,
      for God is our refuge.   *Interlude*

9 From the greatest to the lowliest—
   all are nothing in his sight.
   If you weigh them on the scales,
      they are lighter than a puff of air.
10 Don't try to get rich
      by extortion or robbery.
   And if your wealth increases,
      don't make it the center of your life.

11 God has spoken plainly,
      and I have heard it many times:
   Power, O God, belongs to you;
12   unfailing love, O Lord, is yours.
   Surely you judge all people
      according to what they have done.

*A*s you flip through the book of Ecclesiastes, you can almost hear the sighs of the author, who calls himself "the Teacher." The Teacher had it all: money, success, wisdom, fame. But he still was not truly satisfied. All of those pursuits proved meaningless and empty in themselves, "like chasing the wind."

The phrase translated "meaningless" or "vanity" carries a root meaning of "breath" in the original Hebrew. All your earthly endeavors, he says, are just "hot air."

We see this same word here in Psalm 62:9 with the same basic theme. People put a lot of stock in who's rich and who's poor, who's famous and who's ordinary. But from God's perspective, these people are about as weighty as a breath, a "puff of air." All their wealth, fame, and power does not add one ounce to their weight in the eternal scheme of things. God is looking for us to trust him instead (verse 8) and to live our life in a way that pleases him (verse 12).

So don't invest in hot air; instead, "trust in him at all times" and reap an eternal reward of immeasurable weight.

> Simply trusting ev'ry day,
> Trusting through a stormy way;
> Even when my faith is small,
> Trusting Jesus—that is all.
> EDGAR PAGE STITES

Notable Quotable
"A feather has some weight on the scale [verse 9], vanity has none, and creative confidence has less than that. Yet such is the universal fascination that mankind prefer an arm of flesh to the power of the invisible but almighty Creator."
CHARLES HADDON SPURGEON

Thought to Ponder
When the psalmist says in verse 9 that all people, whether considered great or lowly, amount to only a "puff of air," what does he mean?

PSALM 63:1-5
A psalm of David, regarding a time when David was in the wilderness of Judah.

¹ O God, you are my God;
  I earnestly search for you.
My soul thirsts for you;
  my whole body longs for you
in this parched and weary land
  where there is no water.

² I have seen you in your sanctuary
  and gazed upon your power and glory.
³ Your unfailing love is better to me than life itself;
  how I praise you!
⁴ I will honor you as long as I live,
  lifting up my hands to you in prayer.
⁵ You satisfy me more than the richest of foods.
  I will praise you with songs of joy.

*P*salm 63 was written "regarding a time when David was in the wilderness of Judah." The Bible mentions his being there twice—first running from his predecessor, Saul, and later running from his son, the rebellious Absalom. But the first time he wasn't king yet, as verse 11 suggests (see tomorrow's reading), so this must have been written regarding his escape from Absalom.

In these verses we learn about a trait of David's that his son lacked. Absalom was an angry young man—first wreaking vengeance on his half-brother Amnon, then nursing a grudge against his father. He wanted more than he got, and that irked him. But in this psalm we see that David found satisfaction in God, whose love was "better to [him] than life itself." Even in the desert, temporarily toppled from his throne, David could sing praises.

Another interesting insight about this psalm regards David's comment that his soul thirsts for God. The Judean desert is oppressively dry and difficult terrain, with many canyons, crags, and caves. You can find shade from the sun, but in the dry season you can't find water. The arid air sucks up your perspiration, and your whole body gets thirsty. Perhaps this is the kind of thirst David was speaking about in verse 1.

Which do you resemble most—the father or the son? And does your soul thirst for God as David described?

Better than life itself thy love,
Dearer than all beside to me;
For whom have I in heaven
Or what on earth, compared with thee?
JAMES MONTGOMERY

PSALM 63:6-11

⁶ I lie awake thinking of you,
    meditating on you through the night.
⁷ I think how much you have helped me;
    I sing for joy in the shadow of your protecting wings.
⁸ I follow close behind you;
    your strong right hand holds me securely.

⁹ But those plotting to destroy me will come to ruin.
    They will go down into the depths of the earth.
¹⁰ They will die by the sword
    and become the food of jackals.

¹¹ But the king will rejoice in God.
    All who trust in him will praise him,
    while liars will be silenced.

*I*n many respects Theodore Beza was John Calvin's right-hand man. In the sixteenth century, while Martin Luther was reforming northern Europe, Calvin was changing the face of Switzerland and France. And Beza was right beside Calvin, defending his new teachings about faith, righteousness, and the sovereignty of God. Beza was a noted scholar in his own right, and he translated many psalms into French and Latin verse, allowing these new Reformed churches to "sing a new song" to the Lord.

But Theodore Beza had a problem. Often, after a hard day of teaching or translating, he just couldn't get to sleep. His cure? Psalm 63:6. As he lay awake, he would meditate on the Lord, often reviewing the Psalms in his mind. Sometimes these thoughts carried him into a restful sleep. But even when they didn't, at least he had used the time beneficially.

As you hit the pillow, don't waste time fretting about your enemies or the various struggles in your life. Meditate on the Lord through the night, and let him give your soul the rest it needs.

> *Jesus, give the weary*
> *Calm and sweet repose;*
> *With Thy tend'rest blessing*
> *May mine eyelids close.*
> GEORGE MATHESON

PSALM 64

For the choir director: A psalm of David.

1 O God, listen to my complaint.
  Do not let my enemies' threats overwhelm me.
2 Protect me from the plots of the wicked,
  from the scheming of those who do evil.
3 Sharp tongues are the swords they wield;
  bitter words are the arrows they aim.
4 They shoot from ambush at the innocent,
  attacking suddenly and fearlessly.
5 They encourage each other to do evil
  and plan how to set their traps.
  "Who will ever notice?" they ask.
6 As they plot their crimes, they say,
  "We have devised the perfect plan!"
  Yes, the human heart and mind are cunning.

7 But God himself will shoot them down.
  Suddenly, his arrows will pierce them.
8 Their own words will be turned against them,
    destroying them.
  All who see it happening will shake their heads in
    scorn.
9 Then everyone will stand in awe,
  proclaiming the mighty acts of God,
  realizing all the amazing things he does.

10 The godly will rejoice in the LORD
  and find shelter in him.
  And those who do what is right
  will praise him.

*T*here was a secret plot against the life of Paul. Forty Jews had vowed not to eat or drink until they had killed Paul. They asked the leading priests and other leaders to tell the Romans, who had Paul in custody, to bring him back to the council again for further investigation of his case. These forty men would be waiting in ambush along the road.

Somehow Paul's nephew heard of the plot and told Paul, who sent him to the Roman commander. Because Paul was a Roman citizen, the commander wanted to make sure he got a fair Roman trial, so he sent Paul under armed guard to the Roman governor in Caesarea and avoided the ambush entirely (Acts 23:12-24). Apparently there were forty very hungry people left sitting at a roadside somewhere.

In Psalm 64 David calls for God to protect him from "the plots of the wicked," and he is confident that "the godly will rejoice in the Lord and find shelter in him." This can be seen from Paul's experiences, because the plotters' schemes resulted in Paul's being able to talk about Jesus before two Roman governors and a Jewish king. Later he was sent to Rome in chains, but there he spread the gospel even more. God is able to take what others intend for evil and use it for good (see Genesis 50:20).

> When your enemies assail and your heart begins
>   to fail,
> Don't forget that God in heaven answers prayer;
> He will make a way for you and will lead you safely
>   through—
> Take your burden to the Lord and leave it there.
> CHARLES A. TINDLEY

Bible Networking
For a few tips on avoiding traps and snares (verse 5), see Psalm 91:2-3 and Proverbs 1:17-19.

Notable Quotable
"The deepest and most closely guarded secrets of those opposed to [God's] way are to be fully and utterly exposed. God knows and in time everybody will."
JOHN I. DURHAM

May 16

PSALM 65:1-5
For the choir director: A psalm of David. A song.

¹ What mighty praise, O God,
    belongs to you in Zion.
We will fulfill our vows to you,
²   for you answer our prayers,
    and to you all people will come.
³ Though our hearts are filled with sins,
    you forgive them all.
⁴ What joy for those you choose to bring near,
    those who live in your holy courts.
What joys await us
    inside your holy Temple.

⁵ You faithfully answer our prayers with awesome deeds,
    O God our savior.
You are the hope of everyone on earth,
    even those who sail on distant seas.

*T*he young man finally had a dinner date with Michelle, the young woman he had adored from afar. Afterward, his mother asked him about it.

"Where did you go?"

"I don't know," the boy replied.

"What did you eat?"

"I don't remember."

"What was the restaurant like?"

"I didn't notice."

The mother threw up her hands. "Can you tell me anything about your date?"

"Yes," the smitten boy answered. "Michelle was there."

In a way, going to church should be like that for us. Ultimately our concern should not be how well the choir sang, what hymns were selected, or how good the sermon was. If God is there, that is what is most important. Psalm 65 exclaims: "What joys await us inside your holy Temple!" If that were a question, what would be your answer? The presence of God. Prayer, Bible study, worship—all these things should be motivated by our desire to meet with the Lord.

> Saints below, with heart and voice,
> Still in songs of praise rejoice;
> Learning here, by faith and love,
> Songs of praise to sing above.
> NEEDHAM

A Word on Words

The Hebrew word for "forgive" in verse 3 is kaphar, meaning literally "to cover." Think of it as God's Wite-Out.

Notable Quotable

"The more needy we are, the greater cause there is for going to God."
F. B. MEYER

PSALM 65:6-13

⁶ You formed the mountains by your power
    and armed yourself with mighty strength.
⁷ You quieted the raging oceans
    with their pounding waves
    and silenced the shouting of the nations.
⁸ Those who live at the ends of the earth
    stand in awe of your wonders.
From where the sun rises to where it sets,
    you inspire shouts of joy.

⁹ You take care of the earth and water it,
    making it rich and fertile.
The rivers of God will not run dry;
    they provide a bountiful harvest of grain,
    for you have ordered it so.
¹⁰ You drench the plowed ground with rain,
    melting the clods and leveling the ridges.
You soften the earth with showers
    and bless its abundant crops.
¹¹ You crown the year with a bountiful harvest;
    even the hard pathways overflow with abundance.
¹² The wilderness becomes a lush pasture,
    and the hillsides blossom with joy.
¹³ The meadows are clothed with flocks of sheep,
    and the valleys are carpeted with grain.
    They all shout and sing for joy!

*W*e plow the fields and scatter the good seed on the land,
But it is fed and watered by God's almighty hand.
He sends the snow in winter, the warmth to swell the grain,
The seedtime and the harvest, and soft, refreshing rain.

These old hymn lyrics were being sung by teenagers in motley attire as the first act of *Godspell* drew to a close. This musical, written in the 1960s, tells the story of Jesus in comedy, drama, and song.

The musical continues:

All good gifts around us are sent from heaven above
Then thank the Lord, oh, thank the Lord for all his love.

Then the soloist hits the heights with a beautiful riff: "I really want to thank you, Lord." It's a great moment of simple, joyful expression.

The cast of this particular production included Christians and non-Christians alike. Although much of the script is taken right from the Gospels, and many of the lyrics come straight from old hymns, the musical appeals to people of all religious persuasions (and those with none at all). Part of the musical's universal appeal is no doubt due to the different episodes of joyful expression found throughout the script.

Psalm 65 shows us something similar. It's far more than a weather report; it erupts with delight. God has given us a wonderful world, and we must "shout and sing for joy"!

The joy of the Lord is the strength for life's trials,
And lifts the crushed heart above sorrow and care.
Like the nightingale's notes, it can sing in the darkness,
And rejoice when the fig tree is fruitless and bare.
A. B. SIMPSON

Notable Quotable

"It would be hard to surpass this evocative description of the fertile earth, culminating in the fantasy of hills and fields making merry together."
DEREK KIDNER

Generally when we speak of God, we use one of two names: God or the Lord. For the most part, these two names are interchangeable in our mind.

The Israelites, on the other hand, had several different names or titles for God, each emphasizing some aspect of his character. Here are a few of these names found in the Psalms:

◆ *Yahweh:* More than seven hundred times in Psalms God is referred to as *Yah* or *Yahweh*. This name speaks of his character and his covenant relationship with his people. It is usually translated as LORD in capital letters.

  Example: "The LORD *(Yahweh)* is my shepherd; I have everything I need." (Psalm 23:1)

◆ *El* or *Elohim:* More than four hundred times in the Psalms God is referred to by a name starting with *El*. This name reveals the power and majesty of God and is simply translated "God."

  Example: "You alone are the Most High *(Elyon)*, supreme over all the earth." (Psalm 83:18)

◆ *Adonai:* More than sixty times in the Psalms God is called *Adon* or *Adonai*. This name speaks of God as our Master. It is usually translated as "Lord" in lowercase letters. It is often used in the context of personal communication between the believer and God, and it expresses faith and thanksgiving as well as submission.

Example: "As for me, I am poor and needy, but the Lord *(Adonai)* is thinking about me right now." (Psalm 40:17)

Often the psalm writers used the names of God in various combinations:

"The mighty God, the LORD *(El Elohim Yahweh)*, has spoken;
he had summoned all humanity from east to west." (Psalm 50:1)

"I look to you for help, O Sovereign LORD *(Yahweh Adonai)*.
You are my refuge; don't let them kill me." (Psalm 141:8)

"I come to you for protection, O LORD my God *(Yahweh Elyon)*.
Save me from my persecutors—rescue me!" (Psalm 7:1)

"Don't let those who trust in you stumble because of me,

O Sovereign LORD Almighty
(*Adonai Yahweh Sabaoth*)."
(Psalm 69:6)

"I cry out to God Most High *(Elohim Elyon)*,
to God who will fulfill his purpose for me." (Psalm 57:2)

"O LORD God Almighty *(Yahweh Elohim Sabaoth)*, the God of Israel,
rise up to punish hostile nations." (Psalm 59:5)

What's in a name? It depends. If your name is DiMaggio, you will probably be expected to excel in baseball. If your name is Rockefeller, people will probably ask you for money.

Apparently the psalmists put a lot of stock in names as well—especially regarding God—because they spoke of praising the name of the Lord or trusting his name over one hundred times in the Psalms. But what does all this business about God's name mean? Why is his name so important?

We use the word *God* to refer to the one and only Deity we worship. But we use the same word for the mythological powers of Rome or Greece, only we don't capitalize it.

The Israelites had a similar situation in Old Testament times. They were surrounded by Canaanite tribes who referred to *El* as the supreme deity, under whom was Baal, a fertility god who also was lord of wind and storm. But the *El* that the Canaanites worshiped was certainly not the *El* that the Israel-ites worshiped, for Scripture records that the Canaanites sometimes sacrificed their own children to their gods (Jeremiah 19:4-6). So the Isra-elites differentiated the name of their God from the name of the Canaanite god. They called upon God as *El Elyon* (the Most High God) or *Elohim* (the God possessing intense power and great glory) or *El Shaddai* (the all-sufficient God).

While *El* and *Elohim* speak of God's power, the name *Yahweh* (the LORD) speaks of God's character. It is the name for God that is used most in the Psalms. When the psalmists referred to *Yahweh*, they were speaking of a God who loved his people and kept his promises to them. He was the God who would be their Shepherd.

But eventually the name *Yahweh* became so sacred among the Israel-ites that they hesitated to say it out loud; instead they came to speak of God as *Adonai*, their approachable Master, to whom they could come with their burdens and problems.

As Christians today, we serve the same God that the Israelites wor-shiped. And he still embodies all the characteristics that his many names describe. Let us rejoice that we can call upon the LORD, the Most High God, the sovereign Crea-tor who cares for our smallest concerns.

❧

*With sacred awe pronounce his name,
Whom words nor thoughts can reach;
A broken heart shall please him more
Than the best forms of speech.*
NEEDHAM

PSALM 66:1-7
For the choir director: A psalm. A song.

¹ Shout joyful praises to God, all the earth!
²   Sing about the glory of his name!
   Tell the world how glorious he is.
³ Say to God, "How awesome are your deeds!
   Your enemies cringe before your mighty power.
⁴ Everything on earth will worship you;
   they will sing your praises,
   shouting your name in glorious songs."   *Interlude*

⁵ Come and see what our God has done,
   what awesome miracles he does for his people!
⁶ He made a dry path through the Red Sea,
   and his people went across on foot.
   Come, let us rejoice in who he is.
⁷ For by his great power he rules forever.
   He watches every movement of the nations;
   let no rebel rise in defiance.   *Interlude*

*M*y parents bought me a new bike last week," said ten-year-old Brittany. "It's really cool. And last month they got me three new outfits for school. And next month they're going to get me my own computer."

"Wow," says Kristi, "you must really love your parents for all that."

"Yeah, I guess," Brittany answers. "What have you gotten from your parents?"

Kristi had to think a moment. "Well, they don't have much money, but . . . well, my dad, he's so funny. Every night at the dinner table he tells a joke. Sometimes they're pretty dumb, but even then he's funny about it. And every night before I go to bed, my mom gives me a big hug."

"Wow," says Brittany. "I wish I had your parents."

It's good to thank God for the many things he gives us, but sometimes he just wants us to "rejoice in who he is" (verse 6).

> *Jesus, our only joy be Thou,*
> *As Thou our prize wilt be;*
> *Jesus, be Thou our glory now,*
> *And through eternity.*
> BERNARD OF CLAIRVAUX

Bible Networking
"Come and see," invites the psalmist (verse 5). Look for similar invitations in John 1:35-39, 45-46. Seeing is the first step toward believing. As for God watching everyone (verse 7), see Proverbs 15:3; Exodus 14:24; and Job 31:4.

PSALM 66:8-15

⁸ Let the whole world bless our God
    and sing aloud his praises.
⁹ Our lives are in his hands,
    and he keeps our feet from stumbling.
¹⁰ You have tested us, O God;
    you have purified us like silver melted in a crucible.
¹¹ You captured us in your net
    and laid the burden of slavery on our backs.
¹² You sent troops to ride across our broken bodies.
    We went through fire and flood.
    But you brought us to a place of great abundance.

¹³ Now I come to your Temple with burnt offerings
    to fulfill the vows I made to you—
¹⁴ yes, the sacred vows you heard me make
    when I was in deep trouble.
¹⁵ That is why I am sacrificing burnt offerings to you—
    the best of my rams as a pleasing aroma.
    And I will sacrifice bulls and goats.   *Interlude*

A man is drowning. "Lord, save me," he prays. "If you get me out of this, I'll give you half of everything I own."

But still the sea churns, and he struggles.

"Sixty percent, Lord, if you save me . . . 70. . . . All right, 80 percent. It's yours."

Suddenly the sea calms down, and the man regains his balance and swims safely to shore. As he walks onto the beach, he says, "Now, Lord, about that 10 percent I promised you . . ."

We do it all the time, bargaining with God and then changing the terms. Psalm 66 shows us a person who was in trouble and made vows to God. That may seem like bribery, but God knows that we tend to turn to him in hard times. The question is, what do we do when the danger passes? The psalmist makes good on the vow.

Do you?

> Here, in thy courts, I leave my vow,
> And thy rich grace record;
> Witness, ye saints, who hear me now,
> If I forsake the Lord.
> ISAAC WATTS

*Bible
Networking*
For more on offerings
that please God, see
1 Samuel 15:22 and
Romans 12:1-2.

*Notable
Quotable*
"It is not known what corn will yield, till it comes to the flail; nor what grapes, till they come to the press. Grace is hid in nature, as sweet water in rose-leaves. The fire of affliction fetcheth it out."
F. B. MEYER

PSALM 66:16-20

[16] Come and listen, all you who fear God,
and I will tell you what he did for me.

[17] For I cried out to him for help,
praising him as I spoke.

[18] If I had not confessed the sin in my heart,
my Lord would not have listened.

[19] But God did listen!
He paid attention to my prayer.

[20] Praise God, who did not ignore my prayer
and did not withdraw his unfailing love from me.

*S*he was just going to the well for some water, but there she met a man who changed her life. He talked about giving her "living water," and he knew all about her—including her five husbands—but that didn't keep him from talking with her. He talked about worshiping God in spirit and truth rather than simply in ritual actions. He spoke of a God who wanted to know her. He was certainly a prophet, but could he be the Promised One?

Jesus told her that he was indeed the promised Messiah. Upon hearing this, the Samaritan woman rushed into town to tell others. "Come and meet a man who told me everything I ever did!" she crowed. "Can this be the Messiah?"

Presumably the townspeople knew this woman; some may have despised her for her shady reputation. Then why did they stream out to the well to see Jesus? Maybe they already saw the change in her. Messiah or not, they had to see what she was talking about—and many of them, too, came away believing in Jesus (John 4).

As Psalm 66 closes, the psalmist gives basically the same shout: "Come and listen . . . and I will tell you what he did for me." When it comes right down to it, that's all any of us can do. No one wants lectures in theology or finger-in-the-face attacks on their morality—but they do want an explanation for the changes in your life. If you're a Christian, you're a witness of what God has done for you.

> To God be the glory, great things he hath done,
> So loved he the world that he gave us his Son,
> Who yielded his life an atonement for sin,
> And opened the lifegate that all may go in.
> FANNY J. CROSBY

Fascinating Fact
In his autobiography, John Bunyan (who also wrote The Pilgrim's Progress*) used Psalm 66:16 as the introduction.*

Notable Quotable
"Prayer is the highest use to which speech can be put."
P. T. FORSYTH

PSALM 67

For the choir director: A psalm, to be accompanied by stringed instruments. A song.

¹ May God be merciful and bless us.
    May his face shine with favor upon us.   *Interlude*
² May your ways be known throughout the earth,
    your saving power among people everywhere.
³ May the nations praise you, O God.
    Yes, may all the nations praise you.

⁴ How glad the nations will be, singing for joy,
    because you govern them with justice
    and direct the actions of the whole world.   *Interlude*
⁵ May the nations praise you, O God.
    Yes, may all the nations praise you.

⁶ Then the earth will yield its harvests,
    and God, our God, will richly bless us.
⁷ Yes, God will bless us,
    and people all over the world will fear him.

s the Israelites wandered in the desert, God gave Aaron a blessing to recite over the people, a way to assure them of God's relationship with them (Numbers 6:24-26).

> May the Lord bless you and protect you.
> May the Lord smile on you and be gracious to you.
> May the Lord show you his favor and give you his peace.

Tucked away in the middle of the rule books of Israel, this simple blessing is not about holiness or law keeping but about gracious blessing, and it was to be the identifying mark of the Israelites (Numbers 6:27).

Psalm 67 picks up where that blessing leaves off. But instead of restricting the blessing to the Israelites, it invites the whole world to receive God's favor. When all the nations praise God, "the earth will yield its harvests" (verse 6).

We often mistakenly think of the Old Testament as a book that is concerned only with the Israelites and their status as God's chosen people. But a message of God's love for all people dances throughout the Old Testament. Through Abraham, God promised, "all the families of the earth will be blessed" (Genesis 12:3). We see this highlighted in Psalm 67. Let us join in the psalmist's prayer that all the world would come to praise God!

> Let all the world in every corner sing, "My God and King!"
> The church with psalms must shout; no door can keep them out.
> But more than all, the heart must bear the longest part,
> Let all the world in every corner sing, "My God and King!"
>
> GEORGE HERBERT

Fascinating Fact
Ancient writers called Psalm 67 the Lord's Prayer of the Old Testament.

Notable Quotable
"We can pray . . . boldly for he is our God. But he is not ours to monopolize, nor will he be any less 'our God' when all his rightful subjects bow to him."
DEREK KIDNER

PSALM 68:1-14
For the choir director: A psalm of David. A song.

¹ Arise, O God, and scatter your enemies.
  Let those who hate God run for their lives.
² Drive them off like smoke blown by the wind.
    Melt them like wax in fire.
    Let the wicked perish in the presence of God.
³ But let the godly rejoice.
    Let them be glad in God's presence.
    Let them be filled with joy.

⁴ Sing praises to God and to his name!
    Sing loud praises to him who rides the clouds.
  His name is the LORD—
    rejoice in his presence!

⁵ Father to the fatherless, defender of widows—
    this is God, whose dwelling is holy.
⁶ God places the lonely in families;
    he sets the prisoners free and gives them joy.
    But for rebels, there is only famine and distress.

⁷ O God, when you led your people from Egypt,
    when you marched through the wilderness,   *Interlude*
⁸ the earth trembled, and the heavens poured rain
    before you, the God of Sinai,
    before God, the God of Israel.
⁹ You sent abundant rain, O God,
    to refresh the weary Promised Land.
¹⁰ There your people finally settled,
    and with a bountiful harvest, O God,
    you provided for your needy people.

¹¹ The Lord announces victory,
    and throngs of women shout the happy news.

[12] Enemy kings and their armies flee,
  while the women of Israel divide the plunder.
[13] Though they lived among the sheepfolds,
  now they are covered with silver and gold,
  as a dove is covered by its wings.
[14] The Almighty scattered the enemy kings
  like a blowing snowstorm on Mount Zalmon.

*I*magine being in the company of Israelites when you finally escape from Egypt. God rescues you from harsh slavery and is taking you to a new land. Praise God!

But there's a problem: A sea is in the way, and Pharaoh is sending his war chariots to chase you down.

But God carves a path through the sea. You walk through on dry land and then turn to see the waters closing in on the pursuing Egyptians. You are free!

Centuries later people are still talking about what happened at the Red Sea. Here in Psalm 68 David rehearses the way God led his people, continually working on their behalf and sending rain to them to grow their food.

We serve this same God today, and he is constantly working on our behalf. Nothing is too difficult for him, so we can follow him and know that he will provide for all our needs, just as he did for his people long ago.

*Let all the world in every corner sing, My God
  and King!*
*The heavens are not too high, His praise may
  thither fly:*
The earth is not too low, His praises there may grow.
*Let all the world in every corner sing, My God and
  King.*
GEORGE HERBERT

Fascinating Fact
Antony, father of the monastic movement, used to sing Psalm 68 to celebrate his triumph over spiritual foes. This often puzzled the townspeople, who heard his battle cries but saw no one attacking him.

Bible Networking
This may have been composed for David's procession with the Ark when he took it from the house of Obed-edom to Jerusalem. See 2 Samuel 6:12.

PSALM 68:15-26

15 The majestic mountains of Bashan
stretch high into the sky.
16 Why do you look with envy, O rugged mountains,
at Mount Zion, where God has chosen to live,
where the LORD himself will live forever?

17 Surrounded by unnumbered thousands of chariots,
the Lord came from Mount Sinai into his sanctuary.
18 When you ascended to the heights,
you led a crowd of captives.
You received gifts from the people,
even from those who rebelled against you.
Now the LORD God will live among us here.

19 Praise the Lord; praise God our savior!
For each day he carries us in his arms.   *Interlude*
20 Our God is a God who saves!
The Sovereign LORD rescues us from death.

21 But God will smash the heads of his enemies,
crushing the skulls of those who love their guilty ways.
22 The Lord says, "I will bring my enemies down from
Bashan;
I will bring them up from the depths of the sea.
23 You, my people, will wash your feet in their blood,
and even your dogs will get their share!"

24 Your procession has come into view, O God—
the procession of my God and King
as he goes into the sanctuary.
25 Singers are in front, musicians are behind;
with them are young women playing tambourines.
26 Praise God, all you people of Israel;
praise the LORD, the source of Israel's life.

*I*f you're doing congregational readings of the Psalms in church, you may want to skip over verses 21 and 23 of this psalm. There's some stuff in there that seems pretty nasty.

So what's this doing in the Bible? If Jesus taught us in the New Testament to love our enemies, why are we being invited here to wash our feet in our enemies' blood?

First of all, it's God's battle, not ours. David is not saying, "Let me mangle a few Philistine limbs today, Lord!" He trusts God to fight for him instead.

Second, we can trust God to act with justice. His decisions are always right, though we may not always understand them. He decides if and when judgment will fall upon people, and we are in no place to question God's actions. God wants peace, but apparently it was necessary at this time to rescue his people from their enemies by allowing the wicked to suffer the consequences of their ways.

Finally, note the tenderness with which God treats his own people: "He carries us in his arms" (verse 19). God is ultimately about love, and the New Testament makes it clear that God desires for everyone to come to him and receive mercy (1 Timothy 2:3-4).

> *Stand up, stand up for Jesus, the strife will not be long;*
> *This day the noise of battle, the next, the victor's song;*
> *To him that overcometh, a crown of life shall be;*
> *He with the King of glory shall reign eternally.*
> GEORGE DUFFIELD

Bible Networking
In Ephesians 4:8 Paul refers to Psalm 68:18 and uses it in connection with Christ. In Paul's context the "gifts" are the apostles, the prophets, the evangelists, and the pastors and teachers.

Notable Quotable
"Israel continues to teach the church how to worship with exuberance and jubilation. Public worship is, every time it occurs, a victory celebration."
EUGENE PETERSON

PSALM 68:27-35

[27] Look, the little tribe of Benjamin leads the way.
    Then comes a great throng of rulers from Judah
    and all the rulers of Zebulun and Naphtali.

[28] Summon your might, O God.
    Display your power, O God, as you have in the past.
[29] The kings of the earth are bringing tribute
    to your Temple in Jerusalem.
[30] Rebuke these enemy nations—
    these wild animals lurking in the reeds,
    this herd of bulls among the weaker calves.
Humble those who demand tribute from us.
    Scatter the nations that delight in war.
[31] Let Egypt come with gifts of precious metals;
    let Ethiopia bow in submission to God.
[32] Sing to God, you kingdoms of the earth.
    Sing praises to the Lord.   *Interlude*

[33] Sing to the one who rides across the ancient heavens,
    his mighty voice thundering from the sky.
[34] Tell everyone about God's power.
    His majesty shines down on Israel;
    his strength is mighty in the heavens.
[35] God is awesome in his sanctuary.
    The God of Israel gives power and strength to his
        people.

Praise be to God!

*H*ave you ever seen the poster called "A New Yorker's View of the World"? In the foreground is the familiar skyline of Manhattan with the Bronx off to one side and Brooklyn on another. Across the river is New Jersey, and then off in the distance is Chicago, with Los Angeles being just a blip in the background. A variety of spin-off posters have been made, with the "view" from other cities.

In a similar way the end of Psalm 68 gives us "The Psalmist's View of the World." There in the foreground is the Temple, inhabited by the God of Israel. The kings of all the other nations are coming to pay tribute to the Lord in Jerusalem. Egyptians and Ethiopians come from afar to bow before him, offering their gifts. The mighty nations of the world fade into the background because the Lord is the ruler of all, and he lives right here among his people.

> The whole triumphant host give thanks to God on high;
> "Hail, Father, Son, and Holy Ghost!" they ever cry.
> Hail, Abraham's God and mine! With heaven our songs we raise;
> All might and majesty are thine, and endless praise.

THOMAS OLIVERS

Notable Quotable

"This psalm is a paean of praise; it throbs with exultation; in it we hear the roar of battle, melting in the song of triumph. The Lord is the Victor."
W. GRAHAM SCROGGIE

Thought to Ponder

It is God's presence in Jerusalem that inspires the kings to bear gifts. As John Durham says, "It is the advent and presence of God which makes men different." How has God's presence in your life changed you? What gifts are you bringing him?

The Bible is filled with references to nature. Regarding trees alone, there are over three hundred references! Here are ten references in the Psalms that speak of trees and forests:

◆ *Psalm 1:3*
They are like trees planted along
the riverbank,
bearing fruit each season without fail.

◆ *Psalm 29:5*
The voice of the LORD splits the
mighty cedars;
the LORD shatters the cedars of
Lebanon.

◆ *Psalm 29:9*
The voice of the LORD twists
mighty oaks
and strips the forests bare.
In his Temple everyone shouts,
"Glory!"

◆ *Psalm 52:8*
But I am like an olive tree,
thriving in the house of God.

◆ *Psalm 80:10*
The mountains were covered with
our shade;
the mighty cedars were covered
with our branches.

◆ *Psalm 92:12*
But the godly will flourish like
palm trees
and grow strong like the cedars
of Lebanon.

◆ *Psalm 96:12-13*
Let the trees of the forest rustle
with praise
before the Lord!
For the LORD is coming!

◆ *Psalm 104:16*
The trees of the LORD are well cared
for—
the cedars of Lebanon that he
planted.

◆ *Psalm 137:2*
We put away our lyres,
hanging them on the branches
of the willow trees.

◆ *Psalm 148:7, 9*
Praise the LORD from the earth . . .
    fruit trees and all cedars.

As our world continues to become more urbanized, it is becoming more difficult to see and appreciate the work of our Creator and praise him with great excitement. In the spring, nature explodes with colorful excitement, but we simply do not notice much of the time. We have also grown to see nature in very mechanistic ways. We buy a loaf of bread in the supermarket without much thought of the God who provided it. The weatherman informs us that there is a 50 percent chance of rain, according to the various isobars, highs and lows, and air currents.

The psalmists didn't know as much about isobars, but they could get very excited about what God was doing in nature. They speak of the rivers clapping "their hands in glee" (Psalm 98:8). In Psalm 65, after the psalmist talks about the hillsides blossoming with joy and the valleys being carpeted with grain, he invites all nature to join together to "shout and sing for joy" (65:13).

The psalmists knew that it is God who takes care of the earth and waters it (Psalm 65:9), and he is given credit as Creator throughout the Psalms. The psalmists recognized that God causes "grass to grow for the cattle. [He] cause[s] plants to grow for people to use" (104:14). And as the Psalms conclude, we are reminded that God is the one who "satisfies you with plenty of the finest wheat" (Psalm 147:14).

Make a point this week to praise God for the way he brings color out of drabness, variety out of sameness, beauty out of ugliness. This is the God we worship, and he wants to cause this same transformation in your life as well.

∽

Fair are the meadows, fairer still the
    woodlands,
Robed in the blooming garb of spring:
Jesus is fairer, Jesus is purer,
Who makes the woeful heart to sing.
From the *MÜNSTER GESANGBUCH*

Selah

PSALM 69:1-7

For the choir director: A psalm of David, to be sung to the tune "Lilies."

¹ Save me, O God,
    for the floodwaters are up to my neck.
² Deeper and deeper I sink into the mire;
    I can't find a foothold to stand on.
I am in deep water,
    and the floods overwhelm me.
³ I am exhausted from crying for help;
    my throat is parched and dry.
My eyes are swollen with weeping,
    waiting for my God to help me.

⁴ Those who hate me without cause
    are more numerous than the hairs on my head.
These enemies who seek to destroy me
    are doing so without cause.
They attack me with lies,
    demanding that I give back what I didn't steal.

⁵ O God, you know how foolish I am;
    my sins cannot be hidden from you.
⁶ Don't let those who trust in you stumble because of
        me,
    O Sovereign LORD Almighty.
Don't let me cause them to be humiliated,
    O God of Israel.
⁷ For I am mocked and shamed for your sake;
    humiliation is written all over my face.

*I*t was a tough job, but somebody had to do it. Jeremiah was told to prophesy that the Babylonians would conquer Jerusalem. Everyone else seemed sure that the holy city would be spared, but Jeremiah kept bringing bad news. To silence him, his enemies lowered him into a muddy cistern. As the prophet sank into the mire, surely these words from Psalm 69 would have been running through his head.

Jeremiah never really wanted to be a prophet; he was just obeying God. The religious leaders told him he was dead wrong—God certainly wouldn't let foreigners overrun his Temple! Where was Jeremiah's faith? Jeremiah had to wonder that himself sometimes, worrying that he was getting it wrong, just as David fretted in verses 5 and 6. But he kept doggedly "calling 'em as he saw 'em."

Jesus was in a similar situation, attacked by the religious leaders of his day. We don't usually think of it this way, but Jesus was crucified because he wasn't religious enough—at least not in the eyes of the Pharisees and scribes. He was seen as a Sabbath breaker, a Temple defamer, and ultimately a blasphemer.

Pleasing others should never be our primary concern. If we keep our focus on pleasing God, we may get criticism from others who misunderstand us—just as David, Jeremiah, and Jesus did—but we will have the approval of God.

> On the light of God's own presence
> O'er his ransomed people shed,
> Chasing far the gloom and terror,
> Brightening all the path we tread.
> BERNHARDT SEVERIN INGEMANN

Psalm at a Glance

In this psalm David is, of course, speaking of his own experiences, but it is also a messianic psalm that speaks of the passion and resurrection of our Lord. Keep both perspectives in mind as you read it.

Notable Quotable

"Closeness to God sometimes means alienation from men."
EUGENE PETERSON

PSALM 69:8-21

8 Even my own brothers pretend they don't know me;
   they treat me like a stranger.

9 Passion for your house burns within me,
   so those who insult you are also insulting me.

10 When I weep and fast before the LORD,
   they scoff at me.

11 When I dress in sackcloth to show sorrow,
   they make fun of me.

12 I am the favorite topic of town gossip,
   and all the drunkards sing about me.

13 But I keep right on praying to you, LORD,
   hoping this is the time you will show me favor.
In your unfailing love, O God,
   answer my prayer with your sure salvation.

14 Pull me out of the mud;
   don't let me sink any deeper!
Rescue me from those who hate me,
   and pull me from these deep waters.

15 Don't let the floods overwhelm me,
   or the deep waters swallow me,
   or the pit of death devour me.

16 Answer my prayers, O LORD,
   for your unfailing love is wonderful.
Turn and take care of me,
   for your mercy is so plentiful.

17 Don't hide from your servant;
   answer me quickly, for I am in deep trouble!

18 Come and rescue me;
   free me from all my enemies.

19 You know the insults I endure—
   the humiliation and disgrace.

You have seen all my enemies
and know what they have said.
[20] Their insults have broken my heart,
and I am in despair.
If only one person would show some pity;
if only one would turn and comfort me.
[21] But instead, they give me poison for food;
they offer me sour wine to satisfy my thirst.

*P*salm 69 remarkably describes much of what Jesus experienced on earth. One time Jesus was staying at a house in Galilee, and so many people came to see him that he and his disciples didn't have time to eat. When Jesus' mother and brothers heard about this, they were concerned and hurried over from Nazareth to take Jesus back home (Mark 3:20-21). There were other occasions, too, when Jesus' family just didn't get it. The apostle John tells us, "Even his brothers didn't believe in him" (John 7:5). David's comments in verse 8 of this psalm reflect this sad truth.

Jesus' life further matches this psalm in that he was consumed with a passion for God's house, he was gossiped about, and he was falsely accused. Jesus was also offered "sour wine" on the cross (verse 21; see Matthew 27:48). God answered his prayers (see verse 16), not by removing the suffering he had to go through, but by carrying him through it and raising him from the dead.

> *Abide with me, fast falls the eventide;*
> *The darkness deepens: Lord, with me abide!*
> *When other helpers fail and comforts flee,*
> *Help of the helpless, O Abide with me.*
> HENRY F. LYTE

Notable Quotable
"*Persecution is never so hard to bear as when it is at the hands of near relatives.*"
W. GRAHAM SCROGGIE

PSALM 69:22-36

²² Let the bountiful table set before them become a snare,
and let their security become a trap.
²³ Let their eyes go blind so they cannot see,
and let their bodies grow weaker and weaker.
²⁴ Pour out your fury on them;
consume them with your burning anger.
²⁵ May their homes become desolate
and their tents be deserted.
²⁶ To those you have punished, they add insult to injury;
they scoff at the pain of those you have hurt.
²⁷ Pile their sins up high,
and don't let them go free.
²⁸ Erase their names from the Book of Life;
don't let them be counted among the righteous.

²⁹ I am suffering and in pain.
Rescue me, O God, by your saving power.

³⁰ Then I will praise God's name with singing,
and I will honor him with thanksgiving.
³¹ For this will please the LORD more than sacrificing an ox
or presenting a bull with its horns and hooves.
³² The humble will see their God at work and be glad.
Let all who seek God's help live in joy.
³³ For the LORD hears the cries of his needy ones;
he does not despise his people who are oppressed.

³⁴ Praise him, O heaven and earth,
the seas and all that move in them.
³⁵ For God will save Jerusalem
and rebuild the towns of Judah.
His people will live there
and take possession of the land.

[36] The descendants of those who obey him will
    inherit the land,
    and those who love him will live there in safety.

*I*n the earlier part of Psalm 69, David detailed his sufferings. It's clear he is being falsely accused by those who think that they are doing the right thing (see verse 4). In this last section, he asks God to turn the tables—to punish his powerful accusers and reward "humble" and "needy" people like himself.

This depiction of God as being concerned about the have-nots is a common theme in Scripture. David spoke about it over and over in the Psalms. We may not think of such a great king as having ever been poor, but David spent much of his pre-royal life running from cave to cave. It seems that he was able to remember how much he needed God even amidst all the trappings of luxury.

Jesus also underscored this theme, especially in the Beatitudes (Matthew 5:3-12). "God blesses those who realize their need for him. . . . those who mourn. . . . those who are gentle and lowly." It's the fulfillment of the promise in Psalm 69:32-33. God does hear the cries of the have-nots.

In any society—and sometimes even in the church—some people seem to have it all, while others are needy. The needy ones may be scorned and ignored, vilified and falsely accused, but if they call to the Lord to help them, he will hear them and bless them richly.

> *When we seek relief from a long-felt grief,*
> *When oppressed by new temptations,*
> *Lord, increase and perfect patience;*
> *Show us that bright shore where we weep no more.*
> NIKOLAUS VON ZINZENDORF

Bible Networking
Contrast David's response to persecution (verse 24) with Jesus' response in Luke 23:34.

Notable Quotable
"David's anger was fanned by his zeal for justice, which the Old Testament largely exists to keep before us; but Christ came to crown justice with atonement."
DEREK KIDNER

PSALM 70

For the choir director: A psalm of David, to bring us to the LORD's remembrance.

1 Please, God, rescue me!
    Come quickly, LORD, and help me.
2 May those who try to destroy me
    be humiliated and put to shame.
  May those who take delight in my trouble
    be turned back in disgrace.
3 Let them be horrified by their shame,
    for they said, "Aha! We've got him now!"
4 But may all who search for you
    be filled with joy and gladness.
  May those who love your salvation
    repeatedly shout, "God is great!"
5 But I am poor and needy;
    please hurry to my aid, O God.
  You are my helper and my savior;
    O LORD, do not delay.

Elijah had a "mountaintop experience," literally, on Mount Carmel. He challenged the priests of Baal to a sacrificing duel. If the Lord sent fire from heaven to consume the sacrifice, then he was God. But if Baal sent fire, he was God. Well, Baal didn't show up that day, but God lit up Elijah's altar like a firecracker (1 Kings 18).

But this showdown only made wicked Queen Jezebel even madder. She determined to hunt down Elijah and kill him. Maybe Elijah was expecting a popular revolt to topple the queen and her idolatrous minions. Instead, he had to run for his life.

He went south, down to the Dead Sea area, then farther to the Sinai Desert. He sat and moped, bemoaning his sorry state.

David must have been in a similar situation when he wrote Psalm 70. He begs God to defeat his enemies once and for all, but while Elijah needed a major tutorial from God, complete with wind, earthquake, fire, and finally a gentle whisper (1 Kings 19:9-18), David seems to turn the corner himself in verse 4. Though he's "poor and needy," he knows God is great enough to help him.

> Make haste, O God, and hear my cries;
> Then with the souls who seek thy face,
> And those who thy salvation prize,
> I'll magnify thy matchless grace.
> CHARLES HADDON SPURGEON

A Word on Words
The word for salvation in verse 4 is Yeshua, the Hebrew name for Jesus.

Notable Quotable
"It is not forbidden us, in hours of dire distress, to ask for speed on God's part in his coming to rescue us."
CHARLES HADDON SPURGEON

PSALM 71:1-8

¹ O LORD, you are my refuge;
  never let me be disgraced.
² Rescue me! Save me from my enemies, for you are just.
  Turn your ear to listen and set me free.
³ Be to me a protecting rock of safety,
  where I am always welcome.
  Give the order to save me,
    for you are my rock and my fortress.

⁴ My God, rescue me from the power of the wicked,
  from the clutches of cruel oppressors.
⁵ O Lord, you alone are my hope.
  I've trusted you, O LORD, from childhood.
⁶ Yes, you have been with me from birth;
  from my mother's womb you have cared for me.
  No wonder I am always praising you!

⁷ My life is an example to many,
  because you have been my strength and protection.
⁸ That is why I can never stop praising you;
  I declare your glory all day long.

*W*illiam Wilberforce decided to get serious about his faith at age twenty-five. He had just been elected to the British Parliament, so in the dog-eat-dog world of politics this was not necessarily a good career move.

Young Wilberforce sought advice from a well respected pastor named John Newton. Before Newton's conversion, he had been involved in the slave trade. But now he was campaigning against slavery. Newton encouraged Wilberforce to stay in politics and fight for right. Wilberforce did just that, becoming the strongest voice of his generation against the slave trade.

The slave traders played politics well, making it difficult for Wilberforce to push his abolitionist platform. But Wilberforce pressed on, and in 1807 he succeeded in passing a bill that prohibited the buying and selling of slaves in Britain. Even then, he kept pressing for the total eradication of slavery.

Wilberforce hated making enemies, and he often turned to the Psalms for support. Once, after a particularly heated battle, he told his wife, "The Seventy-first Psalm, which I learned by heart lately, has been a real comfort to me." Indeed, the Lord was a "protecting rock of safety" to Wilberforce, whose faithful government service turned out to be "an example to many."

> *My hope is built on nothing less*
> *Than Jesus' blood and righteousness;*
> *I dare not trust the sweetest frame,*
> *But wholly lean on Jesus' name.*
> *On Christ the solid Rock I stand;*
> *All other ground is sinking sand.*
> EDWARD MOTE

Fascinating Fact
This was the favorite psalm of Athanasius, the much-embattled fourth-century bishop who played a significant role in the establishment of the Nicene Creed.

Notable Quotable
"Our hope is not the glory of heaven, not joy, not rest from labor—nothing which God could create is what we hope for. What we hope for is our Redeeming God himself."
E. B. PUSEY

PSALM 71:9-18

⁹ And now, in my old age, don't set me aside.
　Don't abandon me when my strength is failing.
¹⁰ For my enemies are whispering against me.
　They are plotting together to kill me.
¹¹ They say, "God has abandoned him.
　Let's go and get him,
　for there is no one to help him now."

¹² O God, don't stay away.
　My God, please hurry to help me.
¹³ Bring disgrace and destruction on those who accuse me.
　May humiliation and shame cover
　those who want to harm me.

¹⁴ But I will keep on hoping for you to help me;
　I will praise you more and more.
¹⁵ I will tell everyone about your righteousness.
　All day long I will proclaim your saving power,
　for I am overwhelmed by how much you have done
　for me.
¹⁶ I will praise your mighty deeds, O Sovereign LORD.
　I will tell everyone that you alone are just and good.

¹⁷ O God, you have taught me from my earliest
　childhood,
　and I have constantly told others about the
　wonderful things you do.
¹⁸ Now that I am old and gray,
　do not abandon me, O God.
Let me proclaim your power to this new generation,
　your mighty miracles to all who come after me.

*T*he bishop was at least in his eighties when they came to arrest him. The emperor had decided to crack down on Christians, especially their leaders, because they refused to worship the gods of Rome or the emperor's image. Many believers had been shuttling the bishop from farm to farm as the authorities searched for him.

When the police finally found Bishop Polycarp, he invited them in for lunch, then went peacefully. They took him to an arena, where he stood before a Roman proconsul. He had one more chance to save himself. "Have respect for your old age," the proconsul pleaded. "Curse Christ."

Polycarp's reply was golden: "Eighty-six years have I served him, and he never did me any wrong. How can I blaspheme my king who has saved me?" For his obstinacy, Polycarp was burned to death.

This bishop was a living example of Psalm 71. In his old age he kept trusting Christ, and he kept proclaiming what God had done.

> Yes, broken, timeless, still, O Lord,
> This voice transported, shall record
> Thy goodness, tried so long;
> Till, sinking slow, with calm decay,
> Its feeble murmur melt away
> Into a seraph's song.
> ROBERT GRANT

Bible Networking
For more about teaching that comes from God (verse 17) read John 16:13; Ezekiel 36:26-27; and Psalm 119:98-100.

Notable Quotable
"It is not improper for a man who sees old age coming upon him to pray for special grace to enable him to meet what he cannot but dread."
ALBERT BARNES

PSALM 71:19-24

[19] Your righteousness, O God, reaches to the highest
    heavens.
    You have done such wonderful things.
    Who can compare with you, O God?

[20] You have allowed me to suffer much hardship,
    but you will restore me to life again
    and lift me up from the depths of the earth.

[21] You will restore me to even greater honor
    and comfort me once again.

[22] Then I will praise you with music on the harp,
    because you are faithful to your promises, O God.
    I will sing for you with a lyre,
    O Holy One of Israel.

[23] I will shout for joy and sing your praises,
    for you have redeemed me.

[24] I will tell about your righteous deeds
    all day long,
    for everyone who tried to hurt me
    has been shamed and humiliated.

*M*ichael Jordan is the best there is at what he does. Although there are many other good basketball players, over the course of his career Jordan has proved incomparable. You could make similar claims for actress Meryl Streep, poet Maya Angelou, baseball pitcher Greg Maddux, or even game show host Alex Trebek. In business a Fortune 500 company wants to retain the best consultants in their field. A first-rate hospital searches for the best surgeons. A wealthy crime suspect hires the best lawyers. And what else can brighten a mother's day like the phrase "Mom, you're the best"?

We forget sometimes that the Israelites lived in a world that believed in many gods. The neighboring nations had deities of their own, to whom they prayed for success. Various Scriptures depict the God of the Israelites being pitted against these other gods and emerging victorious.

But the Israelites took it a step farther. Psalm 71:19 asks: "Who can compare with you, O God?" The God of Israel isn't just better than the others, he is incomparable—the best there is. In fact, he is the only one who matters.

Today many people worship the gods of money and entertainment. They are willing to make sacrifices to them, such as giving up their family life to work eighty hours a week. How silly! The true God isn't just better than these other pursuits—he's simply the best. Once you've met him, nothing else compares.

> Great God of wonders!
> All thy ways are matchless, Godlike and divine;
> But the fair glories of thy grace,
> More Godlike and unrivaled shine.
> SAMUEL DAVIES

Bible Networking
To see more on how great our Lord is, see Ephesians 1:21; 3:14-21.

Notable Quotable
"A traveler among the high Alps often feels overwhelmed with awe. Much more is this the case when we survey the holiness of the Lord."
CHARLES HADDON SPURGEON

PSALM 72:1-7
A psalm of Solomon.

¹ Give justice to the king, O God,
and righteousness to the king's son.
² Help him judge your people in the right way;
let the poor always be treated fairly.
³ May the mountains yield prosperity for all,
and may the hills be fruitful,
because the king does what is right.
⁴ Help him to defend the poor,
to rescue the children of the needy,
and to crush their oppressors.
⁵ May he live as long as the sun shines,
as long as the moon continues in the skies.
Yes, forever!
⁶ May his reign be as refreshing as the springtime rains—
like the showers that water the earth.
⁷ May all the godly flourish during his reign.
May there be abundant prosperity until the end of
time.

*I*n April 1822 James Montgomery was speaking at a Methodist missionary conference, and he was planning to close with a hymn he had just written, based on Psalm 72. But in the middle of his remarks the lights went out. People panicked. Then the chairman of the meeting called out, "There is still light within!" The hubbub ceased, and Montgomery resumed speaking.

The incident serves as a parable for our times. Do you feel somewhat panicked by the "darkness" of our culture? Nowadays Christians seem more fearful than faithful. Calm down! There is still light within. God still lives within our heart, and his light shines outward to a world of people groping in the dark. God is still in control.

Montgomery did recite his hymn (shown below) at that missionary meeting. While Psalm 72 was originally an ode to Israel's king, Montgomery drew on its messianic prophecies. This message of hope and triumph needs to be heard today.

> *Hail to the Lord's Anointed,*
> *Great David's greater Son!*
> *Hail in the time appointed,*
> *His reign on earth begun!*
> *He comes to break oppression,*
> *To set the captive free;*
> *To take away transgression,*
> *And rule in equity.*
>
> *He comes with succor speedy*
> *To those who suffer wrong;*
> *To help the poor and needy*
> *And bid the weak be strong;*
> *To give them songs for sighing,*
> *Their darkness turns to light,*
> *Whose souls, condemned and dying,*
> *Are precious in his sight.*

Bible Networking
The beautiful rainfall simile in verses 6-7 may have been prompted by the last words of David (2 Samuel 23:2-4), where the just king is like sun and rain to his subjects. Also, this picture of the king and his realm is very close to the messianic prophecies of Isaiah. (See Isaiah 11:1-5; 60:1–62:12.)

PSALM 72:8-20

8 May he reign from sea to sea,
and from the Euphrates River to the ends of the earth.
9 Desert nomads will bow before him;
his enemies will fall before him in the dust.
10 The western kings of Tarshish and the islands
will bring him tribute.
The eastern kings of Sheba and Seba
will bring him gifts.
11 All kings will bow before him,
and all nations will serve him.

12 He will rescue the poor when they cry to him;
he will help the oppressed, who have no one to
defend them.
13 He feels pity for the weak and the needy,
and he will rescue them.
14 He will save them from oppression and from violence,
for their lives are precious to him.

15 Long live the king!
May the gold of Sheba be given to him.
May the people always pray for him
and bless him all day long.
16 May there be abundant crops throughout the land,
flourishing even on the mountaintops.
May the fruit trees flourish as they do in Lebanon,
sprouting up like grass in a field.
17 May the king's name endure forever;
may it continue as long as the sun shines.
May all nations be blessed through him
and bring him praise.

18 Bless the LORD God, the God of Israel,
who alone does such wonderful things.

[19] Bless his glorious name forever!
Let the whole earth be filled with his glory.
Amen and amen!

[20] (This ends the prayers of David son of Jesse.)

For one brief, shining moment the nation of Israel was a world power. Under Solomon's reign, Israel's borders stretched from Egypt to the Euphrates. Merchants came from all over the world to do business with Israel. And foreign rulers paid tribute to the great Solomon. In other words, the picture painted in Psalm 72 pretty much came true.

It's unclear whether Solomon himself wrote this psalm, whether some poet laureate wrote it to honor Solomon, or whether David wrote it as a prayer for his son. (See verse 20, and compare with 2 Samuel 23.) In any case, there's one part that didn't come true in Solomon's reign. While Solomon received great glory, God didn't. Many of the political marriages that extended Solomon's influence led him away from the Lord and toward foreign gods. There was no international revival. When Solomon died, the nation plunged into chaos.

It took another King to see that "the whole earth" would "be filled with [God's] glory!" As a baby, this King received gifts from great leaders from the East, and he grew up to "rescue the poor" and "help the oppressed." Through this King, Jesus, all nations will be blessed.

> Jesus shall reign where'er the sun
> Does its successive journeys run;
> His kingdom spread from shore to shore,
> Till moons shall wax and wane no more.
> ISAAC WATTS

Bible Networking
This is a beautiful picture of the great King Solomon, yet Solomon placed heavy burdens on his people (see 1 Kings 12:4-14). For Christians, Jesus is King, and his rule is much different than Solomon's. Read Matthew 11:28.

Notable Quotable
"Amen [verse 19] is a short word, but marvelously pregnant, full of spirit. It is a word that seals all the truths of God. . . . It is never likely to rise in the soul, unless there be first an almighty power from heaven . . . unless God . . . brings the heart down, it never will or can say, 'Amen.'"
RICHARD SIBBES

It is about time for you to meet Asaph and his singing family because the next eleven psalms are all credited to the Asaph clan. Throughout many of the Psalms and the other Old Testament books of 1 and 2 Chronicles, Ezra, and Nehemiah, the Asaph family keeps popping up every time music is mentioned. Asaph was the patriarch of one of the three families of Temple musicians who were appointed by King David to be in charge of singing in the Temple. They are even mentioned in one of the apocryphal books (1 Esdras), where they are identified as the "Temple singers." Occasionally they are also described as playing the cymbals, but usually they sing.

Asaph and his family also wrote some of the Psalms. Here are a few lines from Asaph's hymnbook:

◆ *Psalm 50:15*

Trust me in your times of trouble,
   and I will rescue you,
   and you will give me glory.

◆ *Psalm 73:26*

My health may fail, and my spirit
   may grow weak,
  but God remains the strength of
   my heart;
  he is mine forever.

◆ *Psalm 76:4*

You are glorious and more majestic
   than the everlasting mountains.

◆ *Psalm 77:14*

You are the God of miracles and
   wonders!
  You demonstrate your awesome
   power among the nations.

◆ *Psalm 82:3*

Give fair judgment to the poor and
   the orphan;
  uphold the rights of the
   oppressed and the destitute.

In the 1920s and 1930s gospel quartets enjoyed singing a novelty tune called "The Grumblers' Song." It started like this: *"In country, town, or city, some people may be found who spend their lives at grumbling at everything around."* And the chorus went: *"Oh, they grumble on Monday, grumble on Tuesday, grumble on Wednesday, too. Grumble on Thursday, grumble on Friday, grumble the whole week through."*

Asaph's family was not like that at all. Once a vast army was marching against Judah. The people were terrified; so was King Jehoshaphat. The king prayed, "O our God . . . ? We are powerless. . . . We do not know what to do" (2 Chronicles 20:12). But the Spirit of the Lord came upon one of the Asaph family, who gave the people the word from God: "Do not be afraid! . . . the battle is not yours, but God's. . . . Take your positions; then stand still and watch the Lord's victory. He is with you" (verses 14-17). So King Jehoshaphat appointed singers to walk ahead of the army. When they began to give praise to God, the enemy armies began to attack each other! God gave his people a great victory that day—all because they turned to him in praise and thanksgiving.

How do you respond to the struggles of life? Are you a grumbler? Or do you praise God in all circumstances, just as he has commanded us (Ephesians 5:20)? Why not quit the Grumblers Society and become an honorary member of Asaph's clan this week?

∾

There is never a day so dreary,
There is never a night so long,
But the soul that is trusting in Jesus
Will somewhere find a song.
ANNA B. RUSSELL

∾

Follow the "Asaph Family Singers" through the Old Testament: 1 Chronicles 15:19, 27; 16:5-7; 25:1-2, 6, 9; 2 Chronicles 5:12; 29:30; 35:15; Ezra 2:41; 3:10; and Nehemiah 12:46.

Selah

June 6

BOOK THREE (PSALMS 73–89)
PSALM 73:1-6
A psalm of Asaph.

¹ Truly God is good to Israel,
    to those whose hearts are pure.

² But as for me, I came so close to the edge of the cliff!
    My feet were slipping, and I was almost gone.
³ For I envied the proud
    when I saw them prosper despite their wickedness.
⁴ They seem to live such a painless life;
    their bodies are so healthy and strong.
⁵ They aren't troubled like other people
    or plagued with problems like everyone else.
⁶ They wear pride like a jeweled necklace,
    and their clothing is woven of cruelty.

*I*t's not fair! Have you ever said this to God as you watch cheaters get ahead of you on the corporate ladder, immoral people gaining fame and fortune, or speeders in fancy cars zooming past you on the interstate? In those times we've all wondered, *What's wrong with this picture?* That's where Asaph finds himself in Psalm 73.

"Truly God is good to Israel," he begins, but he seems to be mouthing these words. As we read on, we find that he's not very passionate about God's goodness. We see this in verse 2 as Asaph begins "But as for me . . ." Somehow the great promises of God don't seem to apply to him. He sees proud and wicked people living high on the hog, while he struggles in his efforts to live a good, humble life.

We all want to believe that crime doesn't pay, but sometimes it does, at least in the short run. But, as Asaph discovers later on, he is not looking at the big picture. Truly God is good to Israel and to those of us who have joined God's family by faith. But he doesn't always show us that goodness in physical or monetary terms. He gives us himself, and that's an incomparable blessing that the proud and wicked are choosing not to receive.

> *How good is the God we adore,*
> *Our faithful, unchangeable Friend!*
> *His love is as great as his power*
> *And knows neither measure nor end!*
> JOSEPH HART

Bible Networking
See Job 20:5 for an answer to Asaph's predicament.

Notable Quotable
"Envy is a sickness that only faith can heal."
MATTHEW A. CASTILLE

PSALM 73:7-14

[7] These fat cats have everything
   their hearts could ever wish for!

[8] They scoff and speak only evil;
   in their pride they seek to crush others.

[9] They boast against the very heavens,
   and their words strut throughout the earth.

[10] And so the people are dismayed and confused,
   drinking in all their words.

[11] "Does God realize what is going on?" they ask.
   "Is the Most High even aware of what is happening?"

[12] Look at these arrogant people—
   enjoying a life of ease while their riches multiply.

[13] Was it for nothing that I kept my heart pure
   and kept myself from doing wrong?

[14] All I get is trouble all day long;
   every morning brings me pain.

Y ou may have heard the legend that Nero "fiddled" while Rome burned. The truth is that Rome had a terrible fire in the summer of A.D. 64. We don't know whether Emperor Nero was practicing his violin at the time, but he took advantage of the disaster to claim the charred land and build himself a new palace. He also blamed the Christians for the fire, launching a wave of persecution that resulted in the deaths of Peter, Paul, and many others.

Nero was the kind of "fat cat" that Psalm 73 complains about. No matter how you look at it, it's just plain wrong that a moral degenerate like Nero would be given the power to kill two saints like Peter and Paul. Didn't God see what was going on?

And if wicked emperors win out over holy apostles, why bother to be holy? Well, don't overlook the big picture. God sees everything, even though we often don't.

When Jesus predicted Peter's death, he said it would "glorify God" (John 21:19). Paul said, "To me, living is for Christ, and dying is even better" (Philippians 1:21). Nero's victory was temporary. It may seem as if the wicked triumph, but God and his people will be the true winners in the end.

> Through the night of doubt and sorrow,
> Onward goes the pilgrim band,
> Singing songs of expectation,
> Marching to the Promised Land.
> BERNHARDT SEVERIN INGEMANN

A Word on Words
"Fat cats" in verse 7 is not just a slangy paraphrase. The Hebrew text literally says, "Their eyes bulge with fat."

Notable Quotable
"The way to heaven is an afflicted way, a perplexed, persecuted way. . . . Queen Elizabeth is said to have swum to the crown through a sea of sorrows."
JOHN TRAPP

PSALM 73:15-24

[15] If I had really spoken this way,
  I would have been a traitor to your people.
[16] So I tried to understand why the wicked prosper.
  But what a difficult task it is!
[17] Then one day I went into your sanctuary, O God,
  and I thought about the destiny of the wicked.
[18] Truly, you put them on a slippery path
  and send them sliding over the cliff to destruction.
[19] In an instant they are destroyed,
  swept away by terrors.
[20] Their present life is only a dream
  that is gone when they awake.
When you arise, O Lord,
  you will make them vanish from this life.

[21] Then I realized how bitter I had become,
  how pained I had been by all I had seen.
[22] I was so foolish and ignorant—
  I must have seemed like a senseless animal to you.
[23] Yet I still belong to you;
  you are holding my right hand.
[24] You will keep on guiding me with your counsel,
  leading me to a glorious destiny.

*A*s history records momentous conversions, often the site of the decision is considered important. Martin Luther was praying his way up a staircase in Rome when he realized that "the just shall live by faith." John Wesley found his heart "strangely warmed" at a chapel service.

For Asaph, it all began to make sense once he went into the sanctuary of God. For sixteen verses he had been puzzling over the success of the wicked. "Why bother to be good?" he was asking (verse 13). But then in the sanctuary he finally saw the big picture. The wicked were on a slippery path to destruction. Their present riches were just a dream; the solid reality would come later.

Then Asaph confessed how "foolish and ignorant" he had been in doubting God's goodness, and he thanked God for holding his hand through it all. Scripture never shrinks from the hard questions or compromises with easy answers. We see Job, Elijah, and Jeremiah questioning God, and here Asaph does, too. The questioning itself isn't the problem, just the bitterness. When Asaph took his focus off God and started stewing in his envy, that's when he got into trouble.

You will have questions from time to time, perhaps even some doubts. But keep holding onto God's hand, and keep coming back to his sanctuary.

> Come, tell me all that ye have said and done,
> Your victories and failures, hopes and fears.
> I know how hardly souls are wooed and won;
> My choicest wreaths always wet with tears.
> EDWARD H. BICKERSTETH

A Word on Words

The word for "sanctuary" in verse 17 is plural, possibly referring to more than just the visible Temple. It may refer to any place where God resides, such as our own heart.

Notable Quotable

"Walking in Hyde Park one day, I saw a piece of paper on the grass. I picked it up; it was a part of a letter; the beginning was wanting, the end was not there. . . . Such is providence. You cannot see beginning or end, only a part. When you can see the whole, then the mystery will be unveiled."
THOMAS JONES

PSALM 73:25-28

[25] Whom have I in heaven but you?
   I desire you more than anything on earth.
[26] My health may fail, and my spirit may grow weak,
   but God remains the strength of my heart;
   he is mine forever.

[27] But those who desert him will perish,
   for you destroy those who abandon you.
[28] But as for me, how good it is to be near God!
   I have made the Sovereign LORD my shelter,
   and I will tell everyone about the wonderful things
      you do.

Charles Wesley wrote more than seven thousand hymns in his life. If you wrote a hymn a day, you'd have to work for twenty years to match that output. And face it, some gems like "And Can It Be?" and "Hark the Herald Angels Sing" might take two or three days at least. Most Protestant hymnals have dozens of Wesley's hymns. But his last one is little known.

Wesley loved the Psalms, both as inspiration for his hymns and for personal comfort. As he lay on his deathbed at the age of eighty, Wesley was mulling over Psalm 73. Calling his wife to his side, he dictated the lines of his last hymn:

> *In age and feebleness extreme,*
> *What shall a sinful worm redeem?*
> *Jesus, my only hope thou art,*
> *Strength of my failing flesh and heart;*
> *O, could I catch a smile from thee,*
> *And drop into eternity!*

Asaph, the author of this psalm, was no mean hymn writer himself. People think of the Psalms as David's book, but Asaph wrote about twelve of them as well. In Psalm 73 he is going through the wringer emotionally, but he comes out with a stronger faith in God. Through all the pain and doubting, he still desired God more than anything on earth. No doubt Charles Wesley couldn't have agreed more.

> *That, having all things done,*
> *And all your conflicts past,*
> *Ye may o'ercome, through Christ alone,*
> *And stand complete at last.*
> CHARLES WESLEY

Bible Networking
Other people in Scripture have wrestled with Asaph's question about the wicked and learned the same answer that he did in verse 25. Read Job 42:1-6.

Notable Quotable
"The Epicurean, says Augustine, is apt to say, 'It is good for me to enjoy the pleasures of the flesh.' The Stoic is apt to say, 'For me it is good to enjoy the pleasures of the mind.' The Apostle says, 'It is good for me to cleave to God.'"
LORINUS

When you think of Old Testament prophecies about the coming of the Messiah (Jesus), chances are you think of Isaiah. After all, he was the one who prophesied that a virgin would conceive and bear a son, whose name would be Immanuel. He was the one who prophesied that the Suffering Servant, a Man of Sorrows, would be wounded and crushed for our guilt, and that the Lord would lay upon him the sins of us all.

But as you read the Psalms, you find messianic allusions on almost every page. Here are a few messianic prophecies in the Psalms that were fulfilled during Easter week, the week leading up to Jesus' death and resurrection:

♦ Please, LORD, please save us. . . . Bless the one who comes in the name of the LORD.

PSALM 118:25-26 (SEE MARK 11:9)

♦ Even my best friend . . . the one who shared my food, has turned against me.

PSALM 41:9 (SEE JOHN 13:18)

♦ They sneer and shake their heads, saying, "Is this the one who relies on the LORD? Then let the LORD save him!"

PSALM 22:7-8 (SEE MATTHEW 27:42-43)

♦ They have pierced my hands and feet.

PSALM 22:16 (SEE MATTHEW 27:35)

♦ They divide my clothes among themselves and throw dice for my garments.

PSALM 22:18 (SEE JOHN 19:23-24)

♦ They offer me sour wine to satisfy my thirst.

PSALM 69:21 (SEE MARK 15:36)

♦ My God, my God! Why have you forsaken me?

PSALM 22:1 (SEE MARK 15:34)

♦ For you will not leave my soul among the dead or allow your godly one to rot in the grave.

PSALM 16:10 (SEE ACTS 2:27)

◆ The stone rejected by the builders has now become the cornerstone.
PSALM 118:22 (SEE ACTS 4:11)

◆ The LORD said to my Lord, "Sit in honor at my right hand until I humble your enemies."
PSALM 110:1 (SEE HEBREWS 10:13)

It's amazing how much the Psalms teach us about the Messiah (Jesus). Even if we didn't have the New Testament, we would know a great deal about him.

Throughout the Psalms the Messiah is identified as Prophet, Priest, and King. We also learn from Psalm 2 that he is a divine son, belonging to the Deity. This can be seen as God declares someone his "son" and describes him in terms that suggest a person more glorious than David.

Psalm 23 speaks of the Lord as the Good Shepherd, which Jesus called himself in John 10.

Yet Psalm 22 shows us that this Messiah would suffer and die in an ignominious fashion. This psalm graphically describes the details of crucifixion long before the Romans even invented this form of execution. But we also learn that the Messiah would not stay in the grave; he would rise again (Psalm 16).

Ultimately the Messiah would sit in honor at God's right hand (Psalm 110), and as King of kings he would expand the rule of God to the ends of the earth (Psalm 72).

In Luke 24 Jesus walked with two of his followers on the road to Emmaus. He explained to them "everything written about [him] by Moses and the prophets and in the Psalms" (verse 32), and their hearts were strangely warmed. No wonder! The Psalms and other books of the Old Testament are filled with amazing references to him! And it is exciting that all believers will one day be able to share in that Bible study together.

∾

How well your blessed truths agree!
How wise and holy your commands!
Your promises—how firm they be!
How firm our hope and comfort stands!
ISAAC WATTS

Selah

PSALM 74:1-11
A psalm of Asaph.

¹ O God, why have you rejected us forever?
  Why is your anger so intense against the sheep of
    your own pasture?
² Remember that we are the people you chose in ancient
    times,
  the tribe you redeemed as your own special possession!
  And remember Jerusalem, your home here on earth.
³ Walk through the awful ruins of the city;
  see how the enemy has destroyed your sanctuary.
⁴ There your enemies shouted their victorious battle cries;
  there they set up their battle standards.
⁵ They chopped down the entrance
  like woodcutters in a forest.
⁶ With axes and picks,
  they smashed the carved paneling.
⁷ They set the sanctuary on fire, burning it to the ground.
  They utterly defiled the place that bears your holy
    name.
⁸ Then they thought, "Let's destroy everything!"
  So they burned down all the places where God was
    worshiped.

⁹ We see no miraculous signs
  as evidence that you will save us.
  All the prophets are gone;
  no one can tell us when it will end.
¹⁰ How long, O God, will you allow our enemies to mock
    you?
  Will you let them dishonor your name forever?
¹¹ Why do you hold back your strong right hand?
  Unleash your powerful fist and deliver a deathblow.

The fall of Jerusalem in 586 B.C. was the end of a long, humiliating defeat. Several years earlier the Babylonians had forced Judah to submit to their rule and pay massive tribute. Then they set up a puppet king in Judah and carted off most of Jerusalem's nobles into exile. Finally the people rebelled again, so the Babylonian army plundered the city and carried off many more of the people.

Jeremiah watched it all, knowing that God was judging his people. They had mocked this "weeping prophet" and called him a traitor for foretelling of Jerusalem's destruction. The book of Lamentations details Jeremiah's sorrow. "Why do you continue to forget us?" he prays. "Why have you forsaken us for so long?" (Lamentations 5:20).

Psalm 74 is credited to Asaph, but it expresses the sorrow of Jeremiah. Many of us can relate to these feelings. Sometimes things go horribly wrong in our life and we wonder what God is doing. Is he even there? Why does he seem so angry with us?

You may feel guilty for having these feelings, but you shouldn't. Both Psalm 74 and Lamentations show us that these feelings are understandable and acceptable. But also notice that Asaph and Jeremiah kept calling out to God when he seemed so far away. Like Jeremiah and Asaph, let your hard times lead you closer to God, not farther away.

> From the depths of nature's blindness,
> From the hardening power of sin,
> From all malice and unkindness,
> From the pride that lurks within;
> By thy mercy, O deliver us, good Lord.
> JOHN JAMES CUMMINS

Psalm at a Glance
In effect, the prayer of Asaph here is, "Lord, please take your hands out of your pockets and do something."

Bible Networking
Read 2 Kings 25:13-17 to see up close a picture of what happened to the Temple when it was destroyed in 586 B.C.

PSALM 74:12-23

¹² You, O God, are my king from ages past,
  bringing salvation to the earth.

¹³ You split the sea by your strength
  and smashed the sea monster's heads.

¹⁴ You crushed the heads of Leviathan
  and let the desert animals eat him.

¹⁵ You caused the springs and streams to gush forth,
  and you dried up rivers that never run dry.

¹⁶ Both day and night belong to you;
  you made the starlight and the sun.

¹⁷ You set the boundaries of the earth,
  and you make both summer and winter.

¹⁸ See how these enemies scoff at you, LORD.
  A foolish nation has dishonored your name.

¹⁹ Don't let these wild beasts destroy your doves.
  Don't forget your afflicted people forever.

²⁰ Remember your covenant promises,
  for the land is full of darkness and violence!

²¹ Don't let the downtrodden be constantly disgraced!
  Instead, let these poor and needy ones give praise to
    your name.

²² Arise, O God, and defend your cause.
  Remember how these fools insult you all day long.

²³ Don't overlook these things your enemies have said.
  Their uproar of rebellion grows ever louder.

*I*t's the biggest college basketball game of the season. State University has the player of the year, but surprisingly Jackson isn't in the starting lineup for this game. He's on the bench—not injured—he's just not playing.

As the game progresses, the State squad plays hard, but it misses its star center. The team falls behind by twelve points at the half. In the third quarter Jackson's still on the bench, and the team keeps losing ground. The fans are getting angry. "Why is the coach throwing this game away?"

The fourth quarter begins with State down by sixteen points. But then Jackson runs onto the floor to join his teammates, and the crowd's boos turn to cheers. The star center plays with incredible energy, grabbing every rebound, blocking shots, scoring at will. The State team whittles the lead down to ten, to five, to two, and then with a minute left Jackson completes a three-point play to give State the lead for good. The crowd goes wild. What a brilliant coach!

You can't blame the psalmist for wondering why his star player, God himself, isn't entering the game. Why does he sit on the sidelines when his team is getting trounced? Sometimes you may wonder the same thing. But don't fear—the game isn't over yet.

> *Begone, unbelief;*
> *My Savior is near,*
> *And for my relief*
> *Will surely appear;*
> *By prayer let me wrestle,*
> *And he will perform;*
> *With Christ in the vessel,*
> *I smile at the storm.*
> JOHN NEWTON

Bible Networking
Read chapter 8 of Hebrews to find out more about the covenant promises of verse 20.

Notable Quotable
"The man of faith is never blind to the desolation. He sees clearly all the terrible facts. But he sees more. He sees God."
G. CAMPBELL MORGAN

PSALM 75

For the choir director: A psalm of Asaph, to be sung to the tune "Do Not Destroy!" A song.

¹ We thank you, O God!
> We give thanks because you are near.
> People everywhere tell of your mighty miracles.

² God says, "At the time I have planned,
> I will bring justice against the wicked.
³ When the earth quakes and its people live in turmoil,
> I am the one who keeps its foundations firm.   *Interlude*

⁴ "I warned the proud, 'Stop your boasting!'
> I told the wicked, 'Don't raise your fists!
⁵ Don't lift your fists in defiance at the heavens
> or speak with rebellious arrogance.' "

⁶ For no one on earth—from east or west,
> or even from the wilderness—
> can raise another person up.
⁷ It is God alone who judges;
> he decides who will rise and who will fall.
⁸ For the LORD holds a cup in his hand;
> it is full of foaming wine mixed with spices.
> He pours the wine out in judgment,
> and all the wicked must drink it,
> draining it to the dregs.

⁹ But as for me, I will always proclaim what God has
> done;
> I will sing praises to the God of Israel.

¹⁰ For God says, "I will cut off the strength of the wicked,
> but I will increase the power of the godly."

*T*here is no better press agent than a person in love. When you are in love with someone, you want to tell everyone how great your beloved is. Every deed is magnified. Everyone within earshot has to hear about it. This is true for the mother who dearly loves her child as well as for the hopeless romantic who keeps trumpeting the praises of that special someone.

That's the kind of people we meet in the first verse of this psalm. The psalmist, Asaph, is crazy about God and can't stop talking about what he has done (see verse 9).

But then there are the wicked, who raise their fists toward heaven. They can't stop talking about someone either—themselves (verse 4)! Confident in their own power, they see no need for God. Eventually such people will receive God's judgment.

We can see from this psalm that the Lord wants us to praise him—not ourself—as God. He brings down the proud and lifts the lowly. Two of the most beautiful prayers in Scripture, Hannah's and Mary's, focus on this truth (see 1 Samuel 2:1-10 and Luke 1:46-55). And this psalm concludes with a simple statement of the same thing. He increases the power of the righteous and pulls the plug on the proud.

Which kind of person are you? Full of praise for yourself or for God?

> Among the nations He shall judge;
> His judgments truth shall guide;
> His scepter shall protect the just,
> And quell the sinner's pride.
> ANONYMOUS

Bible Networking
To find out more about drinking from the cup of judgment, look up Isaiah 51:17; Jeremiah 25:15; and Habakkuk 2:16.

Notable Quotable
"What a comfort it is to feel that amid the chaos and anarchy which sweep the surface, God is holding fast the foundations on which we build."
F. B. MEYER

PSALM 76

For the choir director: A psalm of Asaph, to be accompanied by stringed instruments. A song.

¹ God is well known in Judah;
  his name is great in Israel.
² Jerusalem is where he lives;
  Mount Zion is his home.
³ There he breaks the arrows of the enemy,
  the shields and swords and weapons of his foes.

Interlude

⁴ You are glorious and more majestic
  than the everlasting mountains.
⁵ The mightiest of our enemies have been plundered.
  They lie before us in the sleep of death.
  No warrior could lift a hand against us.
⁶ When you rebuked them, O God of Jacob,
  their horses and chariots stood still.

⁷ No wonder you are greatly feared!
  Who can stand before you when your anger
    explodes?
⁸ From heaven you sentenced your enemies;
  the earth trembled and stood silent before you.
⁹ You stand up to judge those who do evil, O God,
  and to rescue the oppressed of the earth.   *Interlude*

¹⁰ Human opposition only enhances your glory,
  for you use it as a sword of judgment.

¹¹ Make vows to the LORD your God, and fulfill them.
  Let everyone bring tribute to the Awesome One.
¹² For he breaks the spirit of princes
  and is feared by the kings of the earth.

*I*n the days of Hezekiah, King of Judah, the Assyrian army threatened Jerusalem. Assyria was the superpower of the Near Eastern world at the time, and it was known for its efficient war machine and ruthless methods. So when an Assyrian envoy came knocking at the gates of Jerusalem and proceeded to taunt the people and their God, it was a terrifying, humiliating moment (see the devotional for May 1/Psalm 56:1-7).

But Hezekiah prayed about the matter, and God promised to save his people from the Assyrians. How? God didn't elaborate, but Hezekiah trusted him.

We still don't know exactly how it happened, in natural terms, but the deliverance happened. Food poisoning? An outbreak of some plague? Poisonous gas from some fissure in the earth? God may have used any of these natural forces to accomplish his divine purposes. All we know is that Scripture simply says the "angel of the Lord went out . . . and killed 185,000 Assyrian troops. When the surviving Assyrians woke up the next morning, they found corpses everywhere" (Isaiah 37:36). You can imagine that the remaining soldiers hightailed it home.

After such an experience it would be no surprise if Psalm 76 was the featured psalm for the Temple worship the following Sabbath! The Awesome One had acted.

> *My Savior and my Lord,*
> *My Conqueror and my King,*
> *Thy scepter and thy sword,*
> *Thy reigning grace, I sing:*
> *Thine is the power; behold, I sit*
> *In willing bonds beneath thy feet.*
> ISAAC WATTS

Fascinating Fact
In 1588 copies of this psalm were given out in Edinburgh by Robert Bruce when the news came of the defeat of the Spanish Armada.

Notable Quotable
"God has ever compelled the wrath of man to praise Him."
G. CAMPBELL MORGAN

June 15

PSALM 77:1-12
For Jeduthun, the choir director: A psalm of Asaph.

1 I cry out to God without holding back.
  Oh, that God would listen to me!
2 When I was in deep trouble,
  I searched for the Lord.
  All night long I pray, with hands lifted toward heaven,
    pleading.
  There can be no joy for me until he acts.
3 I think of God, and I moan,
  overwhelmed with longing for his help.   *Interlude*

4 You don't let me sleep.
  I am too distressed even to pray!
5 I think of the good old days, long since ended,
6   when my nights were filled with joyful songs.
  I search my soul and think about the difference now.
7 Has the Lord rejected me forever?
  Will he never again show me favor?
8 Is his unfailing love gone forever?
  Have his promises permanently failed?
9 Has God forgotten to be kind?
  Has he slammed the door on his compassion?

                                              Interlude

10 And I said, "This is my fate,
   that the blessings of the Most High have changed to
     hatred."
11 I recall all you have done, O LORD;
   I remember your wonderful deeds of long ago.
12 They are constantly in my thoughts.
   I cannot stop thinking about them.

*O*ften when believers fall into doubt, it is not really God they are doubting but themselves. They know that God reigns in heaven, but they also know how weak and worldly they are. So they begin to doubt that they are still in God's favor. Perhaps you know the feeling.

John Bunyan, the seventeenth-century preacher who wrote *The Pilgrim's Progress,* was not immune to such doubts. In fact, he detailed them in his autobiography. He went through a period of more than two years when he felt very far from God. He was acutely aware of his own sin and discouraged by his inability to lead a righteous life. The words of Psalm 77 kept invading his mind: "Has the Lord rejected me forever? Will he never again show me favor?"

But then one day, walking through a field and worrying as always, Bunyan suddenly had a new thought: "Your righteousness is in heaven." He realized that God didn't require any more righteousness from him, because Jesus was his righteousness. Bunyan walked home rejoicing and living "at peace with God through Christ."

Yes, Psalm 77 puts into words the thoughts of many worried believers (Bunyan called it one of the "dreadful Scriptures"). But don't get stuck at the "Interlude" after verse 9. Go on to review the great acts of God in history and in your life. He isn't finished with you yet.

> *He who 'mid the raging billows walked upon the sea*
> *Still can hush our wildest tempest, as on Galilee;*
> *He who wept and prayed in anguish in Gethse-*
> *mane,*
> *Drinks with us each cup of trembling, in our agony.*
> *Yesterday, today, forever, Jesus is the same.*
> A. B. SIMPSON

Notable Quotable
"Melancholy and depression are apt at putting questions but faith has an answer ready."
F. B. MEYER

PSALM 77:13-20

¹³ O God, your ways are holy.
   Is there any god as mighty as you?
¹⁴ You are the God of miracles and wonders!
   You demonstrate your awesome power among the
      nations.
¹⁵ You have redeemed your people by your strength,
   the descendants of Jacob and of Joseph by your
      might.   *Interlude*

¹⁶ When the Red Sea saw you, O God,
   its waters looked and trembled!
   The sea quaked to its very depths.
¹⁷ The clouds poured down their rain;
   the thunder rolled and crackled in the sky.
   Your arrows of lightning flashed.
¹⁸ Your thunder roared from the whirlwind;
   the lightning lit up the world!
   The earth trembled and shook.
¹⁹ Your road led through the sea,
   your pathway through the mighty waters—
   a pathway no one knew was there!
²⁰ You led your people along that road like a flock of
      sheep,
   with Moses and Aaron as their shepherds.

*O*ur God is an awesome God, no question about it. He has done amazing things in history, as today's psalm recounts. But we must not forget that the last half of this psalm is attached to the first half.

Take a look back at yesterday's portion, and then reread today's. Don't they seem like totally different situations? Verse 10 wraps up the despair of the preceding verses by saying, essentially, "God must hate me." Then verse 11 sets up the rest of the psalm by recalling God's "wonderful deeds." What's the connection?

Let's pause a moment and recognize that many people never really put the two attitudes together. Sure, God has done great things, but what does that have to do with me? My life is still a disaster area.

Today's verses tell us that God is in the business of doing great things for his people. His great deeds are not just a fireworks display, but an expression of his love. And don't miss the picture in verse 19. God was leading his people, but the road led through the sea. And just as God carved a path through the sea for the Israelites, he can lead us safely through our problems, along a pathway we don't even know is there!

So if you think God has abandoned you, keep looking *down*. God may be constructing a pathway that you can't even see yet.

> Come unto me, ye wanderers, and I will give you light.
> O loving voice of Jesus, which comes to cheer the night!
> Our hearts were filled with sadness, and we had lost our way;
> But morning brings us gladness, and songs the break of day.

WILLIAM CHATTERTON DIX

Bible Networking
Verses 16-20 give us a powerful poetic picture of the historical event found in Exodus 14:21-31. Also read Mark 4:39 to see that the Lord still commands the waves.

Notable Quotable
"As the brook hides the footprints which are imprinted on its soft ooze, so are God's footprints hidden. We cannot detect his great and wonderful secrets. He marches through the ages with steps we cannot track."
F. B. MEYER

One of the sermons that sparked the Great Awakening of the eighteenth century was Jonathan Edwards's "Sinners in the Hands of an Angry God." But you don't hear many sermons about an angry God anymore. Christians often have a hard time dealing with anger—whether it is ours or someone else's. It scares us, and we don't like being around angry people.

Yet, astonishing as it may seem, the Psalms seem preoccupied with the subject of anger. If we are honest, sometimes we feel angry, and rightly so. It's one of the emotions God has given us. We also read of God's anger, which often makes the anger of mere mortals pale in significance.

Here are a few verses from the Psalms describing God's anger:

◆ *Psalm 30:5*
His anger lasts for a moment,
but his favor lasts a lifetime!
Weeping may go on all night,
but joy comes with the morning.

◆ *Psalm 76:7*
No wonder you are greatly feared!
Who can stand before you when your anger explodes?

◆ *Psalm 85:4*
Now turn to us again, O God of our salvation.
Put aside your anger against us.

◆ *Psalm 89:46*
O LORD, how long will this go on?
Will you hide yourself forever?
How long will your anger burn like fire?

◆ *Psalm 95:9*

For there your ancestors tried
my patience;
they courted my wrath
though they had seen my
many miracles.

◆ *Psalm 145:8* (see also Psalm
86:15; 103:8)

The LORD is kind and merciful,
slow to get angry, full of
unfailing love.

Sometimes God is provoked
to anger by his children's way-
wardness. Psalm 78 tells how
God's anger disciplined the
Israelites, and adds, "Many a
time he held back his anger and
did not unleash his fury!"
(verse 38). In several psalms
Asaph asks, "How long will you
be angry and reject our prayers?"

While God's anger with his
children is for the sake of discipline, his complete wrath will
eventually be unleashed on the
ungodly: "Pour out your wrath
on the nations," prays the
psalmist in Psalm 79:6. That
makes many of us uncomfortable because we often concentrate on God's love to such an
extent that we neglect God's
holiness and justice. Yet both
are affirmed in Scripture.

To be sure, the Bible cautions
us to control our own anger,
since our indignation is not
always righteous. "Don't sin by
letting anger gain control over
you," David says. "Think about
it overnight and remain silent"
(4:4). And elsewhere, "Stop
your anger! Turn from your
rage! Do not envy others—it
only leads to harm" (37:8). It
seems that anger is a feeling
that shouldn't be denied, yet we
should take care to see that it is
"tempered."

∾

*Approach, my soul, the mercy seat
where Jesus answers prayer;
There humbly fall before his feet, for
none can perish there.
Bowed down beneath a load of sin, by
Satan sorely pressed,
By wars without and fears within, I
come to you for rest.*
JOHN NEWTON

∾

"The psalmists invite us to deal
with anger rather than skirt negative human emotions. Hence the
Psalms invite us to pray through
anger and thus to be cleansed of
evil emotions and to be filled with
hope in the full inauguration of
God's Kingdom."
WILLEM A. VANGEMEREN

Selah

PSALM 78:1-8
A psalm of Asaph.

¹ O my people, listen to my teaching.
  Open your ears to what I am saying,
²   for I will speak to you in a parable.
  I will teach you hidden lessons from our past—
³   stories we have heard and know,
      stories our ancestors handed down to us.
⁴ We will not hide these truths from our children
    but will tell the next generation about the glorious
      deeds of the LORD.
    We will tell of his power and the mighty miracles he
      did.
⁵ For he issued his decree to Jacob;
    he gave his law to Israel.
  He commanded our ancestors
    to teach them to their children,
⁶ so the next generation might know them—
    even the children not yet born—
    that they in turn might teach their children.
⁷ So each generation can set its hope anew on God,
    remembering his glorious miracles
    and obeying his commands.
⁸ Then they will not be like their ancestors—
    stubborn, rebellious, and unfaithful,
    refusing to give their hearts to God.

*I*magine yourself at an anniversary banquet for a church that has been around for many years. Old pastors return as well as the parishioners who have moved away. People catch up with each other. "How old are your kids now? Why, I remember when they were this tall!"

Sooner or later the conversation turns to the church's own history. "Remember when we bought this land? That was amazing, wasn't it?" "Remember that revival service when everyone in the youth group gave their hearts to Christ?" "Remember how God healed Linda of her cancer? And here she is today, still going strong!"

There are children at this banquet who weren't around when those great events happened, but now these stories become part of their history, too.

There may be other stories not so publicly presented but whispered in corners. "Remember when old man Jones left the church in a huff and took his money with him?" "Remember when that one pastor left with half the congregation?" But even these add to the church's unique history. We learn from our successes and our failures.

Psalm 78 is Israel's "anniversary banquet," a review of what God has done in and through and for his people. But it's not just a time of reminiscing. It's done "so each generation can set its hope anew on God."

> Come, and let us sweetly join, Christ to praise in
>   hymns divine;
> Give we all, with one accord, glory to our common
>   Lord:
> Hands, and hearts, and voices raise; sing as in the
>   ancient days;
> Antedate the joys above, celebrate the feast of love.
> CHARLES WESLEY

Bible Networking
The Lord explicitly commanded Israel to pass on to future generations the stories of his dealings with them throughout history. Read Exodus 10:2; 13:8, 14; and Deuteronomy 4:9.

Notable Quotable
"Everyone who experiences God's grace has an obligation to pass on what he knows."
EUGENE PETERSON

PSALM 78:9-16

9 The warriors of Ephraim, though fully armed,
   turned their backs and fled when the day of battle
      came.
10 They did not keep God's covenant,
   and they refused to live by his law.
11 They forgot what he had done—
   the wonderful miracles he had shown them,
12   the miracles he did for their ancestors in Egypt, on the
      plain of Zoan.
13 For he divided the sea before them and led them
         through!
   The water stood up like walls beside them!
14 In the daytime he led them by a cloud,
   and at night by a pillar of fire.
15 He split open the rocks in the wilderness
   to give them plenty of water, as from a gushing
      spring.
16 He made streams pour from the rock,
   making the waters flow down like a river!

*J*esus' disciples were crossing the sea in a fishing boat, with Jesus zonked out in a corner. Presumably he had had a long day of teaching and healing and needed some sleep. But then a terrible storm came up, with waves splashing into the boat. Even these experienced fishermen were terrified. "Jesus, wake up! We're drowning!"

The master opened his eyes and said to the storm, "Quiet down!" And it did. Then, perhaps as he settled back to sleep, he asked his disciples, "Why are you so afraid? Do you still not have faith in me?" (Mark 4:35-40).

Jesus' disciples had seen him cure leprosy, paralysis, and blindness. He had cast out demons and turned water into wine. If Jesus possessed this kind of power and was in the boat with them, why should they worry about a Galilean squall?

In today's passage Psalm 78 mentions an event we know nothing about. The tribe of Ephraim was especially strong among the tribes of Israel, but in this case they were cowards, turning and running before their foes. But why were they afraid? Hadn't they seen the mighty works of God? Didn't they know that the God who drowned the Egyptians and tamed the desert would continue to fight alongside them?

Take courage in whatever squall you are facing today, knowing that your powerful Lord is fighting for you.

> O Holy Father, who hast led thy children
> In all the ages with the fire and cloud,
> Through seas dry-shod, through weary wastes bewild'ring,
> To thee in rev'rent love our hearts are bowed.
>
> WILLIAM C. DOANE

A Word on Words

Often when Scripture uses the imagery of a rock, as in verses 15-16, you can think of Christ. In 1 Corinthians 10:4 Paul alludes to the same story that's mentioned here in Psalm 78—water from the rock—but he adds, "and that rock was Christ." This, of course, has given the church some rich imagery over the centuries. Christ has been called the rock of ages, the rock of Israel, the rock of our salvation, the rock of refuge, the rock of strength, and the rock that is higher than I—just to name a few.

Notable Quotable

"History is of no use if we don't remember it. The rich heritage of God's mighty works gives neither insight nor inspiration if we are ignorant of it." EUGENE PETERSON

PSALM 78:17-33

¹⁷ Yet they kept on with their sin,
  rebelling against the Most High in the desert.
¹⁸ They willfully tested God in their hearts,
  demanding the foods they craved.
¹⁹ They even spoke against God himself, saying,
  "God can't give us food in the desert.
²⁰ Yes, he can strike a rock so water gushes out,
  but he can't give his people bread and meat."
²¹ When the LORD heard them, he was angry.
  The fire of his wrath burned against Jacob.
  Yes, his anger rose against Israel,
²²   for they did not believe God
  or trust him to care for them.
²³ But he commanded the skies to open—
  he opened the doors of heaven—
²⁴   and rained down manna for them to eat.
  He gave them bread from heaven.
²⁵   They ate the food of angels!
  God gave them all they could hold.
²⁶ He released the east wind in the heavens
  and guided the south wind by his mighty power.
²⁷ He rained down meat as thick as dust—
  birds as plentiful as the sands along the seashore!
²⁸ He caused the birds to fall within their camp
  and all around their tents.
²⁹ The people ate their fill.
  He gave them what they wanted.
³⁰ But before they finished eating this food they had
    craved,
  while the meat was yet in their mouths,
³¹   the anger of God rose against them,
  and he killed their strongest men;
  he struck down the finest of Israel's young men.

³² But in spite of this, the people kept on sinning.
They refused to believe in his miracles.
³³ So he ended their lives in failure
and gave them years of terror.

*T*here you are in the desert. You've just escaped from Egypt and tromped through the Red Sea, with God's convenient parting of the sea to let you through. But now you're getting hungry. "Are we going to starve out here, Moses?'

Well, God himself is taking care of the eating arrangements. The next morning you see white stuff all over the ground. "What is it?" you ask. (In Hebrew, that question is *Man-na?*) Moses tells you to eat it, and you find it's sweet and filling.

A few years go by, and you're getting sick of manna from heaven. You want meat, something substantial. People bring their complaint to Moses, and God sends a wind to blow a flock of quail in from the sea. Now you're eating quail meat to your heart's content, but the worst complainers get sick and die—God's judgment for sin.

Such was the story of Israel after the Exodus. It could be the story of all humanity. God gives and gives and gives, and we still don't trust him to provide for us. Take a moment to thank God for all he has done for you.

> *Praise to the Lord, who doth prosper thy work and defend thee,*
> *Surely his goodness and mercy here daily attend thee.*
> *Ponder anew what the Almighty can do,*
> *If with his love he befriend thee.*
> JOACHIM NEANDER

Bible Networking
The terrible but just anger of God that is alluded to in verse 21 of this psalm can be read about in Numbers 11:1.

Notable Quotable
"There is no if with God; there is no limit to his almightiness but thy unbelief."
F. B. MEYER

PSALM 78:34-39

34 When God killed some of them, the rest finally sought
him.

They repented and turned to God.

35 Then they remembered that God was their rock,
that their redeemer was the Most High.

36 But they followed him only with their words;
they lied to him with their tongues.

37 Their hearts were not loyal to him.
They did not keep his covenant.

38 Yet he was merciful and forgave their sins
and didn't destroy them all.

Many a time he held back his anger
and did not unleash his fury!

39 For he remembered that they were merely mortal,
gone in a moment like a breath of wind, never to
return.

*T*he prophet Hosea was called by God to marry an unfaithful woman. Can you imagine the ups and downs of Hosea's relationship? There must have been times when his wife came running back to him spouting apologies, but then she would dash his hopes by wandering after yet another lover. Could he ever believe what she said?

The pain Hosea felt mirrored the pain that God felt as his beloved bride, Israel, turned away from him. In Hosea 6:1 the prophet tries to put words of repentance in the mouth of his people: "Come let us return to the Lord!" But a few verses later we see the Lord shaking his head: "What should I do with you? . . . For your love vanishes like the morning mist."

In the history lesson of Psalm 78, we find the Israelites following the Lord "only with their words." They knew what to say, but they didn't know how to live. They would come to God's Temple with sacrifices, but they would not offer him their hearts. "I want you to be merciful," God said through Hosea and others. "I don't want your sacrifices" (Hosea 6:6). The people were going through the motions, but not letting God's emotions go through them.

Many of us still live like that. God wants a deep, passionate, loving relationship with you. Don't be like the Israelites and turn away from such a wonderful gift.

> Nought can I bring Thee, Lord, for all I owe;
> Yet let my full heart give what it can bestow;
> Myself my gift; let my devotion prove,
> Forgiven greatly, how I greatly love.
> SAMUEL JOHN STONE

Bible Networking
It may be helpful to read Hosea 5:15–6:6 along with this part of Psalm 78, for both passages speak of God's mercy toward his people's unfaithfulness.

Notable Quotable
"[The Israelites] wanted God's blessing and their own way. Yet, [God] was compassionate."
JOHN I. DURHAM

PSALM 78:40-55

40 Oh, how often they rebelled against him in the desert
  and grieved his heart in the wilderness.

41 Again and again they tested God's patience
  and frustrated the Holy One of Israel.

42 They forgot about his power
  and how he rescued them from their enemies.

43 They forgot his miraculous signs in Egypt,
  his wonders on the plain of Zoan.

44 For he turned their rivers into blood,
  so no one could drink from the streams.

45 He sent vast swarms of flies to consume them
  and hordes of frogs to ruin them.

46 He gave their crops to caterpillars;
  their harvest was consumed by locusts.

47 He destroyed their grapevines with hail
  and shattered their sycamores with sleet.

48 He abandoned their cattle to the hail,
  their livestock to bolts of lightning.

49 He loosed on them his fierce anger—
  all his fury, rage, and hostility.
  He dispatched against them
  a band of destroying angels.

50 He turned his anger against them;
  he did not spare the Egyptians' lives
  but handed them over to the plague.

51 He killed the oldest son in each Egyptian family,
  the flower of youth throughout the land of Egypt.

52 But he led his own people like a flock of sheep,
  guiding them safely through the wilderness.

53 He kept them safe so they were not afraid;
  but the sea closed in upon their enemies.

54 He brought them to the border of his holy land,
  to this land of hills he had won for them.

⁵⁵ He drove out the nations before them;
he gave them their inheritance by lot.
He settled the tribes of Israel into their homes.

*A*lma had worked for her company for forty years, watching and helping it grow. She had started as secretary to a department manager, who, largely through her brilliant ideas and work, rose quickly in the company.

Years later the company was sold. The new owners brought in their own management team. Alma's boss was granted a generous early retirement package, but Alma was bumped down to a secretarial pool.

Soon the company was in serious trouble. Alma grieved that the business she had helped to build was sliding so badly, but what could she do? Whenever she made suggestions, she was ignored. The new owners were frantic to find someone who could fix the company, but like the Israelites in Psalm 78, they had forgotten who had helped them in the past.

This sad trend also takes place in many people's relationship with God. God had worked in amazing ways to rescue the Israelites from Egypt, and he has worked mightily in our life as well. But over time the Israelites forgot about God, and we often do, too. We look for a thousand solutions to our problems, all the while ignoring the God who has helped us so much in the past.

Never, never, never forget what God has done.

> *When all thy mercies, O my God,*
> *My rising soul surveys,*
> *Transported with the view, I'm lost*
> *In wonder, love, and praise.*
> JOSEPH ADDISON

Bible Networking
This psalm gives a sampling of the plagues described in Exodus 7–12.

Notable Quotable
"It must have been difficult to forget [God's power]. Such displays of divine power as those which smote Egypt with astonishment must have needed some more than usual effort to blot from the tablets of memory."
CHARLES HADDON SPURGEON

PSALM 78:56-72

⁵⁶ Yet though he did all this for them,
 they continued to test his patience.
They rebelled against the Most High
 and refused to follow his decrees.

⁵⁷ They turned back and were as faithless as their parents
 had been.
 They were as useless as a crooked bow.

⁵⁸ They made God angry by building altars to other gods;
 they made him jealous with their idols.

⁵⁹ When God heard them, he was very angry,
 and he rejected Israel completely.

⁶⁰ Then he abandoned his dwelling at Shiloh,
 the Tabernacle where he had lived among the people.

⁶¹ He allowed the Ark of his might to be captured;
 he surrendered his glory into enemy hands.

⁶² He gave his people over to be butchered by the sword,
 because he was so angry with his own people—his
 special possession.

⁶³ Their young men were killed by fire;
 their young women died before singing their
 wedding songs.

⁶⁴ Their priests were slaughtered,
 and their widows could not mourn their deaths.

⁶⁵ Then the Lord rose up as though waking from sleep,
 like a mighty man aroused from a drunken stupor.

⁶⁶ He routed his enemies
 and sent them to eternal shame.

⁶⁷ But he rejected Joseph's descendants;
 he did not choose the tribe of Ephraim.

⁶⁸ He chose instead the tribe of Judah,
 Mount Zion, which he loved.

⁶⁹ There he built his towering sanctuary,
 as solid and enduring as the earth itself.

70 He chose his servant David,
  calling him from the sheep pens.
71 He took David from tending the ewes and lambs
  and made him the shepherd of Jacob's descendants—
  God's own people, Israel.
72 He cared for them with a true heart
  and led them with skillful hands.

*S*tephen was as good as dead. As an outspoken leader in the early church, he had been targeted by the authorities. Like his Lord, Stephen had been accused of blasphemy on trumped-up charges. And like Jesus, he would be executed.

But Stephen still had a chance to get a few words in, and he might as well say as much as possible in his final speech.

Stephen began with the story of Abraham responding to God, then Isaac, Jacob, and Joseph. He talked about Moses and the opposition Moses got from his own people. Then he went on to talk about Joshua, David, and Solomon. He accused his accusers of resisting God's plans for them. "Name one prophet your ancestors didn't persecute!" (Acts 7:52). Finally he had riled them enough, and they began stoning him to death.

This martyr's last words were much like Psalm 78—long, yes, but also historical and challenging. God has plans for you. Are you going to fight them or follow them?

> Down in the valley with my Savior I would go,
> Where the storms are sweeping and the dark waters
>   flow;
> With His hand to lead me I will never, never fear,
> Danger cannot fright me if my Lord is near.
> WILLIAM O. CUSHING

Bible Networking
Starting at verse 67 of this psalm we see God making choices. These choices are not based on what people deserve but on what God has planned. See 2 Timothy 1:9.

Notable Quotable
"The wonders of God yet excite men but temporarily; and God is too soon forgotten or forsaken in man's fascination with himself."
JOHN I. DURHAM

Psalms 78, 105, and 106 are three psalms that concentrate almost completely on Israel's history, and many other psalms make allusions to events from God's dealings with his people in the past. In fact, you can find more than fifty references to Old Testament stories in the Psalms, not including all the stories in the life of David. Here are a few of them:

◆ *Creation:* Psalm 19:4
The sun lives in the heavens where God placed it.

◆ *God's Covenant with Abraham:* Psalm 105:9
This is the covenant he made with Abraham
and the oath he swore to Isaac.

◆ *Joseph in Egypt:* Psalm 105:21
Joseph was put in charge of all the king's household;
he became ruler over all the king's possessions.

◆ *The Exodus from Egypt:* Psalm 78:13
For he divided the sea before them and led them through!
The water stood up like walls beside them!

◆ *The Miracle at Meribah:* Psalm 81:7
I tested your faith at Meribah, when you complained that there was no water.

◆ *Guidance through the Wilderness:* Psalm 136:16
Give thanks to him who led his people through the wilderness.

◆ *The Victories of the Judges:* Psalm 83:9

Do to them as you did to the
  Midianites
  or as you did to Sisera and
  Jabin at the Kishon River.

Usually you don't consult poets to learn about history. Shakespeare wrote many historical dramas, but he took a few liberties with the facts here and there. Longfellow also wrote narrative poems like *The Song of Hiawatha* and *The Courtship of Miles Standish*, but these tell more "history" than what actually took place.

Usually you don't go to religion to learn about history either. Most world religions deal with philosophy and ethics. Whatever history is included is often legendary or unessential to the beliefs of the religion.

But Christianity (and Judaism before it) is different. As Christians, we see the acts of God in history as an essential part of our faith. We make a mistake if we think that Christianity is based solely on the catechisms and the teachings of Jesus (the Beatitudes, etc.). Christianity is rooted in history. We believe that our life is critically affected by things that happened in the past.

When the apostle Paul began his discourse on Jesus' resurrection in 1 Corinthians 15, he began with history. Jesus Christ was raised from the dead. More than five hundred people were witnesses to the fact, and most of them were still around to verify it when Paul was writing.

Christians believe that when Jesus Christ was born in Bethlehem over two thousand years ago, God became flesh. The crux of the gospel is not simply his teaching, as marvelous as that is, but his death and resurrection for us on a small hill outside Jerusalem about A.D. 30.

Old Testament history shows God at work for his people. The promises God made to his people were fulfilled in historical events. That's why it was important for Jewish parents to keep reminding their children of them through stories and through historical psalms like Psalms 77, 78, 81, and 83. These examples of God's acting on behalf of his people give new generations, including our own, hope that God will continue to act for us. In this way, we see history truly as his story.

~

When Israel out of Egypt came, they
  left the proud oppressor's land
Supported by the great I AM, safe in
  the hollow of his hand.
And all things, as they change, proclaim,
  the Lord eternally the same.
CHARLES WESLEY

June 25

PSALM 79:1-8
A psalm of Asaph.

¹ O God, pagan nations have conquered your land, your
　　special possession.
　They have defiled your holy Temple
　and made Jerusalem a heap of ruins.
² They have left the bodies of your servants
　as food for the birds of heaven.
　The flesh of your godly ones
　has become food for the wild animals.
³ Blood has flowed like water all around Jerusalem;
　no one is left to bury the dead.
⁴ We are mocked by our neighbors,
　an object of scorn and derision to those around us.

⁵ O LORD, how long will you be angry with us? Forever?
　How long will your jealousy burn like fire?
⁶ Pour out your wrath on the nations that refuse to
　　recognize you—
　on kingdoms that do not call upon your name.
⁷ For they have devoured your people Israel,
　making the land a desolate wilderness.
⁸ Oh, do not hold us guilty for our former sins!
　Let your tenderhearted mercies quickly meet our
　　needs,
　for we are brought low to the dust.

He was a bright young man in a changing world. Aurelius Augustinus had studied philosophy and rhetoric and networked with Roman senators. He even served as a consultant to the emperor.

This was the end of the fourth century, and the Christians had taken over the empire. Bishop Ambrose of Milan was arguably the most powerful man on earth, so it was a good career move for young Aurelius to get to know him. He got more than he bargained for. Ambrose had a strong, passionate faith that intrigued Aurelius, who was officially a Christian (nearly everyone was), but he had never really surrendered his soul.

One day Aurelius was wrestling with these issues as he was sitting in a corner of his backyard. He cried out to God in the words of Psalm 79:5-8: "O Lord, how long will you be angry with us? . . . Oh, do not hold us guilty for our former sins!" Then he heard a child's voice saying, "Pick up and read." Taking a Bible, he opened at random to Romans 13:14: "But let the Lord Jesus Christ take control of you, and don't think of ways to indulge your evil desires."

The rest is history. Aurelius Augustinus let Jesus take control of his life. Giving up his political career, Aurelius used his abilities for the church, where he became the author and bishop we now know as Saint Augustine.

> If a sinner such as I
> May to thy great glory live,
> All my actions sanctify,
> All my words and thoughts receive;
> Claim me for thy service, claim
> All I love, and all I am.
> CHARLES WESLEY

Bible Networking
In Psalm 103, David's words provide soothing comfort to those who plead with God not to hold them guilty for their former sins (verse 8).

Notable Quotable
"A bar of iron, worth 1 pound, when wrought into horseshoes, is worth 2 pounds; if made into needles, it is worth 70 pounds; if into penknife blades, it is worth 650 pounds, into springs for watches it is worth 50,000 pounds. The more it is hammered and passed through the fire and polished, the greater its value. Those who suffer most are capable of yielding most."
F. B. MEYER

PSALM 79:9-13

9 Help us, O God of our salvation!
  Help us for the honor of your name.
  Oh, save us and forgive our sins
    for the sake of your name.
10 Why should pagan nations be allowed to scoff,
    asking, "Where is their God?"
  Show us your vengeance against the nations,
    for they have spilled the blood of your servants.
11 Listen to the moaning of the prisoners.
  Demonstrate your great power by saving those
    condemned to die.

12 O Lord, take sevenfold vengeance on our neighbors
    for the scorn they have hurled at you.
13 Then we your people, the sheep of your pasture,
    will thank you forever and ever,
    praising your greatness from generation to
      generation.

Notable Quotable
"We have an irresistible argument when we plead for God's glory" (John 14:13).
F. B. MEYER

*A*s you might guess, Psalm 79 has been a favorite of persecuted Christians. History tells us that various groups of condemned prisoners have sung it on their way to prison or the gallows. In the sixteenth century the Protestant Huguenots sang it in their French version to annoy their Catholic jailers. In the seventeenth century Puritans sang it in their struggles with the Anglican establishment. In the eighteenth century, as the guillotine claimed the lives of many believers in France, these words were heard again.

That begs a question. All of these people asked God, "Demonstrate your great power by saving those condemned to die." Yet most of them died. No last-minute stays of execution. The guillotine fell anyway.

So, did God save those condemned to die? This depends on what you mean by "save." God always has a bigger perspective than we do. We often look for physical protection and safety from our earthly foes. Sometimes God provides that, but he always offers longer-term support. He saves us spiritually and protects us eternally. In a much, much larger sense, we are all "condemned to die," but he rescues those who turn to him.

One final comment on this psalm addresses the topic of vengeance. The psalmist's vengeful attitude may trouble you, but notice that he takes his problem to God. We, too, can take our anger to God and know that he will deal with those who have wronged us.

> He fills the poor with good,
> He gives the sufferers rest;
> The Lord hath judgments for the proud
> And justice for the oppressed.
> ISAAC WATTS

PSALM 80:1-7

For the choir director: A psalm of Asaph, to be sung to the tune "Lilies of the Covenant."

¹ Please listen, O Shepherd of Israel,
   you who lead Israel like a flock.
O God, enthroned above the cherubim,
   display your radiant glory
² to Ephraim, Benjamin, and Manasseh.
Show us your mighty power.
   Come to rescue us!

³ Turn us again to yourself, O God.
   Make your face shine down upon us.
   Only then will we be saved.

⁴ O LORD God Almighty,
   how long will you be angry and reject our prayers?
⁵ You have fed us with sorrow
   and made us drink tears by the bucketful.
⁶ You have made us the scorn of neighboring nations.
   Our enemies treat us as a joke.

⁷ Turn us again to yourself, O God Almighty.
   Make your face shine down upon us.
   Only then will we be saved.

*T*en sons of Jacob were out in the pasture tending sheep when they noticed their younger brother Joseph walking toward them. "Here comes that dreamer!" they said. Joseph was Papa's favorite son, and he kept having dreams about how he would rule over his family.

So the brothers ambushed Joseph and threw him into a pit. But instead of killing him, they decided to sell him to a passing caravan.

This event sent Joseph on a wild ride of ups and downs. Slavery turned into household management; false accusation and imprisonment turned into prison management; and a bold encounter with the king made him second-in-command. A famine led to a reunion with his brothers and father. Through it all, Joseph maintained his faith that God was shepherding him. "God turned into good what you meant for evil," he later told his brothers (Genesis 50:20).

Psalm 80 seems to echo the sentiments of Joseph. In fact, in Hebrew, the term used for Israel in verse 1 is the name Joseph. No doubt Joseph prayed this sort of prayer many times in the pit and in prison.

Just as Joseph and the psalmist kept turning to God and trusting him to turn evil into good, so we, too, must keep looking to God in difficult times.

> Since all that I meet
> Shall work for my good,
> The bitter is sweet,
> The medicine food;
> Though painful at present,
> 'Twill cease before long;
> And then, O how pleasant
> The Conqueror's song.
> JOHN NEWTON

A Word on Words

This psalm seems to have a strong connection to the patriarch Joseph. In the second line of verse 1, "Israel" is literally "Joseph." In verse 2 it mentions three tribes with strong connections to Joseph. Ephraim and Manasseh were the sons of Joseph, and their tribes became prominent in the northern kingdom of Israel. Benjamin was Joseph's only full brother, and his tribe joined Judah in the southern kingdom. So the psalmist may be asking God to rescue both the northern and the southern kingdoms in the same way he rescued Joseph.

Notable Quotable

In her poem "The Measure," Elizabeth Barrett Browning picked up on the imagery of being fed sorrow and tears (verse 5): "Shall we, then, who have issued from the dust, / And there return shall we, who toil for dust, / And wrap our winnings in this dusty life, / Say, No more tears, Lord God! / The measure runneth o'er?"

PSALM 80:8-19

⁸ You brought us from Egypt as though we were a tender
vine;
you drove away the pagan nations and transplanted
us into your land.
⁹ You cleared the ground for us,
and we took root and filled the land.
¹⁰ The mountains were covered with our shade;
the mighty cedars were covered with our branches.
¹¹ We spread our branches west to the Mediterranean Sea,
our limbs east to the Euphrates River.
¹² But now, why have you broken down our walls
so that all who pass may steal our fruit?
¹³ The boar from the forest devours us,
and the wild animals feed on us.

¹⁴ Come back, we beg you, O God Almighty.
Look down from heaven and see our plight.
Watch over and care for this vine
¹⁵   that you yourself have planted,
this son you have raised for yourself.
¹⁶ For we are chopped up and burned by our enemies.
May they perish at the sight of your frown.
¹⁷ Strengthen the man you love,
the son of your choice.
¹⁸ Then we will never forsake you again.
Revive us so we can call on your name once more.

¹⁹ Turn us again to yourself, O Lord God Almighty.
Make your face shine down upon us.
Only then will we be saved.

A certain landowner planted a vineyard, complete with a wall, winepress, and lookout tower. This was a state-of-the-art vineyard. Then he rented it out to certain grape farmers and moved away from the area. After the next grape harvest, the owner sent servants to collect his rent. Well, the farmers beat up the servants and even killed some of them.

The owner sent more servants, and these were also severely mistreated. Finally the owner decided to send his own son. "Surely they will respect my son," he figured. But the farmers seized the son and killed him.

If this story sounds familiar, it's because Jesus told it in Matthew 21:33-41. Scripture often depicts Israel as a vineyard, and Jesus was making a point about the corrupt leadership of the Pharisees and their ilk. Indeed, they were about to kill the "owner's" Son.

Psalm 80 gives us a similar story but from the perspective of the vines themselves. Mistreated by various enemies, they cry out for God to rescue them. We know that this rescue ultimately comes from the Son, Jesus Christ. And, along those lines, there is a great turn of phrase in verse 17. Literally it says: "Let your [strengthening] hand be on the man at your right side, the son of man you have raised up for yourself." With words like that, it's not hard to see Jesus as the answer to the psalmist's prayer.

> It is a thing most wonderful,
> Almost too wonderful to be,
> That God's own Son
> Should come from heaven,
> And die to save a child like me.
> WILLIAM W. HOW

A Word on Words

In Shakespeare's little known play Timon of Athens, a senator describes a rebel leader in words drawn from the King James Version of Psalm 80:13: "Who, like a boar too savage doth root up / His country's peace."

Notable Quotable

"God will come forward when we acknowledge that we have gone back. There is no forth-shining where there is backsliding."
W. GRAHAM SCROGGIE

PSALM 81:1-10
For the choir director: A psalm of Asaph, to be accompanied by a stringed instrument.

¹ Sing praises to God, our strength.
  Sing to the God of Israel.
² Sing! Beat the tambourine.
  Play the sweet lyre and the harp.
³ Sound the trumpet for a sacred feast
  when the moon is new,
  when the moon is full.
⁴ For this is required by the laws of Israel;
  it is a law of the God of Jacob.
⁵ He made it a decree for Israel
  when he attacked Egypt to set us free.

I heard an unknown voice that said,
⁶ "Now I will relieve your shoulder of its burden;
  I will free your hands from their heavy tasks.
⁷ You cried to me in trouble, and I saved you;
  I answered out of the thundercloud.
I tested your faith at Meribah,
  when you complained that there was no water.

Interlude

⁸ "Listen to me, O my people, while I give you stern
      warnings.
  O Israel, if you would only listen!
⁹ You must never have a foreign god;
  you must not bow down before a false god.
¹⁰ For it was I, the LORD your God,
  who rescued you from the land of Egypt.
  Open your mouth wide, and I will fill it with good
      things."

Can you imagine the apostle Paul walking through the streets of Athens? He was to speak before the city's philosophy council that night, and he had to find some way of explaining his faith to them. In most cities he built his case for Jesus' messiahship from the Hebrew Scriptures, because he usually addressed Jews in synagogues. But these Greek philosophers cared little for Jewish beliefs. They were more intrigued by strange mixes of modern ideas and ancient mythologies.

Paul walked past shrines to all sorts of gods, but then he came to a shrine that was different from the rest. "To an Unknown God," the inscription read. Apparently the people built it in case they had failed to honor any other deities. This gave Paul his hook. Some of the Athenian philosophers were already talking about one nameless god who existed above all the others. Paul knew this was his God.

So Paul told them: "You have been worshiping him without knowing who he is, and now I wish to tell you about him" (Acts 17:22-31).

Verse 5 of this psalm speaks of an "unknown voice" that reminds the people of what has been done for them. This "unknown" voice belonged to the Lord, the same God whom Paul spoke about in his address.

We serve this same God, who has done great things for us. Let us gladly receive his offer to relieve us of our heavy tasks (verse 6).

> And that a higher gift than grace
> Should flesh and blood refine,
> God's presence and His very self,
> And essence all-divine.
> JOHN H. NEWMAN

Bible Networking
The New Testament agrees with the Old Testament on the place of music in true worship. See Ephesians 5:19. But notice in Colossians 2:16-17 that feasts or fasts are "merely a shadow" of the real thing, Christ himself.

Notable Quotable
"Happy the child who in thunder-claps detects the Father's voice. There is no fear in love, because perfect love casteth out the fear that hath torment."
F. B. MEYER

PSALM 81:11-16

¹¹ "But no, my people wouldn't listen.
Israel did not want me around.

¹² So I let them follow their blind and stubborn way,
living according to their own desires.

¹³ But oh, that my people would listen to me!
Oh, that Israel would follow me, walking in my
paths!

¹⁴ How quickly I would then subdue their enemies!
How soon my hands would be upon their foes!

¹⁵ Those who hate the LORD would cringe before him;
their desolation would last forever.

¹⁶ But I would feed you with the best of foods.
I would satisfy you with wild honey from the rock."

*T*he two college roommates went their separate ways after graduation, but they kept in touch. Kristen became a successful actress, while Sandy went into business. When Kristen was touring in a show that came through Sandy's city, she called her old friend and invited her to come and see it on a particular Friday. Both looked forward to the reunion.

That Friday night Sandy got to the theater just before curtain time. All she could afford was a rear balcony seat, but she enjoyed the play from that lofty perch. Meanwhile, Kristen looked out from the stage and saw an empty seat in the front row—the seat she had reserved for Sandy.

Only later did they realize the mix-up. Kristen wanted to treat her friend to the choicest of seats, but Sandy didn't know enough to ask for her reserved ticket.

In Psalm 81 the Lord offers us front-row seats, luxury accommodations. "I would feed you with the best of foods." But too often we settle for seats in the balcony. That's the Lord's complaint about the Israelites in this psalm. He wants to help them, to satisfy them, if only they would listen and follow.

He wants the same for you. Come up close, get a better view of the Lord's goodness. You don't know what you're missing.

> I've a message full of love, hallelujah!
> A message, O my friend, for you;
> 'Tis a message from above, hallelujah!
> Jesus said it, and I know its true:
> Look and live!
> WILLIAM A. OGDEN

Bible Networking
Verse 12 of this psalm speaks of the Israelites following their own desires. Read 2 Peter 1:4 and learn of God's promise to help us escape the decadence that comes from evil desires.

Notable Quotable
"He gives the best, and brings sweetness out of that which is harsh, forbidding, and wholly unpromising."
DEREK KIDNER

PSALM 82
A psalm of Asaph.

¹ God presides over heaven's court;
    he pronounces judgment on the judges:
² "How long will you judges hand down unjust
        decisions?
    How long will you shower special favors on the
        wicked?   *Interlude*

³ "Give fair judgment to the poor and the orphan;
    uphold the rights of the oppressed and the destitute.
⁴ Rescue the poor and helpless;
    deliver them from the grasp of evil people.
⁵ But these oppressors know nothing;
    they are so ignorant!
And because they are in darkness,
    the whole world is shaken to the core.
⁶ I say, 'You are gods
    and children of the Most High.
⁷ But in death you are mere men.
    You will fall as any prince,
    for all must die.' "

⁸ Rise up, O God, and judge the earth,
    for all the nations belong to you.

*I*n Jesus' ongoing struggle with the religious leaders of his day, he nearly got himself stoned to death for blasphemy, claiming to be God. In his defense, Jesus quoted Psalm 82:6, in which God says to the leaders of the people, "You are gods." It was a masterful move, refuting his enemies and getting himself off on a technicality. But there's a powerful point in all this wordplay. Don't miss it.

God puts leaders in a godlike position, giving them authority and allowing them to receive respect from the people. But do they use this authority in a godlike way? Do they act with justice and mercy? Do they care for the poor as God does?

The leaders of Jesus' day did not fulfill their godlike responsibilities—they were unjust and uncaring toward the poor. By contrast, Jesus did many godlike things. "For which one of these good deeds are you killing me?" he taunted (John 10:32). According to Psalm 82, he had a right to be called God, and they had no right to be called leaders.

This takes nothing away from the true divinity of Jesus, but it does make us think about the nature of leadership. Pray for your leaders, that they would exercise their authority in godlike ways. And consider your own leadership: Are you just and merciful toward those you influence?

> *Arm me with jealous care,*
> *As in thy sight to live;*
> *And O thy servant, Lord, prepare*
> *A strict account to give!*
> CHARLES WESLEY

Fascinating Fact
A woman bowed before King Francis I of France, begging him for justice. He said to her, "I owe you justice. If you beg for anything, beg for mercy."

Notable Quotable
"Rulers must understand that they are not placed over stocks and stones, nor over swine and dogs, but over the congregation of God; they must therefore be afraid of acting against God himself when they act unjustly."
MARTIN LUTHER

PSALM 83:1-8
A psalm of Asaph. A song.

[1] O God, don't sit idly by,
  silent and inactive!
[2] Don't you hear the tumult of your enemies?
  Don't you see what your arrogant enemies are doing?
[3] They devise crafty schemes against your people,
  laying plans against your precious ones.
[4] "Come," they say, "let us wipe out Israel as a nation.
  We will destroy the very memory of its existence."
[5] This was their unanimous decision.
They signed a treaty as allies against you—
[6] these Edomites and Ishmaelites,
  Moabites and Hagrites,
[7] Gebalites, Ammonites, and Amalekites,
  and people from Philistia and Tyre.
[8] Assyria has joined them, too,
  and is allied with the descendants of Lot.   *Interlude*

*I*f anyone knew about the kinds of troubles Psalm 83 talks about, it was King Ahaz. Two nations to the north were ganging up against his people and threatening to wipe out the little nation of Judah unless drastic measures were taken. At least that's what King Ahaz thought.

But the prophet Isaiah knew better. The Lord told Isaiah, "Tell him to stop worrying" (Isaiah 7:4). This threat wouldn't amount to anything. "Do not be afraid that some plan conceived behind closed doors will be the end of you. Do not fear anything except the Lord Almighty. . . . If you fear him, you need fear nothing else" (Isaiah 8:12-13).

Unfortunately, Ahaz wouldn't listen. Instead of turning to the Lord in repentance, he turned to the mighty nation of Assyria to rescue him from his enemies. Assyria brought its brutal war machine into the area and defeated Judah's foes, but then it turned on Judah, too (see also Psalm 83:8). Jerusalem was spared only by God's miraculous intervention in response to the faith of Ahaz's godly son, Hezekiah.

Many Christians these days feel as if everyone is conspiring against them, that there's an all-out assault against God's people. We fear the government, the media, and the culture in general—and Psalm 83 can fan those fears. But don't forget the challenge of Isaiah: "Do not fear anything except the Lord Almighty. . . . If you fear him, you need fear nothing else."

> *Fear Him, ye saints, and you will then*
> *Have nothing else to fear;*
> *Make you His service your delight,*
> *Your wants shall be His care.*
> NAHUM TATE

Fascinating Fact
Benedict, the seventh-century monk who founded the Benedictine Rule, spent his last days paralyzed, having the Psalms read to him. The last one he heard was Psalm 83.

PSALM 83:9-16

⁹ Do to them as you did to the Midianites
    or as you did to Sisera and Jabin at the Kishon River.
¹⁰ They were destroyed at Endor,
    and their decaying corpses fertilized the soil.
¹¹ Let their mighty nobles die as Oreb and Zeeb did.
    Let all their princes die like Zebah and Zalmunna,
¹² for they said, "Let us seize for our own use
    these pasturelands of God!"

¹³ O my God, blow them away like whirling dust,
    like chaff before the wind!
¹⁴ As a fire roars through a forest
    and as a flame sets mountains ablaze,
¹⁵ chase them with your fierce storms;
    terrify them with your tempests.
¹⁶ Utterly disgrace them
    until they submit to your name, O LORD.

*I*t must have seemed like a crazy plan. The Midianites had amassed a huge army, far outnumbering the Israelites. So what did General Gideon do? He reduced his force of thirty thousand to ten thousand. And then he reduced it even further to three hundred!

Surely his soldiers must have been thinking, *Is Gideon nuts?*

The fact is that the Lord was calling the shots. He didn't want anyone to boast of their own might, so he saved his people in his own way.

Gideon gave each man a horn and a clay jar with a torch in it. During the night the Israelite soldiers surrounded the Midianite camp and then suddenly blew their horns and broke the jars. The Midianites were terrified and began fighting each other and running away. So the warriors of this huge Midianite force were defeated (Judges 7:1-22).

The last part of Psalm 83 recalls this defeat of the Midianites. Appropriately, Gideon is not mentioned. It wasn't his battle—it was the Lord's.

When you feel surrounded by enemies and totally outnumbered, turn to the Lord for help. He is more than able to save you—though his ways may not make sense to you. As Paul said, "We don't wage war with human plans and methods. We use God's mighty weapons" (2 Corinthians 10:3-4).

> *Stand up, stand up for Jesus,*
> *The trumpet call obey;*
> *Forth to the mighty conflict,*
> *In this His glorious day.*
> *"Ye that are men now serve Him,"*
> *Against unnumbered foes;*
> *Let courage rise with danger,*
> *And strength to strength oppose.*
> GEORGE DUFFIELD

A Word on Words

In verse 12 the enemy is coveting the pastureland. The word here is the same as the one used for the "green pastures" of Psalm 23.

At least six psalms are known as community laments (Psalms 44, 74, 79, 80, 83, and 137), and several others are similar to them. Written in times of national crisis, these psalms call for God to intervene on behalf of the nation.

Here are a few verses from psalms of communal lament:

◆ *Psalm 44:25*
We collapse in the dust,
lying face down in the dirt.

◆ *Psalm 74:9*
We see no miraculous signs
as evidence that you will save us.
All the prophets are gone;
no one can tell us when it will end.

◆ *Psalm 79:9*
Help us, O God of our salvation!
Help us for the honor of your name.
Oh, save us and forgive our sins
for the sake of your name.

◆ *Psalm 80:19*
Turn us again to yourself,
O LORD God Almighty.
Make your face shine down upon us.
Only then will we be saved.

◆ *Psalm 90:16*
Let us see your miracles again;
let our children see your glory at work.

Sometimes we think of the Psalms as expressing individual devotion to God, like "the Lord is my shepherd" (Psalm 23:1). But the Psalms were meant to be the hymnal for the entire nation. At times a godly king like Josiah or Hezekiah or leaders like Ezra or Nehemiah would call the people together for days of fasting, repentance, and seeking God, so there were also communal psalms of lament written for such times.

The year 1857 was not a good one for Americans. A financial crash had shaken the money centers of the world. Industry stood still. Wall Street floundered. The slavery issue divided North and South, Irish and German immigration flooded the labor markets, and interest in religion was at its lowest point in decades. Then a layman, Jeremiah Lanphier, began a noonday prayer meeting in New York City. At first only a few attended. But soon the idea spread to other cities. Pastors in Pittsburgh and Cincinnati called for a day of prayer, fasting, and humbling themselves before the Lord. Then came national revival. Within the next two years between five hundred thousand and one million people were converted to Christ.

How do you pray for your country? Do you ask God to intervene like the psalmists prayed? Are you calling people to repentance as Jeremiah Lanphier did in America in 1857? America has been very blessed and yet has wandered so far away. Are you praying for America to return to God?

∾

Though our sins, our hearts confounding,
Long and loud for vengeance call,
You have mercy more abounding;
Jesus' blood can cleanse them all.
God of nations in the skies,
Now for our deliverance rise.
CONGREGATIONAL COLLECTION

Selah

PSALM 84:1-7

¹ How lovely is your dwelling place,
   O LORD Almighty.
² I long, yes, I faint with longing
   to enter the courts of the LORD.
With my whole being, body and soul,
   I will shout joyfully to the living God.
³ Even the sparrow finds a home there,
   and the swallow builds her nest
   and raises her young—
   at a place near your altar,
   O LORD Almighty, my King and my God!
⁴ How happy are those who can live in your house,
   always singing your praises.   *Interlude*

⁵ Happy are those who are strong in the LORD,
   who set their minds on a pilgrimage to Jerusalem.
⁶ When they walk through the Valley of Weeping,
   it will become a place of refreshing springs,
   where pools of blessing collect after the rains!
⁷ They will continue to grow stronger,
   and each of them will appear before God in
      Jerusalem.

Verse 3 of this psalm speaks of a sparrow finding shelter in the presence of God in the Temple. Jesus spoke of God watching over sparrows as well.

Jesus warned his disciples to expect to suffer persecution for following him, but he told them not to fear those who could kill their body but who couldn't touch their soul (Matthew 10:28-31). Then he added a rather tender assurance: Not a single sparrow falls to the ground without the Father knowing it, and he cares for his people far more than any sparrow.

Sparrows were a dime a dozen in Israel. Everywhere you looked these seemingly worthless birds were flying around. But God takes note of them all.

If God cares so much for sparrows, won't he care for you, too? You are worth more to God than a whole flock of those birds.

Jesus wasn't saying that the sparrows would never fall, and he wasn't saying that his followers would never suffer physical harm. But he was saying that God watches over us and cares for us. Sometimes God rescues his people from their predicaments, and sometimes he allows them to suffer and even die—but he never lets them out of his sight. They remain in his presence eternally.

Psalm 84 shows us people rejoicing in God's presence at the Temple, where even the birds nested peacefully. No matter what kind of valley we may have to walk through, we can find a restful nest in God's presence.

> *Happy birds that sing and fly*
> *Round the altars, O Most High.*
> *Happier souls that find a rest*
> *In their heavenly Father's breast.*
> HENRY F. LYTE

Bible Networking
In verse 7 spiritual growth is closely connected with seeing and knowing God himself. See 2 Corinthians 3:18 for a similar insight.

Notable Quotable
"Pain, sorrow, and disappointment are transmutable: we may climb the rainbow through the rain. Our pilgrimage should be a continuous triumph in and over circumstances."
W. GRAHAM SCROGGIE

PSALM 84:8-12

[8] O LORD God Almighty, hear my prayer.
  Listen, O God of Israel.   *Interlude*

[9] O God, look with favor upon the king, our protector!
  Have mercy on the one you have anointed.

[10] A single day in your courts
  is better than a thousand anywhere else!
I would rather be a gatekeeper in the house of my God
  than live the good life in the homes of the wicked.
[11] For the LORD God is our light and protector.
  He gives us grace and glory.
No good thing will the LORD withhold
  from those who do what is right.
[12] O LORD Almighty,
  happy are those who trust in you.

*H*istory is full of examples of Christians who gave up lucrative careers to serve God full-time, such as Matthew, the tax collector; Augustine, the promising politician; and Martin Luther, who chose not to pursue law but to become a priest.

When Thomas Aquinas, a respected doctor of philosophy, chose to become a monk, he explained his decision by citing Psalm 84:10: "I would rather be a gatekeeper in the house of my God than live the good life in the homes of the wicked."

A gatekeeper was a servant at the Temple. For anyone of status, it would seem to be a major step down. Yet the psalmist considers it an important career move. Serving in God's house is better than being served anywhere else, for God will see that your greatest needs are taken care of.

This is what made Francis of Assisi reject a retailing career, what made track star Eric Liddell become a missionary, and what made David Livingstone take his medical training to the heart of Africa. They were gatekeepers, all of them, serving God by letting people into his presence. Think of all the people who have been ushered into God's presence with the help of such servants!

Not everyone is called to full-time service in the church, but we should all be doing what God has called us to. No matter what else you are doing in life, find a way to be one of God's gatekeepers. It's a great job, and the benefits are tremendous!

> To serve the present age,
> My calling to fulfill;
> O may it all my powers engage
> To do my Master's will!
> CHARLES WESLEY

Bible Networking
See the New Testament job description for a gatekeeper in Matthew 28:19-20.

Notable Quotable
"These poets [the psalmists] knew far less reason than we for loving God. They did not know that He offered them eternal joy; still less that He would die to win it for them. Yet they express a longing for Him, for His mere presence. . . . They long to live all their days in the Temple. . . . Only there can they be at ease, like a bird in the nest (84:3). One day of these 'pleasures' is better than a lifetime spent elsewhere (84:10)."
C. S. LEWIS

PSALM 85:1-7
For the choir director: A psalm of the descendants of Korah.

¹ LORD, you have poured out amazing blessings on your
    land!
    You have restored the fortunes of Israel.
² You have forgiven the guilt of your people—
    yes, you have covered all their sins.   *Interlude*

³ You have withdrawn your fury.
    You have ended your blazing anger.
⁴ Now turn to us again, O God of our salvation.
    Put aside your anger against us.
⁵ Will you be angry with us always?
    Will you prolong your wrath to distant generations?
⁶ Won't you revive us again,
    so your people can rejoice in you?
⁷ Show us your unfailing love, O LORD,
    and grant us your salvation.

England had been in a nasty civil war for several decades when Oliver Cromwell took charge in 1653. As the head of the army, he seized power from Parliament and the king and ushered in a period of relative calm. Cromwell was a Puritan who emphasized personal faith over church establishment. He also loved the Psalms, often quoting them in public and urging others to read them.

In 1656 he opened his second parliamentary session by reading Psalm 85. He went on to talk about his vision for an England where God would be glorified. After the blight of civil war, the people were eager to think that God's anger would be "put aside" and their fortunes restored.

We must be very careful about applying God's promises to Israel to any modern nation. England had a time of peace during Cromwell's reign, but there was more war ahead. England was not God's special representative nation on earth any more than the United States is now. But we do find certain universal truths in God's promises to Israel: Whenever God's people—in any nation—humble themselves, repent, and worship God as it says in 2 Chronicles 7:14, their lives are changed, and that often has a ripple effect on the society around them.

> Many mighty men are lost,
> Daring not to stand,
> Who for God had been a host
> By joining Daniel's band.
> Dare to be a Daniel,
> Dare to stand alone!
> Dare to have a purpose firm;
> Dare to make it known.
> PHILIP P. BLISS

Bible Networking
When people repent of their sin, God's anger is short-lived. See also Psalm 30:5.

Notable Quotable
"O God, when my faith gets overladen with dust, blow it clean with the wind of your Spirit. When my habits of obedience get stiff and rusty, anoint them with the oil of your Spirit. Restore the enthusiasm of my first love for you."
EUGENE PETERSON

PSALM 85:8-13

⁸ I listen carefully to what God the LORD is saying,
  for he speaks peace to his people, his faithful ones.
  But let them not return to their foolish ways.
⁹ Surely his salvation is near to those who honor him;
  our land will be filled with his glory.

¹⁰ Unfailing love and truth have met together.
  Righteousness and peace have kissed!
¹¹ Truth springs up from the earth,
  and righteousness smiles down from heaven.
¹² Yes, the LORD pours down his blessings.
  Our land will yield its bountiful crops.
¹³ Righteousness goes as a herald before him,
  preparing the way for his steps.

*T*he time of captivity had ended for the Israelites, and many had returned to their homeland from Babylon. Nehemiah had masterminded the rebuilding of the wall of Jerusalem, and it was time for a worship service.

Ezra the priest brought out the scroll of God's law and read it from early morning until noon. Apparently these words were new to many of the people.

Ezra praised the Lord, and the people shouted, "Amen!" as they lifted their hands and bowed to the ground. Then the assistant priests began circulating among the people, explaining what the law said. As the people recognized how far they had strayed from God's ways, they began to weep.

But Nehemiah and Ezra tried to cheer up the people by telling them, "The joy of the Lord is your strength!" And then people ate, drank, and had fun (Nehemiah 8:1-12).

Psalm 85 also shows us a nation in transition. As in the days of Ezra, disaster was turning to success, and the people were praising God for it. Like the worshipers in Nehemiah 8, they recognized their past sins but trusted God for forgiveness and looked forward to God's favor in the days to come. Above all, they "listened carefully" to what God said—that's a prescription for revival in any nation.

> O praise ye the Lord!
> Praise Him upon the earth,
> In tuneful accord, ye sons of new birth;
> Praise Him who hath brought you
> His grace from above;
> Praise Him who hath taught you
> To sing of His love.
> HENRY W. BAKER

A Word on Words

Don't overlook the opposites in verse 10. Mercy and truth don't always go together easily. Neither do righteousness and peace. Obviously God is doing some major matchmaking.

Bible Networking

This psalm is speaking from the context of Israel's deliverance from Babylon. Another reference to this great event is Haggai 2:7-9.

PSALM 86:1-10
A prayer of David.

1 Bend down, O LORD, and hear my prayer;
    answer me, for I need your help.
2 Protect me, for I am devoted to you.
    Save me, for I serve you and trust you.
    You are my God.
3 Be merciful, O Lord,
    for I am calling on you constantly.
4 Give me happiness, O Lord,
    for my life depends on you.
5 O Lord, you are so good, so ready to forgive,
    so full of unfailing love for all who ask your aid.
6 Listen closely to my prayer, O LORD;
    hear my urgent cry.
7 I will call to you whenever trouble strikes,
    and you will answer me.

8 Nowhere among the pagan gods is there a god like you,
        O Lord.
    There are no other miracles like yours.
9 All the nations—and you made each one—
    will come and bow before you, Lord;
    they will praise your great and holy name.
10 For you are great and perform great miracles.
    You alone are God.

*I*n most versions of the Bible, the word *Lord* appears sometimes in small capital letters (LORD). Pay attention to this because it tells you something about the original Hebrew.

Whenever you see the word LORD, it refers to God's personal name *(YHWH)*, which some think was originally pronounced "Yahweh." This name became so holy to devout Jews that they refused to speak it. When they came across it in a Scripture reading, they would replace it with the word *Adonai*, which is usually written as "Lord" in English. This Hebrew word means "Master" or "Lord."

Here in Psalm 86 we see two instances (verses 1 and 6) of God's personal name, "LORD," but seven other times in this psalm we see the name "Lord," or *Adonai*. By doing this, David is not simply being repetitive, like some Christians who say the word *Lord* in their prayers over and over. Instead, David is most likely addressing God as a servant addresses his master. "Yes, Master, I will do what you say. Be merciful to me, Master." David takes a humble stance, not declaring his own innocence, demanding God's help, or arguing why God should trounce his enemies (as David does elsewhere).

Let us learn from David's prayer in this psalm and come before God as a servant comes before his master.

> O use me, Lord, use even me,
> Just as Thou wilt, and when, and where;
> Until Thy blessed face I see,
> Thy rest, Thy joy, Thy glory share.
> FRANCES R. HAVERGAL

Fascinating Fact
This psalm is a mosaic of fragments from about twenty other psalms. There are also thoughts from Exodus, Deuteronomy, Isaiah, and Jeremiah.

Notable Quotable
"You have fallen a hundred times and are ashamed to come to God again; it seems too much to expect that He will receive you again. But He will, for He is ready to forgive."
F. B. MEYER

PSALM 86:11-17

[11] Teach me your ways, O LORD,
    that I may live according to your truth!
Grant me purity of heart,
    that I may honor you.
[12] With all my heart I will praise you, O Lord my God.
    I will give glory to your name forever,
[13] for your love for me is very great.
    You have rescued me from the depths of death!

[14] O God, insolent people rise up against me;
    violent people are trying to kill me.
    And you mean nothing to them.
[15] But you, O Lord, are a merciful and gracious God,
    slow to get angry,
    full of unfailing love and truth.
[16] Look down and have mercy on me.
    Give strength to your servant;
    yes, save me, for I am your servant.
[17] Send me a sign of your favor.
    Then those who hate me will be put to shame,
    for you, O LORD, help and comfort me.

*H*ave you ever seen the movie or the play *The Miracle Worker*? Billed as "the Helen Keller story," it was also the Anne Sullivan story. Sullivan was the teacher who helped work the miracle in Helen Keller.

Helen Keller was blind and deaf from an early childhood disease. Her parents hired Anne Sullivan to teach the girl. But how do you teach language to someone who can't see and hear? You can press letter signs into her hands, but how do you teach her that things have names that can be spelled out? And how can you even get this wild child to sit still long enough to learn?

With patience and lots of hard work.

Touchingly, *The Miracle Worker* shows the struggle of teacher and student—establishing discipline, earning trust, going through the motions again and again—until finally the "eureka" moment arrives. "Waa! Waa!" Helen says as her hands splash the cold water. In her babylike speech, she says the name of this thing. The teacher has finally gotten through to her.

"Teach me your ways, O Lord," David prays in this psalm. And sometimes we must seem as blind and deaf as Helen Keller. We close our eyes to God's work and don't want to hear his Word. But, fortunately, we have a great teacher. With patience and lots of hard work, God gets through to us, teaching us to live according to his truth.

Thank God for teachers, and praise him for being a patient teacher to us.

> *Teach me thy way, O Lord, teach me thy way!*
> *Thy guiding grace afford—teach me thy way!*
> *Help me to walk aright, more by faith, less by sight;*
> *Lead me with heavenly light, teach me thy way!*
> B. MANSELL RAMSEY

Bible Networking

The King James Version more literally translates the second half of verse 11, "unite my heart to fear thy name." In other words, David is asking God to change the situation that Paul bemoans in Romans 7:15, where he says that he really wants to do right but doesn't do it.

Notable Quotable

In Alfred Lord Tennyson's poem "Rizpah," one of the characters refers to Psalm 86:15:

Sin? O yes we are sinners, I know let all that be,
And read me a Bible verse of the Lord's goodwill toward men.
"Full of compassion and mercy, the Lord," let me hear it again;
"Full of compassion and mercy long suffering." Yes, O yes!
For the lawyer is born but to murder, the Saviour lives but to bless.

PSALM 87
A psalm of the descendants of Korah. A song.

¹ On the holy mountain stands the city founded by the
  LORD.
² He loves the city of Jerusalem
  more than any other city in Israel.
³ O city of God,
  what glorious things are said of you!   *Interlude*

⁴ I will record Egypt and Babylon among those who
  know me—
  also Philistia and Tyre, and even distant Ethiopia.
  They have all become citizens of Jerusalem!
⁵ And it will be said of Jerusalem,
  "Everyone has become a citizen here."
  And the Most High will personally bless this city.
⁶ When the LORD registers the nations,
  he will say, "This one has become a citizen of
  Jerusalem."   *Interlude*

⁷ At all the festivals, the people will sing,
  "The source of my life is in Jerusalem!"

*S*ome historians are calling the 1900s the "American Century." To be sure, the United States has spread its influence around the globe through military action, industry, and even the media. This has helped to make English the world's common language, and in a way people all over the earth are becoming citizens of America, whether officially or not.

In a way that's the image we find in Psalm 87. The psalmist looks forward to a day when distant nations will come to know the Lord and be considered citizens of Jerusalem. What begins as a nationalistic focus on Israel's capital city becomes an open invitation, welcoming anyone who wants to know the Lord of this city.

This fantasy is essentially fulfilled in Christianity. Christians have always maintained that they worship the God of Israel, and through the spread of the gospel, Gentiles from around the globe have come to worship a Jewish carpenter and study the Hebrew Scriptures (the Old Testament). Jerusalem stands at the center of the Christian faith as the site of Jesus' death and resurrection. In this way it has become "the source of [our] life" (verse 7), and we look forward to God's presence with us in a "new Jerusalem" (Revelation 21). Paul says that Christians have been adopted into the Jewish family, so you might say that all believers are citizens of Jerusalem.

> *With stately towers and bulwarks strong, unrivaled and alone,*
> *Loved theme of many a sacred song, God's holy city shone.*
> *So fair was Zion's chosen seat, the glory of all lands.*
> *Yet, fairer, and in strength complete, the Christian church still stands.*
> ANONYMOUS

Bible Networking
For another beautiful picture of Jerusalem read Isaiah 60.

Notable Quotable
Saint Bernard said of the monastery of Clairvaux: "Glorious things are said of it, because the glorious and wonderful God works great wonders within it!" David says the same of Jerusalem in Psalm 87.

PSALM 88:1-10

For the choir director: A psalm of the descendants of Korah, to be sung to the tune
"The Suffering of Affliction." A psalm of Heman the Ezrahite. A song.

¹ O LORD, God of my salvation,
    I have cried out to you day and night.
² Now hear my prayer;
    listen to my cry.
³ For my life is full of troubles,
    and death draws near.
⁴ I have been dismissed as one who is dead,
    like a strong man with no strength left.
⁵ They have abandoned me to death,
    and I am as good as dead.
I am forgotten,
    cut off from your care.
⁶ You have thrust me down to the lowest pit,
    into the darkest depths.
⁷ Your anger lies heavy on me;
    wave after wave engulfs me.   *Interlude*

⁸ You have caused my friends to loathe me;
    you have sent them all away.
I am in a trap with no way of escape.
⁹   My eyes are blinded by my tears.
Each day I beg for your help, O LORD;
    I lift my pleading hands to you for mercy.
¹⁰ Of what use to the dead are your miracles?
    Do the dead get up and praise you?   *Interlude*

God sent Jonah to the Assyrian capital of Nineveh, but the prophet took a boat in the opposite direction. When a nasty storm threatened to sink the ship, Jonah knew he was the reason. He told the crew to throw him overboard, and as soon as he hit the waves, the storm let up. But Jonah's storm was just beginning because a big fish came along and swallowed him whole.

There in the fish's belly the prophet prayed. His prayer was a lot like Psalm 88, and no wonder. He certainly felt abandoned and forgotten, close to death in a dark place, engulfed by "wave after wave." He begged for God's help and promised to honor him.

The Lord heard Jonah's prayer and caused the fish to get sick, heaving Jonah up on shore. Then Jonah headed to Nineveh to preach God's message to the people there.

Maybe you feel like Heman, who wrote Psalm 88. You're in a bad way, and you don't know why. Or maybe, like Jonah, you know exactly why, and you feel terrible about it. Can God forgive you? Will he restore you?

The New Testament says that Jonah is a picture of Jesus, who also spent three days in a dark place (Matthew 12:40). God's power raised Jesus from the dead, and he can work that same power in your life as well.

> Christian brothers, shout and sing,
> Death has lost its ancient sting!
> Christ, the crucified before,
> Is alive forever more!
> Grave, where is thy vict'ry now?
> See the light upon His brow,
> Empty, see, the stony bed;
> Christ is risen from the dead!
> THOMAS O. CHISHOLM

Psalm at a Glance

This is the most mournful of all the plaintive psalms. There seems to be no mention of hope in the entire psalm.

Bible Networking

In verse 6 the psalmist speaks of being thrust into the "lowest pit." Jesus was sent to the grave as well, and we, too, are called to die to our old, sinful self. In doing this, however, we prepare ourself to be raised to new life, just as Christ was raised from the dead. Read Philippians 3:10-11.

PSALM 88:11-18

¹¹ Can those in the grave declare your unfailing love?
In the place of destruction, can they proclaim your
faithfulness?
¹² Can the darkness speak of your miracles?
Can anyone in the land of forgetfulness talk about
your righteousness?

¹³ O LORD, I cry out to you.
I will keep on pleading day by day.
¹⁴ O LORD, why do you reject me?
Why do you turn your face away from me?
¹⁵ I have been sickly and close to death since my youth.
I stand helpless and desperate before your terrors.
¹⁶ Your fierce anger has overwhelmed me.
Your terrors have cut me off.
¹⁷ They swirl around me like floodwaters all day long.
They have encircled me completely.
¹⁸ You have taken away my companions and loved ones;
only darkness remains.

Things did not look good for King Hezekiah. He had become very ill, and the prophet Isaiah told him, "Set your affairs in order, for you are going to die" (Isaiah 38:1).

Hezekiah's response is heartbreaking. He "turned his face to the wall" and cried out to God, "Remember, O Lord, how I have always tried to be faithful to you. . . ." After this "he broke down and wept bitterly" (Isaiah 38:2-3).

Hezekiah's sadness resembles the sadness of Psalm 88. Like Hezekiah, the psalmist felt close to death. But unlike Hezekiah, the psalmist ends his words with "darkness." Hezekiah got a reprieve instead. After hearing the king's prayer, God sent another message: "I will add fifteen years to your life" (Isaiah 38:5). When Hezekiah recovered, he composed a song of thanks and praise.

At the end of Hezekiah's song, he rejoices: "You have rescued me from death and have forgiven all my sins. . . . Think of it—the Lord has healed me! I will sing his praises with instruments every day of my life in the Temple of the Lord" (Isaiah 38:17-20).

Like Hezekiah and the psalmist, you may be feeling overwhelmed by your present situation. Go ahead and mourn with Psalm 88, but don't stay in the pit. Pray to God, who is more than able to help you, enabling you to climb with Hezekiah into a song of thanksgiving and praise.

> I'll praise Him while He lends me breath;
> And when my voice is lost in death,
> Praise shall employ my nobler powers;
> My days of praise shall ne'er be past,
> While life, and thought, and being last,
> Or immortality endures.
> ISAAC WATTS

Bible Networking
Jesus knew the grief that comes with suffering. Read Isaiah 53:3; Matthew 26:38; Mark 14:33-34; and Luke 22:44.

Notable Quotable
William Wordsworth quotes Psalm 88 in his poem "The Excursion":

Mournful, deep and slow
The cadence, as of psalms—a funeral dirge!
We listened, looking down upon the hut,
But seeing no one; meanwhile from below
The strain continued, spiritual as before;
But now distinctly could I recognize
These words: "Shall in the grave thy love be known,
In death thy faithfulness?"

PSALM 89:1-7
A psalm of Ethan the Ezrahite.

¹ I will sing of the tender mercies of the LORD forever!
    Young and old will hear of your faithfulness.
² Your unfailing love will last forever.
    Your faithfulness is as enduring as the heavens.

³ The LORD said, "I have made a solemn agreement with
    David, my chosen servant.
    I have sworn this oath to him:
⁴ 'I will establish your descendants as kings forever;
    they will sit on your throne from now until eternity.' "

Interlude

⁵ All heaven will praise your miracles, LORD;
    myriads of angels will praise you for your
    faithfulness.
⁶ For who in all of heaven can compare with the LORD?
    What mightiest angel is anything like the LORD?
⁷ The highest angelic powers stand in awe of God.
    He is far more awesome than those who surround
    his throne.

When the Ark of God was carried to the Tabernacle in Jerusalem, three men were given the honor of directing the choir for the festivities: Asaph, who wrote many psalms; Heman, who wrote Psalm 88; and Ethan, who wrote today's psalm (see also 1 Chronicles 15–16).

Ethan takes quite a different approach from his colleague Heman when it comes to writing psalms. In Psalm 88 Heman holds a dour view of life—basically, "Life's a mess and then you die" (see verse 3). But Psalm 89 starts by singing the mercies of God. We get three-quarters of the way through Ethan's song before we realize anything's wrong.

Do you know people like that? Such people have learned a crucial truth: God is bigger than our problems. Obviously Ethan knew that well.

"Oh, the kingdom of Israel is falling apart," Ethan says, "but God is good. His unfailing love will last forever." Ethan's name means "steady, rock-solid," and you can tell that his perspective keeps him steady through the storms of life. No matter what happens, he sees God's great mercy, and he sings about it.

You should also know that Ethan later changed his name to Jeduthun, meaning "the Lord is steady." Because of the Lord's steadiness, we can live with a solid confidence, whatever our circumstances might be.

> Be still, my soul! thy God doth undertake
> To guide the future as he has the past.
> Thy hope, thy confidence let nothing shake;
> All now mysterious shall be bright at last.
> Be still, my soul! the waves and winds still know
> His voice who ruled them while he dwelt below.
> KATHARINA VON SCHLEGEL

Bible Networking
Read God's own words on mercy in Isaiah 55:3.

Notable Quotable
"Mercy is a structure never done, layer on layer, story on story, tier on tier. God's faithfulness is sure as the heavens."
F. B. MEYER

PSALM 89:8-18

⁸ O Lord God Almighty!

Where is there anyone as mighty as you, Lord?

Faithfulness is your very character.

⁹ You are the one who rules the oceans.

When their waves rise in fearful storms, you subdue
them.

¹⁰ You are the one who crushed the great sea monster.

You scattered your enemies with your mighty arm.

¹¹ The heavens are yours, and the earth is yours;

everything in the world is yours—you created it all.

¹² You created north and south.

Mount Tabor and Mount Hermon praise your name.

¹³ Powerful is your arm!

Strong is your hand!

Your right hand is lifted high in glorious strength.

¹⁴ Your throne is founded on two strong

pillars—righteousness and justice.

Unfailing love and truth walk before you as
attendants.

¹⁵ Happy are those who hear the joyful call to worship,

for they will walk in the light of your presence, Lord.

¹⁶ They rejoice all day long in your wonderful reputation.

They exult in your righteousness.

¹⁷ You are their glorious strength.

Our power is based on your favor.

¹⁸ Yes, our protection comes from the Lord,

and he, the Holy One of Israel, has given us our king.

*W*hen the Israelites had to fight the fierce Amalekites, Joshua led the troops into battle, while Moses watched from a nearby hill. Whenever Moses raised his staff, the Israelite army succeeded. Whenever he lowered it, they started losing. Moses' arms grew too tired to hold the staff, however, so Aaron and another man held his arms steady (Exodus 17:8-13).

In the original Hebrew, the word for "steady" in that story is the same word that appears in Psalm 89:8 as "faithfulness." This word also appears as "faith" in Habakkuk 2:4, where the prophet denounces the proud people of his day: "They trust in themselves, and their lives are crooked; but the righteous will live by their faith."

This psalm recognizes that faithfulness is at the very core of God's character. And it's not just that he will *try* to do what he promises—he is mighty enough to do it. His arms are strong enough by themselves (see verse 13); he doesn't need helpers to hold them up! The psalmist tosses around other characteristics of the Lord: righteousness and justice, unfailing love and truth. All of this combines to paint a portrait of a God you can count on—even when everything else in your life seems to be falling apart.

As we steadily trust in God's steadiness and faithfulness, we find life, even when the powers of death surround us. He holds us up in his mighty arms, and he will not let us down.

> *Firm as His throne His promise stands,*
> *And He can well secure*
> *What I've committed to His hands*
> *Till the decisive hour.*
> ISAAC WATTS

Bible Networking
For a look at the mighty right hand of God, read Exodus 15:6-12.

Notable Quotable
Alexander Maclaren believed that verse 15 should be paraphrased as: "Oh! How blessed are the people who are sure that they have God with them, and who, being sure, bow before Him in loving worship."

PSALM 89:19-28

[19] You once spoke in a vision to your prophet and said,
  "I have given help to a warrior.
  I have selected him from the common people to be
    king.
[20] I have found my servant David.
  I have anointed him with my holy oil.
[21] I will steady him,
  and I will make him strong.
[22] His enemies will not get the best of him,
  nor will the wicked overpower him.
[23] I will beat down his adversaries before him
  and destroy those who hate him.
[24] My faithfulness and unfailing love will be with him,
  and he will rise to power because of me.
[25] I will extend his rule from the Mediterranean Sea in the
    west
  to the Tigris and Euphrates rivers in the east.
[26] And he will say to me, 'You are my Father,
  my God, and the Rock of my salvation.'
[27] I will make him my firstborn son,
  the mightiest king on earth.
[28] I will love him and be kind to him forever;
  my covenant with him will never end."

*S*aul just wasn't working out. This first king of Israel kept doing his own thing, not waiting for God's direction. Finally, God decided to make a change. He sent the prophet Samuel to the fields of Bethlehem to find a new ruler, one who would honor and obey him. One of the sons of Jesse would be anointed king. But which one?

It's a Cinderella story, when you think about it. Seven big, strong sons of Jesse came before the prophet for their interviews. God's glass slipper didn't fit any of them. Sure, they looked like king material—but so did Saul. God wanted someone with a heart that would serve him.

They almost forgot about David, the youngest son, who was out in the fields minding the flocks. Somebody had to do the dirty work—and perhaps it was that servant attitude that qualified David for the job. Any fool can be a king, but only a wise king can be a servant.

Psalm 89 celebrates the selection of this shepherd David as king of Israel. He wasn't just second in a long line of monarchs—he was the founder of an enduring dynasty. David's descendants would rule God's people forever. The psalmist, looking ahead to a shaky future, clung to this promise for national security. Christians today look back and see it fulfilled in Jesus, the servant-king, shepherd of God's people, son of David.

> *O come, Thou Key of David, come,*
> *And open wide our heavenly home;*
> *Make safe the way that leads on high,*
> *And close the path to misery.*
> *Rejoice! rejoice! Emanuel shall come to thee, O*
> *   Israel!*
> JOHN M. NEALE

A Word on Words

"[God's] firstborn son" (verse 27) is a term that, in its strictest application, belongs to Christ alone. See Romans 8:29. We need to read this passage with Christ in mind, not just David.

Bible Networking

This part of Psalm 89 concerns God's solemn promise found in 2 Samuel 7:8-16.

PSALM 89:29-37

29 "I will preserve an heir for him;
   his throne will be as endless as the days of heaven.

30 But if his sons forsake my law
   and fail to walk in my ways,

31 if they do not obey my decrees
   and fail to keep my commands,

32 then I will punish their sin with the rod,
   and their disobedience with beating.

33 But I will never stop loving him,
   nor let my promise to him fail.

34 No, I will not break my covenant;
   I will not take back a single word I said.

35 I have sworn an oath to David,
   and in my holiness I cannot lie:

36 His dynasty will go on forever;
   his throne is as secure as the sun,

37   as eternal as the moon,
   my faithful witness in the sky!"   *Interlude*

Most fans who went to Camden Yards to see the Baltimore Orioles game on September 21, 1998, didn't know that they would be attending a game that would go down in the record books. The record, however, didn't involve something they saw but rather something they *didn't* see.

When the Baltimore Orioles trotted out on the field, Cal Ripken Jr. wasn't among the players. That was a momentous nonappearance.

You see, Ripken had played in 2,632 consecutive baseball games over a period of sixteen years. He had never missed a game. But on that September day he decided the streak had gone on long enough, so he told the manager to scratch his name off the lineup card. Ripken's incredible consecutive-game string finally came to an end.

In this world it seems that all streaks eventually come to an end. But God once told David that his streak of love for him would never end (see 2 Samuel 7:15), and this is affirmed in this psalm as well.

God regards us with this same kind of unfailing love. In baseball terms, God says to us, "Though your batting average is below .200, though you strike out twenty times in a row, though you make stupid errors on every easy grounder that is hit to you, I will never stop loving you."

A streak of 2,632 consecutive games? God says that's not much compared to the unbroken streak of love he has for us.

> When we've been there ten thousand years,
> Bright shining as the sun,
> We've no less days to sing God's praise
> Than when we'd first begun.
> JOHN NEWTON

Bible Networking
For more on God's covenant with David, see 2 Samuel 7. Note David's response in verses 18-29 of that chapter.

Notable Quotable
"David's line in the person of Jesus is an endless one, and the race of Jesus shows no sign of failure. No power, human or satanic, can break the Christian succession. . . . A seed and a throne are the two great promises of the covenant. We are the seed who must endure forever, and we are protected and ennobled by that King whose royalty will last forever."
CHARLES HADDON SPURGEON

PSALM 89:38-45

[38] But now you have rejected him.
   Why are you so angry with the one you chose as
      king?

[39] You have renounced your covenant with him,
   for you have thrown his crown in the dust.

[40] You have broken down the walls protecting him
   and laid in ruins every fort defending him.

[41] Everyone who comes along has robbed him
   while his neighbors mock.

[42] You have strengthened his enemies against him
   and made them all rejoice.

[43] You have made his sword useless
   and have refused to help him in battle.

[44] You have ended his splendor
   and overturned his throne.

[45] You have made him old before his time
   and publicly disgraced him.   *Interlude*

*T*he tenth century B.C. was a glorious time for Israel. David's military prowess expanded Israel's borders, and Solomon's wise diplomacy made the nation rich. For a few decades, anyway, Israel was one of the most powerful nations on earth.

But the glory didn't last. When Solomon's son Rehoboam assumed the throne, he rejected good advice and raised taxes, forcing his overworked people to work even harder. Because of this, ten northern tribes seceded and chose a man named Jeroboam to be their king.

Immediately, however, Jeroboam noticed a problem: His subjects had to travel into the southern kingdom to worship God in Jerusalem. So Jeroboam constructed some golden calves and encouraged the people to worship them instead. Rehoboam's two tribes fell into idol worship as well.

From here the once-proud Israel went downhill fast. The ten northern tribes continued to turn away from God, and within two centuries they were obliterated as a nation. The glory years were decidedly over.

Psalm 89 bemoans the consequences of the nation's sin. David's dynasty had been rejected, the throne overturned. We know a little more of the story, however, for God restored the nation once again. Furthermore, in Jesus, David's dynasty lives on, and the sin that ended Israel's splendor met its own defeat at the cross and empty tomb.

> *Israel's strength and consolation,*
> *Hope of all the earth thou art.*
> *Dear desire of every nation,*
> *Joy of every longing heart.*
> CHARLES WESLEY

Notable Quotable
"God is faithful; his will must ultimately triumph; but whether or not we triumph depends upon how we relate ourselves to that will."
W. GRAHAM SCROGGIE

PSALM 89:46-52

⁴⁶ O Lᴏʀᴅ, how long will this go on?
   Will you hide yourself forever?
   How long will your anger burn like fire?
⁴⁷ Remember how short my life is,
   how empty and futile this human existence!
⁴⁸ No one can live forever; all will die.
   No one can escape the power of the grave.   *Interlude*

⁴⁹ Lord, where is your unfailing love?
   You promised it to David with a faithful pledge.
⁵⁰ Consider, Lord, how your servants are disgraced!
   I carry in my heart the insults of so many people.
⁵¹ Your enemies have mocked me, O Lᴏʀᴅ;
   they mock the one you anointed as king.

⁵² Blessed be the Lᴏʀᴅ forever!
   Amen and amen!

*M*artha was ticked. Her brother, Lazarus, had been on his deathbed when she sent word to Jesus. After all the times she had been there for Jesus, you'd think he would come quickly in her time of need. But no, by the time he got there, Lazarus was dead and already rotting in his tomb.

"If you had been here, my brother would not have died!" Martha scolded.

"Your brother will rise again," Jesus told her. Of course. That's what you say to grieving people—think of the hereafter. But Jesus clarified, "I am the resurrection and the life" (John 11:17-25).

Was Jesus speaking of spiritual resurrection? Of course, but he chose to demonstrate his spiritual power in a very physical way. Calling into the tomb, he invited Lazarus back to the land of the living. "Wait," Martha said, "it's going to smell really bad!" But then Lazarus stepped out—he was alive!

The end of Psalm 89 is full of questions. Where is your unfailing love, Lord? Why weren't you here when we needed you? Martha had the same questions, but as she learned to trust the Lord's power and timing, she received a wonderful surprise. As we learn to trust the Lord in the same way, the Lord will surprise us, too, just as he did Martha.

The last verse of Psalm 89 brings it full circle—just attach it to the psalm's first verse and read it all again. No matter how bad things get, we can always count on God's unfailing love to surprise us.

> *If all were easy, if all were bright,*
> *Where would the cross be, where would the fight?*
> *But in the hardness, God gives to you*
> *Chances for proving what He can do.*
> M. D.

A Word on Words

The final verse of this psalm is a benediction much like Psalm 41:13 and 72:18-19. The double "amen" was probably a congregational response.

Notable Quotable

"It is no accident that unchanging love is used five times in this psalm and faithfulness seven times. The congregation is left with the choice between God's integrity and their own."
JOHN I. DURHAM

No fooling. In the Middle Ages theologians really did argue about how many angels could stand on the head of a pin. If someone actually wanted to count them, however, it would be difficult to get them to stand still long enough to count them, because in the Psalms they are always in action!

In bits and pieces the Psalms teach us quite a bit about angels. Here are a few verses about them:

◆ Psalm 34:7
For the angel of the LORD
    guards all who fear him,
    and he rescues them.

◆ Psalm 35:6
Make their path dark and slip-
    pery,

with the angel of the LORD
    pursuing them.

◆ Psalm 91:11
For he orders his angels
    to protect you wherever you
    go.

◆ Psalm 103:20-21
Praise the LORD, you angels of
    his,
    you mighty creatures who
    carry out his plans,
    listening for each of his com-
    mands.
Yes, praise the LORD, you
    armies of angels
who serve him and do his
    will!

◆ Psalm 148:2
Praise him, all his angels!
    Praise him, all the armies of
    heaven!

The Psalms tell us that angels are busy, but they never

do anything for themselves. Other Scriptures confirm this. Angels praise God (compare Psalm 148:2 with Luke 2:13-14). They watch over and rescue believers (compare Psalm 34:7 with Acts 12:6-10). At times they execute judgment on unbelievers (compare Psalm 35:5-6 with 2 Kings 19:35 and Acts 12:23). They care for God's people and protect them (compare Psalm 91:11 with Hebrews 1:14).

At times angels can become visible, but usually they remain unseen. Do you recall the story in 2 Kings 6, when Elisha's servant was afraid of the enemy's army that had surrounded them? "Ah, my lord, what will we do now?" he cried out to the prophet.

"Don't be afraid!" Elisha told him, "For there are more on our side than on theirs" (verses 15-16). Then the servant's eyes were opened to see armies of angels surrounding the enemy. As long as God's angelic hosts were there, Elisha wasn't in any danger. And you aren't either.

The Psalms assure us that the Lord, our Good Shepherd, is leading us and that his angels are surrounding us. With such sure protection, what do we have to be afraid of?

∞

Onward, Christian, though the region
Where you are is dark and lone;
God has set a guardian legion
Very near you, so press on.
SAMUEL JOHNSON

∞

"Seeing we are so dear to God, these angels take this charge upon them with all their hearts, and omit nothing in their duty from our birth to the end of our life."
HENRY LAWRENCE

Selah

BOOK FOUR (PSALMS 90–106)
PSALM 90:1-9
A prayer of Moses, the man of God.

¹ Lord, through all the generations
     you have been our home!
² Before the mountains were created,
          before you made the earth and the world,
          you are God, without beginning or end.

³ You turn people back to dust, saying,
          "Return to dust!"
⁴ For you, a thousand years are as yesterday!
          They are like a few hours!
⁵ You sweep people away like dreams that disappear
          or like grass that springs up in the morning.
⁶ In the morning it blooms and flourishes,
          but by evening it is dry and withered.
⁷ We wither beneath your anger;
          we are overwhelmed by your fury.
⁸ You spread out our sins before you—
          our secret sins—and you see them all.
⁹ We live our lives beneath your wrath.
          We end our lives with a groan.

*I*n 1865 several friends from England climbed the Matterhorn, the great Swiss Alp that had not yet been scaled. They reached the top, but four men lost their footing on the way down and fell to their deaths. One of these was a minister, the Reverend Charles Hudson. When his body was recovered by the others in the expedition, a prayer book was found in his pocket. Someone suggested that a funeral service be held there.

So another minister, named McCormick, used Hudson's prayer book to read Psalm 90 and conduct a brief service. "I am persuaded," McCormick said of his dead friend, "that his soul was filled with joy and gratitude as he stood where no human being had ever stood before and gazed from a new point of view on the great Creator's works."

McCormick found Psalm 90 "singularly appropriate" to the occasion. In that moment God seemed both wonderful and frightening, capable of creating great beauty and of snatching a life. The fleeting quality of human life is a major theme of this psalm. We can be swept away "like dreams that disappear." But our God exists eternally, long before the most majestic mountains were formed and long after they crumble. If the Lord is not our home, what kind of security do we have?

> Before the hills in order stood,
> Or earth received her frame,
> From everlasting thou art God,
> To endless years the same.
> ISAAC WATTS

A Word on Words
Some Jewish rabbis translate verse 3 as "Return unto me, Judge of the human spirit."

Bible Networking
With God time is nothing. Compare verse 4 of this psalm with 2 Peter 3:8.

PSALM 90:10-17

¹⁰ Seventy years are given to us!
    Some may even reach eighty.
    But even the best of these years are filled with pain and
        trouble;
    soon they disappear, and we are gone.
¹¹ Who can comprehend the power of your anger?
    Your wrath is as awesome as the fear you deserve.
¹² Teach us to make the most of our time,
    so that we may grow in wisdom.

¹³ O LORD, come back to us!
    How long will you delay?
    Take pity on your servants!
¹⁴ Satisfy us in the morning with your unfailing love,
    so we may sing for joy to the end of our lives.
¹⁵ Give us gladness in proportion to our former misery!
    Replace the evil years with good.
¹⁶ Let us see your miracles again;
    let our children see your glory at work.
¹⁷ And may the Lord our God show us his approval
    and make our efforts successful.
    Yes, make our efforts successful!

*I*n the sixteenth century Queen Elizabeth I invited an Anglican bishop named Rudd to come and preach at the palace. Rudd was well regarded by the other clergy, and many expected him to be the next archbishop of Canterbury, head of the Anglican Church. When the current archbishop extended the invitation for Rudd to come, he advised him, "The queen is now grown weary of the vanities of wit and eloquence," adding that she now preferred sermons that "come home to her heart."

On this basis Bishop Rudd selected Psalm 90:12: "Teach us to make the most of our time," as his text and used the surrounding verses to discuss the difficulties of the aging process and the inevitability of physical death. He assumed that the queen, now in her old age, would relate to these words.

Maybe she related too much. As it turned out, the queen was highly offended by his direct remarks about her aging and death. She made sure that Bishop Rudd was not the next archbishop of Canterbury. Yet, though his career suffered greatly, Rudd gained a reputation as a preacher who said what God gave him to say, whether the queen liked it or not.

Moses, the author of this psalm, would have smiled at Rudd's actions. He never minced words himself, even before the pharaoh of Egypt. Ultimately, it's the Lord's approval that makes us successful (verse 17) and no one else's.

> *O God, our help in ages past,*
> *Our hope for years to come,*
> *Our shelter from the stormy blast,*
> *And our eternal home!*
> ISAAC WATTS

Bible Networking

Compare the hope that the psalmist prays for in verses 14-15 with an even more glorious hope in 2 Corinthians 4:17-18.

Notable Quotable

T. S. Eliot ends his poem "The Hollow Men" with:

This is the way the world ends
Not with a bang but a whimper.

PSALM 91:1-6

¹ Those who live in the shelter of the Most High
    will find rest in the shadow of the Almighty.
² This I declare of the LORD:
    He alone is my refuge, my place of safety;
    he is my God, and I am trusting him.
³ For he will rescue you from every trap
    and protect you from the fatal plague.
⁴ He will shield you with his wings.
    He will shelter you with his feathers.
    His faithful promises are your armor and protection.
⁵ Do not be afraid of the terrors of the night,
    nor fear the dangers of the day,
⁶ nor dread the plague that stalks in darkness,
    nor the disaster that strikes at midday.

*T*errorism has been a disconcerting reality of life recently—Oklahoma City, the World Trade Center, the Unabomber. Terrorists have various causes, but they share a common weapon—fear. If you can get people worried about taking a bus, going to the market, or even opening their mail, then you've dismantled the normal systems of life. You don't need an army to support your cause—just terror.

All the media's frightening coverage about the food we eat, the fluoride in our water, and global warming makes us want to just stay home—but then there's probably radon gas building up in our house right now!

But the psalmist offers us a better response: Rest secure in God. Let him protect you. The terrors of the night, the dangers of the day—none of these are too great for the Lord Almighty. Trust him to get you through.

That sounds great, but weren't there any Christians who died in, say, the Oklahoma City bombing? Sure there were. But the people of God have a greater, eternal security. We know that death will just give us a new address even closer to God than we are now. With the apostle Paul, we say, "For to me, living is for Christ, and dying is even better" (Philippians 1:21). With this assurance, we need not be terrified by anything or anyone. God is with us, and we are safe in him, no matter what happens. We are safe forever in his protective care.

> *Under His wings I am safely abiding;*
> *Though the night deepens and tempests are wild,*
> *Still I can trust Him; I know He will keep me;*
> *He has redeemed me, and I am His child.*
> WILLIAM O. CUSHING

A Word on Words

The first two verses use four names for God. "Most High" implies a status beyond the gods of any enemy. "The Almighty" emphasizes God's great power to protect his people (see Exodus 6:3). "The LORD" is the personal name Yahweh, the God who had chosen Israel. "My God" shows the intimate nature of the psalmist's relationship with him. Combined, these names for God give us a picture of ultimate protection.

Notable Quotable

"The Lord is our refuge for safety, our fortress for defense, and our God for everything."
W. GRAHAM SCROGGIE

PSALM 91:7-10

⁷ Though a thousand fall at your side,
   though ten thousand are dying around you,
   these evils will not touch you.
⁸ But you will see it with your eyes;
   you will see how the wicked are punished.

⁹ If you make the LORD your refuge,
   if you make the Most High your shelter,
¹⁰ no evil will conquer you;
   no plague will come near your dwelling.

*W*hen the great British preacher Charles Haddon Spurgeon was just starting out at his London church, a terrible epidemic hit the city. In just about every family in his church, somebody came down with the Asiatic cholera, and many died. The young man did his best to minister to his congregation, but there was only so much he could do. He became very weary with the burden of visiting the sick, conducting funerals, and comforting the bereaved.

One day he was walking home from yet another funeral when he saw a sign in the window of a shoemaker's shop. In the owner's handwriting, it said, "Because thou hast made the Lord, which is my refuge, even the most High, thy habitation; there shall no evil befall thee, neither shall any plague come nigh thy dwelling" (Psalm 91:9-10, KJV).

"The effect upon my heart was immediate," Spurgeon wrote. "I felt secure, refreshed, girt with immortality. I went on with my visitation of the dying in a calm and peaceful spirit; I felt no fear of evil, and I suffered no harm." Spurgeon then praised God.

When frightful circumstances surround us, we can remember the promise of Psalm 91. This doesn't mean we will be immune to all disease or danger, but we do know that the Lord will keep us safe from eternal harm.

> *What have I to dread, what have I to fear,*
> *Leaning on the everlasting arms?*
> *I have blessed peace with my Lord so near,*
> *Leaning on the everlasting arms.*
> ELISHA A. HOFFMAN

Bible Networking

Verses 9 and 10 of this psalm are strong, sweeping statements. We find other promises like this in Romans 8:28 and Luke 21:17-19. Nothing can touch God's people unless God allows it.

Notable Quotable

Verse 10 "is a statement of providence, not a charm against adversity."
DEREK KIDNER

PSALM 91:11-16

[11] For he orders his angels
    to protect you wherever you go.
[12] They will hold you with their hands
    to keep you from striking your foot on a stone.
[13] You will trample down lions and poisonous snakes;
    you will crush fierce lions and serpents under your
       feet!

[14] The LORD says, "I will rescue those who love me.
    I will protect those who trust in my name.
[15] When they call on me, I will answer;
    I will be with them in trouble.
    I will rescue them and honor them.
[16] I will satisfy them with a long life
    and give them my salvation."

*I*n the desert the Devil tempted a hungry Jesus to turn stones into bread, but Jesus' main mission was not simply to alleviate physical hunger in himself or anyone else. He could turn every stone in Palestine into a bagel, and people would still be spiritually hungry. They needed to know God.

In Luke's account the next temptation entailed a simple swap (4:1-13): The Devil would give Jesus all the kingdoms of the world; Jesus would worship the Devil. Again, no deal. God alone deserves our worship.

Twice the tempter made his pitch, only to be thwarted when Jesus quoted Scripture. So the Devil took Jesus to a high point of the Temple and found an appropriate text—from Psalm 91. "Jump, Jesus! Doesn't it say that angels will 'keep you from striking your foot on a stone'?"

Jesus answered, "Do not test the Lord your God." The Father does protect, but that doesn't mean we are to go leaping off buildings.

These temptations were all about Jesus' mission. The Devil was doing his best to get Jesus sidetracked, but Jesus stayed with the program.

Matthew says that, when the Devil left Jesus, angels came and cared for him (4:11). So they were protecting him all along! Jesus didn't have to try any daredevil dare—he just had to stay with his mission, and God would get him through it. The same is true for us. He will rescue those who love him.

> Christian, seek not yet repose;
> Hear thy guardian angel say,
> "Thou art in the midst of foes;
> Watch and pray."
> CHARLOTTE ELLIOTT

A Word on Words
Verses 12-13 depict God's servants not merely as survivors but as victors, who trample deadly enemies underfoot.

Bible Networking
Verse 14 says that God will rescue those who love him, but Deuteronomy 7:7-8, 10:15, and 1 John 4:10 remind us that God loved us first.

The Psalms are filled with expressions of worship to God. Here are a few passages that speak of coming before the Lord and giving him honor:

◆ *Psalm 5:7*

Because of your unfailing love, I can enter your house;
with deepest awe I will worship at your Temple.

◆ *Psalm 29:2*

Give honor to the LORD for the glory of his name.
Worship the LORD in the splendor of his holiness.

◆ *Psalm 95:6-7*

Come, let us worship and bow down.
Let us kneel before the LORD our maker,
for he is our God.

◆ *Psalm 99:9*

Exalt the LORD our God
and worship at his holy mountain in Jerusalem,
for the LORD our God is holy!

◆ *Psalm 100:2*

Worship the LORD with gladness.
Come before him, singing with joy.

◆ *Psalm 138:2*

I bow before your holy Temple as I worship.
I will give thanks to your name
for your unfailing love and faithfulness,
because your promises are backed
by all the honor of your name.

"Worship," says John MacArthur, "is all that we are, reacting to all that God is."

But how are we supposed to do this? We come to church and find our mind wandering.

We sit at home reading the Bible, and a dozen things on our "to do" list come to mind. Let's face it. If we were graded according to our attempts at worship during the past month, we would probably be demoted to kindergarten.

But the good news is that the Psalms are user-friendly when it comes to worship. Inside us is a jumble of feelings that the Psalms can help us get out. There is gratitude for what God has done for us and awe as we think about our freedom to come into God's presence. We also have a sense of inadequacy and sorrow for sins. And then there are some questions that are buried more deeply in our heart: Why isn't God answering our prayer for our family? Why did God allow this tragedy to occur?

The Psalms help us understand these questions as well—or at least that it is OK to ask them. The Psalms teach us that tears are OK, even anger is OK. Sometimes we are so confused that we are staggering as we come into God's presence; that's OK, too. God is big enough to handle that, and the Psalms recognize this. God knows us better than we know ourselves, and nothing we tell him about ourselves will shock him. He wants us to come into his presence just as we are, bringing whatever our thoughts and emotions are. He wants us to lay these before him and simply say, "I love you, Lord."

In doing this we prepare ourselves to concentrate on him, and that's when worship really begins.

∾

Just as I am, though tossed about
With many a conflict, many a doubt,
Fightings and fears within, without,
O Lamb of God, I come! I come!
CHARLOTTE ELLIOTT

Selah

PSALM 92:1-8
A psalm to be sung on the LORD's Day. A song.

¹ It is good to give thanks to the LORD,
    to sing praises to the Most High.
² It is good to proclaim your unfailing love in the
        morning,
    your faithfulness in the evening,
³ accompanied by the harp and lute
    and the harmony of the lyre.
⁴ You thrill me, LORD, with all you have done for me!
    I sing for joy because of what you have done.

⁵ O LORD, what great miracles you do!
    And how deep are your thoughts.
⁶ Only an ignorant person would not know this!
    Only a fool would not understand it.
⁷ Although the wicked flourish like weeds,
    and evildoers blossom with success,
    there is only eternal destruction ahead of them.
⁸ But you are exalted in the heavens.
    You, O LORD, continue forever.

*H*ave you ever been explaining something to a friend when you suddenly realized that your friend didn't have a clue about what you were saying? You may have explained your thought very well, but your friend just didn't "get it."

This type of response doesn't necessarily imply that a person is dumb. In fact, people are often brilliant in certain fields but completely lost in others. Part of their lack of understanding may be because they lack a basic familiarity with the subject. If people lack any framework for understanding, all new information they receive will seem completely foreign to them. The words just go in one ear and out the other without hitting much in between.

In Psalm 92:6 the psalmist chides the ignorant person who doesn't know about the Lord's great miracles. God is busy doing thrilling things all around us, but these people don't "get it." The key to seeing these works of God involves an attitude shift that opens a person up to what's really happening. One way to make this attitude shift is by following the instructions of the first part of this psalm. It is good to give thanks and sing praises. A thankful heart is thrilled with what the Lord does. This thankfulness creates a gridwork on which we can place more and more knowledge of the great miracles of God. Let's cultivate that spirit of thankfulness today and every day. And let's open our eyes to the thrills of a life with God.

> O Jesus my Savior, with Thee I am blest,
> My life and salvation, my joy and my rest;
> Thy name be my theme, and Thy love be my song;
> Thy grace shall inspire both my heart and my song.

AUTHOR UNKNOWN

PSALM 92:9-15

⁹ Your enemies, LORD, will surely perish;
   all evildoers will be scattered.

¹⁰ But you have made me as strong as a wild bull.
   How refreshed I am by your power!
¹¹ With my own eyes I have seen the downfall of my
      enemies;
   with my own ears I have heard the defeat of my
      wicked opponents.
¹² But the godly will flourish like palm trees
   and grow strong like the cedars of Lebanon.
¹³ For they are transplanted into the LORD's own house.
   They flourish in the courts of our God.
¹⁴ Even in old age they will still produce fruit;
   they will remain vital and green.
¹⁵ They will declare, "The LORD is just!
   He is my rock!
   There is nothing but goodness in him!"

*J*ohn Emerich was a jolly old soul, a round man with rosy cheeks and wire glasses. Every December he played Santa Claus for the local grammar school—and he didn't have to change his appearance very much.

And Sunday after Sunday he stood in the foyer of his Baptist church, greeting newcomers and hailing friends. He was the first one there and the last one to leave. Visitors remembered his contagious grin. Children loved his impish ways.

He saw his church grow from a handful of folks in a firehouse to a hundred in a renovated barn to three hundred in a brand-new sanctuary. He would never admit it, but he was a major reason for that growth. He was a cedar of Lebanon, a godly man flourishing in the house of the Lord.

A lot of churches have people like John Emerich, faithful servants who might as well be planted at the church door. If there's a service, they're there, welcoming all who come. Such people have a sweet spirit and a gentle servanthood that keeps them producing fruit "even in old age."

Psalm 92 is designated as a song for the Lord's Day, and fittingly it portrays godly people "transplanted" like trees "into the Lord's own house." That may give us all an occasion to thank God for the godly servants we've known, the John Emerichs of the world who reach out with a handshake and a happy word every Lord's Day.

> *O happy servant, he,*
> *In such employment found!*
> *He shall his Lord with rapture see,*
> *And be with honor crowned.*
> PHILIP DODDRIDGE

Notable Quotable

"When we see a noble palm standing erect and growing amid the dearth and drought of the desert, we have a picture of the godly man, independent of outward circumstances, who is made by divine grace to live and thrive where all else perish.
CHARLES HADDON SPURGEON

Thought to Ponder

What a wonderful psalm for senior citizens! We don't retire from God's work. If we live in him, we just get better and better.

PSALM 93

[1] The LORD is king! He is robed in majesty.
  Indeed, the LORD is robed in majesty and armed with
    strength.
The world is firmly established;
  it cannot be shaken.

[2] Your throne, O LORD, has been established from time
    immemorial.
  You yourself are from the everlasting past.
[3] The mighty oceans have roared, O LORD.
  The mighty oceans roar like thunder;
    the mighty oceans roar as they pound the shore.
[4] But mightier than the violent raging of the seas,
  mightier than the breakers on the shore—
    the LORD above is mightier than these!
[5] Your royal decrees cannot be changed.
  The nature of your reign, O LORD, is holiness forever.

From ancient days people have been awestruck by the power of the ocean. Wave after wave pounds onto the shore and pulls itself back. On rocky coastlines waves hit with power, sending spray and sound all around. Out at sea rough water can toss a huge boat. A hurricane can turn waves into weapons.

But there is one mightier than the ocean.

Many people love to sit by the sea and meditate. The pounding waves resonate deep within the human soul. But Christians know the one who made those waves. We have a relationship with the one who first strung the H_2 with the O. We are sustained by one more powerful than the strongest undertow.

We don't honor the ocean; we exalt the Creator of the ocean. We don't just meditate on the gentle drumbeat of the waves on shore; we commune with the heart of the drummer. We worship the Lord, the eternal King, who is our Lord and closest friend.

> God moves in a mysterious way
> His wonders to perform;
> He plants his footsteps in the sea,
> And rides upon the storm.
> WILLIAM COWPER

Fascinating Fact
In medieval times it was thought that the earth remained in a fixed position while the sun and other heavenly bodies circled it. This belief was based in part on Psalm 93:1: "The world is firmly established."

Notable Quotable
"From eternity, before the formation of the world, God always remained the same in himself, not needing creation or any creature, thereby to obtain any new perfection."
LORINUS

PSALM 94:1-7

¹ O LORD, the God to whom vengeance belongs,
   O God of vengeance, let your glorious justice be
      seen!
² Arise, O judge of the earth.
   Sentence the proud to the penalties they deserve.
³ How long, O LORD?
   How long will the wicked be allowed to gloat?
⁴ Hear their arrogance!
   How these evildoers boast!
⁵ They oppress your people, LORD,
   hurting those you love.
⁶ They kill widows and foreigners
   and murder orphans.
⁷ "The LORD isn't looking," they say,
   "and besides, the God of Israel doesn't care."

*H*e was a preacher of the gospel who had given his whole life to serve people in need. When others were abandoning the inner city, that's where he went, caring for poor people and telling everyone about Jesus.

It wasn't easy. He saw the rise of crime. He saw the pushers dealing death on the street corners. Evildoers were taking over the streets, but this preacher kept at it, doggedly doing his work for the Lord—even when he got mugged.

He was hit on the head from behind. He looked up from the pavement to see a few kids—thirteen, fifteen years old maybe—trying to get his wallet. "Stop it!" he said. "Stop terrorizing people! Stop doing this! We're all just tired of this."

They moved back, surprised, but he went on. "I'm a pastor. And if you want to beat up a pastor and take his money, then take your best shot." He prepared for an attack, but the kids ran away. Down the block, the youngest of the group stopped and turned. "Pastor," he said, "would you please ask God for a blessing for me?"

Psalm 94 calls on the "God of vengeance" to set things right, but God has powers we know little about. We might expect God to storm into the enemy's strongholds with guns and tanks, but more often he uses faithful old preachers.

How can he use you to bring about his "glorious justice"?

> We fight for truth; we fight for God;
> Poor slaves of lies and sin!
> He who would fight for thee on earth
> Must first be true within.
> THOMAS HUGHS

A Word on Words
In verse 5 oppress literally means "to break into pieces." The Hebrew word is often used for "to crush underfoot" (see Isaiah 3:15).

Notable Quotable
"The 'How long?' [verse 3] sounds as if it were one of the saddest of all utterances in which misery bemoans itself. Many times this bitter complaint has been heard in the dungeons of the Inquisition, at the whipping posts of slavery, and in the prisons of oppression. In due time God will publish his reply, but the full end is not yet."
CHARLES HADDON SPURGEON

PSALM 94:8-15

8 Think again, you fools!
    When will you finally catch on?
9 Is the one who made your ears deaf?
    Is the one who formed your eyes blind?
10 He punishes the nations—won't he also punish you?
    He knows everything—doesn't he also know what
        you are doing?
11 The LORD knows people's thoughts,
    that they are worthless!

12 Happy are those whom you discipline, LORD,
    and those whom you teach from your law.
13 You give them relief from troubled times
    until a pit is dug for the wicked.
14 The LORD will not reject his people;
    he will not abandon his own special possession.
15 Judgment will come again for the righteous,
    and those who are upright will have a reward.

*N*owadays we think of judgment as a bad thing. Surfing the TV talk shows, we come to the painful conclusion that the only Bible verse anyone cares about is Matthew 7:1: "Stop judging others." Even when Christians talk about God as judge, we are quick to temper this by recognizing his mercy. That is not to say that this is not based on good New Testament theology. We are sinners, deserving the Judge's death penalty, but through Christ's death we can receive a pardon. Kneeling at the holy rail, you never boast of your own holiness. No, you throw yourself on the mercy of the Judge.

But the Psalms have another perspective on judgment. The people of God welcome God's judgment because it's true and right—unlike the decisions of the corrupt leaders they know. The world is like the Wild West without a sheriff. Good people long for a Wyatt Earp to come in, guns blazing, and restore order. And it's up to him to determine how it gets done.

At first glance, Psalm 94 seems very heavy—all this talk about punishment from God. But look deeper into it. "The Lord will not reject his people." Judgment comes along "for the righteous." Those who live right get rewarded. Those evil crime bosses who think they can get away with murder have another think coming. God sees their deeds and will see that justice is done. The sheriff has arrived, and law-abiding citizens can rejoice.

> *Arm of the Lord, awake, awake!*
> *Thine own immortal strength put on;*
> *With terror clothed, hell's kingdom shake,*
> *And cast thy foes with fury down.*
> CHARLES WESLEY

Bible Networking

Reread verse 14, and then turn to John 10:28. These are mighty words of encouragement to all believers.

Notable Quotable

"God sees the sorrows of life are very good for us; for as seeds that are deepest covered with snow in winter flourish most in spring; or as the wind by beating down the flame raiseth it higher and hotter; even so, when the Lord would increase our joy and thankfulness, he allays it with the tears of affliction."
H. G. SALTER

PSALM 94:16-23

16 Who will protect me from the wicked?
  Who will stand up for me against evildoers?
17 Unless the LORD had helped me,
  I would soon have died.
18 I cried out, "I'm slipping!"
  and your unfailing love, O LORD, supported me.
19 When doubts filled my mind,
  your comfort gave me renewed hope and cheer.

20 Can unjust leaders claim that God is on their side—
  leaders who permit injustice by their laws?
21 They attack the righteous
  and condemn the innocent to death.
22 But the LORD is my fortress;
  my God is a mighty rock where I can hide.
23 God will make the sins of evil people fall back upon
    them.
  He will destroy them for their sins.
  The LORD our God will destroy them.

*T*his is a junior high parable. Ben came to Middletown Middle School as a seventh grader and immediately faced several disadvantages. He was new. He was short. He was clumsy. He was shy. He wore thick glasses.

Ben was immediately the target of mockery and even mild violence. The other boys stole his lunch money nearly every day. When he reported that, they beat him up, so he learned to keep quiet. What could he do?

One day another boy named Josh came to sit with Ben at lunch. Josh was a well-liked eighth grader, active in the school sports program, popular with the girls. But that morning Josh had seen some boys teasing Ben, and he wanted to help.

As usual, a bully came by to grab Ben's food, but Josh grabbed his wrist. "Ben is my friend," Josh said sternly. "Don't mess with him." After school Josh waited for Ben and walked home with him. When some tormentors came by, Josh kept them from bothering Ben.

With Josh as his friend and protector, Ben was spared the mistreatment of earlier days. He became less shy and more accepted. His torment was over. But then he noticed some guys picking on a poor seventh grader. What do you think he did?

Today's text starts with Ben's question: Who will protect me? The Lord. And we praise him for his support. But the stern talk to leaders in verses 20-21 implies that we need to protect others, too.

> *I know that my Redeemer lives.*
> *What joy this blest assurance gives! . . .*
> *He lives, my hungry soul to feed;*
> *He lives, to help in time of need.*
> SAMUEL MEDLEY

Bible Networking

We hear echoes of these trials in other passages of Scripture. The loneliness of verse 16 we see in 2 Timothy 4:16. The plight of the psalmist in verse 18 we see also in Psalm 73:2. In both cases the Lord meets the need.

Notable Quotable

"God has proven himself equal to anything the enemy can send."
DEREK KIDNER

Why do we turn to the Psalms when we are discouraged or when we visit someone who has gone through a trying time? We turn to them because the psalmists—from David to Asaph to Moses—wrote from experience, and as you read the Psalms in those difficult times, they ring true. The psalmists have been there, done that, felt that. David, for example, probably knew more about discouragement than most people. His boss threw spears at him; his wife chided him; his son revolted against him; and on and on.

Here are a few verses from the Psalms that can help you when you are feeling discouraged:

◆ Psalm 9:18
For the needy will not be forgotten forever;
the hopes of the poor will not always be crushed.

◆ *Psalm 78:7*
So each generation can set its hope anew on God,
remembering his glorious miracles
and obeying his commands.

◆ *Psalm 33:18, 22*
But the LORD watches over those who fear him,
those who rely on his unfailing love. . . .
Let your unfailing love surround us, LORD,
for our hope is in you alone.

◆ *Psalm 138:8*
The LORD will work out his plans for my life—
for your faithful love, O LORD, endures forever.

◆ *Psalm 130:7*
With the LORD there is unfailing love
and an overflowing supply of salvation.

◆ *Psalm 102:17*
He will listen to the prayers of the destitute.
He will not reject their pleas.

◆ *Psalm 94:18-19*
I cried out, "I'm slipping!"
  and your unfailing love,
    O LORD, supported me.
When doubts filled my mind,
  your comfort gave me renewed
    hope and cheer.

As you read the Psalms that speak about discouraging times, you will soon notice that many of them end on a positive note. What's their secret? Why do the psalmists come out of almost every psalm smiling and praising the Lord? How have they conquered discouragement?

It is because the psalmists knew three big truths about God that can act like pills against depression and discouragement: God's promises, God's love, and God's unchanging character. Over and over again these three divine qualities are rehearsed:

God's promises: "The Lord . . . will not abandon his own special possession" (Psalm 94:14). He will always be faithful to his people and to the promises that he has given them. We can trust him to hold on to us even when times are tough.

God's love: "His unfailing love continues forever" (Psalm 100:5). We can always count on God's love for us. No matter how bad we feel about ourselves or how bad others feel about us, we can know that God cares for us.

God's unchangingness: "He is our God forever and ever, and he will be our guide until we die"

(Psalm 48:14). God is eternal. He is certain, and we can stake everything on him. Everything around us may seem temporary and uncertain, but God is always the same.

Someone has said that discouragement is the Devil's all-purpose tool. When he can't get us down with anything else, he will use the D-tool. The next time he tries it on you, find those three pills in the Psalms, take all three before going to bed at night, and see if you don't sleep soundly and feel better in the morning!

∞
We hope in you, O God!
The day wears on to night,
Thick shadows lie across our world,
In you alone is light.
MARIANNE HEARN

Selah

PSALM 95:1-7a

¹ Come, let us sing to the LORD!
  Let us give a joyous shout to the rock of our
    salvation!
² Let us come before him with thanksgiving.
  Let us sing him psalms of praise.
³ For the LORD is a great God,
  the great King above all gods.
⁴ He owns the depths of the earth,
  and even the mightiest mountains are his.
⁵ The sea belongs to him, for he made it.
  His hands formed the dry land, too.

⁶ Come, let us worship and bow down.
  Let us kneel before the LORD our maker,
⁷ for he is our God.
  We are the people he watches over,
    the sheep under his care.

*I*n the late 1700s William Carey, a simple shoemaker, had a dream to reach the whole world for Jesus Christ. But his fellow Englishmen weren't crazy about his ideas. If God wanted to save the heathen, they figured, he would find a way to do it. Carey kept insisting that he and other British Christians were the way.

"Expect great things from God. Attempt great things for God." That was Carey's motto as he awakened a complacent church. He believed that since God created the whole world and loves everyone, his worshipers should help spread the worship of the true God throughout the world. So Carey founded the Baptist Missionary Society and sailed to India in 1793.

It must have been a lonely time for Carey. He had to debate with other Christians over the value of foreign missions. His journey was long and uncertain. His wife and children only grudgingly agreed to join him. At times Carey must have wondered how carefully God was watching over him. Was he really a "sheep under his care" (verse 7)?

Well, it turned out that a German named Christian Friedrich Schwartz had been sent forty years earlier by the Danish Missionary Society and had started churches in various areas of India and Ceylon. William Carey was greatly comforted when he saw the inscription Schwartz had placed over the door to the mission church: "Come, let us worship and bow down" (Psalm 95:6).

> *Where no fruit appears to cheer them*
> *And they seem to toil in vain,*
> *Then in mercy, Lord, draw near them,*
> *Then their sinking hopes sustain,*
> *Thus supported, let their zeal revive again.*
> THOMAS KELLY

Notable Quotable
"When the heart is full, it brims over in some outward act of devotion."
F. B. MEYER

PSALM 95:7b-11

⁷ Oh, that you would listen to his voice today!

⁸ The LORD says, "Don't harden your hearts as Israel did
at Meribah,
as they did at Massah in the wilderness.

⁹ For there your ancestors tried my patience;
they courted my wrath though they had seen my
many miracles.

¹⁰ For forty years I was angry with them, and I said,
'They are a people whose hearts turn away from me.
They refuse to do what I tell them.'

¹¹ So in my anger I made a vow:
'They will never enter my place of rest.' "

*W*andering through the desert, the Israelites had an attitude problem. God had parted the sea for them and provided a miraculous food supply. But now they were thirsty, so they complained.

"Why are you testing the Lord?" Moses asked the people. Then he turned to God and asked, "What am I going to do with these people?" So God told Moses to take his staff, hit a rock, and water would come gushing out. Moses did as he was told, and water flowed from the rock, just as God promised (Exodus 17:1-7).

The Israelites' same attitude problem resurfaced again and again in the desert. The worst of it came when the leaders decided they should not enter Canaan because the inhabitants were too big—even though God had promised that he had given the Israelites the land. For this, God kept his people wandering in the desert for forty more years. That generation died off, and only their children were able to enter God's "place of rest."

The book of Hebrews quotes this psalm at length, repeating verse 7 as a refrain: Listen to his voice! Come to God in faith and avoid the attitude problems of those unfortunate Israelites. Only then can you find true rest with God.

So are you worrying about some giant issues in your life? Are you wondering how your needs will be met? Listen to the Lord's voice! The Good Shepherd wants to care for you. Let him!

> *Fear not, brethren, joyful stand*
> *On the borders of our land;*
> *Jesus Christ, our Father's Son,*
> *Bids us undismayed go on.*
> JOHN CENNICK

Bible Networking
To learn more about God's "rest," read Hebrews 4:9-10.

Notable Quotable
Psalm 95 "has about it a ring like that of the church bells, and like the bells it sounds both merrily and solemnly, at first ringing out a lively peal, and then dropping into funeral knell as if tolling at the funeral of the generation which perished in the wilderness."
CHARLES HADDON SPURGEON

PSALM 96:1-6

¹ Sing a new song to the LORD!
  Let the whole earth sing to the LORD!
² Sing to the LORD; bless his name.
  Each day proclaim the good news that he saves.
³ Publish his glorious deeds among the nations.
  Tell everyone about the amazing things he does.
⁴ Great is the LORD! He is most worthy of praise!
  He is to be revered above all the gods.
⁵ The gods of other nations are merely idols,
  but the LORD made the heavens!
⁶ Honor and majesty surround him;
  strength and beauty are in his sanctuary.

*I*n the early fourth century Constantine legalized Christianity in the Roman Empire and made it the official religion. But less than fifty years later Constantine's nephew Julian tried to undo those reforms. Julian was committed to the traditional pagan gods of Rome, and he tried to force those beliefs on Roman society. He arranged for paganism to be taught in the schools, repaired the old pagan temples, and reserved high government posts for his fellow pagans. He did everything he could to undermine Christianity.

Christians were surprised by this sudden opposition, for Julian himself (later called "the Apostate") had professed to be a Christian until he took office. Christians had enjoyed a free ride for half a century. Now they had to defend their beliefs, showing their pagan neighbors that Jesus Christ really is the answer.

One of the church's favorite psalms during this time was Psalm 96, and it's no wonder. It asserts that the Lord "is to be revered above all the gods" (verse 4). All other gods (*elohim* in Hebrew) are merely idols *(elilim)*. You can hear the wordplay there, and the word for idols can carry the sense of "useless objects."

Eventually Julian was killed in a battle with the Persians, and Christians regained control of the empire. Once again their God had emerged victorious over "the gods of other nations."

> Let all on earth their voices raise
> To sing the great Jehovah's praise
> And bless his holy name.
> His glory let the people know,
> His wonders to the nations show,
> His saving grace proclaim.
> ISAAC WATTS

Psalm at a Glance

There's a subtle direction change in verse 2. Those who have been singing to the Lord are now to tell the world. Worship and evangelism are intimately connected.

Thought to Ponder

Notice that even though the psalmist was proving a point—the Lord's superiority over other gods—he kept singing. God's people are always strongest when their lives are characterized by joy and singing.

PSALM 96:7-13

⁷ O nations of the world, recognize the LORD;
  recognize that the LORD is glorious and strong.
⁸ Give to the LORD the glory he deserves!
  Bring your offering and come to worship him.
⁹ Worship the LORD in all his holy splendor.
  Let all the earth tremble before him.
¹⁰ Tell all the nations that the LORD is king.
  The world is firmly established and cannot be
      shaken.
  He will judge all peoples fairly.

¹¹ Let the heavens be glad, and let the earth rejoice!
  Let the sea and everything in it shout his praise!
¹² Let the fields and their crops burst forth with joy!
  Let the trees of the forest rustle with praise
¹³   before the LORD!
For the LORD is coming!
  He is coming to judge the earth.
He will judge the world with righteousness
  and all the nations with his truth.

*T*he Ark of God made its ascent up Mount Zion, into the special tent that David had prepared. People sang and shouted, trumpets blasted, and David danced. They gave gifts of food, and the Levites sang a song of thanksgiving that David had written for the occasion.

Apparently the song was so well received that they included part of it among the hymns of the community, for the words of Psalm 96 are also found in David's song as it is recorded in 1 Chronicles 16:8-36.

These verses depict the entire universe—heavens, sea, fields, trees—joining with people of every nation in giving glory to God. "Recognize the Lord," our text says, and that's a good way to render the Hebrew word here. The word for "recognize" comes from one of the words for "give." In modern slang, a TV host might tell an audience, "Give it up for our special guest!" and they would applaud. That's what the psalmist is saying here: "Recognize the Lord—give it up" for him, and grant him the glory he deserves.

This psalm also mentions the Lord's "holy splendor." The King James Version says: "Worship the Lord in the beauty of holiness." There is something beautiful about holiness, and the Lord shares his holiness with us. Through Jesus Christ, we become holy in his eyes—and that's a beautiful thing.

> He framed the globe, He built the sky;
> He made the shining worlds on high
> And reigns in glory there.
> His beams are majesty and light,
> His beauties, how divinely bright!
> His dwelling place, how fair!
> ISAAC WATTS

Fascinating Fact
Some scholars think Psalm 96 is a pastiche of quotations from other Scriptures. In this section alone we find references to Psalms 86:9; 100:4; 29:2; and 97:1.

Notable Quotable
"How high and glorious must be the beauty of His holiness, which is the perfect combination of all his infinite perfections."
JOSEPH LE CONTE

PSALM 97:1-6

1 The Lord is king! Let the earth rejoice!
   Let the farthest islands be glad.
2 Clouds and darkness surround him.
   Righteousness and justice are the foundation of his
      throne.
3 Fire goes forth before him
   and burns up all his foes.
4 His lightning flashes out across the world.
   The earth sees and trembles.
5 The mountains melt like wax before the Lord,
   before the Lord of all the earth.
6 The heavens declare his righteousness;
   every nation sees his glory.

requently a city decides to demolish an old building to make way for a new one. Demolition experts are called in to place dynamite at strategic points. With a huge boom and a cloud of dust, the building essentially vanishes. What was a huge block of brick and metal only a moment ago is now a pile of rubble. Sometimes such an event is publicized, and people watch on TV to see the building go down. Why? Because they love to see such an awesome display of power, especially when it's harnessed for a good purpose.

Many still recall the images of twisted metal and heaps of debris from the Oklahoma City bombing of 1994. That was a demonstration of awesome power employed for a destructive purpose. We still watched the television coverage with amazement, but also with horror.

Power can be used for good or evil. This is underscored by the fact that the inventor of dynamite was Alfred Nobel, for whom the peace prize is named.

The psalmist sees the Lord as powerful, a consuming fire burning up his enemies. These verses speak of events that rival any Hollywood special effects. Visualize the lightning flashing and the mountains melting "like wax." Of course, this isn't good news for the enemies. But we who love the Lord don't need to be afraid. He is our King. His mighty power will benefit those who follow his ways. Let the whole earth rejoice at his coming!

> Before Jehovah's aweful throne,
> Ye nations, bow with sacred joy,
> Know that the Lord is God alone;
> He can create, and He destroy.
> ISAAC WATTS

Bible Networking

Verse 1 speaks of God's coming as the universal King. For other such passages read Isaiah 66:15-16; 2 Thessalonians 1:7-10; and 2 Peter 3:3-10.

Notable Quotable

"The strain of 'Hallelujah' is impossible till it can be said in heart and universe, 'The Lord God Omnipotent reigneth.'"
F. B. MEYER

PSALM 97:7-12

7 Those who worship idols are disgraced—
    all who brag about their worthless gods—
    for every god must bow to him.
8 Jerusalem has heard and rejoiced,
    and all the cities of Judah are glad
    because of your justice, LORD!
9 For you, O LORD, are most high over all the earth;
    you are exalted far above all gods.

10 You who love the LORD, hate evil!
    He protects the lives of his godly people
    and rescues them from the power of the wicked.
11 Light shines on the godly,
    and joy on those who do right.
12 May all who are godly be happy in the LORD
    and praise his holy name!

The town of Antioch on the Mediterranean Sea was an early center of Christian ministry. This was the church that pioneered outreach to the Gentiles, sending Paul and Barnabas on their first missionary journey.

During the persecution in the third century, the beloved bishop of Antioch, Babylas, was martyred. His body was buried in a grove by the Orontes River. His burial place was the former site of a shrine to Apollo. The persecution of Christians died away, but then in the fourth century, the emperor Julian came to power.

As was mentioned in the devotional for August 5, Julian was trying to steer the empire back to the pagan gods. Part of his strategy involved sprucing up pagan worship centers—like the one on the banks of the Orontes River. For that to happen, the bishop's body had to be moved. Julian ordered the exhumation of the bishop's body.

What could the poor Christians in Antioch do? Well, they decided to make a worship service out of it. They carried the bishop's body in a sacred procession to another burial site. As they proceeded, they sang Psalm 97.

"You can have your Apollo," they seemed to be saying. "We have a God who rules over all the earth. You can make us move our bishop's body, but we know where his soul is. You can make life difficult for us, but we have a source of light and joy you know nothing about. The Lord protects us, and so we are happy in him."

> My God, how wonderful thou art,
> Thy majesty how bright,
> How beautiful thy mercy seat
> In depths of burning light!
> FREDERICK W. FABER

Bible Networking
Each of us needs to exercise our happiness and joy in the Lord (verses 11-12). Read Habakkuk 3:17-18.

Notable Quotable
"Each act of self-denial is a seed-germ of the harvest of gladness."
F. B. MEYER

PSALM 98:1-9
A psalm.

¹ Sing a new song to the LORD,
    for he has done wonderful deeds.
He has won a mighty victory
    by his power and holiness.
² The LORD has announced his victory
    and has revealed his righteousness to every nation!
³ He has remembered his promise to love and be faithful
        to Israel.
    The whole earth has seen the salvation of our God.

⁴ Shout to the LORD, all the earth;
    break out in praise and sing for joy!
⁵ Sing your praise to the LORD with the harp,
    with the harp and melodious song,
⁶   with trumpets and the sound of the ram's horn.
Make a joyful symphony before the LORD, the King!

⁷ Let the sea and everything in it shout his praise!
    Let the earth and all living things join in.
⁸   Let the rivers clap their hands in glee!
    Let the hills sing out their songs of joy
⁹   before the LORD.
For the LORD is coming to judge the earth.
    He will judge the world with justice,
    and the nations with fairness.

A young peasant girl named Mary had just gotten the shock of her life, and it would change her life forever. A being clothed in brightness appeared to her. After calming her fears, the angel announced that Mary would give birth to God's own child, even though she was a virgin. "Nothing is impossible with God," the angel told her.

It was all a bit much to deal with, but Mary was an extraordinary young woman. After conferring with her cousin Elizabeth (who was already miraculously pregnant with the child who would become John the Baptist), Mary composed a song of praise.

Nowadays a teenage minstrel would probably write something very introspective: "Something strange is happening to me." But Mary understood that her situation was part of God's great work in human history, and her song reflects this.

Perhaps the words of Psalm 98 inspired her. The psalm calls people to "sing a new song," telling about God's deeds, and Mary did just that. The psalm speaks of God's "power and holiness," and so does she. "He has remembered his promise," says the psalm, and Mary adds, "He has not forgotten his promise to be merciful" (Luke 1:54). And there's one more fascinating connection: The word for "victory" in Psalm 98:1 is related to the Hebrew word *Yeshua*. And that's exactly what Mary named her son. It translates into Greek as "Jesus."

> Joy to the world! the Lord is come;
> Let earth receive her King;
> Let every heart prepare him room,
> And heaven and nature sing.
> ISAAC WATTS

Bible Networking
"Break out" in joyful praise (verse 4) is a favorite expression in Isaiah. (See Isaiah 44:23 and 55:12.) Also, this psalm is one great orchestra of praise, similar to that in Revelation 5:12-14.

Notable Quotable
"There are two levels to the scene; one, God's day of power, at His coming; the other, its anticipation in every act of worship. The psalms we sing now are a rehearsal, and God's presence among His worshipers is a prelude to His appearing to the world."
DEREK KIDNER

Some of the Psalms contain super-scriptions that give musical instructions. The superscriptions can refer to what instruments are to accompany the psalm, how the psalm is to be sung, or what tune is to be used with the psalm. Psalm 4 was to be accompanied by stringed instruments, Psalm 5 by a flute, and Psalm 6 by an eight-stringed instrument. Psalm 8 was to be accompanied probably by a Gittite lyre.

Here is a list of the instruments referred to in the superscriptions, along with a verse from the Psalms that mentions the instrument:

STRINGED INSTRUMENTS

- The ten-stringed harp or Phoeni-cian zither. "Make music for him on the ten-stringed harp" (Psalm 33:2).

- David's harp, probably more of a lyre, with strings made of sheep tripe and a sounding box at the bottom of the instrument. "Play the sweet lyre" (Psalm 81:2).

- Harp *(nebel)*, larger and louder than David's harp. It was shaped something like a bottle with a belly-shaped sounding box underneath it. "Wake up, O harp and lyre! I will waken the dawn with my song" (Psalm 57:8).

WIND INSTRUMENTS

- Trumpet, made of silver or gold, about three feet long with a pro-nounced bell, and played exclu-sively by priests. "Sing your praise to the LORD . . . with trum-pets. . . . Make a joyful symphony before the LORD, the King!" (Psalm 98:5-6).

- Ram's horn. Later horns were straighter and made from other materials. It was used not so much for music as for signals. "Sing your praise to the LORD with . . . the sound of the ram's horn" (Psalm 98:5-6).

◆ Flute, a pipe used commonly in Egypt. Double flutes were played at King Solomon's coronation but are not referred to in the Psalms. "Praise him with stringed instruments and flutes!" (Psalm 150:4).

PERCUSSION INSTRUMENTS

◆ Cymbals. These were the only percussion instruments included in Temple music. Two different kinds are mentioned in Psalm 150, perhaps indicating different sizes or materials. "Praise him with a clash of cymbals" (Psalm 150:5).

◆ Tambourine. This was a hand drum used mainly by women. It was similar to modern tambourines but perhaps without the jangles. "Sing! Beat the tambourine" (Psalm 81:2).

◆ Castanets and rattles. David was also familiar with these (2 Samuel 6:5), but they are not referred to in the Psalms.

As we mentioned above, some of the Psalms contain instructions about how they were to be sung. The superscription for Psalm 46 uses the Hebrew word *alamoth*, probably indicating that it was to be sung by young women. Psalm 53 is called a meditation, which may mean it should be sung slowly or quietly. Psalm 9 says that it is to be sung to the tune of "Death of the Son." Other tunes mentioned include "Doe of the Dawn" (Psalm 22), "Lilies" (Psalm 45), "Dove on Distant Oaks" (Psalm 56), and "Do Not Destroy!" (Psalm 57). These were probably popular melodies of the day that the psalmists used to help the people sing praises to God.

There are more "probably's" in translating the superscriptions than in any other part of the Bible. But there is no "probably" in how the psalmists viewed the Lord. The Lord is a rock, a fortress, a shield. And we can count on him today as much as David did three thousand years ago, even though we don't know what the tune "Do Not Destroy!" sounds like or what a Gittite lyre, if there was such a thing, looks like. Our faith rests on something far more secure than Gittite lyres.

∾

I know not why God's wondrous grace to me he hath made known,
Nor why, unworthy, Christ in love redeemed me for his own.
But "I know whom I have believed and am persuaded that he is able
To keep that which I've committed unto him against that day."

DANIEL W. WHITTLE

PSALM 99:1-5

¹ The LORD is king!
　　Let the nations tremble!
　He sits on his throne between the cherubim.
　　Let the whole earth quake!
² The LORD sits in majesty in Jerusalem,
　　supreme above all the nations.
³ Let them praise your great and awesome name.
　　Your name is holy!
⁴ Mighty king, lover of justice,
　　you have established fairness.
　You have acted with justice
　　and righteousness throughout Israel.
⁵ Exalt the LORD our God!
　　Bow low before his feet, for he is holy!

*A*fter decades of religious corruption, King Uzziah worked hard to bring the nation of Judah back to the Lord. But toward the end of Uzziah's long and prosperous reign, he became proud and burned incense himself on the altar in the Temple, a job reserved for the priests. As punishment, Uzziah contracted leprosy, which forced him to live in isolation the rest of his life. It was a sad last chapter to a great career.

In the year King Uzziah died, a young man named Isaiah saw a vision. God was on a lofty throne, with the train of his robe spilling over the throne and filling the Temple. The whole place was filled with smoke, probably incense, and seraphim surrounded him singing, "Holy, holy, holy is the Lord Almighty. The whole earth is filled with his glory!" (Isaiah 6:1-3).

Isaiah immediately knew he was out of place. If a great king like Uzziah was punished for burning incense, what would happen to him? He loudly confessed his unworthiness. But one of the seraphim picked up a burning coal from the altar with a pair of tongs, touched Isaiah's lips with it, and said, "Now your guilt is removed, and your sins are forgiven" (verse 7).

Throughout his prophetic ministry, Isaiah understood the message of Psalm 99—that God is holy, frighteningly holy. Such a vision of the holy, holy, holy Lord keeps us bowing low before his feet.

> Holy, holy, holy! Lord God Almighty!
> All thy works shall praise thy name, in earth, and sky, and sea;
> Holy, holy, holy! Merciful and mighty!
> God in three persons, blessed Trinity!
> GERALD S. HENDERSON

Bible Networking

This psalm uses the word holy *three times (verses 3, 5, and 9). For other places in Scripture where this word appears three times, see Isaiah 6:3 and Revelation 4:8.*

Notable Quotable

"The more we abase ourselves before God, the more we exalt Him."
F. B. MEYER

PSALM 99:6-9

[6] Moses and Aaron were among his priests;
    Samuel also called on his name.
They cried to the LORD for help,
    and he answered them.
[7] He spoke to them from the pillar of cloud,
    and they followed the decrees and principles he gave
      them.
[8] O LORD our God, you answered them.
    You were a forgiving God,
    but you punished them when they went wrong.

[9] Exalt the LORD our God
    and worship at his holy mountain in Jerusalem,
    for the LORD our God is holy!

*I*t was the third time that night! Little Samuel kept having nightmares, hearing voices in the darkness, and waking up Eli the priest to see if he had called him.

The boy insisted he had heard his name clear as day. "Samuel! Samuel!"

"Go back to bed," the old priest said, probably figuring it was the boy's imagination.

By the third time, Eli figured that maybe it wasn't Samuel's imagination. Maybe it was God trying to get his attention. God had spoken to Moses in a burning bush and to Gideon under an oak tree. Why couldn't he be calling this boy in his bedroom?

"Go and lie down again," Eli instructed. "If someone calls again, say, 'Yes, Lord, your servant is listening'" (1 Samuel 3:8-9).

The voice did call his name once again, and God gave young Samuel a message for the nation—the first of many this prophet would receive. And throughout his life, Samuel, in turn, called on God's name, just as Moses and Aaron did, and the Lord communicated with them. This is the wonder that Psalm 99 describes: God shakes the earth, but he talks with his people on earth. He gets his point across not only with thunder and lightning but also with midnight whispers. We exalt the Lord because he is awesome, yet he also calls us his children.

> *Sinners, whose love can ne'er forget*
> *The wormwood and the gall,*
> *Go, spread your trophies at his feet,*
> *And crown him Lord of all.*
> EDWARD PERRONET

Notable Quotable
"He forgave the sinners, but he slew their sins."
CHARLES HADDON SPURGEON

Thought to Ponder
God's holiness demands a response from us. See 1 Peter 1:16.

PSALM 100:1-3
A psalm of thanksgiving.

1   Shout with joy to the LORD, O earth!
2   Worship the LORD with gladness.
        Come before him, singing with joy.
3   Acknowledge that the LORD is God!
        He made us, and we are his.
        We are his people, the sheep of his pasture.

Nine-year-old Joey worked for nearly a year carving and crafting a toy boat. When he finished, he took it down to the river to test it. But the wind was too strong, pushing the little boat out into the middle of the river. Heartbroken, Joey watched his prize creation drift out of sight.

A few months later Joey was walking downtown and was stunned to see his boat in a storefront window. When he told the manager that it was his boat, the man told him, "That may well be true, but somebody found that boat down by the river and sold it to me. I've got to get back my investment."

Over the next few weeks Joey worked feverishly to earn the money to buy back his boat. When he finally earned enough money, he rushed back to the store and bought his boat. Cradling the boat in his arms, Joey said, "Little boat, you're mine twice. I made you, and I bought you."

God must feel the same way about us, his prize creation. We chose to drift away, but God bought us back. "He made us," Psalm 100:3 tells us, "and we are his." It is fitting that the same verse calls us "the sheep of his pasture," for sheep tend to wander off. Isaiah says, "All of us have strayed away like sheep. We have left God's paths to follow our own. Yet the Lord laid on [Jesus] the guilt and sins of us all" (Isaiah 53:6). The Good Shepherd laid down his life for the sheep (John 10:15) to buy us back for the one who made us. So, as the psalm says, "We are his"—twice.

Let those refuse to sing
Who never knew our God,
But children of the heavenly King
May speak their joys abroad.
ISAAC WATTS

Fascinating Fact
British Christians attached this psalm to a tune that became known as "Old Hundredth." In The Courtship of Miles Standish, *Longfellow calls the "Old Hundredth" "the grand old Puritan anthem."*

Bible Networking
It is possible this psalm was sung in connection with an offering of thanksgiving for the good gifts of God. That offering is described in Leviticus 7:11-18.

Notable Quotable
"When I think of God, my heart is so full of joy that the notes leap and dance as they leave my pen; and since God has given me a cheerful heart, I serve him with a cheerful spirit."
FRANZ JOSEPH HAYDN

PSALM 100:4-5

⁴ Enter his gates with thanksgiving;
go into his courts with praise.
Give thanks to him and bless his name.
⁵ For the LORD is good.
His unfailing love continues forever,
and his faithfulness continues to each generation.

A man threw a party, sending out invitations to all his friends. But when the time arrived, those invited started offering excuses.

"I'm buying some real estate, and I need to inspect it."

"I just got some new software, and I need to try it out."

"I just got married and have some things to take care of."

Meanwhile the host was sitting there with a live band, bowls of crab dip, and no guests. What did he do? Well, he went out to the streets, inviting to his party anyone he saw: travelers, cops, cab drivers, hookers, pushers, beggars. "Come on over! There's plenty of food and festivity for all!"

Jesus told a story much like this one to describe God's kingdom (Luke 14:16-24). Since the original guest list was filled with names of people who didn't come, God threw open his gates to everyone—rich and poor, Jew and Gentile, good and bad. While the first group of people greeted the invitation with yawns, the second group was excited. They would certainly "enter his gates with thanksgiving."

Psalm 100 gives us a glimpse of God's great party. There's plenty of singing and shouting, laughter and merriment, thanks and praise. The whole earth is invited to respond to the Lord's "unfailing love." The Lord has taken care of everything, so all you have to do is show up.

> For why? the Lord our God is good,
> His mercy is forever sure;
> His truth at all times firmly stood,
> And shall from age to age endure.
> WILLIAM KETHE

Fascinating Fact
The first part of the psalm may have been chanted by those who gave burnt offerings, and the last verses may have been the response, sung by the whole company of singers when the fire was applied to the offering.

Notable Quotable
"Most of the bars have what is called a 'happy hour.' I wish we had a 'happy hour' in church, without the liquid."
Radio Preacher
J. VERNON MCGEE
Commenting on
Psalm 100

PSALM 101:1-8
A psalm of David.

¹ I will sing of your love and justice.
    I will praise you, LORD, with songs.
² I will be careful to live a blameless life—
    when will you come to my aid?
  I will lead a life of integrity
    in my own home.
³ I will refuse to look at
    anything vile and vulgar.
  I hate all crooked dealings;
    I will have nothing to do with them.
⁴ I will reject perverse ideas
    and stay away from every evil.
⁵ I will not tolerate people who slander their neighbors.
    I will not endure conceit and pride.

⁶ I will keep a protective eye on the godly,
    so they may dwell with me in safety.
  Only those who are above reproach
    will be allowed to serve me.
⁷ I will not allow deceivers to serve me,
    and liars will not be allowed to enter my presence.
⁸ My daily task will be to ferret out criminals
    and free the city of the LORD from their grip.

arly in his life, Ernest found the second verse of this psalm and decided to make it his motto, committing himself to live a "blameless life." Perhaps that's why he became known as Ernest the Pious—though it's not clear whether the nickname arose out of mockery or admiration.

Ernest was a prince in Germany in the seventeenth century, a time of great upheaval. The Protestant Reformation had torn countries apart along religious, ethnic, and economic lines. Ernest found himself in the midst of the Thirty Years' War (1618–1648), which might be considered the first of the "world wars," with European leaders allying and conniving to carve out for themselves bigger chunks of territory. "Crooked dealings" were common practice. More than half of Germany's population was lost in the vicious fighting.

In the wake of that war, Ernest tried to rebuild Germany, reestablishing churches, hospitals, courts, and other public institutions. Psalm 101 was foundational to this effort. If he heard that some public official had done something wrong, he would send him a copy of this psalm. In fact, it became a catchphrase in that country—to get scolded was to "receive the prince's psalm to read."

But the psalm itself is not a tongue-lashing. Instead it's a commitment to an honest, holy way of life, a commitment we could all stand to make.

> Sing, pray, and swerve not from His ways,
> But do thine own part faithfully;
> Trust His rich promises of grace,
> So shall they be fulfilled in thee;
> God never yet forsook a need
> The soul that trusted Him indeed.
> GEORG NEUMARK

Bible Networking
Read Romans 13:1-2. Could Paul have been thinking of a ruler who followed David's commitments in Psalm 101?

Notable Quotable
"The modern ruler makes promises to the people; this king's promises are made to God—the real source of power of government."
JOHN I. DURHAM

PSALM 102:1-11

A prayer of one overwhelmed with trouble, pouring out problems before the LORD.

1 LORD, hear my prayer!
    Listen to my plea!
2 Don't turn away from me
    in my time of distress.
Bend down your ear
    and answer me quickly when I call to you,
3   for my days disappear like smoke,
    and my bones burn like red-hot coals.
4 My heart is sick, withered like grass,
    and I have lost my appetite.
5 Because of my groaning,
    I am reduced to skin and bones.
6 I am like an owl in the desert,
    like a lonely owl in a far-off wilderness.
7 I lie awake,
    lonely as a solitary bird on the roof.
8 My enemies taunt me day after day.
    They mock and curse me.
9 I eat ashes instead of my food.
    My tears run down into my drink
10 because of your anger and wrath.
    For you have picked me up and thrown me out.
11 My life passes as swiftly as the evening shadows.
    I am withering like grass.

*H*ave you ever noticed how birds often line up on telephone wires? Who knows why they do this, but they look like a church choir getting in place for the anthem. One bird flies up to join the already crowded line, and the others make room.

You've certainly seen how geese form V's as they migrate north or south. How do they decide who gets to be the leader? Do they have some official pecking order?

Have you heard birds calling to one another in the night or exciting one another into an early morning chorus? Birds are social creatures. They instinctively relate to other birds, so that often a whole flock seems to act as one.

And that's why there's nothing quite as lonely as a solitary bird (see verses 6-7). It calls, and no one answers. It flies, but without a formation. The psalmist felt like that, and often we do, too.

But here's an encouraging bit of trivia for you. One of the odder symbols the early Christians used for Christ was a pelican, based on an alternate translation of the Hebrew word that is translated "owl" in verse 6. Whichever bird the author was referring to, when we consider it an image of Christ, it can be a source of comfort. Jesus knew what it feels like to be alone, too, and he can identify with us when we are lonely, struggling, and as out of place as . . . well, as a pelican in the desert.

> *We would leave, O God, to Thee*
> *Every anxious care and fear;*
> *Thou the troubled thought can see,*
> *Thou canst dry the bitter tear.*
> B. L. GASKELL

Fascinating Fact
There's an ancient sundial in Venice with the words of verse 11 inscribed on it.

Notable Quotable
"The Lord allows his babbling children to speak to Him in their own form of speech."
DAVID DICKSON

PSALM 102:12-17

¹² But you, O LORD, will rule forever.
  Your fame will endure to every generation.
¹³ You will arise and have mercy on Jerusalem—
  and now is the time to pity her,
  now is the time you promised to help.
¹⁴ For your people love every stone in her walls
  and show favor even to the dust in her streets.
¹⁵ And the nations will tremble before the LORD.
  The kings of the earth will tremble before his glory.
¹⁶ For the LORD will rebuild Jerusalem.
  He will appear in his glory.
¹⁷ He will listen to the prayers of the destitute.
  He will not reject their pleas.

They call it the Wailing Wall. It's the western courtyard wall of what used to be the Temple in Jerusalem, the only remaining piece of that once-majestic structure. What the Romans didn't level in A.D. 70, the ravages of time, vandals, and crusaders have destroyed or carted off—all except this wall, which now shares its hilltop perch with two Muslim shrines.

The psalmist says of Jerusalem, "Your people love every stone in her walls." You can sense that as the Orthodox Jews come to pray at the Wailing Wall, rocking back and forth in their customary way and raising their voices in chants and cries. Some write down their requests or the names of loved ones and stick the folded paper in the wall's cracks. Surely God will remember his people, just as they remember him.

"The Lord will rebuild Jerusalem," the psalm promises, and theologians have long debated just when and how that will happen. Physically? Spiritually? Through the church? In the end times? We won't settle the questions in these few paragraphs, but we can still learn something from these verses.

God is still at work. He will reveal his glory. He can rebuild cities, and he can rebuild people's lives. People come to wail at the Wailing Wall because they are convinced that God is still working. We can have the same assurance as we kneel in faithful prayer.

> *Lord, teach us how to pray aright*
> *With reverence and with fear;*
> *Though weak and sinful in your sight,*
> *We may, we must draw near.*
> JAMES MONTGOMERY

A Word on Words

The main verbs of verses 16-17 are translated as future tense. The context of the passage requires that. But in the original Hebrew the verbs are present—God is building, appearing, listening, and not rejecting. The psalmist is so sure of this that he speaks of these future events as already taking place.

Notable Quotable

"A man that is destitute knows how to pray. He needs not an instructor. His miseries indoctrinate him wonderfully in the art of prayer. Let us know ourselves destitute that we might know how to pray."
STEPHEN MARSHALL

PSALM 102:18-28

¹⁸ Let this be recorded for future generations,
so that a nation yet to be created will praise the LORD.
¹⁹ Tell them the LORD looked down
from his heavenly sanctuary.
He looked to the earth from heaven
²⁰ to hear the groans of the prisoners,
to release those condemned to die.
²¹ And so the LORD's fame will be celebrated in Zion,
his praises in Jerusalem,
²² when multitudes gather together
and kingdoms come to worship the LORD.

²³ He has cut me down in midlife,
shortening my days.
²⁴ But I cried to him, "My God, who lives forever,
don't take my life while I am still so young!
²⁵ In ages past you laid the foundation of the earth,
and the heavens are the work of your hands.
²⁶ Even they will perish, but you remain forever;
they will wear out like old clothing.
You will change them like a garment,
and they will fade away.
²⁷ But you are always the same;
your years never end.
²⁸ The children of your people
will live in security.
Their children's children
will thrive in your presence."

*W*e're hearing a lot about generations these days. Advertisers are furiously targeting every imaginable age division—*Builders, Boomers, Busters, Boomlets* and Generations X and Y.

Churches are joining in the positioning frenzy as well. Some churches are still run by the pre–World War II generation, but amazing growth has been happening in Boomer churches. These churches have replaced some of the old ways with new styles that appeal to the sixties generation. A few churches are experimenting with alternative services that target Generations X or Y.

All the talk about "targeting" and "positioning" may leave you cold. And you can't help but sympathize with the Builders who wonder if they're leaving any valuable traditions for the succeeding generations to carry on.

Psalm 102 ends with a forward look toward future generations. And what can the psalmist offer to those who will follow? Stories. The record of how God has worked among his people. If the older generation faithfully celebrates the Lord's fame, the younger generation will "thrive" in the Lord's presence. That was true back then, and it's true today. Styles may change, but let's all keep telling the stories of God's mighty acts in any way we can.

> *In heavenly love abiding,*
> *No change my heart shall fear;*
> *And safe is such confiding,*
> *For nothing changes here.*
> *The storm may roar around me,*
> *My heart may low be laid;*
> *But God is round about me,*
> *And can I be dismayed?*
> ANNA L. WARING

Bible Networking
Verse 27 speaks of God always being the same, and Hebrews 13:8 says the same thing about Jesus Christ. Also verses 25-27 of this psalm are quoted in Hebrews 1:10-12, which gives us reason to see this as a messianic psalm.

PSALM 103:1-7
A psalm of David.

1. Praise the LORD, I tell myself;
   with my whole heart, I will praise his holy name.
2. Praise the LORD, I tell myself,
   and never forget the good things he does for me.
3. He forgives all my sins
   and heals all my diseases.
4. He ransoms me from death
   and surrounds me with love and tender mercies.
5. He fills my life with good things.
   My youth is renewed like the eagle's!
6. The LORD gives righteousness
   and justice to all who are treated unfairly.
7. He revealed his character to Moses
   and his deeds to the people of Israel.

*P*salm 103 sounds too good to be true. Surely God can forgive all my sins, but does he really "heal all my diseases"? I still catch an occasional sniffle, and I know devout believers who have died from their diseases. Where was the healing then? Yes, God fills my life with "good things," but why doesn't he take away the bad things?

Those are good questions, but we need to take a step back to get a better view. God does heal all our diseases, but not now necessarily. We are headed for a Kingdom, where there will be no more tears, no more sickness, and no more death. There will be final, complete healing for all. When we pray, "Thy Kingdom come," that's what we're looking forward to. When we ask God to heal a dying loved one, we're asking him to bring a piece of his future Kingdom into the present. Sometimes he does, and sometimes he asks us to wait.

Waiting for the Lord is a common theme in the Psalms (40:1) and other Scriptures. Those who wait patiently for God to act eventually find answers to their cries but not always the answers they expect. They also find themselves strengthened by the Lord. Isaiah promised, "Those who wait on the Lord will find new strength. They will fly high on wings like eagles. They will run and not grow weary. They will walk and not faint" (Isaiah 40:31).

> O praise ye the Lord! Thanksgiving and song
> To Him be outpoured all ages along;
> For love in creation, for heaven restored,
> For grace of salvation, O praise ye the Lord!
> AUTHOR UNKNOWN

Bible Networking
Compare Deuteronomy 6:12 and 8:11, 14 with Psalm 103:2.

Notable Quotable
"Memory is very treacherous, by a strange perversity—it treasures up the refuse of the past and permits priceless treasures to lie neglected."
CHARLES HADDON SPURGEON

PSALM 103:8-14

[8] The LORD is merciful and gracious;
    he is slow to get angry and full of unfailing love.
[9] He will not constantly accuse us,
    nor remain angry forever.
[10] He has not punished us for all our sins,
    nor does he deal with us as we deserve.
[11] For his unfailing love toward those who fear him
    is as great as the height of the heavens above the
    earth.
[12] He has removed our rebellious acts
    as far away from us as the east is from the west.
[13] The LORD is like a father to his children,
    tender and compassionate to those who fear him.
[14] For he understands how weak we are;
    he knows we are only dust.

It's time for the second grade math test. The students are ready with their pencils, but as the test sheets are handed out, they become totally confused. It's a college-level calculus test! The students can't even understand the symbols, much less solve the problems. They are ready for two plus two, but they're being asked to find the functional coordinates for simultaneous equations.

One kid tremulously raises a hand. "Uh, Miss Jones? We can't do these problems."

"What's wrong with you?" she barks. "You're supposed to be smart kids. If you ever want a degree in math, you'll have to solve problems like this. Get busy."

But they're in second grade! They need a teacher who understands their level, who pushes them gently but doesn't demand answers that are beyond them.

Some people seem to think God is like that overdemanding teacher, insisting on perfection when they keep slipping up. They worry about all the "bad grades" God must be giving them as they struggle to do the right thing but often fall short. But Psalm 103 assures us that God understands our weakness. He is "tender and compassionate," a loving Father. He is still troubled by our sin, but he keeps loving us. And through the blood of Christ, he removes our sin from us "as far as the east is from the west."

> O how in this thy quire of souls I stand—
> Propt by thy hand—A heap of sand!
> With busy thoughts—like winds—would scatter quite,
> And put to flight / But for thy might;
> Thy hand alone doth tame
> Those blasts, and knit my frame.
> HENRY VAUGHAN

Bible Networking
The fatherly love and mercy we see here is echoed in Jesus' story of the lost son (Luke 15:11-32).

Notable Quotable
"When sin is pardoned, it is never charged again; the guilt of it can no more return than east can become west."
STEPHEN CHARNOCK

PSALM 103:15-22

¹⁵ Our days on earth are like grass;
    like wildflowers, we bloom and die.
¹⁶ The wind blows, and we are gone—
    as though we had never been here.
¹⁷ But the love of the LORD remains forever
    with those who fear him.
His salvation extends to the children's children
¹⁸   of those who are faithful to his covenant,
    of those who obey his commandments!

¹⁹ The LORD has made the heavens his throne;
    from there he rules over everything.
²⁰ Praise the LORD, you angels of his,
    you mighty creatures who carry out his plans,
    listening for each of his commands.
²¹ Yes, praise the LORD, you armies of angels
    who serve him and do his will!
²² Praise the LORD, everything he has created,
    everywhere in his kingdom.
    As for me—I, too, will praise the LORD.

*T*here comes a time in every child's life when he or she wants desperately to be included. "Me too!" is the common response. If you're headed out the door, the child wants to tag along. If you express your opinion on anything—from your favorite color to the national debt—the child is likely to agree . . . "Yes, that's what I think, too."

In some ways we never outgrow this. "Me too" is what crazes are made of. The kid next door has a Hula Hoop, so you want one, too. The family across the street buys a sports utility vehicle, so you've got to get one, too. If a crowd of people stands on a street corner staring up into the sky, what do you do? Join them! If there's something interesting going on up there, you want to see it!

This last section of Psalm 103 sees something very interesting going on up there and all around. The Lord rules from the heavens, and angels are poised to do his bidding. Everything in the whole universe is summoned to a massive praisefest, extolling the mighty Maker. "Me too," the psalmist pipes up. As insignificant as he is in terms of his lifespan, the psalmist wants to join in the choir of praise.

Will you?

> Let all things their Creator bless,
> And worship him in humbleness,
> O praise him, Alleluia!
> Praise, praise the Father, praise the Son,
> And praise the Spirit, Three in One.
> WILLIAM HENRY DRAPER

Bible Networking
Angels wait for a chance to do God's bidding (verse 20). See Matthew 26:53.

Notable Quotable
"There is too much in this psalm for a thousand pens to write. As in the lofty Alps, some peaks rise above all others, so this psalm overtops the rest."
CHARLES HADDON SPURGEON

PSALM 104:1-12

¹ Praise the LORD, I tell myself;
    O LORD my God, how great you are!
You are robed with honor and with majesty;
²   you are dressed in a robe of light.
You stretch out the starry curtain of the heavens;
³   you lay out the rafters of your home in the rain clouds.
You make the clouds your chariots;
    you ride upon the wings of the wind.
⁴ The winds are your messengers;
    flames of fire are your servants.

⁵ You placed the world on its foundation
    so it would never be moved.
⁶ You clothed the earth with floods of water,
    water that covered even the mountains.
⁷ At the sound of your rebuke, the water fled;
    at the sound of your thunder, it fled away.
⁸ Mountains rose and valleys sank
    to the levels you decreed.
⁹ Then you set a firm boundary for the seas,
    so they would never again cover the earth.

¹⁰ You make the springs pour water into ravines,
    so streams gush down from the mountains.
¹¹ They provide water for all the animals,
    and the wild donkeys quench their thirst.
¹² The birds nest beside the streams
    and sing among the branches of the trees.

*T*he traveler was on his way back from a jungle expedition, on which he studied primitive cultures for his latest book. In England he met a new friend who plied him with questions about his many adventures around the world.

This friend turned out to be well connected in British society. He invited the traveler to stay at his home for a few days to meet his wife and a few friends. There would be a formal dinner that weekend with a duchess, who would love to hear the traveler's stories.

The traveler's head was spinning. A week earlier he had been camping out with people from a stone-age culture. Now he would be dining with a duchess. One problem, though—he had nothing to wear. His traveling clothes were stained and tattered; he had no formal attire worthy of royalty.

"No matter," his host replied. "I'll buy you a suitable outfit." So the traveler was decked out in Britain's best finery, and he saluted the duchess in style.

Psalm 104 addresses royalty, too—the Lord God. He himself is "dressed in a robe of light" (verse 2), but he makes sure the universe is appropriately attired as well (verse 6). This foreshadows a New Testament truth that God clothes us in the righteousness of Jesus in order to prepare us to dine at his table.

> O tell of his might, O sing of his grace,
> Whose robe is the light, whose canopy space.
> His chariots of wrath the deep thunderclouds form,
> And dark is his path on the wings of the storm.
> ROBERT GRANT

Bible Networking
Light is often associated with the Lord. See Matthew 17:2; 1 Timothy 6:16; and 1 John 1:5.

Notable Quotable
Verse 2 "is a picture of God providing the sky like a curtain so that men may not be blinded by the blaze of His glory."
W. E. BARNES

PSALM 104:13-23

¹³ You send rain on the mountains from your heavenly
　　　home,
　　and you fill the earth with the fruit of your labor.
¹⁴ You cause grass to grow for the cattle.
　　You cause plants to grow for people to use.
　　You allow them to produce food from the earth—
¹⁵ 　　wine to make them glad,
　　olive oil as lotion for their skin,
　　and bread to give them strength.
¹⁶ The trees of the LORD are well cared for—
　　the cedars of Lebanon that he planted.
¹⁷ There the birds make their nests,
　　and the storks make their homes in the firs.
¹⁸ High in the mountains are pastures for the wild goats,
　　and the rocks form a refuge for rock badgers.
¹⁹ You made the moon to mark the seasons
　　and the sun that knows when to set.
²⁰ You send the darkness, and it becomes night,
　　when all the forest animals prowl about.
²¹ Then the young lions roar for their food,
　　but they are dependent on God.
²² At dawn they slink back
　　into their dens to rest.
²³ Then people go off to their work;
　　they labor until the evening shadows fall again.

*I*n the sixteenth century two scholars were debating the merits of ancient poetry. One insisted that nothing could measure up to the work of the great classical poets like Ovid or Sophocles. His companion, Henry Stephanus, was working on a commentary on the Psalms. He suggested that his strongly opinionated friend might want to consider classical Hebrew poetry as well.

The classical scholar laughed. The Psalms, he felt, were primitive, coarse. He had heard of one poet who was translating the Psalms into Latin poetry, a project doomed to failure. He said it was like trying "to put seeds in dry sand."

"But have you really heard the Psalms lately?" Stephanus asked, and he read him the 104th Psalm. Could anything be as poetic and inspiring as these old lyrics?

The other scholar listened with growing wonder. Yes, he admitted, he had underestimated this poetry. In a few broad strokes, the psalmist had painted the whole universe. The Lord's majestic handiwork is mirrored in the poet's deft wording. With specific images and crisp verbs, the earth is set in motion.

Any translation may fail, Stephanus acknowledged, but that's the fault of the sower, not the soil. Psalm 104 is a brilliant testimony to a brilliant Creator. Be sure you don't underestimate the psalm—or its subject.

> He built the earth, He spread the sky,
> And fixed the starry lights on high;
> Wonders of grace to God belong,
> Repeat His mercies in your song.
> ISAAC WATTS

Bible Networking

References to the sun setting (verse 19) and people working (verse 23) call to mind some portions of Ecclesiastes (1:5; 2:20-23; 12:1-2)—but the psalmist has a much brighter attitude.

Notable Quotable

"The more we learn about the wonders of our universe, the more clearly we are going to perceive the hand of God."
FRANK BORMAN

PSALM 104:24-35

24 O LORD, what a variety of things you have made!
    In wisdom you have made them all.
    The earth is full of your creatures.
25 Here is the ocean, vast and wide,
    teeming with life of every kind,
    both great and small.
26 See the ships sailing along,
    and Leviathan, which you made to play in the sea.
27 Every one of these depends on you
    to give them their food as they need it.
28 When you supply it, they gather it.
    You open your hand to feed them, and they are
        satisfied.
29 But if you turn away from them, they panic.
    When you take away their breath, they die
    and turn again to dust.
30 When you send your Spirit, new life is born
    to replenish all the living of the earth.

31 May the glory of the LORD last forever!
    The LORD rejoices in all he has made!
32 The earth trembles at his glance;
    the mountains burst into flame at his touch.
33 I will sing to the LORD as long as I live.
    I will praise my God to my last breath!
34 May he be pleased by all these thoughts about him,
    for I rejoice in the LORD.
35 Let all sinners vanish from the face of the earth;
    let the wicked disappear forever.
    As for me—I will praise the LORD!

    Praise the LORD!

Lady Jane Grey was caught in the middle of a political-religious war in England. It was Catholic versus Protestant in the sixteenth century, and she (a Protestant) was suddenly crowned queen. She held the title for nine days. Then she was deposed, held prisoner, and condemned to death.

Shortly before her execution, she wrote to her father, reassuring him that all would be well. She used Psalm 104:29-30. Yes, she was telling him, people die and return to dust. But the Spirit brings new life. That's what she was counting on.

The psalmist is using a very old image. Making the first man, God molded him from the dust of the earth and then breathed into him, giving him life (Genesis 2:7). The word for "spirit" also means "breath" or "wind."

A popular song from a few decades ago was entitled "(All We Are Is) Dust in the Wind." It sounds pretty depressing, but for Christians this title speaks of hope, for if the "Wind" (Spirit) of God blows on us, we know that we will be filled with life. It only makes sense to "praise [our] God to [our] last breath!"

> Through all eternity to Thee
> A joyful song I'll raise;
> But O! eternity's too short
> To utter all Thy praise.
> JOHN ADDISON

Bible Networking

In Scripture the sea (verse 26) is always awe inspiring. Read Job 38:16 and Psalm 74:13.

Notable Quotable

"This psalm . . . never loses sight of the sheer majesty and holiness of God, and at the same time . . . sees that God is in the world which he has made."
WILLIAM BARCLAY

A few years ago a garbage collector's strike in New York City became not only an unsightly embarrassment but also a health hazard. Garbage was heaped upon garbage, and no one would remove it.

Nauseating, isn't it? This is how God sees our sin.

But is that it? Are we condemned to have our sins ever piled before God so that they are all he ever sees in us? In the Psalms we see that God hates the garbage of sin, but we also see that God can do something about it. It's called forgiveness.

Here are some passages from the Psalms that speak of sin and forgiveness:

SIN

◆ *Psalm 102:4*
My heart is sick, withered like grass,
and I have lost my appetite.

◆ *Psalm 38:4*
My guilt overwhelms me—
it is a burden too heavy to bear.

◆ *Psalm 32:3*
When I refused to confess my sin,
I was weak and miserable.

◆ *Psalm 51:4*
Against you, and you alone, have I sinned;
I have done what is evil in your sight.

◆ *Psalm 51:8*
Oh, give me back my joy again.

FORGIVENESS

◆ *Psalm 103:3*
He forgives all my sins
and heals all my diseases.

◆ *Psalm 103:12*
He has removed our rebellious acts
as far away from us as the east is from the west.

◆ *Psalm 32:1-2*
Oh, what joy for those whose rebellion is forgiven,
whose sin is put out of sight!
Yes, what joy for those whose record the LORD has cleared of sin,
whose lives are lived in complete honesty!

Three different Hebrew words are used to describe sin in Psalm 32:1-2: (1) *pesha,* meaning rebellion or mutiny against God; (2) *hataah,* meaning a missing of the mark, as when an arrow falls short of its target; and (3) *avon,* meaning a curving from God's path, which makes us twisted ourselves.

Three other Hebrew words are used for God's forgiveness: (1) *nasa,* meaning our sin taken away like garbage; (2) *kasah,* meaning our sin is covered, atoned for by the blood of the Lamb; and (3) *hashav,* meaning our sin is no longer charged against us—our record is cleared and the bill is paid in full.

By using three different ways to express sin and three ways to express forgiveness for those sins, the psalmist makes it clear that *all* sins can be removed by the Lord. There is nothing—no rebellion, no shortcoming, no perversion of his ways—that cannot be forgiven.

And this sin pervades the heart of each of one of us. A columnist for *The Times* of London regularly concluded his columns by asking the question "What's wrong with the world?" After reading several such entries, the famous British author G. K. Chesterton wrote a letter to the editor:

> Dear Editor:
>
> What's wrong with the world?
> I am.
>
> Faithfully yours,
> G. K. Chesterton

That's what the psalmist concluded, too. Before reading very far in the Psalms, you discover that sin pervades not only heathen nations and David's foes in Israel but also David the king himself—yes, even this one whom God called "a man after [my] own heart" (1 Samuel 13:14). Yet, as we have seen, there is also forgiveness.

The noted psychiatrist Karl Menninger once said that if he could convince the patients in his psychiatric hospital that their sins were forgiven, three-fourths of them could walk out the next day. He knew how sin can shackle people, and he knew that forgiveness was the answer.

So when God says that he has removed our rebellious acts "as far away . . . as the east is from the west" (Psalm 103:12), you'd better believe it.

∾

No condemnation now I dread; Jesus, and
    all in him, is mine!
Alive in him, my living head, and clothed
    in righteousness divine,
Bold I approach the eternal throne, and
    claim the crown, through Christ my
    own.
Amazing love! How can it be that thou,
    my God, shouldst die for me?
CHARLES WESLEY

PSALM 105:1-8

1 Give thanks to the LORD and proclaim his greatness.
   Let the whole world know what he has done.

2 Sing to him; yes, sing his praises.
   Tell everyone about his miracles.

3 Exult in his holy name;
   O worshipers of the LORD, rejoice!

4 Search for the LORD and for his strength,
   and keep on searching.

5 Think of the wonderful works he has done,
   the miracles and the judgments he handed down,

6 O children of Abraham, God's servant,
   O descendants of Jacob, God's chosen one.

7 He is the LORD our God.
   His rule is seen throughout the land.

8 He always stands by his covenant—
   the commitment he made to a thousand generations.

The end of the twentieth century may go down in church history as the era of the "seeker church." Many congregations today seek out the seeker, making their services more attractive to those who may not already be believers. The trend has spawned more entertaining worship services (for good or ill) and friendlier church lobbies.

Many Christians debate whether this is a good thing. We won't solve the issue in these few paragraphs. But this emphasis on seekers does make us reflect on our own spiritual walk. Are we seeking God as we should?

Just because we make a commitment to follow Christ does not mean that our spiritual journey is complete. Many Christians seem to shut down somewhere along the way. Soon after they "get their tickets punched" for the pearly gates, they grab an upper berth and go to sleep. But Christians should be seeking to know God better. Paul prayed for believers to "keep on growing in your knowledge and understanding" (Philippians 1:9) and desired that Christ would "be more and more at home in your hearts" (Ephesians 3:17).

Psalm 105 begins with an awesome worship service—thanking, proclaiming, praising, exulting—and searching. "Search for the Lord," it advises us, "and keep on searching." May we all strive to know more and more of this God who seeks a growing relationship with us.

> Spread, O spread, thou mighty word
> Spread the Kingdom of the Lord,
> Wheresoe'er His breath has given
> Life to beings meant for heaven.
> JONATHAN FRIEDRICH BAHNMAIER

Notable Quotable
"Christianity is a tissue of miracles, and every part of the work of grace on the soul is a miracle. Genuine Christian converts may talk of miracles from morning to night."
ADAM CLARKE

PSALM 105:9-22

⁹ This is the covenant he made with Abraham
   and the oath he swore to Isaac.
¹⁰ He confirmed it to Jacob as a decree,
   to the people of Israel as a never-ending treaty:
¹¹ "I will give you the land of Canaan
   as your special possession."

¹² He said this when they were few in number,
   a tiny group of strangers in Canaan.
¹³ They wandered back and forth between nations,
   from one kingdom to another.
¹⁴ Yet he did not let anyone oppress them.
   He warned kings on their behalf:
¹⁵ "Do not touch these people I have chosen,
   and do not hurt my prophets."
¹⁶ He called for a famine on the land of Canaan,
   cutting off its food supply.
¹⁷ Then he sent someone to Egypt ahead of them—
   Joseph, who was sold as a slave.
¹⁸ There in prison, they bruised his feet with fetters
   and placed his neck in an iron collar.
¹⁹ Until the time came to fulfill his word,
   the LORD tested Joseph's character.
²⁰ Then Pharaoh sent for him and set him free;
   the ruler of the nation opened his prison door.
²¹ Joseph was put in charge of all the king's household;
   he became ruler over all the king's possessions.
²² He could instruct the king's aides as he pleased
   and teach the king's advisers.

*H*e had served the family faithfully. He was chief of staff in a high-class household. The husband trusted this servant to manage his finances and to be alone with his wife. But one day the wife claimed that the servant had attacked her, and she offered as evidence the torn shirt he left behind. You can imagine how the master glared as the servant was led away in chains. *I trusted you! How could you betray me like this?*

The problem was, the servant was innocent. The wife had often tried to seduce the servant, and finally she cooked up this story to pay him back for his rejection of her. The plan worked. The servant, Joseph, now languished in an Egyptian dungeon. *He* was the one betrayed—by the wife, by the master, by the brothers who had sold him into slavery, and seemingly by the God who had promised great things and hadn't come through.

But this was all a test of character, Psalm 105 tells us, and Joseph passed with flying colors. So "the ruler of the nation opened his prison door" and set Joseph free.

What kind of prison are you in? Have you been betrayed? Do you wonder whether God will keep his word? He will, though you may have to wait a bit. Keep the faith, as Joseph did, and soon you'll see the ruler of the universe opening your prison door.

> Yes, come! then tried as in the fire,
> From every lie set free,
> Thy perfect truth shall dwell in us,
> And we shall live in thee.
> THOMAS HUGHS

A Word on Words
Verse 18 speaks of Joseph's neck being placed in an iron collar. Actually, the image is even more striking in Hebrew, for it reads more literally, "his soul (nephesh) entered iron."

Notable Quotable
"Few can bear great and sudden mercies without pride and wantonness, till they are hampered and humbled to carry it moderately."
SAMUEL LEE

PSALM 105:23-36

²³ Then Israel arrived in Egypt;
  Jacob lived as a foreigner in the land of Ham.
²⁴ And the LORD multiplied the people of Israel
  until they became too mighty for their enemies.
²⁵ Then he turned the Egyptians against the Israelites,
  and they plotted against the LORD's servants.

²⁶ But the LORD sent Moses his servant,
  along with Aaron, whom he had chosen.
²⁷ They performed miraculous signs among the Egyptians,
  and miracles in the land of Ham.
²⁸ The LORD blanketed Egypt in darkness,
  for they had defied his commands to let his people
    go.
²⁹ He turned the nation's water into blood,
  poisoning all the fish.
³⁰ Then frogs overran the land;
  they were found even in the king's private rooms.
³¹ When he spoke, flies descended on the Egyptians,
  and gnats swarmed across Egypt.
³² Instead of rain, he sent murderous hail,
  and flashes of lightning overwhelmed the land.
³³ He ruined their grapevines and fig trees
  and shattered all the trees.
³⁴ He spoke, and hordes of locusts came—
  locusts beyond number.
³⁵ They ate up everything green in the land,
  destroying all the crops.
³⁶ Then he killed the oldest child in each Egyptian home,
  the pride and joy of each family.

*P*ut yourself in the sandals of an Israelite slave in Egypt. You spend your days making bricks for Pharaoh. Then Moses shows up, claiming that the Lord is going to set you free and give you a homeland. Moses is an Israelite, but he has been raised in Pharaoh's household. His initial discussions with Pharaoh result in a double workload for you and lower quality materials to work with. Thanks a lot, Moses!

Then the world starts to fall apart—literally. The Nile turns to blood. Frogs overrun the land. Flies and gnats swarm around, and locusts eat the crops. Even the weather goes wacky with hail and lightning.

Just when you think the end of the world has arrived, you notice that these plagues have fallen only on the Egyptians. You, an Israelite, are unscathed. Strange! Maybe this really is the Lord's doing. Could Moses be right?

Then comes word that you should put lamb's blood on your door to save your firstborn son from the angel of death. A month ago you might have scoffed, but the locusts and lightning have made you a believer. You eat supper in your traveling clothes, ready to leave as soon as the signal is given. This last dreadful plague is what finally sets you free.

No doubt many Israelites forgot about the God of Abraham, Isaac, and Jacob while they were in Egypt. But that was then, and God has powerfully invaded the now.

> God the Omnipotent King who ordainest
> Thunder thy clarion, the lightning thy sword;
> Show forth thy pity on high, where thou reignest;
> Give to us peace in our time, O Lord.
> HENRY F. CHORLEY

Bible Networking
Verse 28 speaks of the plague of darkness that descended upon Egypt. Darkness is used as judgment elsewhere as well. Read Joel 2:2 and Revelation 16:10-11.

Notable Quotable
"God is stronger than fire and destruction, and even in the valleys of deepest darkness, rod and staff are put into our hands and bridges are thrown across the abyss."
HELMUT THIELECKE

PSALM 105:37-45

[37] But he brought his people safely out of Egypt, loaded
     with silver and gold;
   there were no sick or feeble people among them.
[38] Egypt was glad when they were gone,
     for the dread of them was great.
[39] The LORD spread out a cloud above them as a covering
     and gave them a great fire to light the darkness.
[40] They asked for meat, and he sent them quail;
     he gave them manna—bread from heaven.
[41] He opened up a rock, and water gushed out
     to form a river through the dry and barren land.
[42] For he remembered his sacred promise
     to Abraham his servant.
[43] So he brought his people out of Egypt with joy,
     his chosen ones with rejoicing.
[44] He gave his people the lands of pagan nations,
     and they harvested crops that others had planted.
[45] All this happened so they would follow his principles
     and obey his laws.

Praise the LORD!

*R*ichard Baxter was a pain in the neck. He was just so . . . so . . . Christian, and he kept influencing others to take their faith seriously, too. Baxter was one of the first Puritans, a reforming group within the Church of England in the seventeenth century. Nowadays Puritans have a bad reputation as fun-hating zealots, but actually they just wanted people to be passionate about following Jesus Christ.

Baxter was a gifted preacher. His lengthy ministry in the town of Kidderminster reformed the whole town. It was said, "On the Lord's day there was no disorder to be seen in the streets; but you might hear a hundred families singing psalms and repeating sermons."

Still, Baxter had his enemies. His emphasis on living for the glory of God made some people uncomfortable. He probably identified with the Israelites in Psalm 105 when "Egypt was glad when they were gone" (verse 38). You may find that true in your own life as well. When God is active in your life, people notice. Some may be excited by it, but others feel threatened.

Don't sweat it. Keep looking for God's guidance and provision, step by step. Just as he led and fed the Israelites, he will care for you. Just continue to follow the verse that was carved on the pulpit of Baxter's church at Kidderminster: "Call upon his name, and make known his deeds among the people" (Psalm 105:1, KJV).

> Through each perplexing path of life
> Our wandering footsteps guide;
> Give us each day our daily bread
> And raiment fit provide.
> PHILIP DODDRIDGE

Psalm at a Glance

This psalm ends as it began, on a positive note. God is to be praised, even though his people have strayed. He keeps showing mercy to those he loves.

Thought to Ponder

As verse 44 reminds us, God's people came into the land by God's grace, not because of their own efforts. Of course, that's also true in a spiritual sense as well. We enter our heavenly home by grace, not by our works. (See Romans 4:14; 6:23; Ephesians 2:8-9).

EXODUS 15:1-2, 11-13, 17-18 (Song of Moses)

¹ "I will sing to the LORD, for he has triumphed
  gloriously;
   he has thrown both horse and rider into the sea.
² The LORD is my strength and my song;
   he has become my victory.
He is my God, and I will praise him;
   he is my father's God, and I will exalt him!

¹¹ "Who else among the gods is like you, O LORD?
   Who is glorious in holiness like you—
so awesome in splendor,
   performing such wonders?
¹² You raised up your hand,
   and the earth swallowed our enemies.

¹³ "With unfailing love you will lead
   this people whom you have ransomed.
You will guide them in your strength
   to the place where your holiness dwells.

¹⁷ "You will bring them in and plant them on your own
  mountain—
   the place you have made as your home, O LORD,
   the sanctuary, O Lord, that your hands have made.
¹⁸ The LORD will reign forever and ever!"

Psalm Link
PSALM 105:42-43

⁴² For he remembered his sacred promise
   to Abraham his servant.
⁴³ So he brought his people out of Egypt with joy, his
   chosen ones with rejoicing.

*I*magine what it must have been like to be Moses. Only a few months earlier he had been herding sheep on a desolate hillside. Then God speaks to him from a burning bush, calling him to lead his people out of Egypt. Despite Moses' excuses, he is soon standing in front of the most powerful man on earth, saying, "Let my people go."

Ten plagues later Moses leads the Israelites from Egypt with the Egyptian military in hot pursuit. Miraculously, the sea opens, the Israelites cross over, and Pharaoh's army is trapped.

How do you feel now, Moses? A mighty victory had been won, and it must have been tempting for Moses to take some of the credit for himself. After all, he was the one who went toe-to-toe with Pharaoh and raised his staff to part the sea. But Moses knew that God deserved the glory for all that had happened.

God had a lot more for Moses to do. But first things first, and, according to Exodus 15, the first thing to do was praise God. All those other important tasks certainly needed to get done, but they could wait until Moses took time to thank God for all he had done. That's what this song in Exodus 15 is all about—praising God for rescuing his people from Egypt.

What has God done for you that you can praise him for today?

> When Moses and the Israelites from Egypt's land did flee,
> Their enemies behind them and in front of them the sea;
> God raised the waters like a wall and opened up their way,
> And the God that lived in Moses' time is just the same today.
>
> J. C. ADDIE

Bible Networking
Why did God choose the Israelites as his people? See Deuteronomy 7:6-9.

Notable Quotable
"Dare to believe that one day, when you know as you are known, you shall understand the lovingkindness that underlay your darkest experience."
F. B. MEYER

PSALM 106:1-12

¹ Praise the LORD!

Give thanks to the LORD, for he is good!
    His faithful love endures forever.
² Who can list the glorious miracles of the LORD?
    Who can ever praise him half enough?
³ Happy are those who deal justly with others
    and always do what is right.

⁴ Remember me, too, LORD, when you show favor to your
        people;
    come to me with your salvation.
⁵ Let me share in the prosperity of your chosen ones.
    Let me rejoice in the joy of your people;
    let me praise you with those who are your heritage.

⁶ Both we and our ancestors have sinned.
    We have done wrong! We have acted wickedly!
⁷ Our ancestors in Egypt
    were not impressed by the LORD's miracles.
They soon forgot his many acts of kindness to them.
    Instead, they rebelled against him at the Red Sea.
⁸ Even so, he saved them—
    to defend the honor of his name
    and to demonstrate his mighty power.
⁹ He commanded the Red Sea to divide, and a dry path
        appeared.
    He led Israel across the sea bottom that was as dry as
        a desert.
¹⁰ So he rescued them from their enemies
    and redeemed them from their foes.

¹¹ Then the water returned and covered their enemies;
  not one of them survived.
¹² Then at last his people believed his promises.
  Then they finally sang his praise.

The final moments of the musical *Camelot* are heartbreaking.

King Arthur had a marvelous hope: that his nation would be ruled by law, not just by whim. He set up the famous Round Table, inviting knights to discuss their disputes rather than go to battle over them. He tried to create a civilization based on justice. And for "one brief shining moment" it worked.

Then, as the story goes, Lancelot and Guenevere fell in love, and Arthur himself was forced to go to war against his best friend. His kingdom was crumbling. All the glories were forgotten. People simply forgot how to be civilized.

But Arthur found hope in a young boy who showed up, ready to go into battle. Instead, the king sent him home, ordering him to tell the story of Camelot to "every living person, far and near."

Forgetfulness brings disaster. That's a common theme of the Old Testament. When people forget God's "many acts of kindness," they drift away from him. Again and again God worked miracles for his people. Again and again they forgot. But that's why the psalmist tells the story—again and again. As we hear the tales of God saving his people, we remember that God remembers us.

I will tell the wondrous story,
How, my lost estate to save,
In his boundless love and mercy
He the ransom freely gave.
PHILIP P. BLISS

Fascinating Fact
Louis IX of France, before judging his people's disputes, would often quote Psalm 106:3.

Bible Networking
In verse 3 we read one of the many beatitudes in the Psalms. See also Psalm 1:1, and compare it with Matthew 5:3-12.

Notable Quotable
"We inherit from our fathers much sin and little wisdom. They could only leave us what they themselves possessed. The sin of the understanding leads on to the sin of the memory. What is not understood will soon be forgotten."
CHARLES HADDON SPURGEON

PSALM 106:13-23

¹³ Yet how quickly they forgot what he had done!
    They wouldn't wait for his counsel!
¹⁴ In the wilderness, their desires ran wild,
    testing God's patience in that dry land.
¹⁵ So he gave them what they asked for,
    but he sent a plague along with it.
¹⁶ The people in the camp were jealous of Moses
    and envious of Aaron, the LORD's holy priest.
¹⁷ Because of this, the earth opened up;
    it swallowed Dathan
    and buried Abiram and the other rebels.
¹⁸ Fire fell upon their followers;
    a flame consumed the wicked.

¹⁹ The people made a calf at Mount Sinai;
    they bowed before an image made of gold.
²⁰ They traded their glorious God
    for a statue of a grass-eating ox!
²¹ They forgot God, their savior,
    who had done such great things in Egypt—
²² such wonderful things in that land,
    such awesome deeds at the Red Sea.
²³ So he declared he would destroy them.
    But Moses, his chosen one, stepped between the
        LORD and the people.
    He begged him to turn from his anger and not
        destroy them.

*I*t had been a month since Moses disappeared on Mount Sinai, and the people were thinking that he was not coming back. No doubt some of them reasoned, "Moses has been up on that mountain for an awfully long time. We're just not sure about his leadership. He has led us through some amazing things, but now we're in the desert. Moses keeps talking about a 'Promised Land,' but it seems like he hasn't thought this trip through much."

Had they been abandoned by Moses and the Lord? What could they do?

They thought back to their days in Egypt. Those Egyptians worshiped some sort of cattle god. Maybe that deity would help the Israelites, too. They went to Aaron with their golden earrings: "Melt these into a cow idol." And Aaron, who should have known better, did just that.

When the last nostril of the golden calf was hammered into shape, a party began—a drunken, licentious rave. Of course that's when Moses finally showed up, angrily smashing the stone tablets of God's commandments. He scolded Aaron, who responded with one of the great excuses of all time: "I threw [the gold earrings] into the fire—and out came this calf!" (Exodus 32:24).

How easy it is for us to forget God. We turn quickly to the idols around us—money, success, pleasure—and rationalize our actions. We must be careful not to follow the example of the Israelites but to learn from their mistakes.

> *Prone to wander, Lord, I feel it;*
> *Prone to leave the God I love.*
> *Here's my heart, O take and seal it;*
> *Seal it for Thy courts above.*
> ROBERT ROBINSON

Bible Networking
For other passages on jealousy (verse 16), read Numbers 16:3 and Matthew 27:18.

Notable Quotable
"It is hoped we shall never live to see a time when the miracles of our redemption shall be forgotten; when the return of Jesus Christ from heaven shall be despaired of; and when people shall fabricate a new philosophical deity for them to worship, instead of the God of their ancestors, to whom glory has been ascribed from generation to generation."
GEORGE HORNE

PSALM 106:24-31

²⁴ The people refused to enter the pleasant land,
   for they wouldn't believe his promise to care for them.
²⁵ Instead, they grumbled in their tents
   and refused to obey the LORD.
²⁶ Therefore, he swore
   that he would kill them in the wilderness,
²⁷ that he would scatter their descendants among the nations,
   exiling them to distant lands.

²⁸ Then our ancestors joined in the worship of Baal at Peor;
   they even ate sacrifices offered to the dead!
²⁹ They angered the LORD with all these things,
   so a plague broke out among them.
³⁰ But Phinehas had the courage to step in,
   and the plague was stopped.
³¹ So he has been regarded as a righteous man
   ever since that time.

Joshua and Caleb hurried back to safety after completing their assignment to spy out the land of Canaan. After a couple of years wandering in the desert, they were thrilled with the lush farmland they encountered. Joshua and Caleb must have been ecstatic on the way back to the camp, chattering about what life would be like in this land God had promised them.

When they reached the camp, they cheerfully reported the good news: It's a magnificent land, flowing with milk and honey!

But five other pairs of spies had returned with a different story: The people living there are huge. They make us look like grasshoppers. We'll never displace them.

Joshua and Caleb had seen those people, too, and they did look big—but they knew God is bigger. If God had promised this land to Israel, no one could stand in their way.

But the Israelites bought the majority report, rejecting Caleb and Joshua's call to arms. As a result, the Lord allowed none of the people except Joshua and Caleb to enter the land. It was an early example of that great comic-strip saying: "We have met the enemy, and he is us."

God's people are still making that mistake. We cower from new experiences because we fear the opposition. God wants to lead us forward, but we feel like grasshoppers. Don't be like the Israelites, who "grumbled in their tents and refused to obey the Lord" (Psalm 106:25).

> To an inheritance divine
> He taught our hearts to rise;
> 'Tis uncorrupted, undefiled,
> Unfading in the skies.
> ISAAC WATTS

Bible Networking
Phinehas (verse 30) was a grandson of Aaron, the high priest, and thus a great-nephew of Moses. Find this story in Numbers 25.

Notable Quotable
"Generally speaking, the soul and body fare inversely. When the body is pampered with every luxury, the soul starves."
F. B. MEYER

PSALM 106:32-39

³² At Meribah, too, they angered the LORD,
causing Moses serious trouble.

³³ They made Moses angry,
and he spoke foolishly.

³⁴ Israel failed to destroy the nations in the land,
as the LORD had told them to.

³⁵ Instead, they mingled among the pagans
and adopted their evil customs.

³⁶ They worshiped their idols,
and this led to their downfall.

³⁷ They even sacrificed their sons
and their daughters to the demons.

³⁸ They shed innocent blood,
the blood of their sons and daughters.
By sacrificing them to the idols of Canaan,
they polluted the land with murder.

³⁹ They defiled themselves by their evil deeds,
and their love of idols was adultery in the LORD's
sight.

*A*fter church on Sunday, the young couple climbed into their classy sports car and began the drive home.

"So, what did you think about the pastor's message?" the husband asked, turning on the radio.

"Well, it was interesting," the wife replied, "but I don't think it really applied to—ooh, turn the radio up. I love this song."

"Don't you love this car's sound system?" he added as the music swelled. "I paid an arm and a leg for this car, but it's worth it."

She suddenly thought of something. "Honey, could we swing by my office? I need to pick up some reports to work on this afternoon."

"Working again?" he chided. "You never rest, do you?"

"Well, I assume you want to keep making the payments on this car. Besides, you work as much as I do."

"Not today," he countered. "Football season is starting. I'm going to camp out on that sofa all afternoon."

"Oh yeah," she said, "I forgot." Then, as her favorite song ended, she asked, "So what did you think about the pastor's message?"

"Well, it was all right, I guess. But I wish he'd make it more relevant. I just don't see what idol worship has to do with us today."

His mighty works and ways
By Moses he made known,
But gave the world his truth and grace
By his beloved Son.
ISAAC WATTS

Bible Networking
For more on the life of a believer in the midst of an unbelieving culture (verse 35), read 1 Corinthians 10:19-22.

Notable Quotable
"The grace of God is as necessary to create a right temper in a Christian on the breaking of a china plate as on the death of an only son."
JOHN NEWTON

PSALM 106:40-48

40 That is why the LORD's anger burned against his people,
   and he abhorred his own special possession.
41 He handed them over to pagan nations,
   and those who hated them ruled over them.
42 Their enemies crushed them
   and brought them under their cruel power.
43 Again and again he delivered them,
   but they continued to rebel against him,
   and they were finally destroyed by their sin.
44 Even so, he pitied them in their distress
   and listened to their cries.
45 He remembered his covenant with them
   and relented because of his unfailing love.
46 He even caused their captors
   to treat them with kindness.

47 O LORD our God, save us!
   Gather us back from among the nations,
so we can thank your holy name
   and rejoice and praise you.

48 Blessed be the LORD, the God of Israel,
   from everlasting to everlasting!
Let all the people say, "Amen!"

Praise the LORD!

*L*ittle Billy was acting up regularly, and his parents didn't know what to do. They tried to punish him appropriately, but nothing seemed to work.

The family had been planning a trip to Disney World for some time. At one point Billy got his mom so exasperated that she threatened, "Keep that up and you won't go to Disney World." For a while the threat seemed to work. Billy was looking forward to the trip and didn't want to jeopardize it. But eventually Billy went on another defiant streak. His parents had to follow through on their threat. They canceled the trip, making arrangements for Billy to go to a camp for troubled kids.

But Mom and Dad kept thinking about Billy the whole time. They called him every night to let him know they loved him, and when he returned, they had several gifts for him. Even though he was being punished, they wanted him to know that he was still part of the family.

That's a picture of God with his people. He often warned them: If you reject me, things will go badly for you. And they did. Ultimately, the Babylonians overran Jerusalem and captured its citizens. But even during this punishment, the Lord "pitied them in their distress." The stories of Nehemiah, Esther, and Daniel show that God was working even within his people's captivity, "remember[ing] his covenant" and "caus[ing] their captors to treat them with kindness."

> And I, poor sinner, cast it away;
> Lived for the toil or pleasure of each day,
> As if no Christ had shed His precious blood,
> As if I owed no homage to my God.
> HENRY W. BAKER

Notable Quotable
"Penitence is never out of place in praise, nor praise in an act of penitence."
DEREK KIDNER

Poverty is a major concern of the entire Old Testament, and no Old Testament book has more references to this subject than the Psalms. Here are a few references regarding the poor and the oppressed:

◆ Psalm 72:13
He feels pity for the weak and the needy,
   and he will rescue them.

◆ Psalm 10:17
LORD, you know the hopes of the helpless.
   Surely you will listen to their cries and comfort them.

◆ Psalm 74:21
Don't let the downtrodden be constantly disgraced!
   Instead, let these poor and needy ones give praise to your name.

◆ Psalm 109:31
He stands beside the needy,
   ready to save them from those who condemn them.

◆ Psalm 113:7
He lifts the poor from the dirt
   and the needy from the garbage dump.

◆ Psalm 146:9
The LORD protects the foreigners among us.
   He cares for the orphans and widows.

◆ Psalm 112:1, 9
Happy are those who fear the LORD. . . .
   They give generously to those in need.

◆ Psalm 41:1
Oh, the joys of those who are kind to the poor.
   The LORD rescues them in times of trouble.

God set up many systems in the Old Testament to relieve poverty: (1) Judges were warned not to deny justice to the poor in court cases (Exodus 23:6); (2) farmers were instructed to leave any grain and grapes that were missed in the harvesting process for foreigners, orphans, and widows (Deuteronomy 24:21); (3) the wealthy were encouraged to give loans to the poor, and every seventh year all outstanding debts were cancelled (Deuteronomy 15:1, 9); (4) tithes were to be given not only to the Levites and the Temple but also to the "foreigners living among you, the orphans, and the widows" (Deuteronomy 14:29); (5) property rights of the poor were safeguarded so that the rich could not permanently take over their land (Leviticus 25:24-28); and (6) while the poor could sell themselves into voluntary servitude, they had to be released after seven years and provided with resources to get a fresh start in life (Deuteronomy 15:12-14).

Despite these provisions, however, poverty and oppression were always a problem in Israel. We can see this by how frequently the Psalms speak about this issue. At first it might seem surprising that a king like David, who became increasingly wealthy during his lifetime, would be so concerned about such social issues. But David probably never forgot that his great-grandmother, Ruth, was a foreigner in Israel and had to glean in the fields. He never forgot that he himself had been a fugitive for many years, a hunted man living in caves and foraging for food.

It might have seemed strange for Israelites to sing psalms written by their king, saying, "I am poor and needy" (Psalm 70:5), but a psalm like that brings all of us to the same level before God, which is where we need to be.

∾

To comfort and to bless, to find a balm for woe,
To tend the lone and fatherless is angels' work below.
And we believe thy word, though dim our faith may be:
Whate'er for thine we do, O Lord, we do it unto thee.
WILLIAM W. HOW

∾

How did David the psalmist deal with the needy and handicapped? Read the story of Mephibosheth in 2 Samuel 4:4 and 2 Samuel 9.

Selah

BOOK FIVE (PSALMS 107–150)
PSALM 107:1-9

¹ Give thanks to the LORD, for he is good!
His faithful love endures forever.
² Has the LORD redeemed you? Then speak out!
Tell others he has saved you from your enemies.
³ For he has gathered the exiles from many lands,
from east and west, from north and south.

⁴ Some wandered in the desert,
lost and homeless.
⁵ Hungry and thirsty,
they nearly died.
⁶ "LORD, help!" they cried in their trouble,
and he rescued them from their distress.
⁷ He led them straight to safety,
to a city where they could live.
⁸ Let them praise the LORD for his great love
and for all his wonderful deeds to them.
⁹ For he satisfies the thirsty
and fills the hungry with good things.

*T*his is a beautiful and fascinating psalm. After a three-verse introduction, there are four stanzas, each beginning with the word *some* and each ending with "Let them praise the Lord." Then the last ten verses offer a conclusion with a very surprising twist.

At first glance the four sections seem to describe four different groups of people: (1) wanderers who got lost in the desert; (2) prisoners condemned to hopelessness; (3) sufferers of incurable illnesses; and (4) sailors about to be shipwrecked. But commentator Derek Kidner points out that the psalmist was using all four figures to describe Israel—and they all can describe us as well.

The New Testament presents Jesus Christ as the answer. He is the way (John 14:6) for lost wanderers. He is the one who breaks the chains of sin and declares that there is no condemnation (Romans 8:1) for hopeless prisoners. He is the Great Physician (Luke 5:31), bringing relief for sufferers. He is the calmer of storms (Mark 4:39-41) for those about to sink beneath the waves.

If Christ has rescued you from any of these four situations, then your natural response should be as the second verse indicates: "Speak out! Tell others he has saved you."

> All my life long I had panted for a drink from
>   some cool spring
> That I hoped would quench the burning of the thirst
>   I felt within.
> Hallelujah! I have found him whom my soul so long
>   has craved!
> Jesus satisfies my longings; through his blood I
>   now am saved.
> CLARA T. WILLIAMS

Bible Networking
What city is the psalmist talking about in verse 7? Maybe it's the one in Hebrews 12:22 or in Revelation 21:1-4.

Notable Quotable
"Every furrow in the book of Psalms is sown with seeds of thanksgiving."
JEREMY TAYLOR

PSALM 107:10-22

[10] Some sat in darkness and deepest gloom,
  miserable prisoners in chains.

[11] They rebelled against the words of God,
  scorning the counsel of the Most High.

[12] That is why he broke them with hard labor;
  they fell, and no one helped them rise again.

[13] "LORD, help!" they cried in their trouble,
  and he saved them from their distress.

[14] He led them from the darkness and deepest gloom;
  he snapped their chains.

[15] Let them praise the LORD for his great love
  and for all his wonderful deeds to them.

[16] For he broke down their prison gates of bronze;
  he cut apart their bars of iron.

[17] Some were fools in their rebellion;
  they suffered for their sins.

[18] Their appetites were gone,
  and death was near.

[19] "LORD, help!" they cried in their trouble,
  and he saved them from their distress.

[20] He spoke, and they were healed—
  snatched from the door of death.

[21] Let them praise the LORD for his great love
  and for all his wonderful deeds to them.

[22] Let them offer sacrifices of thanksgiving
  and sing joyfully about his glorious acts.

*I*n 1544 Psalm 107:20 was the text on which Cambridge-educated George Wishart preached to plague-stricken Dundee, Scotland. When he heard that a deadly epidemic was ravaging the town, he had hurried to get there. "They are in trouble and need comfort," he said. Wishart also hoped that the plague would soften the hearts of the people so they would respond spiritually to the gospel message.

This preacher's arrival was greeted with great joy. He visited the sick, assisted the poverty-stricken, and in the process exposed himself to the dreaded plague day after day. But Wishart had a custom—which in that day was thought to be very strange—of taking a bath in a tub every night. Along with the mercy of God, that custom may have preserved his life in Dundee.

Day after day more citizens, both those who were well and those who were dying, responded to Wishart's gospel message. Eventually Dundee became a key city in the Scottish Reformation. A young man who came along as Wishart's bodyguard and valet was increasingly impressed with the message, too. That young man was John Knox, who became the founder of Presbyterianism.

Sometimes, as in Psalm 107, it takes some terrible situation to move us to cry out, "Lord, help!" But once we do turn to him, he is ready to respond and help us.

> Long my imprisoned spirit lay
> Fast bound in sin and nature's night;
> Thine eye diffused a quickening ray;
> I woke—the dungeon flamed with light!
> My chains fell off, my heart was free,
> I rose, went forth, and followed Thee.
> CHARLES WESLEY

A Word on Words

In Scripture the word *fool (verse 17)* does not refer primarily to someone of low intelligence or someone who is ignorant, but rather it refers to someone who is willfully perverse, choosing to adopt destructive behaviors and lifestyles. See 1 Samuel 25:23-25 for the story of Nabal, whose very name means "fool."

Bible Networking

For another reference to gates of bronze and bars of iron *(verse 16)*, see Isaiah 45:2.

PSALM 107:23-32

²³ Some went off in ships,
    plying the trade routes of the world.
²⁴ They, too, observed the LORD's power in action,
    his impressive works on the deepest seas.
²⁵ He spoke, and the winds rose,
    stirring up the waves.
²⁶ Their ships were tossed to the heavens
    and sank again to the depths;
    the sailors cringed in terror.
²⁷ They reeled and staggered like drunkards
    and were at their wits' end.
²⁸ "LORD, help!" they cried in their trouble,
    and he saved them from their distress.
²⁹ He calmed the storm to a whisper
    and stilled the waves.
³⁰ What a blessing was that stillness
    as he brought them safely into harbor!
³¹ Let them praise the LORD for his great love
    and for all his wonderful deeds to them.
³² Let them exalt him publicly before the congregation
    and before the leaders of the nation.

*I*n a storm like the one described in Psalm 107, John Newton experienced God's amazing grace. He was so notorious for his swearing, his atheism, and his promiscuity that he shamed even his fellow sailors.

But in early March, 1748, a violent storm arose. Water poured into Newton's cabin, and he heard a cry, "The ship is sinking!" Newton rushed on deck, and there he saw the sails in shreds and the upper timbers of the ship shattered. Drenched by icy waves, he struggled for hours to keep the ship afloat. His teeth were chattering, and his strength was gone.

In such straits he wanted to pray, but he didn't think God, if he existed, would hear him. His mind ran through Scriptures he had learned as a child, but they all spoke of judgment for someone like himself. When the storm subsided, Newton began reading the New Testament. Although bleary eyed, he kept reading, and one message struck home: "The Prodigal Son was myself."

He called on the Lord, who showed him amazing grace. Newton later wrote a famous hymn by the same name. In many ways God calmed the storms in Newton's life, making them die down to a whisper.

Sometimes we forget that God wants to show us not only his amazing grace but also his ability to calm the storms in our life. What storms are you facing in your life today? Call out to God to help you through them.

> *Thy way is on the deep, O Lord!*
> *Even there we'll go with Thee;*
> *We'll meet the tempest at Thy word*
> *And walk upon the sea.*
> MARTINEAU'S COLLECTION

Bible Networking

Compare this psalm with Jonah 1–2; Mark 4:35-41; and Acts 27.

Notable Quotable

"Prayer is good in a storm. We may pray staggering and reeling, and pray when we are at our wit's end. God will hear us amid the thunder and answer us out of the storm. . . . And when God makes peace, it is peace indeed, the peace of God that passes all understanding."
CHARLES HADDON SPURGEON

PSALM 107:33-43

³³ He changes rivers into deserts,
   and springs of water into dry land.
³⁴ He turns the fruitful land into salty wastelands,
   because of the wickedness of those who live there.
³⁵ But he also turns deserts into pools of water,
   the dry land into flowing springs.
³⁶ He brings the hungry to settle there
   and build their cities.
³⁷ They sow their fields, plant their vineyards,
   and harvest their bumper crops.
³⁸ How he blesses them!
   They raise large families there,
   and their herds of cattle increase.

³⁹ When they decrease in number and become
      impoverished
   through oppression, trouble, and sorrow,
⁴⁰ the LORD pours contempt on their princes,
   causing them to wander in trackless wastelands.
⁴¹ But he rescues the poor from their distress
   and increases their families like vast flocks of sheep.
⁴² The godly will see these things and be glad,
   while the wicked are stricken silent.
⁴³ Those who are wise will take all this to heart;
   they will see in our history the faithful love of the
      LORD.

*I*n mid-February 1830, Alexander Duff preached a sermon on the last verse of Psalm 107. It was not a sermon that he wanted to preach nor a text he wanted to use.

Four months earlier he and his wife had sailed from England, bound for India, where they would be the first missionaries of the Presbyterian Church of Scotland. On board the ship with him was his eight-hundred-volume library, which would be helpful in establishing a Christian college in India.

But as they rounded the southern tip of Africa, the ship ran aground, the masts were cut away, and waves began dashing over the deck. Eventually the passengers found safety on a small island.

The next morning a sailor found two books from the wreckage, Duff's Bible and his Scottish Psalm Book. So the group knelt down on the sand and listened as Duff read Psalm 107 and preached from the last verse.

In this last verse the psalmist wants to make sure that his listeners don't miss the point: God saves us, and he does it not just once but over and over again in many different ways. His grace is truly amazing. His salvation is so wonderful that it spills over into all of life. And as Alexander Duff learned, even in our losses we can learn something of God's goodness.

> *My times of sorrow and of joy,*
> *Great God, are in your hand;*
> *My choicest comforts come from you*
> *And go at your command.*
> *If you would take them all away,*
> *And all my world be gone,*
> *I'd still seek lasting happiness*
> *In you and you alone.*
> BENJAMIN BEDDOME

Notable Quotable
"Consider the various vignettes of this psalm. Love broods over the weary caravan that faints in the desert; visits the prison house with its captives; watches by our beds of pain; notices each lurch of the tempest-driven vessel; brings the weary hosts from the wilderness into the fruitful soil. Detected everywhere is the loving-kindness of the Lord."
F. B. MEYER

PSALM 108:1-5

A psalm of David. A song.

¹ My heart is confident in you, O God;
   no wonder I can sing your praises!
Wake up, my soul!
²   Wake up, O harp and lyre!
   I will waken the dawn with my song.
³ I will thank you, LORD, in front of all the people.
   I will sing your praises among the nations.
⁴ For your unfailing love is higher than the heavens.
   Your faithfulness reaches to the clouds.
⁵ Be exalted, O God, above the highest heavens.
   May your glory shine over all the earth.

The great Italian tenor Enrico Caruso was often unsure of himself prior to a performance. Sometimes when he was facing a very demanding role, a little voice inside of him seemed to say, "You can't do it, Enrico! You can't do it!"

Enrico decided that he must have two personalities within him, the Little Me and the Big Me. The Little Me told him he couldn't do it. It was always negative and doubtful. The Big Me, however, told him he could do it. It was positive and full of confidence.

Sometimes offstage before a large concert, Caruso could be heard muttering to himself, "Get out, Little Me! Get out, Little Me!" Then the Big Me would take over as he went on stage.

For Christians, the Big Me takes over when we say, along with the apostle Paul, "I can do everything with the help of Christ who gives me the strength I need" (Philippians 4:13).

In this psalm David expresses his confidence in his big God in verse 1, and throughout the first five verses he exalts God for his love and faithfulness. That's a good way for us to begin when the Little Me takes over in our life. Because David starts the psalm in this way, he can end the psalm by saying, "With God's help we will do mighty things" (verse 13).

> My God is reconciled, His pardoning voice I hear.
> He owns me for His child; I can no longer fear,
> With confidence I now draw nigh,
> With confidence I now draw nigh,
> And "Father, Abba, Father," cry.
> CHARLES WESLEY

Fascinating Fact
Note that it isn't the dawn (or the rooster crowing or the alarm clock ringing) that wakes up the psalmist. It is the psalmist who wakes up the dawn (verse 2). He is so eager to sing praise to God that he tells the sun that it is time to wake up.

Notable Quotable
"How deeply God loves his people, and how true He is to His word—these are experiences that keep growing on God's children as long as they draw breath here on earth. Surely both are as high as the heavens or as high as the clouds."
H. C. LEUPOLD

PSALM 108:6-13

⁶ Use your strong right arm to save me,
    and rescue your beloved people.
⁷ God has promised this by his holiness:
    "I will divide up Shechem with joy.
    I will measure out the valley of Succoth.
⁸ Gilead is mine,
    and Manasseh is mine.
    Ephraim will produce my warriors,
    and Judah will produce my kings.
⁹ Moab will become my lowly servant,
    and Edom will be my slave.
    I will shout in triumph over the Philistines."

¹⁰ But who will bring me into the fortified city?
    Who will bring me victory over Edom?
¹¹ Have you rejected us, O God?
    Will you no longer march with our armies?
¹² Oh, please help us against our enemies,
    for all human help is useless.
¹³ With God's help we will do mighty things,
    for he will trample down our foes.

*I*f you think you have troubles, think of Israel. Whether you think of modern Israel or ancient Israel, you will come up with the same conclusion: Israel has always been surrounded by enemies.

As you read verses 7-10, you'll find eleven first-person pronouns—*I, me, my,* and *mine.* This is the almighty God speaking. It's as if God is looking at a map of the Middle East and pointing his finger, first at the sections of Israel and then at the nations surrounding it. They are all his. Even though the enemy nations worshiped other gods, they were all his. He controlled them.

Among these enemies of Israel was the small nation of Edom. One of the fortified strongholds of this nation was Petra, which was built into the towering rock southeast of the Dead Sea. Tourists still marvel at the sights of this ancient Edomite city. Could such a remote fortified city ever be taken? Yes, even Edom's Petra was in God's hands.

Think of the problems surrounding you. Let God put his finger on each one and declare, "It is mine. I am in charge there, too." Then think of that impenetrable Petra, and see if the Lord won't lead you into that enemy stronghold.

> Conquering now and still to conquer, Jesus thou
>   ruler of all,
> Thrones and their scepters all shall perish; crowns
>   and their splendor shall fall.
> Not to the strong is the battle, not to the swift is the
>   race,
> But to the true and the faithful, victory is prom-
>   ised through grace.
> SALLIE MARTIN

A Word on Words

A literal rendering of verse 9 would be "Moab is my washbasin; on Edom I throw my sandals." A lowly servant would wash his master's feet in the washbasin after the master had taken off his dusty sandals and tossed them in the general direction of his slave.

Fascinating Fact

The verses in this psalm are almost identical to Psalm 57:7-11 and Psalm 60:5-12. But there are some differences. See if you can find them.

PSALM 109:1-8
For the choir director: A psalm of David.

¹ O God, whom I praise,
   don't stand silent and aloof
² while the wicked slander me
   and tell lies about me.
³ They are all around me with their hateful words,
   and they fight against me for no reason.
⁴ I love them, but they try to destroy me—
   even as I am praying for them!
⁵ They return evil for good,
   and hatred for my love.

⁶ Arrange for an evil person to turn on him.
   Send an accuser to bring him to trial.
⁷ When his case is called for judgment,
   let him be pronounced guilty.
   Count his prayers as sins.
⁸ Let his years be few;
   let his position be given to someone else.

*B*enedict Arnold, a brilliant general on the colonists' side in the early days of the American Revolution, jumped to the British side in 1780 and arranged to turn the strategic post of West Point over to the British. In exchange, Arnold was handed a considerable sum of money and was named a brigadier general in the British army. This treachery made his name synonymous with the word *traitor*.

David felt betrayed when Ahithophel went over to Absalom's side. Paul felt betrayed when Demas deserted him, but of course the deepest betrayal in Scripture was when Judas sold Jesus for thirty pieces of silver.

About seven weeks after Judas committed suicide, the apostle Peter quoted verse 8 of this psalm to sanction the selection of a new apostle to take the traitor's place.

Interesting, isn't it, that Peter was the one who quoted this passage about the traitor. After all, it was Peter who had denied his Lord three times. In those hours before the Crucifixion, whose side was Peter really on?

Perhaps there is a little bit of traitor in all of us, and we need to confess those times when someone looking on might really think that we have switched sides. Maybe it's clear which side you're on when you're sitting in church, but what about during the week? Whose side are you really on?

> Jesus, thou hast bought us, not with gold or gem,
> But with thine own lifeblood, for thy diadem.
> With thy blessing filling each who comes to thee,
> Thou hast made us willing, thou hast made us free.
> By thy grand redemption, by thy grace divine,
> We are on the Lord's side, Savior, we are thine.
> FRANCES R. HAVERGAL

A Word on Words

From the root meaning of the word for "sin" (to miss the mark), verse 7 could be translated as "May his prayers be misses."

Notable Quotable

"Truly this is one of the hard places of Scripture, a passage which the soul trembles to read; yet as it is a psalm unto God and given by inspiration, it is not ours to sit in judgment upon it but to bow our ear to what God the Lord would speak to us therein."
CHARLES HADDON SPURGEON

PSALM 109:9-19

⁹ May his children become fatherless,
    and may his wife become a widow.
¹⁰ May his children wander as beggars;
    may they be evicted from their ruined homes.
¹¹ May creditors seize his entire estate,
    and strangers take all he has earned.
¹² Let no one be kind to him;
    let no one pity his fatherless children.
¹³ May all his offspring die.
    May his family name be blotted out in a single
        generation.
¹⁴ May the LORD never forget the sins of his ancestors;
    may his mother's sins never be erased from the
        record.
¹⁵ May these sins always remain before the LORD,
    but may his name be cut off from human memory.
¹⁶ For he refused all kindness to others;
    he persecuted the poor and needy,
    and he hounded the brokenhearted to death.
¹⁷ He loved to curse others;
    now you curse him.
He never blessed others;
    now don't you bless him.
¹⁸ Cursing is as much a part of him as his clothing,
    or as the water he drinks,
        or the rich food he eats.
¹⁹ Now may his curses return and cling to him like
        clothing;
    may they be tied around him like a belt.

*I*t was said of Archbishop Thomas Cranmer of England that if you wished to be sure he would do you a good turn, you would have to do something bad to him.

This is certainly the New Testament's teaching. Jesus taught: "Love your enemies! Pray for those who persecute you!" (Matthew 5:44). Paul wrote, "Conquer evil by doing good" (Romans 12:21).

Yet the difference between this psalm and New Testament teachings cannot be explained simply by saying that the Old Testament teaching was different. After all, in Romans 12, Paul also quotes a passage from Deuteronomy 32:35: " 'I will repay those who deserve it,' says the Lord."

That may be part of the answer. David was not seeking to execute judgment himself, even though he was the absolute monarch. He was merely seeking justice—God's justice. As F. G. Hibbard put it a century ago: "If a murderer broke into [your] house and murdered your mother, and then escaped, and the sheriff went after him to arrest him, don't you think that you would pray to God that the murderer would be caught and brought to justice?"

How can you pray for both justice and mercy in your work today?

> Depth of mercy! can there be mercy still reserved
> for me?
> Can my God His wrath forbear—me, the chief of
> sinners, spare?
> There for me my Savior stands, holding forth His
> wounded hands;
> God is love! I know, I feel, Jesus weeps and loves
> me still.
> CHARLES WESLEY

Bible Networking
This is one of the six imprecatory psalms. The other five are Psalms 35, 58, 69, 83, and 137. In these psalms the psalmist calls for the Lord's judgment on the enemies of God's people.

Notable Quotable
"If we choose to curse, cursing is the environment we finally inhabit, inescapably. If we oppress, oppression is the context in which we exist, unavoidably. Our words and our acts create conditions in which we ourselves must live. Unrepentant and unforgiven, we live with the curses and pitiless actions which we set loose in the world."
EUGENE PETERSON

PSALM 109:20-31

²⁰ May those curses become the LORD's punishment for
    my accusers
    who are plotting against my life.
²¹ But deal well with me, O Sovereign LORD,
    for the sake of your own reputation!
    Rescue me because you are so faithful and good.
²²   For I am poor and needy,
    and my heart is full of pain.
²³ I am fading like a shadow at dusk;
    I am falling like a grasshopper that is brushed aside.
²⁴ My knees are weak from fasting,
    and I am skin and bones.
²⁵ I am an object of mockery to people everywhere;
    when they see me, they shake their heads.

²⁶ Help me, O LORD my God!
    Save me because of your unfailing love.
²⁷ Let them see that this is your doing,
    that you yourself have done it, LORD.
²⁸ Then let them curse me if they like,
    but you will bless me!
    When they attack me, they will be disgraced!
    But I, your servant, will go right on rejoicing!
²⁹ Make their humiliation obvious to all;
    clothe my accusers with disgrace.
³⁰ But I will give repeated thanks to the LORD,
    praising him to everyone.
³¹ For he stands beside the needy,
    ready to save them from those who condemn them.

avid had a personal fortune worth millions, perhaps billions, of dollars, much of which he later donated for the construction of a temple for the Lord. It included 112 tons of gold and 262 tons of refined silver (see 1 Chronicles 29:4-5). So he certainly wasn't poverty stricken. Yet several times in the Psalms he refers to himself as being poor and needy.

What did he mean by that? The poor and needy person is one who cannot get himself out of the jam he is in; he has no resources to deliver himself, and he depends completely on others for help. Sometimes the poor and needy person may be financially destitute, but often the trouble is in other areas of life. According to these verses, David may have been physically and emotionally without resources—perhaps Absalom was threatening to take over the kingdom, and David felt powerless. Whatever the reason, David knew that he was completely dependent upon the Lord.

Are you poor and needy? Is there an area of your life in which you feel powerless? Depend on the Lord, "for he stands beside the needy, ready to save them from those who condemn them" (verse 31).

> Poor and naked, sick and blind,
> Bound fast in misery,
> Friend of the needy, let me find
> My help, my all in thee.
> CHARLES WESLEY

PSALM 110:1-3
A psalm of David.

¹ The LORD said to my Lord,
　"Sit in honor at my right hand
until I humble your enemies,
　making them a footstool under your feet."

² The LORD will extend your powerful dominion from
　　Jerusalem;
　you will rule over your enemies.
³ In that day of battle,
　your people will serve you willingly.
Arrayed in holy garments,
　your vigor will be renewed each day like the morning
　　dew.

*I*t was only a few days before Passover, and the Temple courts were bustling with people. The crowd's attention was riveted to Jesus, who was being plied with theological questions by the Pharisees and Sadducees. The crowds were amazed at how Jesus answered each puzzling question. When the religious leaders ran out of questions, it was Jesus' turn: "What do you think about the Messiah?" he asked. "Whose son is he?"

"David's son," came the quick response.

"Then why does David call him Lord?" replied Jesus. Then he quoted the first verse of Psalm 110 and silenced the scholars of his day.

As the writer of the psalm, David called his messianic descendent "my Lord," declaring that the Messiah would be more than just a human king. A purely human king would have looked up to David as his great ancestor, but David was looking up to this coming King, honoring him in divine terms. Jesus, who was certainly aware of his own messiahship, didn't deny that he was descended from David, but he affirmed an even greater connection with God the Father. Peter spelled out the implications in the same location less than two months later at the culmination of his Pentecost sermon (Acts 2:34-35).

But what does it mean to us? Surely, if David bowed in awe, and if the enemies will eventually be forced to bow before him, it's the least we can do.

A Word on Words

Why does this psalm use the imagery of a "footstool" (verse 1)? It was an ancient Near Eastern practice for victorious generals to place their feet on the necks of the vanquished leaders (see Joshua 10:24).

Bible Networking

No other Old Testament prophecy is quoted as frequently in the New Testament as the one in verse 1. See Matthew 22:44-45; Mark 12:36-37; Luke 20:42-44; Acts 2:34-35; Hebrews 1:13; and 10:12-13.

> *Look, ye saints, the sight is glorious:*
> *See the Man of Sorrows now;*
> *From the fight return victorious,*
> *Every knee to him shall bow:*
> *Crown him! Crown him! Crowns become the*
> *   Victor's brow.*
> THOMAS KELLY

PSALM 110:4-7

⁴ The LORD has taken an oath and will not break his vow:
  "You are a priest forever in the line of Melchizedek."
⁵ The Lord stands at your right hand to protect you.
  He will strike down many kings in the day of his
    anger.
⁶ He will punish the nations
    and fill them with their dead;
  he will shatter heads
    over the whole earth.
⁷ But he himself will be refreshed from brooks along the
    way.
  He will be victorious.

Melchizedek is a man of mystery. Three verses in Genesis (14:18-20) tell us all we really know about him. Wearily, Abram returns from battle. Then Melchizedek, king of Salem and a priest of God Most High, comes, refreshing him with a supply of bread and wine and bestowing a blessing on him in the name of God Most High, Creator of heaven and earth.

Abram then gave him an offering.

Even though only three verses in Genesis tell us about Melchizedek, he is a key figure in the letter to the Hebrews. In Hebrews 5–7 the writer says that Jesus is like Melchizedek, both a king and a priest. But how could Jesus be a priest, one might ask, since he wasn't from the priestly tribe of Levi? Well, neither was Melchizedek, the writer of Hebrews responds, quoting Psalm 110:4. While other priests live and die, Jesus is a "priest forever." At the right hand of God, he continues to intercede for us. "He lives forever to plead with God" on our behalf (Hebrews 7:25).

What a great High Priest we have! Besides being our sacrifice, our Savior, and our Intercessor, he is the one who comes to us when we are completely worn out from our daily battles and gives the refreshment that we need, just as Melchizedek did for Abram.

> Before the throne of God above
> I have a strong, a perfect plea;
> A great High Priest, whose name is Love,
> Who ever lives and pleads for me.
> CHARITIE BANCROFT

Bible Networking
Note how Hebrews 10:11-14 refers to both the first and fourth verses of Psalm 110.

Notable Quotable
"Many are willing enough to have him as priest who refuse to accept him as king. But it will not do. He must be king, or he will not be priest. And he must be king in this order; first making you right, then giving you his peace that passes all understanding. Let your heart be the Salem, the city of peace, where he, the priest-king, shall reign forever."
F. B. MEYER

PSALM 111:1-4

¹ Praise the LORD!

I will thank the LORD with all my heart
    as I meet with his godly people.
² How amazing are the deeds of the LORD!
    All who delight in him should ponder them.
³ Everything he does reveals his glory and majesty.
    His righteousness never fails.
⁴ Who can forget the wonders he performs?
    How gracious and merciful is our LORD!

*P*oet John Milton, author of *Paradise Lost* and *Paradise Regained*, was raised on the Psalms. He, his older sister, Anne, and his younger brother, Kit, would often sprawl in front of the fireplace as they discussed a Bible passage with their parents and then sing several psalms together.

It is not surprising that the earliest of Milton's poems were paraphrases of psalms, written when he was about fifteen years old. He began: "Let us with a gladsome mind / Praise the Lord, for He is kind." As he was going completely blind in his forties, he wrote a paraphrase of Psalm 6, including the words: "My bed I water with my tears; my eye through grief consumed, is waxen old and dark."

But despite his blindness, Milton could always recall the beauties and the majesties of God's creation, as he did in his epics. He paraphrased Psalm 111:4 as:

> For wonderful indeed are all his works,
> Pleasant to know and worthiest to be all
> Had in remembrance always with delight.

"Who can forget?" asked the psalmist. The answer is simple: We do, over and over again. Very quickly we forget the wonderful things God has done for us. Pause a moment to bring to remembrance a few of the things God did for you yesterday.

> Show my forgetful feet the way
> That leads to joys on high.
> There knowledge grows without decay,
> And love shall never die.
> ISAAC WATTS

Fascinating Fact

This psalm, when combined with Psalm 112, is another acrostic poem with each verse (or sometimes each sentence) beginning with the next letter of the Hebrew alphabet. Undoubtedly, it was a learning device, which is reinforced by the reminder in verse 4 not to forget.

Notable Quotable

"We must study, apprehend, reason, and compare, if we would remember. Memory is but the treasure-house of the things we put in it, and we can only store it with the facts of God's universe by the exercise of all the intellectual powers. But memory is fickle, hence the necessity of constantly examining it to see if its contents are still there and in their right places."
J. W. BURN

PSALM 111:5-10

5 He gives food to those who trust him;
  he always remembers his covenant.
6 He has shown his great power to his people
  by giving them the lands of other nations.
7 All he does is just and good,
  and all his commandments are trustworthy.
8 They are forever true,
  to be obeyed faithfully and with integrity.
9 He has paid a full ransom for his people.
  He has guaranteed his covenant with them forever.
  What a holy, awe-inspiring name he has!
10 Reverence for the LORD is the foundation of true
    wisdom.
  The rewards of wisdom come to all who obey him.

Praise his name forever!

What do you think the pharaoh of the Exodus would have said if you had told him that the Hebrew slaves, who were making bricks for him, would have a strong kingdom of their own and conquer other nations (as Psalm 111:6 says)?

What do you think Adolf Hitler would have said if you had told him that there would be a new nation called Israel and that it would become a formidable Middle Eastern power?

What do you think those fearful disciples in the upper room would have said if you had told them that they would become instruments of world change?

And what do you think Billy Graham's mother would have said if you had told her that the little boy playing baseball in the field out back would win millions to the Kingdom of God?

God delights in doing surprising things—things that we cannot imagine. What do you think God might be starting to do through you today? Maybe a chance meeting with someone, maybe a letter you write, maybe an unexpected phone call could be the start of something beyond your wildest dreams. Just because God doesn't show you the end result within twenty-four hours doesn't mean that he isn't starting to do something big. And don't expect fireworks. More likely your contact with tomorrow's greatness will come through something that is seemingly insignificant today. That's the way God often works.

> O give me faith, and faith's increase;
> Finish the work begun in me.
> Preserve my soul in perfect peace,
> And let me always rest on thee.
> CHARLES WESLEY

Bible Networking
The reverence-wisdom connection in verse 10 is a familiar theme in the book of Proverbs. See Proverbs 1:7 and 9:10. It also appears in Job 28:28 and Ecclesiastes 12:11-13. Note the subtle differences in each reference.

Notable Quotable
"The thought in the psalmist's mind (verse 6) was the conquest of Canaan, which could only have been effected by the miraculous arm of God. Equally unlikely has it been for the simple preaching of the gospel of Christ crucified to be the power by which God has changed the face of the world."
J. W. BURN

PSALM 112:1-5

¹ Praise the LORD!

Happy are those who fear the LORD.
  Yes, happy are those who delight in doing what he
    commands.
² Their children will be successful everywhere;
  an entire generation of godly people will be blessed.
³ They themselves will be wealthy,
  and their good deeds will never be forgotten.
⁴ When darkness overtakes the godly, light will come
    bursting in.
  They are generous, compassionate, and righteous.
⁵ All goes well for those who are generous,
  who lend freely and conduct their business fairly.

Walter Petherick, a wealthy London merchant in the seventeenth century, was the kind of person that Psalm 112 talks about—godly, devoted to his family, generous—but the darkness of verse 4 had not tested him yet.

Then on a Sunday morning in 1665 he listened to a preacher speak on Habakkuk. The minister talked about the prophet sitting in the midst of desolate Jerusalem, singing and rejoicing in spite of total devastation. At this time London was like Habakkuk's Jerusalem. For two years a plague had ravaged the city, and more desolation was yet to come. But, thus far, Petherick and his family had been spared.

Petherick went home from church and prayed for each of the members of his family, anguishing over whether he could rejoice in the Lord if they were taken by the plague. But that night Petherick acknowledged the Giver to be more important than his gifts, and he surrendered all his possessions to him.

A year later the London fire swept through the city, and Petherick's warehouse was consumed by the blaze. But he was able to pray, "O Lord, . . . you threatened me with the loss of your choicest gifts in order that I might set my affections more upon their Giver. Accept the thanks of your servant this day and help him to rejoice in the Lord."

Has the Giver become more important to you than his gifts?

> And must I part with all I have,
> My dearest Lord, for thee?
> It is but right, since thou hast done
> Much more than that for me.
> BENJAMIN BEDDOME

Notable Quotable
"It is a small thing to lose the gifts as long as you possess the Giver; the supreme tragedy lies in losing the Giver and retaining only the gifts."
F. W. BOREHAM

PSALM 112:6-10

6 Such people will not be overcome by evil
  circumstances.
  Those who are righteous will be long remembered.
7 They do not fear bad news;
  they confidently trust the LORD to care for them.
8 They are confident and fearless
  and can face their foes triumphantly.
9 They give generously to those in need.
  Their good deeds will never be forgotten.
  They will have influence and honor.
10 The wicked will be infuriated when they see this.
  They will grind their teeth in anger;
  they will slink away, their hopes thwarted.

*I*n *Silas Marner,* George Eliot's classic novel, the title character became a recluse, his personality twisted by a problem with church "friends." So he fled to a remote village. There, as a miser, he retreated within himself. "Year after year, Silas Marner lived in solitude, his guineas [coins] rising in the iron pot, and his life narrowing and hardening itself more and more. . . . His life had reduced itself to weaving and hoarding." Another character in the novel describes him as "a poor mushed creature."

And so he was. Having been hurt, he became a hoarder, and then his whole life hardened on him. The characterization of the godly in Psalm 112 is just the opposite. The godly are compassionate and confident.

But if you are similar to Silas Marner, how do you turn yourself around? How do you halt the inward spiral?

In Marner's case it was an orphan girl named Eppie who opened up a larger world to him. And this is what Jesus came to do as well. He can heal your wounded spirit, give you something to live for, and open you up to a larger world where you can live compassionately and confidently.

> A whispered word may touch the heart and call it back to life.
> A look of love bid sin depart and calm unholy strife.
> No act falls fruitless; none can tell how vast its power may be.
> Nor what results enfolded dwell within it silently.
> AUTHOR UNKNOWN

Bible Networking
Read 2 Corinthians 9:6-15 to learn how generosity affects the giver. Notice how the apostle Paul refers to Psalm 112:9 in 2 Corinthians 9:9.

Notable Quotable
"Charity empties the heart of one gift that it may make room for a larger."
J. PARKER

In the time of Christ, boys and girls may have carried little parchment scrolls on which were written Psalms 113 through 118. Why these portions of Scripture? Because these chapters, which were called the *Hallel,* or Hallel of Egypt, were recited at the important Jewish feasts.

Here are some verses from these psalms:

◆ *Psalm 113:5*
Who can be compared with the LORD our God,
   who is enthroned on high?

◆ *Psalm 114:8*
He turned the rock into pools of water;
   yes, springs of water came from solid rock.

◆ *Psalm 115:1*
Not to us, O LORD, but to you goes all the glory
   for your unfailing love and faithfulness.

◆ *Psalm 116:8*
He has saved me from death,
   my eyes from tears,
   my feet from stumbling.

◆ *Psalm 118:22*
The stone rejected by the builders
   has now become the cornerstone.

◆ *Psalm 118:24*
This is the day the LORD has made.
   We will rejoice and be glad in it.

You may notice that *hallel* is part of *hallelujah,* which means "Praise the Lord." That's the phrase that starts or ends most of these six psalms. By itself, the word *hallel* simply means "praise," so this is designated the praise section of the Psalms. Because Psalm 114:1 refers to Egypt, these psalms were also known as the Hallel of Egypt.

No one knows exactly when these psalms were written, but it was certainly after David's time. All the Jews needed to know these psalms, for they were festival psalms, recited not only at Passover but also at the Festival of Harvest, the Festival of Shelters, the Festival of Dedication (Hanukkah), and usually at the new moon festivals.

At Passover, for instance, Psalms 113 and 114 were sung before the meal and Psalms 115 to 118 after it. When Jesus and the disciples celebrated the Last Supper in the upper room, it was a Passover meal. So, when Scripture says they sang a hymn before going out to Gethsemane, it must refer to the last four psalms of the *Hallel*. These psalms were probably sung antiphonally with Jesus, who, as the leader, would have sung the lines, and the disciples would have responded with "Hallelujah."

The disciples never forgot some of the closing verses that Jesus sang: "The stone rejected by the builders," "This is the Lord's doing," and "Bring forward the sacrifice and put it on the altar." They had known these verses since they were little children with parchment scrolls up their sleeves, but now they saw them being fulfilled before their eyes.

∾

*Praise ye the Father! for His loving
  kindness,
Tenderly cares He for his erring
  children;
Praise Him, ye angels, praise Him in
  the heavens,
Praise ye Jehovah!*
AUTHOR UNKNOWN

∾

For a fuller explanation of the annual Jewish feasts, see Leviticus 23.

Selah

PSALM 113

¹ Praise the LORD!

Yes, give praise, O servants of the LORD.
    Praise the name of the LORD!
² Blessed be the name of the LORD
    forever and ever.
³ Everywhere—from east to west—
    praise the name of the LORD.
⁴ For the LORD is high above the nations;
    his glory is far greater than the heavens.

⁵ Who can be compared with the LORD our God,
    who is enthroned on high?
⁶ Far below him are the heavens and the earth.
    He stoops to look,
⁷ and he lifts the poor from the dirt
    and the needy from the garbage dump.
⁸ He sets them among princes,
    even the princes of his own people!
⁹ He gives the barren woman a home,
    so that she becomes a happy mother.

Praise the LORD!

Early in the 1600s a Dutch optician named Hans Lippershey developed the telescope. Another Dutchman, Zacharias Janssen, made the first microscope about the same time. Before long, astronomers like Galileo were looking upward through telescopes, and biologists like William Harvey were looking downward through microscopes.

The telescope shows that the earth is only a grain of sand in the vast universe, but the microscope shows us that every grain of sand is a fascinating universe in itself. Thomas Chalmers said, "The one told me of the insignificance of the world I tread on, the other redeems it from all insignificance." So whether you look upward through a telescope or downward through a microscope, you can see the greatness of our God.

As the psalmist looks, he realizes that God's glory is greater than anything he can see, with or without a telescope. Yet he notes that God is also interested in the poor and needy on the garbage dump. That's the wonder of our God. You can never sink so far down—emotionally, physically, or even spiritually—that he can't lift you up. Through Jesus Christ, he offers us the opportunity to become his children, setting us among princes (see verse 8).

> He can raise the poor to stand
> With the princes of the land,
> Wealth upon the needy shower,
> Set the smallest high in power.
> Who is like our God most high,
> Infinite in majesty?
> JOSIAH CONDER

Fascinating Fact
We don't normally think of the reformer John Calvin as a musician, yet he was the editor of the first printed edition of metrical psalms for church worship. Of the seventeen psalms that were included, he was personally responsible for the metrical translations of five. In addition to the metrical versions, one psalm (Psalm 113) was printed in prose.

Notable Quotable
"Gideon is fetched from threshing, Saul from seeking the asses, David from keeping the sheep, and the apostles from fishing. The treasure of the gospel is put into earthen vessels, and the weak and the foolish ones of the world confound the wise and mighty that the excellency of the power may be of God."
MATTHEW HENRY

PSALM 114

1 When the Israelites escaped from Egypt—
   when the family of Jacob left that foreign land—
2 the land of Judah became God's sanctuary,
   and Israel became his kingdom.

3 The Red Sea saw them coming and hurried out of their
      way!
   The water of the Jordan River turned away.
4 The mountains skipped like rams,
   the little hills like lambs!
5 What's wrong, Red Sea, that made you hurry out of
      their way?
   What happened, Jordan River, that you turned away?
6 Why, mountains, did you skip like rams?
   Why, little hills, like lambs?

7 Tremble, O earth, at the presence of the Lord,
   at the presence of the God of Israel.
8 He turned the rock into pools of water;
   yes, springs of water came from solid rock.

*H*ave you ever returned from a trip to the Rocky Mountains or the Alps and tried to convey to others what these mountains are like? Words are inadequate, and even slides and films fall woefully short.

So it is with all of God's wonders. How do you pass along to others the greatness of what he has done? How do you describe the indescribable?

For Hebrew parents who wanted to convey to their children the excitement of the Exodus from Egypt and the miraculous entry into Canaan, this psalm was the next best thing to being there. The exuberant excitement of the expressions still makes us wide-eyed. Yes, God did a remarkable thing for the children of Israel, and it was important to communicate the emotion of it from generation to generation. There is a place for being matter-of-fact in retelling the stories of great life-changing experiences, but matter-of-factness can quickly degenerate into ho-humness.

Has God done a remarkable thing for you? How are you passing it along from one generation to another? How are you conveying it to those you see every day?

> The sea beheld his power and fled;
> Jordan ran backward to its head.
> The mountains skipped like frightened rams;
> The hills leaped after them like lambs.
> And all things, as they change, proclaim
> The Lord eternally is the same.
> CHARLES WESLEY

Bible Networking
Check to see when the Red Sea hurried out of the way (Exodus 14:21) and when the Jordan turned away (Joshua 3:14-16). For the reference to the mountains, see Exodus 19:18 and Judges 5:4-5.

Notable Quotable
"Here is the Exodus, not as a familiar item in Israel's creed, but as an astounding event: as startling as a clap of thunder, as shattering as an earthquake."
DEREK KIDNER

PSALM 115:1-8

¹ Not to us, O Lord, but to you goes all the glory
  for your unfailing love and faithfulness.
² Why let the nations say,
  "Where is their God?"
³ For our God is in the heavens,
  and he does as he wishes.
⁴ Their idols are merely things of silver and gold,
  shaped by human hands.
⁵ They cannot talk, though they have mouths,
  or see, though they have eyes!
⁶ They cannot hear with their ears,
  or smell with their noses,
⁷   or feel with their hands,
  or walk with their feet,
  or utter sounds with their throats!
⁸ And those who make them are just like them,
  as are all who trust in them.

*A*t the age of twenty-six, William Wilberforce became a Christian. It wasn't an easy conversion because Wilberforce, despite his diminutive stature, tipped-up nose, and shortsightedness, was a playboy. For months he wrestled with the decision, realizing that if he decided for Christ, he might lose his popularity and have to abandon his political ambition.

Wilberforce decided to follow Christ, but instead of abandoning his political ambition, he used it for God's purposes. In the British Parliament in the early nineteenth century, Wilberforce proposed a bill to abolish slavery, and he kept on proposing bills until eventually one was passed. After slavery was abolished in England, he fought to abolish it internationally. It was said of Wilberforce that he was willing to compromise on almost anything except the slavery issue and the fundamentals of Christianity.

Wilberforce loved the Psalms and enjoyed comparing different Bible versions of the Psalms. When he finally won passage of his antislavery bill after years of tireless work, he went home and meditated on Psalm 115:1: "Not to us, O Lord, but to you goes all the glory." For the ex-playboy, personal glory was no longer important.

It's a great verse to tuck away for occasions like that. In heaven we will cast our crowns at Jesus' feet, but it's good practice for us to start giving him all the glory now.

> Not I, but Christ be honored, loved, exalted;
> Not I, but Christ be seen, be known, be heard;
> Not I, but Christ, in every look and action;
> Not I, but Christ, in every thought and word.
> A. B. SIMPSON

Bible Networking

Compare verses 4-7 with Isaiah 44:9-20 and Isaiah 46:1-7.

Notable Quotable

"There are many precious texts of Scripture that we will carry to heaven with us and will form the theme of our song. But if there is one text that must break forth from every redeemed one as he enters heaven, it is the first verse of this psalm."
BARTON BOUCHIER

PSALM 115:9-18

⁹ O Israel, trust the LORD!
    He is your helper; he is your shield.
¹⁰ O priests of Aaron, trust the LORD!
    He is your helper; he is your shield.
¹¹ All you who fear the LORD, trust the LORD!
    He is your helper; he is your shield.

¹² The LORD remembers us,
    and he will surely bless us.
He will bless the people of Israel
    and the family of Aaron, the priests.
¹³ He will bless those who fear the LORD,
    both great and small.

¹⁴ May the LORD richly bless
    both you and your children.
¹⁵ May you be blessed by the LORD,
    who made heaven and earth.
¹⁶ The heavens belong to the LORD,
    but he has given the earth to all humanity.

¹⁷ The dead cannot sing praises to the LORD,
    for they have gone into the silence of the grave.
¹⁸ But we can praise the LORD
    both now and forever!

Praise the LORD!

*W*e usually remember Caleb as one of the two spies who came back to Moses and advised the Israelites to go ahead with the invasion of the land of Canaan. The other ten spies gave a fearful report and advised the people not to invade. Because the Israelites followed the advice of the ten spies, they were condemned to wander in the wilderness for another generation.

Psalm 115 repeats two major truths: We should trust God, and God will bless us. This is what set Caleb and Joshua apart from the other ten spies. These two trusted God to bless the nation, despite the difficulties that lay ahead of them. While God judged the rest of his people for their unbelief, he promised to bless Caleb and Joshua for their faith and courage.

The second time we meet Caleb is forty-five years later when he reminds Joshua of the blessing God had promised (Joshua 14:6-15). He was still trusting God to bless! And, because he asked, he was given the hill country of Hebron, south of Jerusalem. Of course, there was a slight hitch: Enemies were still alive and well in that area. But the eighty-five-year-old Caleb responded, "If the Lord is with me, I will drive them out of the land, just as the Lord said" (verse 12).

The presence and promise of the Lord were all Caleb needed, and that's all we need to face life's challenges as well.

> Sure I must fight if I would reign;
> Increase my courage, Lord;
> I'll bear the toil, endure the pain,
> Supported by thy word.
> ISAAC WATTS

Notable Quotable
"One by one the singers in the consecrated choir of saints steal away from us, and we miss their music. Thank God, they have gone above to swell the harmonies of the skies, but as far as we are concerned, we have need to sing all the more earnestly because so many songsters have left our choirs."
CHARLES HADDON SPURGEON

PSALM 116:1-9

¹ I love the LORD because he hears
  and answers my prayers.
² Because he bends down and listens,
  I will pray as long as I have breath!
³ Death had its hands around my throat;
  the terrors of the grave overtook me.
  I saw only trouble and sorrow.
⁴ Then I called on the name of the LORD:
  "Please, LORD, save me!"
⁵ How kind the LORD is! How good he is!
  So merciful, this God of ours!
⁶ The LORD protects those of childlike faith;
  I was facing death, and then he saved me.
⁷ Now I can rest again,
  for the LORD has been so good to me.
⁸ He has saved me from death,
  my eyes from tears,
  my feet from stumbling.
⁹ And so I walk in the LORD's presence
  as I live here on earth!

*T*o the Jews of Jesus' time, this was a psalm of thanksgiving to be sung at the Passover celebration. Coming after Psalms 114 and 115, which refer to deliverance from bondage in Egypt, this psalm reminds us that each of us is individually redeemed from bondage as well. In the early church it was used as a burial song, reminding mourners to look beyond death into a glorious life to come. In the Anglican prayer book this psalm is suggested as a psalm of thanksgiving after childbirth.

For every believer, this psalm serves as a reminder of the complete salvation we have in Jesus Christ. Spiritually, he has delivered our soul from eternal death. Emotionally, he puts a song in our heart and wipes away our tears. Physically, he strengthens us and keeps us from stumbling.

Genesis 21:14-20 tells the story of God's loving care for Hagar and her son Ishmael. Alone in the desert, Hagar sobbed because her son was dying of thirst. God sent an angel, who directed her to a well of water. Then Scripture says: "God was with the boy as he grew up" (verse 20). God saved Hagar and Ishmael from death, he wiped away their tears, and he kept their feet from stumbling. Can you recall times when he has done the same for you?

> *I love the Lord; he bowed his ear,*
> *And chased my grief away!*
> *O let my heart no more despair,*
> *While I have breath to pray.*
> ISAAC WATTS

A Word on Words

Verse 7 can be more literally rendered: *"Return, O my soul, to your rest,"* and the word *rest* is plural, indicating its thoroughness. Now that God has delivered him, the psalmist can truly sleep in peace, knowing that God will keep him safe.

Bible Networking

How does verse 1 differ from 1 John 4:19?

PSALM 116:10-19

¹⁰ I believed in you, so I prayed,
  "I am deeply troubled, LORD."
¹¹ In my anxiety I cried out to you,
  "These people are all liars!"
¹² What can I offer the LORD
  for all he has done for me?
¹³ I will lift up a cup symbolizing his salvation;
  I will praise the LORD's name for saving me.
¹⁴ I will keep my promises to the LORD
  in the presence of all his people.

¹⁵ The LORD's loved ones are precious to him;
  it grieves him when they die.
¹⁶ O LORD, I am your servant;
  yes, I am your servant, the son of your handmaid,
  and you have freed me from my bonds!
¹⁷ I will offer you a sacrifice of thanksgiving
  and call on the name of the LORD.
¹⁸ I will keep my promises to the LORD
  in the presence of all his people,
¹⁹ in the house of the LORD,
  in the heart of Jerusalem.

Praise the LORD!

O n vacation in Germany, Frances Ridley Havergal was tired from a busy day of sightseeing. As she sat down to rest, she noticed a painting of the crucified Christ on the wall. The eyes of Jesus seemed to be focused on her. Then she noticed that underneath the painting was the inscription: "I did this for thee; what hast thou done for me?"

Immediately, an idea for a hymn flashed through her mind, and she took a pencil and scribbled down some words on a scrap of paper. Then as she read the words again, she thought the poem was very poor, so she crumpled the paper up and tossed it into the fire. It fell to the side of the flames, however, and didn't burn. She then picked up the crumpled paper and put it in her purse.

Months later she showed it to her father, who suggested that the poem was worth publishing, and soon her hymn "I Gave My Life for Thee" was being sung in churches on both sides of the Atlantic.

"What can I offer the Lord for all he has done for me?" asked the psalmist. It's a daunting question for any of us. Scottish minister Samuel Rutherford called himself a "drowned debtor to God's mercy" and explained that he was "over head and ears in debt to God."

Aren't we all?

> I gave my life for thee, my precious blood I shed,
> That thou might'st ransomed be, and quickened
> from the dead;
> I gave, I gave my life for thee; what hast thou
> given for me?
> FRANCES R. HAVERGAL

Bible Networking
Notice how verse 10 is cited in 2 Corinthians 4:13. We have the same kind of faith the psalmist had.

Notable Quotable
Regarding verse 12: "[God] awakened us into being, he ennobled us with understanding, he taught us arts to enrich us, he commanded the earth to yield crops for us, he bade the animals to own us as lords. For us the rains descend, the sun sheds its rays, the mountains rise, the valleys bloom, the rivers flow. All nature pours her treasures at our feet."
BASIL THE GREAT

PSALM 117

1 Praise the LORD, all you nations.
    Praise him, all you people of the earth.
2 For he loves us with unfailing love;
    the faithfulness of the LORD endures forever.

Praise the LORD!

*M*any children find it difficult to share. Often one of the first things they learn to say is, "Mine! Mine!" But adults can have the same problem. This has been true of God's people over the centuries.

God told Abraham that his descendants were to be a testimony to the Gentiles, but this was hard for his people to learn. Jonah certainly didn't get it at first. Isaiah had to spell it out for the people of his day: "Arise, Jerusalem! Let your light shine for all the nations to see!" (Isaiah 60:1). The religious leaders of Jesus' day must have missed that page, because they deplored Jesus' outreach efforts. The apostles needed the extra incentive of persecution to begin spreading the gospel to the Gentiles, although Jesus told them clearly to "go and make disciples of all the nations" (Matthew 28:19). In 1786, when young William Carey suggested that missionaries be sent out from his denomination, he was told, "If God wants to save the heathen, he doesn't need human aid to do it."

"Praise the Lord, all you nations," sings the psalmist. In Revelation we read of a vast choir in heaven "too great to count, from every nation and tribe and people and language, standing in front of the throne and before the Lamb" (Revelation 7:9). Are you helping to get the choir together?

A Word on Words

While the word translated "nations" in verse 1 is a broader term referring to Gentile nations, the word translated "people" is more specific and could be translated "people groups" or even "clans" or "tribes."

Psalm at a Glance

Though it's the shortest chapter in the Bible, Psalm 117 emphasizes the vastness of God's vision and the length of his love.

Bible Networking

Notice the point that Paul makes from this little psalm in Romans 15:11.

> Let every kindred, every tribe, on this terrestrial ball,
> To him all majesty ascribe, and crown him Lord of all;
> O that with yonder sacred throng, we at his feet may fall!
> We'll join the everlasting song, and crown him Lord of all.
> EDWARD PERRONET

JUDGES 5:12-14 (Deborah's Song, Part 2)

[12] "Wake up, Deborah, wake up!
Wake up, wake up, and sing a song!
Arise, Barak!
Lead your captives away, son of Abinoam!

[13] "Down from Tabor marched the remnant against the
mighty.
The people of the LORD marched down against
mighty warriors.

[14] They came down from Ephraim—a land that once
belonged to the Amalekites,
and Benjamin also followed you.
From Makir the commanders marched down;
from Zebulun came those who carry the rod of
authority."

Psalm Link
PSALM 118:15

[15] Songs of joy and victory are sung in the camp of the
godly.
The strong right arm of the LORD has done glorious
things!

Fear paralyzes; faith frees. And a fearless faith inspires others.

In the time of the judges, fear had paralyzed all the Israelites—except for a woman named Deborah. The Canaanites had been ruthlessly oppressing them for twenty years, and she was the answer to the Israelites' prayers.

Deborah told Barak that he was to lead the army of Israel, but he, too, was paralyzed with fear. He refused to go to war unless Deborah went with him. Determined to obey the Lord at any cost, Deborah went with Barak into battle.

Sisera, the general of the Canaanite army, must have snickered when he heard that Israel's general had to be led into battle by a woman. But Deborah's faith overcame the fear of Barak and his troops. Deborah's victory song reveals that some of the tribes didn't follow her lead (Judges 5:15-17). But those who followed her won a great victory.

Joan of Arc, who has been called the Deborah of France, led her army into battle with priests singing psalms and hymns. Her faith, like that of Deborah, inspired confidence and courage in her followers.

Are you facing your challenges in fear or with Deborah's faith? If you share Deborah's faith, you might be surprised at how it will inspire others as well.

> Encamped along the hills of light, ye Christian soldiers rise,
> And press the battle ere the night shall veil the glowing skies.
> Against the foe in vales below, let all our strength be hurled;
> Faith is the victory, we know, that overcomes the world.
> JOHN H. YATES

Bible Networking
Deborah and Barak close their song with a prayer that their victory may serve as a pattern for future battles. See Psalm 68:1-2.

Notable Quotable
"The first step on the way to victory is to recognize the enemy."
CORRIE TEN BOOM

PSALM 118:1-9

1 Give thanks to the LORD, for he is good!
   His faithful love endures forever.

2 Let the congregation of Israel repeat:
   "His faithful love endures forever."
3 Let Aaron's descendants, the priests, repeat:
   "His faithful love endures forever."
4 Let all who fear the LORD repeat:
   "His faithful love endures forever."

5 In my distress I prayed to the LORD,
   and the LORD answered me and rescued me.
6 The LORD is for me, so I will not be afraid.
   What can mere mortals do to me?
7 Yes, the LORD is for me; he will help me.
   I will look in triumph at those who hate me.
8 It is better to trust the LORD
   than to put confidence in people.
9 It is better to trust the LORD
   than to put confidence in princes.

Of the Psalms, Martin Luther said, "I love them all. . . . But this psalm [118] is nearest my heart, and I have a familiar right to call it mine. It has saved me from many dangers. . . . It is my friend, dearer to me than all the honors and power of the earth."

The Reformer loved many parts of this psalm. He had a copy of verse 17 up on his wall and referred frequently to the messianic verses in the latter part of the psalm. But the psalm truly became "his" when he entered Worms with the promise that the Lord was for him.

Summoned to the city of Worms to face the charges against him, he was warned by friends not to go. But quoting Psalm 118:6, Luther said, "The Lord is for me, so I will not be afraid. I am determined to go though as many devils should oppose me as there are tiles upon all the houses."

As he entered the assembly hall, an old soldier put his arm on Luther's shoulder and said, "Little monk, you need more courage for your battle today than any soldier I know. But if God is for you, go ahead and do not be afraid."

Later Luther made his famous statement: "I cannot and will not recant; here I stand, I can do no other."

> And though this world, with devils filled, should
> threaten to undo us,
> We will not fear, for God hath willed his truth to
> triumph through us.
> The Prince of Darkness grim, we tremble not for
> him;
> His rage we can endure, for lo, his doom is sure;
> One little word shall fell him.
> MARTIN LUTHER

Fascinating Fact
The eighth verse of this psalm is the middle verse in the Bible, with 31,174 verses on either side of it. Curiously, the middle verse in the Bible is located between the shortest chapter in the Bible and the longest chapter in the Bible. But it is far better to learn the truth of this verse than to spend your time counting to double-check this fascinating fact!

Bible Networking
Compare the song sung by the Levites in Ezra 3:10-11 with the opening verses of this psalm.

PSALM 118:10-18

¹⁰ Though hostile nations surrounded me,
    I destroyed them all in the name of the LORD.

¹¹ Yes, they surrounded and attacked me,
    but I destroyed them all in the name of the LORD.

¹² They swarmed around me like bees;
    they blazed against me like a roaring flame.
    But I destroyed them all in the name of the LORD.

¹³ You did your best to kill me, O my enemy,
    but the LORD helped me.

¹⁴ The LORD is my strength and my song;
    he has become my victory.

¹⁵ Songs of joy and victory are sung in the camp
    of the godly.
    The strong right arm of the LORD has done
    glorious things!

¹⁶ The strong right arm of the LORD is raised in triumph.
    The strong right arm of the LORD has done
    glorious things!

¹⁷ I will not die, but I will live
    to tell what the LORD has done.

¹⁸ The LORD has punished me severely,
    but he has not handed me over to death.

John Wycliffe lay dying in Lutterworth, England. The year was 1384, and most of his influential friends in church and state had deserted him. Many thought he had gone too far.

For one thing, Wycliffe had dared to translate the Bible into English. He also urged a separation of church and state in order to reform the church. He attacked the corruption and the abuses of power that he observed—particularly among the friars. But most of all he preached that the Bible should be made available in every language.

It sounded like heresy, and since Wycliffe was now at the point of death, some felt he should reconsider his statements. So four friars and four senators crowded into his bedroom. They spoke sternly to him, reminding him of all he had advocated. Now was the time to confess the error of his ways.

Wycliffe was surprisingly alert. He asked if he could be raised in his bed so he could speak more clearly. Then he summoned all his remaining strength to quote Psalm 118:17, or at least part of it: "I will not die, but I will live, and will again declare the evil deeds of the friars."

Wycliffe died, but his message and work lived on. English Bible available to the common people. People die, but what they have begun is not halted by death. The trail they have left behind them goes on ahead of them.

> Shrink not, Christian, will you yield?
> Will you quit the painful field?
> Will you flee in danger's hour?
> Don't you know your Captain's power?
> Oft in danger, oft in woe,
> Onward, Christian, onward go.
> H. K. WHITE

Bible Networking

For other bees (verse 12) in the Bible, look up Deuteronomy 1:44. To read about hornets, turn to Exodus 23:28.

Notable Quotable

"Good songs, good promises, good proverbs, and good doctrines are none the worse for age. What was sung just after the passage of the Red Sea (Exodus 15:2) is here sung again and shall be sung to the end of the world by the saints of the Most High."
WILLIAM S. PLUMER

PSALM 118:19-29

[19] Open for me the gates where the righteous enter,
and I will go in and thank the LORD.

[20] Those gates lead to the presence of the LORD,
and the godly enter there.

[21] I thank you for answering my prayer
and saving me!

[22] The stone rejected by the builders
has now become the cornerstone.

[23] This is the LORD's doing,
and it is marvelous to see.

[24] This is the day the LORD has made.
We will rejoice and be glad in it.

[25] Please, LORD, please save us.
Please, LORD, please give us success.

[26] Bless the one who comes in the name of the LORD.
We bless you from the house of the LORD.

[27] The LORD is God, shining upon us.
Bring forward the sacrifice and put it on the altar.

[28] You are my God, and I will praise you!
You are my God, and I will exalt you!

[29] Give thanks to the LORD, for he is good!
His faithful love endures forever.

To students of English literature, William Cowper is a brilliant eighteenth-century poet. To church musicians, he is the author of hymns like "There Is a Fountain Filled with Blood" and "O for a Closer Walk with God."

But those who were close to him knew Cowper was a very troubled young man. Three times he attempted suicide; twice he was pronounced insane; and if it weren't for Christian friends and for Psalm 118, he probably wouldn't have written anything.

A delicate child, Cowper was bullied and beaten by an older boy, but as a lad, Cowper found comfort in Psalm 118:6. After a bout with insanity during his twenties, he was strengthened by the fourteenth and eighteenth verses of this psalm.

For several years Cowper found a happy companionship with John Newton, the former slave trader turned pastor. They enjoyed walking, joking, and writing hymns together. For a while they tried to write a hymn every week. When he was feeling stable, Cowper rejoiced in the twenty-ninth verse: "Give thanks to the Lord, for he is good!"

The friendship of these two men enriched the church with hymns like Newton's "Amazing Grace" and Cowper's "God Moves in a Mysterious Way." In the words of verse 23: "This [was] the Lord's doing, and it [was] marvelous to see."

You fearful saints, fresh courage take,
The clouds you so much dread
Are big with mercy, and shall break
In blessings on your head.
WILLIAM COWPER

A Word on Words

"Save us" in verse 25 is hoshi'ah na in Hebrew, or hosanna as it's transliterated into Greek. It became a phrase of praise, but it's rooted in this plea for help. (Whom would you ask for help? Someone strong enough to help you!) The annual Festival of Shelters used this psalm—and this word—prominently. The seventh day of the festival was known as the Great Hosanna, during which palm branches would be waved. Those branches were also called hosannas.

Bible Networking

The New Testament quotes several verses in this section and finds them fulfilled in Jesus Christ. But note in particular the references to Jesus as the cornerstone: Matthew 21:42; Ephesians 2:20; and 1 Peter 2:7.

PSALM 119:1-16

¹ Happy are people of integrity,
    who follow the law of the LORD.
² Happy are those who obey his decrees
    and search for him with all their hearts.
³ They do not compromise with evil,
    and they walk only in his paths.
⁴ You have charged us
    to keep your commandments carefully.
⁵ Oh, that my actions would consistently
    reflect your principles!
⁶ Then I will not be disgraced
    when I compare my life with your commands.
⁷ When I learn your righteous laws,
    I will thank you by living as I should!
⁸ I will obey your principles.
    Please don't give up on me!

⁹ How can a young person stay pure?
    By obeying your word and following its rules.
¹⁰ I have tried my best to find you—
    don't let me wander from your commands.
¹¹ I have hidden your word in my heart,
    that I might not sin against you.
¹² Blessed are you, O LORD;
    teach me your principles.
¹³ I have recited aloud
    all the laws you have given us.
¹⁴ I have rejoiced in your decrees
    as much as in riches.
¹⁵ I will study your commandments
    and reflect on your ways.
¹⁶ I will delight in your principles
    and not forget your word.

*I*f you are going to memorize an entire chapter of Scripture, it is much simpler to memorize Psalm 117 than it is to memorize Psalm 119. But it's Psalm 119 that reminds us to hide God's Word in our heart, to recite it aloud, to study it, to reflect on it, and not to forget it.

David Livingstone, the intrepid explorer-missionary to Africa, memorized this entire psalm when he was nine years old and won a New Testament from his Sunday school teacher for doing so.

Another who memorized the entire psalm was John Ruskin, the brilliant writer and art critic of the nineteenth century. Later he admitted, "It is strange that of all the pieces of the Bible that my mother taught me, that which cost me most to learn, and which was to my child's mind most repulsive, the 119th psalm, has now become, of all, the most precious to me."

Many of us may have the same sentiment as seventeenth-century British minister Thomas Fuller, who confessed, "Lord, I discover an errant laziness in my soul. For when I am to read a chapter in the Bible, before I begin it, I look where it endeth, and if it endeth not on the same side, I cannot keep my hand from turning over the leaf to measure the length thereof. . . . Were I truly hungry after heavenly food, I would not complain of meat. Make the reading of thy Word not a penance but a pleasure for me, so that I may esteem that chapter in thy Word the best which is the longest."

> Who can tell the pleasure, who recount the treasure,
> By your Word imparted to the simple-hearted?
> O that we, discerning its most holy learning,
> May always love and fear you, and evermore be
>   near you.
> HENRY W. BAKER

Notable Quotable
"If you have the Word in your mouth only, it shall be taken from you. If you have it in your book only, you shall miss it when you need it most; but if you lay it up in your heart, as Mary did the words of the angel, no enemy shall ever be able to take it from you, and you shall find it a comfortable treasure in your time of need."
WILLIAM COWPER

PSALM 119:17-32

17 Be good to your servant,
   that I may live and obey your word.
18 Open my eyes to see
   the wonderful truths in your law.
19 I am but a foreigner here on earth;
   I need the guidance of your commands.
   Don't hide them from me!
20 I am overwhelmed continually
   with a desire for your laws.
21 You rebuke those cursed proud ones
   who wander from your commands.
22 Don't let them scorn and insult me,
   for I have obeyed your decrees.
23 Even princes sit and speak against me,
   but I will meditate on your principles.
24 Your decrees please me;
   they give me wise advice.

25 I lie in the dust, completely discouraged;
   revive me by your word.
26 I told you my plans, and you answered.
   Now teach me your principles.
27 Help me understand the meaning of your
      commandments,
   and I will meditate on your wonderful miracles.
28 I weep with grief;
   encourage me by your word.
29 Keep me from lying to myself;
   give me the privilege of knowing your law.
30 I have chosen to be faithful;
   I have determined to live by your laws.
31 I cling to your decrees.
   LORD, don't let me be put to shame!

³² If you will help me,
   I will run to follow your commands.

Jonathan Edwards was never accused of being an emotional man. Even when he preached his famous sermon, "Sinners in the Hands of an Angry God," it was given with few gestures and with sober dignity. When his wife, Sarah, got caught up in the emotion of the Great Awakening, he was suspicious.

But as the great theologian carefully analyzed his wife's experience, he was amazed at her "constant sweet peace, calm and serenity of soul." He decided that because his wife's experience focused on Jesus Christ, it had a lasting effect on her.

Later, as he preached on Psalm 119, he focused on verses 20 and 28: "I am overwhelmed continually" and "I weep with grief." He admitted that he longed for more holiness. "My heart seemed to be full, ready to break, which often brought me back to the words of the psalmist in Psalm 119." These emotions of "godly sorrow" and "holy thirst" are what Edwards later called the distinguishing traits of true saints. "Godly sorrow and brokenness of heart is peculiarly acceptable and pleasing to God" and "Holy thirst is a condition of participation of the blessings of eternal life."

Are godly sorrow and holy thirst distinguishing qualities of your life?

> Oh, may these heavenly pages be
> My ever dear delight;
> And still new beauties may I see
> And still increasing light.
> ANNE STEELE

Bible Networking
Note the strong verbs in the last three verses: "I have chosen," "I cling," and "I will run." See New Testament parallels in Hebrews 11:25; 10:23; and Philippians 3:14.

Notable Quotable
"The writer knew that there were vast treasures in the Word which he had not yet fully seen, marvels he had not yet beheld. The Bible is a wonder-land; it not only relates miracles, but it is itself a world of wonders. . . . Scripture needs opening, but not half so much as our eyes do; the veil is not on the book, but on our eyes."
CHARLES HADDON SPURGEON

PSALM 119:33-48

[33] Teach me, O LORD,
   to follow every one of your principles.

[34] Give me understanding and I will obey your law;
   I will put it into practice with all my heart.

[35] Make me walk along the path of your commands,
   for that is where my happiness is found.

[36] Give me an eagerness for your decrees;
   do not inflict me with love for money!

[37] Turn my eyes from worthless things,
   and give me life through your word.

[38] Reassure me of your promise,
   which is for those who honor you.

[39] Help me abandon my shameful ways;
   your laws are all I want in life.

[40] I long to obey your commandments!
   Renew my life with your goodness.

[41] LORD, give to me your unfailing love,
   the salvation that you promised me.

[42] Then I will have an answer for those who taunt me,
   for I trust in your word.

[43] Do not snatch your word of truth from me,
   for my only hope is in your laws.

[44] I will keep on obeying your law
   forever and forever.

[45] I will walk in freedom,
   for I have devoted myself to your commandments.

[46] I will speak to kings about your decrees,
   and I will not be ashamed.

[47] How I delight in your commands!
   How I love them!

[48] I honor and love your commands.
   I meditate on your principles.

The man who almost became Jonathan Edwards's son-in-law was quite different from the intellectual minister. David Brainerd, pioneer missionary to the American Indians in New Jersey, was engaged to Edwards's daughter but died of tuberculosis at the age of thirty before they could get married.

Jonathan Edwards was so impressed with Brainerd that he published the account of his life, including Brainerd's journal. God used this remarkable book to fire the lives of missionaries like David Livingstone, William Carey, Henry Martyn, and others.

Brainerd had struggled for nearness to God. Unlike Edwards, Brainerd was not afraid of expressing his emotions. He went through anguish before coming to a "full assurance of hope." Afterward, he seemed to concentrate more on the Psalms, and his aspirations stemmed from various verses in the book.

One of the marks of a true Christian, Brainerd said, was delight in God's Word. Verses like Psalm 119:47 became his experience. Earlier he had read the Bible out of a sense of duty, but later he delighted in it. He didn't feel as though he were in bondage, but rather he saw obedience to God's Word as liberating. He quoted verse 45: "I will walk in freedom."

Jesus described this freedom that comes from God's Word as he said, "And you will know the truth, and the truth will set you free" (John 8:32).

> I hear your Word in love;
> In faith your Word obey;
> O send your Spirit from above
> To teach me, Lord, your way.
> ISAAC WATTS

Bible Networking
Relate Acts 4:29 with verses 42-46 of this psalm.

Notable Quotable
"Saints feel no bondage in sanctity. The Spirit of holiness is a free spirit; he sets men at liberty and enables them to resist every effort to bring them under subjection."
CHARLES HADDON SPURGEON

PSALM 119:49-64

⁴⁹ Remember your promise to me,
for it is my only hope.
⁵⁰ Your promise revives me;
it comforts me in all my troubles.
⁵¹ The proud hold me in utter contempt,
but I do not turn away from your law.
⁵² I meditate on your age-old laws;
O LORD, they comfort me.
⁵³ I am furious with the wicked,
those who reject your law.
⁵⁴ Your principles have been the music of my life
throughout the years of my pilgrimage.
⁵⁵ I reflect at night on who you are, O LORD,
and I obey your law because of this.
⁵⁶ This is my happy way of life:
obeying your commandments.

⁵⁷ LORD, you are mine!
I promise to obey your words!
⁵⁸ With all my heart I want your blessings.
Be merciful just as you promised.
⁵⁹ I pondered the direction of my life,
and I turned to follow your statutes.
⁶⁰ I will hurry, without lingering,
to obey your commands.
⁶¹ Evil people try to drag me into sin,
but I am firmly anchored to your law.
⁶² At midnight I rise to thank you
for your just laws.
⁶³ Anyone who fears you is my friend—
anyone who obeys your commandments.
⁶⁴ O LORD, the earth is full of your unfailing love;
teach me your principles.

*P*romises, promises. Life is full of them. Boy Scouts and politicians, wedding ceremonies and labor agreements, international negotiations and United Way pledges.

Yesterday's section (verses 44-46) was filled with "I will's," all promises on our part. Today's section begins with God's promises and how they comfort and revive us and give us hope. The Bible is built on promises. The Jewish nation was established on God's promises to Abraham and underwritten by God's promises to Moses. Throughout the Old Testament, God promised a Messiah to redeem his people, and throughout the New Testament, we receive God's promises of his presence and his guidance through the Holy Spirit.

When the Canadian Pacific Railroad was ready to lay tracks from Medicine Hat to Calgary in southern Alberta, it had to negotiate with Crowfoot, the chief of the Blackfoot confederacy that controlled the land. Crowfoot granted permission, in return for a lifetime railroad pass on the Canadian Pacific. He put it in a leather case and carried it around his neck until he died—but he never used it. He never availed himself of the railroad's promise.

Sometimes we're like that regarding God's promises. We admire them and put them up on our walls, but we don't make use of them. Instead, let us determine to trust all that God has told us and enjoy his promised blessings.

> *Standing on the promises that cannot fail,*
> *When the howling storms of doubt and fear assail,*
> *By the living Word of God I shall prevail,*
> *Standing on the promises of God.*
> R. KELSO CARTER

Fascinating Fact
God is referred to, either explicitly or implied, in every verse of Psalm 119; the psalmist refers to himself more than three hundred times in this psalm. Obviously, this is a very personal psalm.

Notable Quotable
"When we hear any promise in the Word of God, let us turn it into a prayer. God's promises are his bond. He loves it when we wrestle with him by his promises."
RICHARD SIBBES

PSALM 119:65-80

⁶⁵ You have done many good things for me, LORD,
  just as you promised.
⁶⁶ I believe in your commands;
  now teach me good judgment and knowledge.
⁶⁷ I used to wander off until you disciplined me;
  but now I closely follow your word.
⁶⁸ You are good and do only good;
  teach me your principles.
⁶⁹ Arrogant people have made up lies about me,
   but in truth I obey your commandments
    with all my heart.
⁷⁰ Their hearts are dull and stupid,
  but I delight in your law.
⁷¹ The suffering you sent was good for me,
  for it taught me to pay attention to your principles.
⁷² Your law is more valuable to me
  than millions in gold and silver!

⁷³ You made me; you created me.
  Now give me the sense to follow your commands.
⁷⁴ May all who fear you find in me a cause for joy,
  for I have put my hope in your word.
⁷⁵ I know, O LORD, that your decisions are fair;
  you disciplined me because I needed it.
⁷⁶ Now let your unfailing love comfort me,
  just as you promised me, your servant.
⁷⁷ Surround me with your tender mercies so I may live,
  for your law is my delight.
⁷⁸ Bring disgrace upon the arrogant people
   who lied about me;
   meanwhile, I will concentrate on your
    commandments.

⁷⁹ Let me be reconciled
     with all who fear you and know your decrees.
⁸⁰ May I be blameless in keeping your principles;
     then I will never have to be ashamed.

Francis I, king of France in the 1500s, is not a good example of how to read the Psalms.

Francis was captured in a battle in Italy and was taken to a church. There he heard monks singing Psalm 119. Although ill from the battle, Francis recovered enough to join in the singing of verse 71: "The suffering you sent was good for me."

When Francis finally signed a treaty and returned to Pais, many thought he would be more tolerant. The Sorbonne had issued an edict banning the singing of psalms, and Reformed forces hoped Francis would reverse that order. He delayed enforcing the ban, but finally Francis bowed to political pressures. He executed hundreds of French Huguenots, who defiantly sang psalms as they were led to their death. Yet even Francis himself continued to sing the Psalms.

It seems that Francis loved the Psalms but never learned from them. He had sung Psalm 119:71 in prison, which was intended to teach him "to pay attention to [God's] principles," but Francis never paid attention.

Consider what God has allowed to come across your path. Have you used it to learn to pay attention to God's principles?

> *I cannot call affliction sweet;*
> *And yet 'twas good to bear;*
> *Affliction brought me to your feet,*
> *And I found comfort there.*
> JAMES MONTGOMERY

A Word on Words
In verse 66 the word for "judgment" is more literally "taste," as in Job 34:3. See also Hebrews 5:14.

PSALM 119:81-96

⁸¹ I faint with longing for your salvation;
    but I have put my hope in your word.
⁸² My eyes are straining to see your promises come true.
    When will you comfort me?
⁸³ I am shriveled like a wineskin in the smoke, exhausted
        with waiting.
    But I cling to your principles and obey them.
⁸⁴ How long must I wait?
    When will you punish those who persecute me?
⁸⁵ These arrogant people who hate your law
    have dug deep pits for me to fall into.
⁸⁶ All your commands are trustworthy.
    Protect me from those who hunt me down
        without cause.
⁸⁷ They almost finished me off,
    but I refused to abandon your commandments.
⁸⁸ In your unfailing love, spare my life;
    then I can continue to obey your decrees.

⁸⁹ Forever, O Lord,
    your word stands firm in heaven.
⁹⁰ Your faithfulness extends to every generation,
    as enduring as the earth you created.
⁹¹ Your laws remain true today,
    for everything serves your plans.
⁹² If your law hadn't sustained me with joy,
    I would have died in my misery.
⁹³ I will never forget your commandments,
    for you have used them to restore my joy and health.
⁹⁴ I am yours; save me!
    For I have applied myself to obey your
        commandments.

⁹⁵ Though the wicked hide along the way to kill me,
    I will quietly keep my mind on your decrees.
⁹⁶ Even perfection has its limits,
    but your commands have no limit.

At the 1939 World's Fair on Long Island, New York, a torpedo-shaped time capsule was placed underground, to be exhumed five thousand years later. Among the many objects in the capsule were two books. One was a book explaining the capsule and what it included; the other was a Bible.

Why a Bible? An official explained, "The Holy Bible, of all books familiar to us today, will most likely survive through the ages. . . . It will be a sort of connecting link between the past, present, and future."

That's what verses 89 and 90 say when they use words like *forever, to every generation,* and *as enduring as the earth.*

The Bible has been burned and banned. Its demise has been predicted by every generation, but it lives on. You can go to the Amazon jungle or to Wall Street and find it being read and studied. You can find professional athletes as well as senior citizens in nursing homes looking for guidance in its pages. No wonder the World's Fair executive chose it as "the book most likely to survive."

Almighty Lord, the sun shall fail, and moon forget
    her nightly tale,
But fixed for everlasting years, unmoved amid the
    wreck of spheres,
Your Word shall shine in cloudless day
When heaven and earth shall pass away.
ROBERT GRANT

Notable Quotable
"The shadow of the sun and moon in the water seems to shake as much as the water it shines upon. Yet for all this seeming shaking here below, the sun and moon go on in a steadfast course in heaven. So the psalmist tells us that, however our hearts stagger at a promise through unbelief, and our unbelief makes us think that the promise is shaken, God's Word stands firm, though not in our hearts, but in heaven."
ANTHONY TUCKNEY

PSALM 119:97-112

[97] Oh, how I love your law!
   I think about it all day long.
[98] Your commands make me wiser than my enemies,
   for your commands are my constant guide.
[99] Yes, I have more insight than my teachers,
   for I am always thinking of your decrees.
[100] I am even wiser than my elders,
   for I have kept your commandments.
[101] I have refused to walk on any path of evil,
   that I may remain obedient to your word.
[102] I haven't turned away from your laws,
   for you have taught me well.
[103] How sweet are your words to my taste;
   they are sweeter than honey.
[104] Your commandments give me understanding;
   no wonder I hate every false way of life.

[105] Your word is a lamp for my feet
   and a light for my path.
[106] I've promised it once, and I'll promise again:
   I will obey your wonderful laws.
[107] I have suffered much, O LORD;
   restore my life again, just as you promised.
[108] LORD, accept my grateful thanks
   and teach me your laws.
[109] My life constantly hangs in the balance,
   but I will not stop obeying your law.
[110] The wicked have set their traps for me along your path,
   but I will not turn from your commandments.
[111] Your decrees are my treasure;
   they are truly my heart's delight.
[112] I am determined to keep your principles,
   even forever, to the very end.

George Washington Carver, the brilliant biochemist, revolutionized Southern agriculture by discovering hundreds of valuable uses for the sweet potato and the peanut.

In 1921 this black scientist was invited to testify in Washington, D.C., before the House Ways and Means Committee about the potential of the peanut.

The committee was captivated by his presentation. He talked for an hour and forty-five minutes, long past the normal adjournment time. After he finished, the chairman asked, "Dr. Carver, how did you learn all these things?"

Carver answered, "From an old book."

"What book?"

"The Bible."

"Did the Bible tell you about peanuts?"

"No sir," replied the scientist, "but it told me about the God who made the peanut. And then I asked him to show me what to do with the peanut, and he did."

Through God's Word the psalmist gained "more insight than [his] teachers" (verse 99), and God's commandments gave him understanding (verse 104). This is what Dr. Carver discovered as well.

If you need wisdom, said James, just ask God (James 1:5). His "word is a lamp for [your] feet" (Psalm 119:105). "Seek his will in all you do, and he will direct your paths" (Proverbs 3:6).

> How glorious is your Word, O God!
> 'Tis for our light and guidance given;
> It sheds a luster all abroad,
> And points the path to bliss and heaven.
> FRANK BOTTOME

Bible Networking

It's time to check the "lamps" throughout the house. Find out what kinds of lamps you have: Proverbs 6:23; 20:27; Matthew 25:1-13; Luke 8:16; and Revelation 22:5.

Notable Quotable

"Unless God's Word illumines our way, our whole life is shrouded in darkness and mist, so that we cannot help but miserably stray."
JOHN CALVIN

PSALM 119:113-128

[113] I hate those who are undecided about you,
    but my choice is clear—I love your law.

[114] You are my refuge and my shield;
    your word is my only source of hope.

[115] Get out of my life, you evil-minded people,
    for I intend to obey the commands of my God.

[116] LORD, sustain me as you promised, that I may live!
    Do not let my hope be crushed.

[117] Sustain me, and I will be saved;
    then I will meditate on your principles continually.

[118] But you have rejected all who stray from your
        principles.
    They are only fooling themselves.

[119] All the wicked of the earth are the scum you skim off;
    no wonder I love to obey your decrees!

[120] I tremble in fear of you;
    I fear your judgments.

[121] Don't leave me to the mercy of my enemies,
    for I have done what is just and right.

[122] Please guarantee a blessing for me.
    Don't let those who are arrogant oppress me!

[123] My eyes strain to see your deliverance,
    to see the truth of your promise fulfilled.

[124] I am your servant;
    deal with me in unfailing love,
    and teach me your principles.

[125] Give discernment to me, your servant;
    then I will understand your decrees.

[126] LORD, it is time for you to act,
    for these evil people have broken your law.

[127] Truly, I love your commands
    more than gold, even the finest gold.

128 Truly, each of your commandments is right.
That is why I hate every false way.

L iving about 150 years after the apostles, Tertullian had been trained for a career in politics and oratory. He had a razor-sharp mind that was quick and keen. At the age of thirty-five, he embraced Christianity, and he chose to leave a lucrative career in politics to become an ardent preacher, writer, and defender of the faith.

Like the psalmist (see verse 113), Tertullian couldn't understand halfhearted Christians. One day he was talking with another Christian, who was involved in some questionable business practices. Defending his actions, the man said, "But I must live."

Tersely, Tertullian retorted, "Why?"

Why, indeed? When you think about it, how important is living compared with pleasing the Lord? Like Tertullian's friend, we make many compromises because we consider them necessary to maintain a certain way of life. But how necessary is that way of life? What kind of life does God call us to lead?

Jesus Christ called people to forsake everything and follow him (Mark 10:21; Luke 9:23), but how easily we dilute those words. As a result, our choices are seldom clear, and we become undecided not only about the smaller things but also about the greater things of life.

> O let me feel thee near me; the world is ever near;
> I see the sights that dazzle, the tempting sounds I hear:
> My foes are ever near me, around me and within;
> But, Jesus, draw thou nearer, and shield my soul
>   from sin.
>
> JOHN BODE

A Word on Words
The "scum" of verse 119 probably refers to dross in metalworking. When a precious metal is being refined, a layer of impurities forms on the top and is skimmed off and discarded by the metalsmith. See also Isaiah 1:22.

PSALM 119:129-144

¹²⁹ Your decrees are wonderful.
No wonder I obey them!

¹³⁰ As your words are taught, they give light;
even the simple can understand them.

¹³¹ I open my mouth, panting expectantly,
longing for your commands.

¹³² Come and show me your mercy,
as you do for all who love your name.

¹³³ Guide my steps by your word,
so I will not be overcome by any evil.

¹³⁴ Rescue me from the oppression of evil people;
then I can obey your commandments.

¹³⁵ Look down on me with love;
teach me all your principles.

¹³⁶ Rivers of tears gush from my eyes
because people disobey your law.

¹³⁷ O LORD, you are righteous,
and your decisions are fair.

¹³⁸ Your decrees are perfect;
they are entirely worthy of our trust.

¹³⁹ I am overwhelmed with rage,
for my enemies have disregarded your words.

¹⁴⁰ Your promises have been thoroughly tested;
that is why I love them so much.

¹⁴¹ I am insignificant and despised,
but I don't forget your commandments.

¹⁴² Your justice is eternal,
and your law is perfectly true.

¹⁴³ As pressure and stress bear down on me,
I find joy in your commands.

¹⁴⁴ Your decrees are always fair;
help me to understand them, that I may live.

*T*he young French philosopher Emile Cailliet had been disillusioned by World War I. Sitting in the trenches, he saw that his naturalistic philosophy didn't work. He sought for a book that would make sense out of life, and more than that, "a book that would understand me."

Not finding such a book, he decided to put it together himself, finding wise sayings wherever he could and putting them in a scrapbook. One day he sat under a tree, reading his self-made book with his self-made philosophy. After reading it, he was more disillusioned than ever. His own collection of wisdom wouldn't work either.

Just then his wife came out of the house with a Bible, which she had chanced upon at a nearby chapel. Despite his education, Cailliet had never seen a Bible before. "As I read it, I could not find words to express my awe and wonder. Suddenly the realization dawned upon me. This was the Book that would understand me."

Throughout this psalm, the psalmist expresses amazement at what God's Word is, just as Cailliet discovered. Later the French philosopher, who became a devout Christian, admitted that it seemed strange to speak of a book understanding a person, but it could be said only "because its pages were animated by the presence of the living God."

> The Hand that gave it still supplies
> The gracious light and heat,
> His truths upon its readers rise,
> They rise but never set.
> JOHN NEWTON

Fascinating Fact
Verse 132 is one of only four verses in this psalm that do not have a direct reference to God's Word. The other verses are 90, 121, and 122.

Notable Quotable
"This light [verse 130] has excellent properties. (1) It is a manifesting light; it lays open all the frauds of the world; (2) it is a directing light; it shows us how to manage ourselves in all situations; (3) it is a quickening light; it shows us Jesus, the light who gives life; (4) it is a refreshing light; it brings daily comfort."
THOMAS MANTON

PSALM 119:145-160

¹⁴⁵ I pray with all my heart; answer me, LORD!
    I will obey your principles.
¹⁴⁶ I cry out to you; save me,
    that I may obey your decrees.
¹⁴⁷ I rise early, before the sun is up;
    I cry out for help and put my hope in your words.
¹⁴⁸ I stay awake through the night,
    thinking about your promise.
¹⁴⁹ In your faithful love, O LORD, hear my cry;
    in your justice, save my life.
¹⁵⁰ Those lawless people are coming near to attack me;
    they live far from your law.
¹⁵¹ But you are near, O LORD,
    and all your commands are true.
¹⁵² I have known from my earliest days
    that your decrees never change.

¹⁵³ Look down upon my sorrows and rescue me,
    for I have not forgotten your law.
¹⁵⁴ Argue my case; take my side!
    Protect my life as you promised.
¹⁵⁵ The wicked are far from salvation,
    for they do not bother with your principles.
¹⁵⁶ LORD, how great is your mercy;
    in your justice, give me back my life.
¹⁵⁷ Many persecute and trouble me,
    yet I have not swerved from your decrees.
¹⁵⁸ I hate these traitors
    because they care nothing for your word.
¹⁵⁹ See how I love your commandments, LORD.
    Give back my life because of your unfailing love.
¹⁶⁰ All your words are true;
    all your just laws will stand forever.

During World War II, Jacob DeShazer hated the Japanese. They were the enemy, and as a pilot he enjoyed the chance to rain flaming death on them. But then his plane was shot down, and he began a thirty-two month period of solitary confinement in a Japanese prison camp. There he turned to the Bible. Through its pages he became a Christian. He resolved that, if he ever made it out alive, he would become a missionary to Japan, bringing them the love of Jesus Christ instead of bombs.

In less than four years after his release, he returned to Japan as a missionary and wrote a tract about his experiences. Mitsuo Fuchida, the Japanese squadron commander who led the air raid on Pearl Harbor in 1941, was one who read the tract. DeShazer had testified of the power of the Bible in his life, so Fuchida decided to read the Bible for himself. Before finishing the first thirty pages the Japanese officer accepted Christ as his Savior. Shortly afterward, DeShazer and Fuchida sat together on a platform at an evangelistic meeting in Tokyo. The two former enemies were now brothers in Jesus Christ.

Throughout this section of Psalm 119, the psalmist expresses his confidence in God's Word and his concern about his enemies. As DeShazer discovered, it is possible, through the power of the Word, for enemies to become friends.

Are you willing to pray for your enemies in that way?

> Thy word is power and life;
> It bids confusion cease.
> And changes envy, hatred, strife
> To love and joy and peace.
> JAMES MONTGOMERY

A Word on Words

In Hebrew, verses 150 and 151 both begin with the words be near. The enemy is closing in and the Lord is nearby. At such a time it is good to remember that you can count on God's Word (see verse 152).

PSALM 119:161-176

161 Powerful people harass me without cause,
 but my heart trembles only at your word.

162 I rejoice in your word
 like one who finds a great treasure.

163 I hate and abhor all falsehood,
 but I love your law.

164 I will praise you seven times a day
 because all your laws are just.

165 Those who love your law have great peace
 and do not stumble.

166 I long for your salvation, LORD,
 so I have obeyed your commands.

167 I have obeyed your decrees,
 and I love them very much.

168 Yes, I obey your commandments and decrees,
 because you know everything I do.

169 O LORD, listen to my cry;
 give me the discerning mind you promised.

170 Listen to my prayer;
 rescue me as you promised.

171 Let my lips burst forth with praise,
 for you have taught me your principles.

172 Let my tongue sing about your word,
 for all your commands are right.

173 Stand ready to help me,
 for I have chosen to follow your commandments.

174 O LORD, I have longed for your salvation,
 and your law is my delight.

175 Let me live so I can praise you,
 and may your laws sustain me.

[176] I have wandered away like a lost sheep;
   come and find me,
   for I have not forgotten your commands.

*P*salm 119 is known for the fact that almost every verse mentions God's Word. But you will find even more frequent references to God (count how often *you* and *your* are used in these verses) and to the psalmist (count the occurrences of *I* and *me*). The main point of this psalm is not the Word but the relationship between people and God through the Word. Verse 176 makes this very clear.

The university library in Kansas has an unusual Bible. At first it looks rather ordinary, but when the gilt edges of the pages are slightly parted, you see a picture of Christ with his disciples in the upper room. Underneath this picture are the words "It is I myself; handle me and see."

That's the message of the Bible and indeed the message of Psalm 119. When the pages are open, Christ can be seen; but more than that, through these pages you can find a personal relationship with him. The aim of the Scriptures is not simply that you may know about God. It is that you may know him personally.

> Holy Bible, book divine, precious treasure, thou
>   art mine;
> Mine to tell me whence I came; mine to teach me
>   what I am;
> Mine to chide me when I rove; mine to show a
>   Savior's love;
> Mine thou art to guide and guard; mine to punish
>   or reward.

JOHN BURTON

Bible Networking

Does verse 176 remind you of any other Bible passages? What about Isaiah 53:6; Jeremiah 50:6; Ezekiel 34:12; Matthew 18:12-14; John 10:14-16; or 1 Peter 2:25?

Notable Quotable

"I do not think there could possibly be a more appropriate conclusion of such a psalm, so full of the ever-changing frames and feelings even of a child of God, in the sunshine and the cloud, in the calm and in the storm, than this ever-clinging sense of his propensity to wander and the expression of his utter inability to find his way back without the Lord's guiding hand."
BARTON BOUCHIER

For Psalms 120–134, we find the interesting inscription "A song for the ascent to Jerusalem," or, more literally, "A song of ascents." What does this mean? What kind of psalms must these be?

Here are a few verses from these psalms:

◆ *Psalm 121:3*
He will not let you stumble
    and fall;
    the one who watches over
    you will not sleep.

◆ *Psalm 122:1*
I was glad when they said
    to me,
    "Let us go to the house of
    the LORD."

◆ *Psalm 126:5*
Those who plant in tears
    will harvest with shouts
    of joy.

◆ *Psalm 127:1*
Unless the LORD builds a house,
    the work of the builders is
    useless.

◆ *Psalm 130:3-4*
LORD, if you kept a record of
    our sins,
    who, O Lord, could ever
    survive?
But you offer forgiveness.

◆ *Psalm 133:1*
How wonderful it is, how
    pleasant,
    when brothers live together
    in harmony!

Ever take a long journey with children? It isn't easy. Most families, out of desperation, develop an assortment of games, puzzles, and songs to make the trip feel shorter. If you can find a song with a dozen verses, you're doing well. "The Twelve Days of Christmas" is good for at least ten minutes, and that means ten miles closer to the next rest stop.

In biblical times parents had the same kind of problem, but, of course, in those days ten minutes didn't mean ten fewer miles. Families were obliged to make three trips each year to Jerusalem to commemorate Passover, Pentecost, and the Festival of Shelters. If you had one donkey and five children, even fifty miles was a long journey. For safety reasons, you usually tried to travel with other families from your village, and this also helped to keep the kids entertained.

Adding to the challenge was the fact that much of the trip to Jerusalem was uphill. Mount Zion (where the Temple was located) certainly wasn't anything like Mount Everest or Kilimanjaro, but traveling with children from Jericho, which is nine hundred feet below sea level, to Jerusalem, with an elevation of about twenty-six hundred feet, was a good climb for everyone.

This is probably where the "songs for the ascent to Jerusalem" (Psalms 120–134) came in handy. Pilgrims on their way to Jerusalem would sing them as they climbed up toward the city. It should be noted that these psalms were probably not originally written as "Music to Climb Hills By." Instead, they were probably written for worship in the Temple (Psalms 122, 124, 134), for public singing (Psalms 123, 125), for national celebration (Psalms 121, 126, 129, 132, 133), or for private or family use (120, 127, 128, 130, 131). But because these psalms are all rather short and speak of things that were appropriate for a pilgrimage to the Temple, they were good for communal singing as a caravan plodded its way up toward Jerusalem.

What wonderful family vacations those must have been— with a spiritual end in view. Not a bad idea for these days as well. Why not use these psalms to give you refreshment as you make your spiritual "climb"?

∾

A hand divine shall lead you on
And up the blissful road,
Till to the sacred mount you ri⸱⸱
And see your smiling God.
PHILIP DODDRIDGE

October 15

PSALM 120
A song for the ascent to Jerusalem.

¹ I took my troubles to the LORD;
    I cried out to him, and he answered my prayer.
² Rescue me, O LORD, from liars
    and from all deceitful people.
³ O deceptive tongue, what will God do to you?
    How will he increase your punishment?
⁴ You will be pierced with sharp arrows
    and burned with glowing coals.

⁵ How I suffer among these scoundrels of Meshech!
    It pains me to live with these people from Kedar!
⁶ I am tired of living here
    among people who hate peace.
⁷ As for me, I am for peace;
    but when I speak, they are for war!

*E*vidently Thomas Carlisle, the clever English writer, did not appreciate the company he had at a London dinner party. He described it to a friend as "babble, babble," and then, referring to Psalm 120:5, commented, "Woe is me, that I in Meshech am!"

Several hundred years earlier some Benedictine monks were dismayed by the lack of the spirituality in their order, and they described their plight as "sojourning in the tents of Kedar."

What is this Meshech and Kedar language all about?

Meshech was a barbaric tribe far north of Israel; Kedar was an amoral clan to the southeast. The psalmist was probably not actually living in their midst, but he felt as if his neighbors were living like barbarians (as Carlisle felt) or lacking any spiritual sensitivity (as those Benedictine monks felt).

It isn't easy to live in such circumstances where gossip, slander, and filthy talk are commonplace. But as Charles Spurgeon once said, it's sometimes easier to "live a holy life in a city warehouse than it is in a divinity school." We can always choose to follow God's way, regardless of the fact that we are surrounded by the people of Meshech and Kedar.

> Should burning arrows smite thee through,
> Strict justice would approve.
> But I had rather spare my foe
> And melt his heart with love.
> ISAAC WATTS

Bible Networking
The Bible has a lot to say about the devastation a "deceptive tongue" (verse 3) can cause. See Jeremiah 9:8; James 3:6; Matthew 15:11; and Romans 3:13.

Notable Quotable
"This little passage is a classic comment on the incompatibility of light and darkness. The New Testament counsels the Christian in this context against two opposite errors: compromise (2 Corinthians 6:14ff; 1 John 2:15ff) and animosity (Romans 12:14-21)."
DEREK KIDNER

October 16

PSALM 121:1-4

A song for the ascent to Jerusalem.

1 I look up to the mountains—
    does my help come from there?
2 My help comes from the LORD,
    who made the heavens and the earth!

3 He will not let you stumble and fall;
    the one who watches over you will not sleep.
4 Indeed, he who watches over Israel
    never tires and never sleeps.

*I*n the seventeenth century the English envoy to Sweden was extremely disturbed by reports he was receiving from his home country. Unable to sleep, he began pacing the floor.

His servant piped up, "Do you mind, sir, if I asked a question?"

"Go ahead," responded the envoy.

"Do you think God governed the world very well before you came into it?"

"Yes, of course."

"And do you think that he will govern the world equally well when you have gone out of it."

"Certainly."

"Then don't you think that you may trust him to govern it for the few years that you are alive?"

We have a never-sleeping God, who is watching over us and ours.

The Old Testament pilgrims who came to Jerusalem for their annual feasts often traveled roads where bandits roamed. Obviously, parents had concerns about the safety of their children, so this psalm addressed some very deep fears.

The pilgrim found assurance in the fact that the God who loved and preserved the nation (verse 4) is the same God who loves and preserves you (verse 3). And that is just as true for you today as it was for the pilgrim of the psalmist's day.

> *What God's almighty power hath made, his gracious mercy keepeth;*
> *By morning glow or evening shade, his watchful eye ne'er sleepeth;*
> *Within the kingdom of his might, lo! all is just and all is right:*
> *To God all praise and glory.*
> J. J. SCHÜTZ

Bible Networking

This psalm reminds us that the Lord never sleeps. But do you remember the story of Elijah's contest with the prophets of Baal on Mount Carmel? When the prophets of Baal were unable to bring down fire from heaven, Elijah prodded them to yell louder to Baal, "Maybe he is away on a trip, or he is asleep and needs to be wakened!" (1 Kings 18:27).

Notable Quotable

"We are all tempted to look at the mountains, to the creature rather than the Creator, to things and people beneath the heavens, instead of to Him who dwells above the heavens, in His infinite majesty, and to whom all power is given in heaven and in earth."
F. B. MEYER

PSALM 121:5-8

5 The LORD himself watches over you!
  The LORD stands beside you as your protective shade.
6 The sun will not hurt you by day,
  nor the moon at night.
7 The LORD keeps you from all evil
  and preserves your life.
8 The LORD keeps watch over you as you come and go,
  both now and forever.

*I*t was dark and cold that November morning when the Livingstone family woke up to say farewell to their son David. He was leaving Scotland that day for the heart of Africa. Mrs. Livingstone made coffee; Mr. Livingstone dressed warmly to walk his son to Glasgow. David got the family Bible and read the comforting words of Psalm 121 with the family.

A dozen years later, Dr. Livingstone was contemplating a trip deeper into the unexplored interior of Africa along with his wife and children. Just before he left, he received a letter from his mother-in-law, Mary Moffat, who was also a missionary. "My dear Livingstone," she began. "Hitherto I have kept up my spirits and have been enabled to believe that our Great Master may yet bring you out in safety." She said that she was clinging to the promises of Psalm 121 and Psalm 91. "Unceasing prayer is made for you." Then she added, "Every petition, however fervent, must be with submission to his will."

Protected? Yes. Submissive to his will? That, too.

Sometimes we can be confused by that. Neither David Livingstone nor the apostle Paul were immune from trouble, and Jesus guaranteed us that in this world we will have trouble (John 16:33). But no matter what happens, we can never be separated from God's love or God's purposes. He promises to preserve us from evil but not to pave over every pothole in life's road.

> From God the Lord does come your certain aid;
> From God the Lord who heaven and earth has made.
> Above you watching, He whom you adore
> Shall keep you henceforth, yes, for evermore.
> JOHN CAMPBELL

Fascinating Fact

Notice all the phrases in this psalm that say that the Lord "watches over," "keeps," "stands beside," "preserves," and "never sleeps." Do you think the Lord is trying to tell you something?

Notable Quotable

"Christians travel the same ground that everyone else walks on, breathe the same air, drink the same water. . . . The difference is that each step we walk, we know we are accompanied by God, we know we are ruled by God, and therefore no matter what accidents we experience, the Lord will preserve us from evil."
EUGENE PETERSON

PSALM 122:1-5
A song for the ascent to Jerusalem. A psalm of David.

1 I was glad when they said to me,
"Let us go to the house of the LORD."
2 And now we are standing here
inside your gates, O Jerusalem.
3 Jerusalem is a well-built city,
knit together as a single unit.
4 All the people of Israel—the LORD's people—
make their pilgrimage here.
They come to give thanks to the name of the LORD
as the law requires.
5 Here stand the thrones where judgment is given,
the thrones of the dynasty of David.

C an you imagine the Israelite families' excitement as they close in upon Jerusalem around the time of the festivals—some from Galilee to the north, some from Egypt in the south, some from Cyprus or even Greece across the Mediterranean. As they draw nearer, they join other pilgrims, and the crowd grows noisier as the excitement becomes almost feverish.

"Aw, Mom, can't we wait five minutes more before going to Sunday school? This is my favorite cartoon on TV."

As the throngs make their way to the brow of the last hill, they see Jerusalem and its famous Temple, and they let out shrieks of joy in anticipation.

"I'm not sure we need to go to church today. I don't think the pastor is preaching on anything important."

And through the gates of the city the pilgrims come at a faster pace, and into the Temple courts they rush. Some fall on their faces and kiss the marble floors. At last, at last—"Hallelujah, Shalom Jerusalem!"

"Well, maybe we'd better go anyway. Someone might get the wrong idea if we don't."

> Come, we that love the Lord
> And let your joys be known,
> Join in a song with sweet accord,
> And thus surround the throne.
> ISAAC WATTS

A Word on Words

The Hebrew word translated "knit together" in verse 3 can also refer to people joining forces or finding fellowship together.

Bible Networking

For more on Jerusalem's gates, see 2 Chronicles 8:14; 31:2; Nehemiah 1:3; 12:30; Psalms 24:7; 100:4; Proverbs 8:1-5; Lamentations 2:9; and Revelation 21:21.

PSALM 122:6-9

[6] Pray for the peace of Jerusalem.
May all who love this city prosper.

[7] O Jerusalem, may there be peace within your walls
and prosperity in your palaces.

[8] For the sake of my family and friends, I will say,
"Peace be with you."

[9] For the sake of the house of the LORD our God,
I will seek what is best for you, O Jerusalem.

No doubt when pilgrims came within sight of Jerusalem's glorious skyline, they were exuberant in their joyful praise.

But when Jesus Christ approached the city in that final week before his crucifixion, he wept over it. "I wish that even today you would find the way of peace. But now it is too late, and peace is hidden from you" (Luke 19:42). Jesus foresaw the destruction of the city by the Romans, which would take place a generation later.

Probably no city in history has heard the word *peace*, or *shalom*, sounded more often within its walls, yet perhaps no city has been so devastated over and over again by invading armies. The Babylonians, the Greeks, the Romans, the Persians, the Muslims, the Turks, the Crusaders, the British—all have besieged it and captured it, some several times. Strange, isn't it, that peace has so eluded this city, which is held sacred by three religions. Strange, isn't it, that the Prince of Peace was crucified there.

Christians should continue to pray for the troubled city of Jerusalem. We should also remember that the church is to the Christian what Jerusalem was to pilgrims. In language reminiscent of the way Jews approached Jerusalem, the book of Hebrews tells us: "You have come to Mount Zion, to the city of the living God" (12:22). And the way to bring peace is to "continue to love each other with true Christian love" (13:1).

> Peace, perfect peace, our future all unknown?
> Jesus we know, and he is on the throne.
> EDWARD H. BICKERSTETH

Bible Networking
For inspiring implications of verse 9 read Hebrews 12:22-24.

Notable Quotable
"What Jerusalem was to the Israelite, the church is to the Christian. Here are his closest ties, his brethren and companions, known and unknown, drawn with him to the one center as fellow pilgrims."
DEREK KIDNER

PSALM 123
A song for the ascent to Jerusalem.

[1] I lift my eyes to you,
O God, enthroned in heaven.
[2] We look to the LORD our God for his mercy,
just as servants keep their eyes on their master,
as a slave girl watches her mistress for the slightest
signal.

[3] Have mercy on us, LORD, have mercy,
for we have had our fill of contempt.
[4] We have had our fill of the scoffing of the proud
and the contempt of the arrogant.

*I*magine that it's the last minute of the Super Bowl. Behind by one touchdown, the quarterback throws a long pass into the end zone, and his swiftest wide receiver races down the field and reaches out to grab the football. An opponent is also in pursuit, and just as the catch is about to be made, the opponent grabs the arm of the receiver. The pass is dropped, and the opponent gloats exultingly. He thinks he has gotten away with it. Nobody saw him grab the wide receiver's arm, or so he thinks.

On the ground the receiver has his eyes on the referee. Has the referee signaled a penalty? Where's the flag? Didn't the referee notice the infraction? What if the game is lost because the opponent got away without a penalty?

Nehemiah felt like that (Nehemiah 4:4). He had come back to Jerusalem to rebuild its walls, and all had been going well—that is, until the enemies started their scoffing. So Nehemiah prayed, "Hear us, O our God." Didn't he notice what the enemy was doing? Why wasn't he penalizing them?

That's also what the psalmist felt like in this psalm. Actually, we all feel like that from time to time. We look for instant replay to vindicate us instead of keeping our eyes on the referee.

What Nehemiah did was to keep on praying and to keep on working. And we need to do the same. The signals are already being called for the next play. Get in the action.

> Awake, our souls! Away our fears!
> Let every anxious thought be gone!
> Awake, and run the heavenly race,
> And put a cheerful courage on.
> ISAAC WATTS

A Word on Words
Contempt (verse 3) can be more murderous than anger (Matthew 5:22), but it is an honor to receive it if it is for the sake of the gospel (Acts 5:41).

Notable Quotable
"We must use our eyes with resolution, for they will not go upward to the Lord of themselves, but they incline to look downward, or inward, or anywhere but to the Lord."
CHARLES HADDON SPURGEON

You might think that the Israelites would have been at a disadvantage in describing their God. After all, the first commandment forbade them from making any images of God, and that meant they couldn't draw pictures.

So how did the Israelites describe God? Here are a few verses from the Psalms:

◆ God is just
The LORD is known for his justice.
   The wicked have trapped themselves in their own snares (9:16).

◆ God is fair
Tell all the nations that the LORD is king. . . .
   He will judge all peoples fairly (96:10).

◆ God is compassionate
The LORD is like a father to his children,
   tender and compassionate to those who fear him (103:13).

◆ God is merciful
With all my heart I want your blessings.
   Be merciful just as you promised (119:58).

◆ God is good
Praise the LORD, for the LORD is good;
   celebrate his wonderful name with music (135:3).

◆ God is eternally loving
Give thanks to the God of gods.
   His faithful love endures forever (136:2).

◆ God is righteous
Everyone will share the story of your wonderful goodness;
   they will sing with joy of your righteousness (145:7).

Instead of making pictures of God with a brush or chisel, the Israelites drew word pictures. In the Psalms they called God a rock, a fortress, a shield, a shepherd. God isn't literally a rock or a shepherd, but the people got the picture. Sometimes they spoke of God sheltering his people under his wings or holding them in his arms, but they knew God didn't actually have wings or arms. And they spoke of God by different names— God the Provider, God the Healer, God my Righteousness—but they knew there was only one God.

Yet in the various word pictures, the thing the psalmists emphasized most about God was his character. As we noted above, God is known for his justice (9:16); he is fair (96:10); he is compassionate (103:13); he is merciful (119:58); he is good (135:3); he is characterized by his faithful love (136:2); and he is righteous (145:7). What an amazing God we serve!

If you were to draw a word picture of God, which of these divine attributes would you emphasize the most? And which of them do you need to appreciate more in the future? Perhaps you can search through the Psalms to help you think of attributes that God possesses.

∾

This, this is the God we adore,
Our faithful, unchangeable Friend.
Whose love is as great as his power,
And neither knows measure nor end.
JOSEPH HART

∾

What else can you find out about God? See Psalm 5:4 and Isaiah 6:3; Psalm 90:2 and 1 Timothy 1:17; Psalm 147:5 and Romans 11:33 to start with.

Selah

PSALM 124:1-5
A song for the ascent to Jerusalem. A psalm of David.

¹ If the LORD had not been on our side—
  let Israel now say—
² if the LORD had not been on our side
  when people rose up against us,
³ they would have swallowed us alive
  because of their burning anger against us.
⁴ The waters would have engulfed us;
  a torrent would have overwhelmed us.
⁵ Yes, the raging waters of their fury
  would have overwhelmed our very lives.

*I*t's hard to know when this psalm was written, but the first five verses remind us of an incident in King David's life.

He had just been acclaimed king of the entire nation of Israel. Then the Philistines amassed their armies and spread out across the valley of Rephaim. From there they could invade south to where David had his headquarters in Hebron, or they could invade north to where most of the Israelite tribes were located. Or both.

Newly crowned king, David hadn't had a chance yet to recruit a national army, so he was greatly outnumbered. If the Lord hadn't been on his side, he and the struggling nation would have been "swallowed alive."

"What should I do?" prayed David. After getting his directions from God, David used his small troop of guerrilla soldiers and devastated the Philistines in a surprise attack.

David's reaction is interesting (2 Samuel 5:20): "The Lord has done it!" David exclaimed. "He burst through my enemies like a raging flood!" But wasn't David the general? Weren't his guerrilla troops the victorious army? Yes, but David knew the limits of his own power. If God hadn't been running the show, the outcome would have been totally different. So David gave credit where credit was due.

Look back over the successes of your life during the past week. Who got the credit?

> We are daily led by one who never lost a battle,
> And our adversary is a conquered foe;
> We are more than conquerors through our Captain's triumph;
> Let us shout the victory as we onward go.
>
> A. B. SIMPSON

Bible Networking
Verses 4-5 depict a conquering army, rolling to victory. For a similar picture, see Isaiah 8:7-8.

Notable Quotable
"What an If is this [verses 1-2]! One shudders to think what and where we might have been without the delivering, preserving hand of our God."
F. B. MEYER

PSALM 124:6-8

6 Blessed be the LORD,
   who did not let their teeth tear us apart!
7 We escaped like a bird from a hunter's trap.
   The trap is broken, and we are free!
8 Our help is from the LORD,
   who made the heavens and the earth.

*I*n the British Museum there's a piece of stone with an ancient message that dates back to 691 B.C.. Sennacherib's Prism tells how he captured forty-six towns of the tiny nation of Judah and trapped their king in the capital city "like a bird in a cage."

But the prism doesn't tell the rest of the story. Yes, the Assyrians surrounded Jerusalem, and King Hezekiah was caged like a bird. But then Hezekiah prayed.

The Bible says that the angel of the Lord came and decimated the Assyrian army. The Greek historian Herodotus reports that a plague of field mice gnawed the bowstrings of the Assyrian soldiers. Other historians say that the field mice may have done more than gnaw bowstrings; they may have started a bubonic plague among the soldiers. Still others say an insurrection arose against Sennacherib, forcing him to withdraw. Whatever the actions of the "angel of the Lord" were, the Assyrian troops were gone by morning, and the "caged bird" could sing again.

Often David was surrounded by enemy forces as well, and God made a way of escape for him. That's why he could sing, "We escaped like a bird from a hunter's trap. The trap is broken, and we are free!" (verse 7).

That's a song you should be able to sing, too. The Bible tells us that it is only by God's mercy that we could "escape from the Devil's trap" (2 Timothy 2:26).

> *He breaks the power of cancelled sin,*
> *He sets the prisoner free;*
> *His blood can make the foulest clean;*
> *His blood availed for me.*
> CHARLES WESLEY

Bible Networking
Hezekiah was also trapped like a caged bird (see verse 7) under the onslaught of Sennacherib. Read 2 Kings 19:19, 35-36 to see how God set that bird free.

Notable Quotable
"All the help of Omnipotence is pledged on the side of the weakest of the saints. Lean back upon it and be strong."
F. B. MEYER

PSALM 125
A song for the ascent to Jerusalem.

¹ Those who trust in the LORD are as secure as
   Mount Zion;
      they will not be defeated but will endure forever.
² Just as the mountains surround and protect Jerusalem,
      so the LORD surrounds and protects his people, both
         now and forever.
³ The wicked will not rule the godly,
      for then the godly might be forced to do wrong.
⁴ O LORD, do good to those who are good,
      whose hearts are in tune with you.
⁵ But banish those who turn to crooked ways, O LORD.
      Take them away with those who do evil.
      And let Israel have quietness and peace.

Life under Louis XIV was not easy for the French Huguenots. They loved to sing psalms, but the king made an edict that forbade the singing of the Psalms almost everywhere. So the Huguenots went out to the fields and forests and continued their singing. Psalm 125 was a favorite of theirs, maybe because it said that the wicked would not rule the godly. Or maybe it was because the Huguenots could see something that Louis XIV couldn't see.

Remember the story of Elisha and his servant (2 Kings 6:8-23)? The servant couldn't understand why Elisha wasn't bothered about the hordes of enemy soldiers surrounding them. It looked like disaster, but Elisha could see horses and chariots of fire surrounding the enemy soldiers.

The same has been true for many other saints, including Paul and Silas, who sang at midnight in the Philippian jail, and Shadrach, Meshech, and Abednego, who calmly entered the fiery furnace.

When John Woolman, a Quaker missionary to American Indians, was faced with danger, he wrote: "I found my soul filled with comfort as I meditated on the love of God."

John Paton, missionary to South Sea Island natives, was surrounded by men seeking to assassinate him, but he wrote: "I was never left without hearing that promise 'Lo, I am with you always.'"

How does it look to you today? Hopeless? Then take another look.

> When I tread the verge of Jordan,
> Bid my anxious fears subside;
> Death of death, and hell's destruction,
> Land me safe on Canaan's side:
> Songs of praises, I will ever give to thee.
> WILLIAM WILLIAMS

Bible Networking
When our heart is right (verse 4), all is right. See Proverbs 4:23.

Notable Quotable
"Faith is a living, daring confidence in God's grace. It is so sure and certain that a man could stake his life on it a thousand times."
MARTIN LUTHER

PSALM 126

A song for the ascent to Jerusalem.

¹ When the LORD restored his exiles to Jerusalem,
  it was like a dream!
² We were filled with laughter,
  and we sang for joy.
And the other nations said,
  "What amazing things the LORD has done for them."
³ Yes, the LORD has done amazing things for us!
  What joy!

⁴ Restore our fortunes, LORD,
  as streams renew the desert.
⁵ Those who plant in tears
  will harvest with shouts of joy.
⁶ They weep as they go to plant their seed,
  but they sing as they return with the harvest.

Cyrus the Great of Persia did something unheard of. He recorded his astonishing deed on a ten-inch piece of clay, now located in the British Museum. The Cyrus Cylinder announces: "I [Cyrus] gathered all their inhabitants and returned [to them] their habitations." In other words, he let his captives return home.

This was a revolutionary policy in the ancient world. Assyria and Babylon took their captives and made them slaves. But when Persia defeated Babylon, Cyrus sent the captives back to their homes. No wonder the Israelites thought it was like a dream.

The Roman historian Livy records a similar event that happened two hundred years later when Rome conquered Greece. The Greeks were expecting the worst. Then, as tens of thousands of Greeks packed an arena to witness the Isthmian Games, the word came that liberty was restored to all the Greek cities. The crowd was stunned; they "were like them that dream," the historian wrote, unintentionally echoing this psalm.

That's the way it is with the gospel. "The gospel is nothing else than laughter and joy," said Luther. "It is good tidings of great joy."

The Lord has done, is doing, and will continue to do great things for us—and not merely great things, but amazing things. How many of these things have you already witnessed in your own life?

> Low we bow before thy face;
> Sons of God, O wondrous place;
> Great the riches of thy grace.
> Father, we adore thee.
> SAMUEL TREVOR FRANCIS

A Word on Words

The "streams of the desert" (verse 4) were gullies that a rainstorm would fill suddenly with rushing water. For a short time after such a watering, these streambeds would burst into bloom with wildflowers. Eugene Peterson comments, "With such suddenness are long, dry periods of waiting interrupted by God's invasion into our lives in Jesus Christ."

Bible Networking

Like this psalm, the story of Joseph's life begins with a dream and includes an amazing harvest (Genesis 37–50). Do you see any other parallels between this psalm and Joseph's life?

1 SAMUEL 2:8-10 (Hannah's Song, Part 2)

[8] "He lifts the poor from the dust—
    yes, from a pile of ashes!
He treats them like princes,
    placing them in seats of honor.

"For all the earth is the LORD's,
    and he has set the world in order.
[9] He will protect his godly ones,
    but the wicked will perish in darkness.
No one will succeed by strength alone.
[10]   Those who fight against the LORD will be broken.
He thunders against them from heaven;
    the LORD judges throughout the earth.
He gives mighty strength to his king;
    he increases the might of his anointed one."

Psalm Link
PSALM 32:10-11

[10] Many sorrows come to the wicked,
    but unfailing love surrounds those who trust the
        LORD.
[11] So rejoice in the LORD and be glad, all you who obey
        him!
    Shout for joy, all you whose hearts are pure!

*A*lthough Hannah may not have been recognized for her leadership as were Miriam and Deborah, she was still quite remarkable.

A woman of prayer, Hannah went to the Tabernacle and prayed in deep anguish. Because of her prayer, her son Samuel was born. She kept a promise she had made to God and gave Samuel to the priests in the Tabernacle, and he became a prophet and a priest himself.

Hannah praised God because "he has set the world in order." And every year, as sure as clockwork, Hannah made a new coat for her son Samuel and brought it to him in the Tabernacle.

Hannah was also a poet. Her beautiful hymn of praise served as a model for the psalmists of the Old Testament as well as for Mary, the mother of Jesus, in the New Testament.

It seems that Hannah, in this song, was also acting as a prophet. In the last verse of her song, she speaks of a king and of the "anointed one," using the Hebrew word *messiah*. There was no king in Israel yet, so who was she talking about? Was God allowing her to see that her son Samuel would eventually anoint the first two kings of Israel? Historically, both Jewish and Christian scholars have felt that Hannah was speaking prophetically of the Messiah who was to come. If so, Hannah had written the first Christmas carol. No wonder Hannah could sing, "He lifts the poor from the dust. . . . He treats them like princes."

> Then pealed the bells more loud and deep:
> "God is not dead, nor doth he sleep;
> The wrong shall fail, the right prevail,
> With peace on earth, goodwill to men."
> HENRY W. LONGFELLOW

Bible Networking
Hannah is claiming God's protection in verse 9. See what David says in Psalm 32:6-7.

Notable Quotable
"No calamity of this world, no troubles of this life, no terrors of death, no guiltiness of sin, can be so great, but that the godly by means of his faith in Christ can wade out of them."
THOMAS PLAYFERE

PSALM 127

A song for the ascent to Jerusalem. A psalm of Solomon.

¹ Unless the LORD builds a house,
    the work of the builders is useless.
Unless the LORD protects a city,
    guarding it with sentries will do no good.
² It is useless for you to work so hard
    from early morning until late at night,
anxiously working for food to eat;
    for God gives rest to his loved ones.

³ Children are a gift from the LORD;
    they are a reward from him.
⁴ Children born to a young man
    are like sharp arrows in a warrior's hands.
⁵ How happy is the man whose quiver is full of them!
    He will not be put to shame when he confronts his
        accusers at the city gates.

Benjamin Franklin is best known for his inventions (the lightning rod) and his aphorisms ("Early to bed and early to rise, makes a man healthy, wealthy, and wise"). But he was also a key figure when the thirteen colonies were giving birth to a new nation.

At the age of eighty-one, Franklin was the oldest representative at the 1787 Constitutional Convention in Philadelphia. Weeks after the convention began, representatives were still haggling about the relative voting power of large states and small states. Then Franklin stood up and said,

> "In the beginning of the contest with Britain, when we were sensible of danger, we had daily prayers in this room for the divine protection. Our prayers, sir, were heard, and they were graciously answered. . . . Have we now forgotten this powerful Friend? Do we imagine that we no longer need his assistance? I have lived a long time, and the longer I live the more convincing proof I see of this truth, that God governs in the affairs of men. . . . We have been assured, sir, that 'except the Lord builds the house, they labor in vain that build it,' and without his concurring aid, we shall succeed in this political building no better than the builders of Babel."

The verse from Psalm 127 had its effect. A compromise was soon worked out, and a Constitution was ratified by the states the following year.

> *O happy home, where Thou art not forgotten,*
> *When joy is overflowing full and free;*
> *O happy home, where every wounded spirit*
> *Is brought, Physician, Comforter, to Thee.*
> CARL J. SPITTA

Bible Networking
Building without God is foolish, as seen in the stories of the Tower of Babel (Genesis 11:1-9) and the house built on sand (Matthew 7:24-27).

Notable Quotable
"Down they come, one after another; down they come, and every time for lack of righteousness. . . . When a nation no longer possesses a real effective belief in things spiritual, strong enough to inspire and to direct action, it decays."
MATTHEW ARNOLD

PSALM 128
A song for the ascent to Jerusalem.

¹ How happy are those who fear the LORD—
　　all who follow his ways!
² You will enjoy the fruit of your labor.
　　How happy you will be! How rich your life!
³ Your wife will be like a fruitful vine,
　　flourishing within your home.
　And look at all those children!
　　There they sit around your table
　　as vigorous and healthy as young olive trees.
⁴ That is the LORD's reward
　　for those who fear him.

⁵ May the LORD continually bless you from Zion.
　　May you see Jerusalem prosper as long as you live.
⁶ May you live to enjoy your grandchildren.
　　And may Israel have quietness and peace.

*P*salms 127 and 128 both speak about the family. There are some things, however, that we must be careful not to misunderstand from these psalms. They are *not* saying:

♦ Every good Christian will enjoy marital bliss.

♦ The primary purpose of a woman is to bear lots of children.

♦ Every good Christian couple will have scores of children and grandchildren descending on their homes every Christmas.

But what *do* these psalms teach us?

♦ Family blessings are from the Lord. If you have a wonderful family, praise God for them.

♦ Joy and peace should characterize the family.

♦ God cares about your home just as he cares about the church and nation.

But we live in a sinful world, and evil encroaches upon us and our families. Some of the finest saints have not enjoyed all the blessings of this psalm. In some cases they never married, although they wanted to; in other cases, they had childless marriages; and still in other cases, children died at an early age, a spouse died, or a child got into serious trouble.

Luther made a good point when he said, "Let the Lord build the home and keep it.... The concern for these matters is his, not yours." In other words, live verse 1 day by day, and let God concern himself with the rest.

> *O perfect Love, all human thought transcending,*
> *Lowly we kneel in prayer before thy throne,*
> *That theirs may be the love that has no ending,*
> *Whom thou forevermore dost join in one.*
> DOROTHY GURNEY

Notable Quotable
"The fear (verse 1) is an inward principle; the walk is an outward expression. No one really fears the Lord who does not walk in his ways. The Christian life is ethical as well as emotional."
W. GRAHAM SCROGGIE

PSALM 129
A song for the ascent to Jerusalem.

¹ From my earliest youth my enemies have persecuted
      me—
    let Israel now say—
² from my earliest youth my enemies have persecuted
      me,
    but they have never been able to finish me off.
³ My back is covered with cuts,
    as if a farmer had plowed long furrows.
⁴ But the LORD is good;
    he has cut the cords used by the ungodly to bind me.

⁵ May all who hate Jerusalem
    be turned back in shameful defeat.
⁶ May they be as useless as grass on a rooftop,
    turning yellow when only half grown,
⁷   ignored by the harvester,
    despised by the binder.
⁸ And may those who pass by refuse to give them this
      blessing:
    "The LORD's blessings be upon you;
    we bless you in the LORD's name."

*D*uring the 1660s Alexander Peden was sort of a Scottish Robin Hood. In England, Cromwell had been overthrown, the monarchy had been restored, and Scottish Presbyterian ministers, of whom Peden was one, were treated as outlaws.

Ejected from his church, imprisoned in an isolated jail, and banished to a life of slavery in America, Peden escaped to London and was "dogged by spies and hunted by dragoons." One historian writes: "Dogs sniffed at the entrance of the cave in which he was hiding. . . . Soldiers stabbed the beds or heaps of unthreshed wheat under which he lay." Once closely pursued on horseback, Peden prayed to God to "cast the lap of thy cloak over old Sandy [himself]," and within minutes a mist covered the hills so he could escape.

Perhaps all these experiences are why Peden loved the Psalms—especially Psalm 129. No doubt he could identify with the suffering that David had endured, and he looked for the day when the tables would be turned.

For most of us, our suffering is nothing compared to what the psalmist and Alexander Peden have gone through, but we, too, long for the day when the tables are turned. Until that day, we can sing Alexander Peden's other favorite psalm, Psalm 32:

> Thou art my hiding place, thou shalt
> From trouble keep me free;
> Thou with songs of deliverance,
> About shalt compass me.
> OLD SCOTTISH PSALTER

A Word on Words
Regarding verse 6: "As the roofs of the common dwellings are flat, and instead of being built of stone or wood, are coated with plaster or hardened earth, a slight crop of grass frequently springs up. Such vegetation, having no soil into which it can strike its roots, and being exposed to a scorching sun, rarely attains to any great height, or continues long. It is a feeble stunted product and soon withers away." WILLIAM JOWETT

PSALM 130

A song for the ascent to Jerusalem.

¹ From the depths of despair, O LORD,
  I call for your help.
² Hear my cry, O Lord.
  Pay attention to my prayer.

³ LORD, if you kept a record of our sins,
  who, O Lord, could ever survive?
⁴ But you offer forgiveness,
  that we might learn to fear you.

⁵ I am counting on the LORD;
  yes, I am counting on him.
  I have put my hope in his word.
⁶ I long for the Lord
  more than sentries long for the dawn,
  yes, more than sentries long for the dawn.

⁷ O Israel, hope in the LORD;
  for with the LORD there is unfailing love
  and an overflowing supply of salvation.
⁸ He himself will free Israel
  from every kind of sin.

*O*n May 24, 1738, John Wesley was depressed. He had been wrestling with spiritual questions. Was faith alone enough for salvation? If so, could a man be converted instantaneously?

That afternoon at London's St. Paul's Cathedral, he heard an anthem sung that opened his heart. Based on Psalm 130, it began, "Out of the deeps of long distress, the borders of despair..." He was greatly moved because the anthem from Psalm 130 told his personal story. That evening he attended a meeting in a little chapel on Aldersgate Street, heard a reading from the introduction to Luther's commentary on Romans, and felt his heart "strangely warmed." He had taken the leap from verse 1 to verse 5 of the psalm.

Many outstanding Christians have loved this psalm. One of them was John Owen, who wrote an extended commentary on it—with nearly three hundred pages on verse 4 alone! He loved that verse because once when he was "brought to the mouth of grace" and when his soul was "oppressed with horror and darkness," that fourth verse brought him close to God.

God offers forgiveness, verse 4 says. Forgiveness is God's free gift. Have you accepted it yet?

> In tenderness he sought me, weary and sick with
> sin,
> And on his shoulders brought me back to his fold
> again.
> While angels in his presence sang
> Until the courts of heaven rang.
> W. SPENCER WALTON

***Bible
Networking***
*A companion verse to
this mighty psalm on
forgiveness is Romans
5:20.*

***Notable
Quotable***
*"Waiting is vigilance
plus expectation; it is
wide awake to God."*
EUGENE
PETERSON

PSALM 131
A song for the ascent to Jerusalem. A psalm of David.

¹ LORD, my heart is not proud;
  my eyes are not haughty.
I don't concern myself with matters too great
  or awesome for me.
² But I have stilled and quieted myself,
  just as a small child is quiet with its mother.
  Yes, like a small child is my soul within me.

³ O Israel, put your hope in the LORD—
  now and always.

*I*n the second part of *The Pilgrim's Progress*, John Bunyan tells of Christiana's journey through the same dangerous territory that her husband had previously taken. She is fearful as she approaches the Valley of Humiliation, but her guide, Mr. Great-Heart, consoles her: "It is the best and most fruitful piece of ground in all these parts . . . for God resists the proud but gives grace to the humble."

Then they notice a shepherd boy feeding his father's sheep. The boy is singing:

> *He that is down, needs fear no fall;*
> *He that is low, no pride.*
> *He that is humble ever shall*
> *Have God to be his guide.*

Mr. Great-Heart continues, "Our Lord loved much to be here, and I must tell you that men have met with angels here, have found pearls here, and have in this place found the words of life."

It sounds strange, perhaps, to extol the blessings of humiliation. But maybe that is what Philippians 2:5-11 is all about. At the beginning of that passage that spells out the humility of Jesus is the verse "Your attitude should be the same that Christ Jesus had."

> *He came down to earth from heaven*
> *Who is God and Lord of all,*
> *And his shelter was a stable,*
> *And his cradle was a stall:*
> *With the poor and mean and lowly*
> *Lived on earth, our Savior holy.*
> CECIL FRANCES ALEXANDER

Bible Networking

This psalm exudes humility. We find the best picture of humility in Philippians 2:5-11, but also check out Proverbs 15:33; John 13:14-15; 2 Corinthians 8:9; and 1 Peter 5:5-6.

Notable Quotable

"That which first overcame the human race is the last thing it overcomes."
SAINT AUGUSTINE

PSALM 132:1-9
A song for the ascent to Jerusalem.

¹ LORD, remember David
   and all that he suffered.
² He took an oath before the LORD.
   He vowed to the Mighty One of Israel,
³ "I will not go home;
   I will not let myself rest.
⁴ I will not let my eyes sleep
   nor close my eyelids in slumber
⁵   until I find a place to build a house for the LORD,
   a sanctuary for the Mighty One of Israel."
⁶ We heard that the Ark was in Ephrathah;
   then we found it in the distant countryside of Jaar.
⁷ Let us go to the dwelling place of the LORD;
   let us bow low before him.
⁸ Arise, O LORD, and enter your sanctuary,
   along with the Ark, the symbol of your power.
⁹ Your priests will be agents of salvation;
   may your loyal servants sing for joy.

"Our life," said Martin Luther, "is a beginning and a progress, not a consummation."

Paul recognized this as well when he said, "My job was to plant the seed in your hearts, and Apollos watered it, but it was God, not we, who made it grow" (1 Corinthians 3:6).

On the job, in the church, or in the home, we may not always see our plans come to completion. A missionary may spend her life translating, preaching, and teaching but see only a handful respond to the gospel. A businessman may labor a lifetime and then find his dreams ruined by an embezzling partner. A wife, after thirty years of marriage, may find that her husband no longer loves her.

This psalm speaks of David's vision to build a Temple for the Lord. But David never witnessed the fulfillment of his dream, and his family was a disaster. Does this make David a failure? Didn't the Lord still call him a "man after his own heart"?

God wants you to have dreams and goals and ambitions, but don't analyze your progress at every bend in the road. How God measures you and how you measure yourself may be two different things.

> Lord Jesus Christ, the work is thine,
> Not ours, but thine alone;
> And prospered by thy power divine
> Can ne'er be overthrown.
> GERMAN HYMN, Translated by Frank Houghton

Bible Networking
The mention of Ephrathah and Jaar in verse 6 refers to the reclaiming of the Ark of God in Kiriath-jearim. See 1 Samuel 7:1-2. The rival Philistines had captured this holy box in battle, yet it brought them nothing but misfortune, so they returned it.

Notable Quotable
"He remembers us individually. . . . He remembers our afflictions, troubles, humblings. . . . He remembers what we purpose in our hearts for His glory. The Lord who is asked to remember is the mighty God."
W. GRAHAM SCROGGIE

PSALM 132:10-18

¹⁰ For the sake of your servant David,
do not reject the king you chose for your people.

¹¹ The LORD swore to David
a promise he will never take back:
"I will place one of your descendants on your throne.

¹² If your descendants obey the terms of my covenant
and follow the decrees that I teach them,
then your royal line will never end."

¹³ For the LORD has chosen Jerusalem;
he has desired it as his home.

¹⁴ "This is my home where I will live forever," he said.
"I will live here, for this is the place I desired.

¹⁵ I will make this city prosperous
and satisfy its poor with food.

¹⁶ I will make its priests the agents of salvation;
its godly people will sing for joy.

¹⁷ Here I will increase the power of David;
my anointed one will be a light for my people.

¹⁸ I will clothe his enemies with shame,
but he will be a glorious king."

*I*t's no secret that poets often use concrete images to describe deeper, abstract concepts. The poets of the Psalms do this as well in order to communicate important messages to God's people.

For instance, the first line of verse 17 literally reads: "I will make a horn sprout for David." To the Israelites, an animal horn symbolized strength and power. Spurgeon draws the comparison: "As the stag is made noble and strong by the development of his horns, so the house of David shall advance from strength to strength."

Verse 17 also says that God's anointed one will be a light to the world—literally, "a glowing lamp." The same symbol is used elsewhere for King David (2 Samuel 21:17) and for Jesus (Luke 2:32; John 9:5).

The third symbol is somewhat veiled in our translation. God promises to place a "gleaming crown" on the head of David (and his descendants). The word for "crown" is the same as that used for the high priest's miter. Thus, this Kingdom would be a glorious one characterized by holiness.

And when you put it all together—the horn, the lamp, and the crown—you get the symbols for power, illumination, and holy authority. Jesus Christ turns out to be a striking image of all three, don't you think?

> Crown him with many crowns, the Lamb upon his throne;
> Hark! how the heavenly anthem drowns all music but its own;
> Awake, my soul, and sing of him who died for thee,
> And hail him as thy matchless King through all eternity.
> MATTHEW BRIDGES

A Word on Words

There are messianic implications in verses 17-18 you don't want to miss. "Anointed one" in Hebrew is messiah. Thus, it refers to both David and to God's greater Son, the Lord Jesus.

Bible Networking

Zechariah, referred to this psalm in his prayer about the birth of his son, John the Baptist (Luke 1:69).

Notable Quotable

"The psalm is saying . . . that the hope of Israel rested, not on any particular pious acts of the sinner, King David, but on the . . . promise of God."
GEORGE A. F. KNIGHT

PSALM 133
A song for the ascent to Jerusalem. A psalm of David.

¹ How wonderful it is, how pleasant,
    when brothers live together in harmony!
² For harmony is as precious as the fragrant anointing oil
        that was poured over Aaron's head,
        that ran down his beard
        and onto the border of his robe.
³ Harmony is as refreshing as the dew from Mount
            Hermon
        that falls on the mountains of Zion.
    And the LORD has pronounced his blessing,
        even life forevermore.

*I*n 1881 the American Greeley Expedition faced a long winter in the Arctic Circle. With a four-and-a-half-month night ahead of them, the commander knew that if his men didn't live together in harmony, the expedition would fail. So they gathered in their winter house and read Psalm 133.

We don't know if this psalm had been written when David was crowned king over all twelve Israelite tribes. It certainly would have been appropriate then.

But three centuries later there was another celebration of unity when King Hezekiah invited the northern kingdom to come to worship in Jerusalem in the southern kingdom (2 Chronicles 30). Ever since the division of the kingdom after Solomon, the people of the northern kingdom had never gone to Jerusalem to worship. Many laughed at the invitation, but some went, and what a time they had—so much so that they continued the celebration for seven additional days. The Jewish historian Josephus records how the Levites sang psalms and played on their harps, and the rest of the priests responded with blasts on their trumpets. No doubt Psalm 133 would have been a favorite.

What a day that will be as well when all Christians come together in harmony in the heavenly Jerusalem. But why wait until then? Let's try to get some dress rehearsals organized before then.

> *Be this our common enterprise:*
> *That truth be preached and prayer arise,*
> *That each may seek the other's good,*
> *And live and love as Jesus would.*
> FREDERICK K. BREWSTER

Bible Networking
The oil in verse 2 becomes especially precious when we realize that it symbolizes the Holy Spirit. See also 1 John 2:20, 27.

Notable Quotable
"Love in the Spirit is the dew which is a symbol and channel of the eternal love and blessing of God."
F. B. MEYER

PSALM 134
A song for the ascent to Jerusalem.

¹ Oh, bless the LORD, all you servants of the LORD,
  you who serve as night watchmen in the house of the
    LORD.
² Lift your hands in holiness,
  and bless the LORD.

³ May the LORD, who made heaven and earth,
  bless you from Jerusalem.

*I*t is never easy to work in the dark. And that is true no matter what kind of dark you are in.

In the Temple the Levites served various shifts night and day. It is probable that the first two verses of this psalm were sung by the Israelites who came to the Temple at night, and the final verse was sung back to the people by the Levites. Then the Levites went back in the Temple to serve the Lord in the shadows of the dark.

The shadows of the night can often be terrifying—even more than darkness by itself. Shakespeare speaks of King Richard's terror of shadows: "Shadows tonight have struck more terror than can the substance of ten thousand soldiers."

The poet John Milton also struggled with the darkness of his blindness: "Doth God exact daylabor, light denied?" he asked in his classic poem, "On His Blindness." But then he got his reply: "God doth not need man's work or his own gifts. Who best bear his mild yoke, they serve him best. . . . They also serve who only stand and wait."

Whether your way is shrouded in shadows, whether your work is completely in the dark, or whether you feel, like Milton, that you're merely standing and waiting, your task is to bless the Lord anyway. And don't forget that Milton, whose blindness hit him in his forties, wrote his masterpieces in darkness.

> *Bless, O my soul! the living God;*
> *Call home thy thoughts that rove abroad;*
> *Let all the powers within me join*
> *In work and worship so divine.*
> ISAAC WATTS

Fascinating Fact
The word LORD (Yahweh) appears five times in these three verses.

Notable Quotable
"To bless God (verse 1) is to acknowledge gratefully what he is; but to bless man (verse 3) God must make of him what he is not, and give him what he has not."
DEREK KIDNER

In the play *Green Pastures*, the angel Gabriel reports to God about the situation down on the earth, and the report isn't good. "Everything nailed down is comin' loose," he says.

Sometimes it seems that way. Things seem out of control, and you feel that if God doesn't take action soon, everything is going to go completely haywire. No one knew these feelings better than David and his fellow psalmists. The big Ds—disorientation, despair, and doubt—plagued them. Some of their psalms sound as if it was hard to know which way was up, much less which way to go.

But David and the other psalmists knew the key to surviving these difficult times: trust. Here are a few verses from the Psalms that spell this out:

◆ *Psalm 27:1*
The LORD protects me from danger—
    so why should I tremble?

◆ *Psalm 31:14-15*
But I am trusting you, O LORD,
    saying, "You are my God!"
My future is in your hands.

◆ *Psalm 44:6-7*
I do not trust my bow;
    I do not count on my sword to save me.
It is you who gives us victory over
    our enemies.

◆ *Psalm 56:3*
But when I am afraid,
    I put my trust in you.

◆ *Psalm 62:8*
O my people, trust in him at all times.
    Pour out your heart to him,
    for God is our refuge.

◆ *Psalm 94:19*
When doubts filled my mind,
    your comfort gave me renewed hope and cheer.

◆ *Psalm 112:7*
They do not fear bad news;
  they confidently trust the LORD
    to care for them.

◆ *Psalm 119:42*
Then I will have an answer for
    those who taunt me,
  for I trust in your word.

◆ *Psalm 146:3, 5*
Don't put your confidence in pow-
    erful people. . . .
But happy are those . . . whose
    hope is in the LORD their
    God.

Sometimes the psalmists flail around, telling God what he should do to his enemies: "String them all up by their thumbs. . . . May his children wander as beggars. . . . May creditors seize his entire estate" or worse. Those violent statements don't just shock us—they embarrass us because we often do wish for such things in our heart. Vengeance belongs to the Lord, not to us, even when everything that is nailed down seems to be coming loose.

Sometimes the psalmists look around at others who counted on their own power or wealth to get them out of jams. Some nations would depend on their armed forces. Others would expect their false gods to put things in order. When things are coming apart at the seams, it's tempting to try something new.

But the Psalms keep leading us back to a simple prescription for life's ills. What should we do

when we don't know what to do? Trust. When the wicked seem to be winning, trust God. When nothing seems to make sense anymore, keep trusting God. Even when he seems to be far away, he is near you. He will hear your anguished cry.

What do you need to trust God for today?

∾

*Then trust him for today as your unfailing
    friend,
And let him lead you all the way who loves
    you to the end;
And let tomorrow rest in his beloved hand;
His good is better than our best, as you
    will understand,
So trusting him who fails you never, just
    rest on him today, forever.*
FRANCES R. HAVERGAL

∾

For some New Testament insights on trusting God, check out Matthew 6:30 and 2 Corinthians 5:7.

Selah

PSALM 135:1-12

¹ Praise the LORD!

Praise the name of the LORD!
Praise him, you who serve the LORD,
²   you who serve in the house of the LORD,
    in the courts of the house of our God.
³ Praise the LORD, for the LORD is good;
    celebrate his wonderful name with music.
⁴ For the LORD has chosen Jacob for himself,
    Israel for his own special treasure.

⁵ I know the greatness of the LORD—
    that our Lord is greater than any other god.
⁶ The LORD does whatever pleases him
    throughout all heaven and earth,
    and on the seas and in their depths.
⁷ He causes the clouds to rise over the earth.
    He sends the lightning with the rain
    and releases the wind from his storehouses.
⁸ He destroyed the firstborn in each Egyptian home,
    both people and animals.
⁹ He performed miraculous signs and wonders in Egypt;
    Pharaoh and all his people watched.
¹⁰ He struck down great nations
    and slaughtered mighty kings—
¹¹   Sihon king of the Amorites,
    Og king of Bashan,
    and all the kings of Canaan.
¹² He gave their land as an inheritance,
    a special possession to his people Israel.

*T*his psalm begins with "Praise the Lord" and it ends with "Praise the Lord." That's the way Billy Bray started and ended things, too.

In the early 1800s Billy Bray was known as a no-good drunken miner in the village of Twelveheads in Cornwall, England. Then, through the reading of a book by John Bunyan, Billy was converted to Christ, and he was never the same again.

"I can't help praising God," he once said. "As I go along the street, I lift up one foot, and it seems to say, 'Glory,' and I lift up the other, and it seems to say, 'Amen.' If they would put me into a barrel to keep me quiet, I would shout, 'Glory' out of the bunghole. Praise the Lord."

Billy would often say about the Lord, "He has made me glad and no one can make me sad; he makes me shout and no one can make me doubt; he makes me leap, and no one can hold down my feet."

Shortly before his death, Billy was asked if he was afraid, and he answered, "My Savior conquered death. If I was to go down to hell, I would shout, 'Glory, glory' to my blessed Jesus until I made the bottomless pit ring again, and then old Satan would say, 'Billy, Billy, this is no place for you; get out of here.' Then up to heaven I should go, shouting, 'Glory, glory, praise the Lord.'"

The following tribute was written for him:

> *His dress was always homely;*
> *His dwelling somewhat poor,*
> *But the presence of his Savior*
> *Made up for that and more.*
> AUTHOR UNKNOWN

Psalm at a Glance
This psalm gives four reasons for praising God: (1) He is good (verse 3); (2) his choice of Israel as his people (verse 4); (3) his creative power (verses 5-7); and (4) his deeds throughout history (verses 8-12).

Notable Quotable
"Israel's election (as ours) was an election to responsibility more than privilege."
W. T. PURKISER

PSALM 135:13-21

¹³ Your name, O LORD, endures forever;
　　your fame, O LORD, is known to every generation.
¹⁴ For the LORD will vindicate his people
　　and have compassion on his servants.

¹⁵ Their idols are merely things of silver and gold,
　　shaped by human hands.
¹⁶ They cannot talk, though they have mouths,
　　or see, though they have eyes!
¹⁷ They cannot hear with their ears
　　or smell with their noses.
¹⁸ And those who make them are just like them,
　　as are all who trust in them.

¹⁹ O Israel, praise the LORD!
　　O priests of Aaron, praise the LORD!
²⁰ O Levites, praise the LORD!
　　All you who fear the LORD, praise the LORD!
²¹ The LORD be praised from Zion,
　　for he lives here in Jerusalem.

Praise the LORD!

*O*ften we are good at sending missionaries to a far off mission field, but how do we cope with a mission field when it comes to us?

That's what's been happening in the last few decades. Millions of people who practice other religions have been coming into our neighborhoods, and often we don't know how to respond.

In a way, that's what was happening throughout the Old Testament as well. The people of Canaan had an amazing pantheon of gods, such as Baal, Molech, Chemosh, Ashtoreth, and Tammuz. At one point the prophet Jeremiah said that there were as many gods in Judah as there were cities. The worship of these gods involved cult prostitution, child sacrifice, mediums, soothsayers, and spiritists.

It is in this context that the psalmist was trying to show what was unique about the God the Israelites worshiped. He is not merely a tribal deity; he reigns over all the earth. He created all things, so he is powerful. Yet he is also compassionate and loving. Yes, he is an awesome God.

In the New Testament world this God invaded the world in Jesus Christ, and his death and resurrection provide us with unique points of conversation as we witness to non-Christian neighbors. Other religions have philosophies and holy books, but none of them has a risen Savior like Jesus Christ.

> *O God of sovereign grace,*
> *We bow before your throne,*
> *And plead for all the human race*
> *The merits of your Son.*
> BAPTIST COLLECTION

Bible Networking

For a similar description of the so-called "gods" worshiped by the heathen, read Jeremiah 10:3-10.

Notable Quotable

"The makers of idols become like that which they make—a man becomes like his god, approximates in character and conduct that to which he yields his homage. The difference between true and false religion is that, in the former, worship is to the One who is forever greater than ourselves, and the others worship their creation, which is forever less than themselves."
G. CAMPBELL MORGAN

PSALM 136:1-9

¹ Give thanks to the LORD, for he is good!

His faithful love endures forever.

² Give thanks to the God of gods.

His faithful love endures forever.

³ Give thanks to the Lord of lords.

His faithful love endures forever.

⁴ Give thanks to him who alone does mighty miracles.

His faithful love endures forever.

⁵ Give thanks to him who made the heavens so skillfully.

His faithful love endures forever.

⁶ Give thanks to him who placed the earth on the water.

His faithful love endures forever.

⁷ Give thanks to him who made the heavenly lights—

His faithful love endures forever.

⁸ the sun to rule the day,

His faithful love endures forever.

⁹ and the moon and stars to rule the night.

His faithful love endures forever.

*I*t was midnight on Thursday, February 8, A.D. 356, and Athanasius, a leader in the early Christian church and passionate defender of the deity of Jesus Christ, was leading a worship service. Suddenly loud shouts and clashing armor could be heard outside the church. Soldiers had come to arrest him.

But Athanasius said, "I didn't think it right, at such a time, to leave my people," so he continued the service. He asked a deacon to read Psalm 136 and then requested the congregation to respond with the refrain "His faithful love endures forever," which they did twenty-six times over the din of the soldiers outside.

Just as the final verse was completed, the soldiers rushed into the church, brandishing their swords and spears and crowding forward up the nave toward Athanasius. The people yelled for Athanasius to run, but he refused to go until he had given a benediction. Then some of his assistants gathered tightly around him, and, as he recounts it, "I passed through the crowd of people unseen and escaped, giving thanks to God that I had not betrayed my people, but had seen to their safety before I thought of my own."

Athanasius was portraying to his people God's love, which endures forever. He was willing to lay down his life for his flock—just as Jesus had laid down his life for his flock a few centuries earlier.

Since God's "faithful love endures forever," why is there ever any need to worry?

> *Let us with a gladsome mind,*
> *Praise the Lord for he is kind;*
> *For his mercies aye endure,*
> *Ever faithful, ever sure.*
> JOHN MILTON

A Word on Words

The word translated as "faithful love" throughout this psalm has also been translated as "mercy," "steadfast love," "kindness," "loyalty," and even "covenant faithfulness."

Bible Networking

God's "faithful love" flows out of the solemn covenant he made with his people in Genesis 15:18.

PSALM 136:10-16

[10] Give thanks to him who killed the firstborn of Egypt.
> *His faithful love endures forever.*

[11] He brought Israel out of Egypt.
> *His faithful love endures forever.*

[12] He acted with a strong hand and powerful arm.
> *His faithful love endures forever.*

[13] Give thanks to him who parted the Red Sea.
> *His faithful love endures forever.*

[14] He led Israel safely through,
> *His faithful love endures forever.*

[15] but he hurled Pharaoh and his army into the sea.
> *His faithful love endures forever.*

[16] Give thanks to him who led his people through the
wilderness.
> *His faithful love endures forever.*

*I*t should have been heresy for any Hebrew schoolboy to say, "I hate history." He could hate arithmetic, spelling, even reading—but never history.

There's just no way to talk about the faith of the Israelites without considering the exodus from Egypt—a historical event. Skeptics can argue about the ten plagues or the miracles, but somehow these people got away from an Egyptian pharaoh and ended up in Canaan. That's history. His story. God's actions in the lives of his people.

Christianity is rooted in history, too. We adopt Old Testament history, to be sure, but the pivotal point for us is the death and resurrection of Jesus Christ. Skeptics can argue about the miracles of turning water into wine or feeding the five thousand, but somehow the body of a crucified rabbi disappeared, and his followers were willing to die for the historical fact of the Resurrection. Without that historical grounding, our faith makes no sense.

But we have more than a historical past. There's a glorious future, too. Psalm 136 ends each verse with the same refrain: "His faithful love endures forever." That gives us strength for the present and hope for the future.

Let's face it, our love does not endure; his does. Because of this, we can confidently hope in another resurrection—our own.

> *I love to tell the story of unseen things above,*
> *Of Jesus and his glory, of Jesus and his love.*
> *I love to tell the story because I know 'tis true;*
> *It satisfies my longings as nothing else can do.*
> A. CATHERINE HANKEY

Bible Networking

Verse 16 speaks of the Lord leading his people through the wilderness, but in Psalm 23:2-3 he leads his people in different paths.

Notable Quotable

"God's own people—his chosen—he led through the wilderness; and this because 'His mercy endureth forever.' It is one of the Lord's sweet truths that so perplex those that are without, but which are so full of consolation to his own children, that the wilderness and mercy are linked together by God in indissoluable union here."
BARTON BOUCHIER

PSALM 136:17-26

17 Give thanks to him who struck down mighty kings.
> *His faithful love endures forever.*

18 He killed powerful kings—
> *His faithful love endures forever.*

19   Sihon king of the Amorites,
> *His faithful love endures forever.*

20   and Og king of Bashan.
> *His faithful love endures forever.*

21 God gave the land of these kings as an inheritance—
> *His faithful love endures forever.*

22   a special possession to his servant Israel.
> *His faithful love endures forever.*

23 He remembered our utter weakness.
> *His faithful love endures forever.*

24 He saved us from our enemies.
> *His faithful love endures forever.*

25 He gives food to every living thing.
> *His faithful love endures forever.*

26 Give thanks to the God of heaven.
> *His faithful love endures forever.*

Edward Taylor, a colonial minister in New England, was known for his colorful prayers, earning him the nickname "The Sailor Preacher of Boston." One Sunday as he was about to sail to England for a visit, he took considerable time and flowery speech entreating God to watch over his flock during his absence. Then suddenly he halted his prayer and burst out, "What have I done? Distrust the providence of heaven? A God who gives a whale a ton of herrings for a breakfast, will he not care for my children?" Then having exhausted his emotion, he continued his prayer in a more subdued manner.

When Jesus was given a boy's lunch of five barley loaves and two fish to feed a crowd of thousands, "Jesus took the loaves, gave thanks to God, and passed them out to the people" (John 6:11). He thanked his heavenly Father for what little he was given and asked him to make use of it. He knew that his Father could provide anything he needed, for God "gives food to every living thing," and "his faithful love endures forever."

"His faithful love" not only gives us our salvation and our victory over the enemy, but it also gives us food on our table, a roof over our head, and clothes on our back. Give thanks today for his faithful love that provides for the necessities of our daily life.

> Things future nor things that are now,
> Nor all things below or above,
> Can make Him His purpose forego
> Or sever my soul from His love.
> AUGUSTUS TOPLADY

Bible Networking
Check up on the stories behind Sihon and Og in Numbers 21. Why do you think they are singled out in this psalm?

Notable Quotable
"The birds rise in the morning and are saluting the rising sun with their sweet notes on the air. Thus, should we strike up our harps in praising God at the first appearance of a mercy."
WILLIAM GURNALL

PSALM 137:1-4

1 Beside the rivers of Babylon, we sat and wept
   as we thought of Jerusalem.
2 We put away our lyres,
   hanging them on the branches of the willow trees.
3 For there our captors demanded a song of us.
   Our tormentors requested a joyful hymn:
   "Sing us one of those songs of Jerusalem!"
4 But how can we sing the songs of the LORD
   while in a foreign land?

*I*n captivity in Babylon, the Jews wept for their homeland and prayed for the day when they might return. But when the day of their release from captivity finally came and they were allowed to return, only about fifty thousand (out of hundreds of thousands) made the trek back to Jerusalem.

Why?

For one thing, some of the Jews were making a good living in Babylon—a better living than their fathers had made in Jerusalem. Others had married Babylonian spouses and become assimilated into Babylonian culture. They had forgotten Jerusalem. Can you blame them? Seventy years of captivity is a long time.

Whatever the reason, some of the Jews weren't like the writer of this psalm, which apparently was written shortly after their return from exile.

The Bible speaks of heaven as our Jerusalem and suggests that where we are now living is Babylon on earth.

How comfortable are you in your Babylon? How are you faring there? Have you forgotten Jerusalem? Have you forgotten that you, too, are an exile, a pilgrim in a foreign land? What are you looking ahead to?

> A tent or a cottage, why should I care?
> They're building a palace for me over there;
> Though exiled from home, yet still I may sing:
> "All glory to God, I'm a child of the King."
> HARRIETT E. BUELL

Bible Networking
Read the melancholy tale of Judah's captivity in 2 Chronicles 36:14-20.

Notable Quotable
"Every true Christian loves praise. But when the believer falls into sin and darkness, his lyre is on the willows, and he cannot sing the Lord's song, for he is in a strange land."
ROBERT MURRAY MCCHEYNE

PSALM 137:5-9

[5] If I forget you, O Jerusalem,
    let my right hand forget its skill upon the harp.

[6] May my tongue stick to the roof of my mouth
    if I fail to remember you,
    if I don't make Jerusalem my highest joy.

[7] O LORD, remember what the Edomites did
    on the day the armies of Babylon captured Jerusalem.
    "Destroy it!" they yelled.
    "Level it to the ground!"

[8] O Babylon, you will be destroyed.
    Happy is the one who pays you back
    for what you have done to us.

[9] Happy is the one who takes your babies
    and smashes them against the rocks!

*P*salm 137:9 probably ranks among those verses in Scripture that you wish weren't there. Why is this in the inspired Word of God?

Because it is the true, human desire of the psalmist. The Psalms can be inspirational, comforting, and instructive, but more than anything, they're honest expressions of the human heart in relationship with God.

After the Armenian massacres in Turkey in the early 1900s, a Christian relief worker visited a village where almost every man had been killed and fifteen hundred orphans were left roaming the streets. He brought some food for the starving women and children and then arranged for a church service. When he suggested they sing one of their hymns, they replied that they hadn't been able to sing since the massacre.

Can you blame them? Which of the Psalms would you give them to sing? It's easy to criticize the intemperate language of Psalm 137:9, but as Charles Spurgeon writes: "Let those find fault with it who have never seen their temple burned, their city ruined, their wives ravished, and their children slain; they might not perhaps be so velvet-mouthed."

Strong emotion against inhuman violence is not wrong when it comes as a cry to God. But make sure you leave the outcome in his hands. God says, "I will take vengeance; I will repay those who deserve it" (Deuteronomy 32:35; Romans 12:19).

> *Come, ye disconsolate, where'er ye languish;*
> *Come to the mercy seat, fervently kneel;*
> *Here bring your wounded hearts, here tell your anguish;*
> *Earth has no sorrow that heaven cannot heal.*
> THOMAS MOORE

Bible Networking
Verse 8 seems like the macabre flip side of Jesus' Golden Rule (Matthew 7:12). For another version of this principle, read Job 4:8.

Notable Quotable
"Let all the secret and open enemies of God's church take heed how they employ their tongues and hands against God's own. They that presume to do either may here read their fatal doom written in the dust of Eden, and in the ashes of Babylon."
DANIEL FEATLEY

In the fear-filled days of the Great Depression, Franklin D. Roosevelt said, "The only thing we have to fear is fear itself." Yet today psychiatrists' couches are filled with people who fear everything from heights to cream-filled doughnuts. Parents fear for their children's safety when they send them to school, and doors and windows are locked even in the best of neighborhoods.

Some children grow up boasting about their fearlessness. It's cool to mock everyone in authority—parents, principal, police, or president. Yet many adults find it difficult to relate to God because of fears instilled in them by authority figures, especially fathers, who have bedeviled their past. Yes, it's a crazy, mixed-up, fearful world.

The Psalms contain more than seventy-five references to fear—more than any other book of the Bible. Most often these refer to fear of God, sometimes to fear of nature, and sometimes to fear of other people.

Here are some references to fear in the Psalms:

FEAR OF OTHER PEOPLE AND EVENTS

♦ *Psalm 23:4*
I will not be afraid,
　for you are close beside me.

♦ *Psalm 27:1*
The LORD is my light and my salvation—
　so why should I be afraid?

♦ *Psalm 46:2*
So we will not fear, even if earthquakes come.

♦ Psalm 56:4
I trust in God, so why should I be afraid?
　What can mere mortals do to me?

♦ *Psalm 118:6*
The LORD is for me, so I will not be afraid.

FEAR OF GOD, SOMETIMES TRANSLATED "AWE" OR "REVERENCE OF GOD"

♦ *Psalm 2:11*
Serve the LORD with reverent fear,
　and rejoice with trembling.

◆ *Psalm 5:7*
With deepest awe I will worship at
    your Temple.

◆ *Psalm 22:23*
Praise the LORD, all you who fear
    him!

◆ *Psalm 25:14*
Friendship with the LORD is
    reserved for those who fear him.

◆ *Psalm 33:18*
But the LORD watches over those
    who fear him,
  those who rely on his unfailing
    love.

◆ *Psalm 103:11*
For his unfailing love toward those
    who fear him
  is as great as the height of the
    heavens above the earth.

◆ *Psalm 111:10*
Reverence for the LORD is the foun-
    dation of true wisdom.

◆ *Psalm 135:20*
All you who fear the LORD, praise
    the LORD!

What's all this talk about fear
doing in the Psalms? Well, neighboring nations were constantly
marauding Israel, and in his early
days David was constantly on the
run. In light of these circumstances, the references to the fear of
others are quite understandable.
But notice that the psalmists seem
to have had an underlying confidence that God is big enough to
deal with their enemies, so they
left all their fears with him.

But what about the fear of God?

Why do the psalmists talk about
fearing God, who is supposed to
love us?

The more we know about people, often the less we are in awe of
them. But the more we know of
God, the more awestruck we are.
Reverential fear comes upon us. At
the same time, throughout the Old
Testament the fear of God is linked
with his love and tender care for
us. Hence, the word *fear* is often
translated "honor," "awe," or "reverence." When Psalm 128:1 tells us
that we are happy when we fear the
Lord, it sounds like an oxymoron,
a contradiction of terms. But it
isn't. Over and over again the
Psalms remind us that if we fear
the Lord, we need not be afraid of
anything or anyone else. Thus, we
have confidence in our daily living
and joy in our daily walk.

The psalmists also tell us that the
fear of God is the beginning of true
wisdom, the basis for friendship
with God, the key to divine comfort, and the basis for holy living.

So let us come before our great
and loving God with reverential
fear and trust that he will take care
of all our other fears.

∽
O fearful saint, fear not the foe
Who madly seeks your overthrow.
Be of good cheer, your cause belongs
To him who can avenge your wrongs.
GERMAN HYMN, Translator Unknown

PSALM 138
A psalm of David.

¹ I give you thanks, O LORD, with all my heart;
  I will sing your praises before the gods.
² I bow before your holy Temple as I worship.
  I will give thanks to your name
  for your unfailing love and faithfulness,
because your promises are backed
  by all the honor of your name.
³ When I pray, you answer me;
  you encourage me by giving me the strength I need.

⁴ Every king in all the earth will give you thanks, O LORD,
  for all of them will hear your words.
⁵ Yes, they will sing about the LORD's ways,
  for the glory of the LORD is very great.
⁶ Though the LORD is great, he cares for the humble,
  but he keeps his distance from the proud.

⁷ Though I am surrounded by troubles,
  you will preserve me against the anger of my
    enemies.
You will clench your fist against my angry enemies!
  Your power will save me.
⁸ The LORD will work out his plans for my life—
  for your faithful love, O LORD, endures forever.
  Don't abandon me, for you made me.

Psalm 138 is a *Reader's Digest* version of the life of Elijah. As we meet Elijah in 1 Kings 17, he is trusting the promises of God. God had warned that, if the people began worshiping idols, it wouldn't rain in Israel. So that's what Elijah told King Ahab: "As surely as the Lord, the God of Israel lives . . . there will be no dew or rain." How could Elijah say this? Because he believed the truth of Psalm 138:2: "Your promises are backed by all the honor of your name."

In hiding, Elijah was fed by ravens, "giving [him] the strength [he] need[ed]" (verse 3). When Elijah went to live with the poor widow of Zarephath, God was near to her, providing her with food and raising her son to life. But God remained aloof from Ahab (verse 6). Later Elijah faced off with his enemies on Mount Carmel, and God's power saved Elijah (verse 7).

Unfortunately, Elijah must have skipped verse 8. After his victory on Mount Carmel, he ran to the desert in a deep funk. Apparently, he forgot that God still had a plan to work out in his life; he forgot that God's love endures forever.

Sometimes that's the story of our life, too. Looking back, we can see how God has brought us through difficult times and kept his promises to us. But what now? Has God's plan for us screeched to a sudden stop? No, the Lord still has plans for each of us, as verse 8 says. Listen, as Elijah eventually did, to God's gentle whisper, assuring you that he will never abandon you.

> *The work which his goodness began*
> *The arm of his strength will complete.*
> *His promise is Yea and Amen,*
> *And never was forfeited yet.*
> AUGUSTUS TOPLADY

Bible Networking

Will God abandon what he has made (verse 8)? Even humans love their own works. We have museums to honor the works of human hands. So how do you think God will treat the people he has created? See Isaiah 64:8.

Notable Quotable

"Grace will complete what grace begins. God does not abandon his work in an incomplete state."
WILLIAM JONES

PSALM 139:1-6
For the choir director: A psalm of David.

¹ O Lord, you have examined my heart
and know everything about me.
² You know when I sit down or stand up.
You know my every thought when far away.
³ You chart the path ahead of me
and tell me where to stop and rest.
Every moment you know where I am.
⁴ You know what I am going to say
even before I say it, Lord.
⁵ You both precede and follow me.
You place your hand of blessing on my head.
⁶ Such knowledge is too wonderful for me,
too great for me to know!

*W*hen the Russian cosmonaut returned to earth from the world's first trip into outer space, he said flippantly that he didn't see God up there. Maybe it would have been better to ask if God saw him up there.

The Marquis de Lafayette, who fought with George Washington during the Revolutionary War, returned afterward to France and led a French army against Austria. Captured, he was confined to a small cell. In the door to the cell was a small hole. A soldier was placed at the hole day and night to watch him. When Lafayette looked out, all he could see was the soldier's eye. It was dreadful, he said. There was no escape from that eye. It was always there, watching his every movement.

For some, it may be equally terrifying to know that God is all-seeing and all-knowing. But to the Christian it is full of comfort, and that's the way David meant it when he wrote this psalm. It reminds us of the Twenty-third Psalm with the Shepherd going ahead and goodness and mercy following behind us.

A theologian would say that these verses tell us that God is omniscient, or all-knowing. But these verses show us more than that; they show us that God knows each of us. These verses are warmly personal. In every line is a first person pronoun (I, me, or my). If that Russian cosmonaut were looking for this kind of God, he might have seen him in outer space—or in the inner space of his own heart.

> I need thy presence every passing hour;
> What but thy grace can foil the tempter's power?
> Who, like thyself, my guide and stay can be?
> Through cloud and sunshine, Lord, abide with me.
> HENRY F. LYTE

Psalm at a Glance

This psalm is divided into four sections of six verses each, and each section focuses on a different attribute of God:

1-6: God's omniscience (God is all-seeing and all-knowing)

7-12: God's omnipresence (God is always present)

13-18: God's omnipotence (God the all-powerful Creator)

19-24: God's holiness (God is perfectly pure and righteous)

Notable Quotable

"An atheist does not find God for the same reason a thief does not find a policeman. He is not looking for him."
WENDELL BAXTER

PSALM 139:7-12

[7] I can never escape from your spirit!
    I can never get away from your presence!
[8] If I go up to heaven, you are there;
    if I go down to the place of the dead, you are there.
[9] If I ride the wings of the morning,
    if I dwell by the farthest oceans,
[10] even there your hand will guide me,
    and your strength will support me.
[11] I could ask the darkness to hide me
    and the light around me to become night—
[12]   but even in darkness I cannot hide from you.
To you the night shines as bright as day.
    Darkness and light are both alike to you.

Eight years after Columbus discovered America, an English sea captain showed a map to King Henry VII. The map revealed all the unexplored territories of the world. Over some of these territories were the words "Here be dragons," "Here be demons," etc.

But if King David drew up such a map, over the unexplored territories on his map would be the words "Here be God."

Bishop Selwyn, a pioneer missionary to New Zealand, knew that he would soon face the Maori natives, reputed to be vicious cannibals. On arriving, Selwyn wrote: "All visible things are new and strange, but the things that are unseen remain the same." So he preached his first sermon on Psalm 139:9-10. In a way he was writing, "Here be God," on his map.

John Franklin, the Arctic explorer who was searching for the Northwest Passage, wrote to his sister about the wonderful ways the Bible had become meaningful to him in the silence of the frozen north. Franklin never returned from that expedition. But years later another Arctic explorer came across Franklin's ship and found his Bible, in which Psalm 139:9-10 was marked and underlined. Maybe Franklin, too, was saying, "Here be God."

If it was true for Selwyn and Franklin facing treacherous unknowns, you can confidently write across the unknowns on your calendar: "Here be God."

> I know not where his islands lift
> Their fronded palms in air,
> I only know I cannot drift
> Beyond his love and care.
> JOHN GREENLEAF WHITTIER

*Bible
Networking*
For more about how impossible it is to escape God's watchful eye, read Amos 9:2-4.

*Notable
Quotable*
"A heathen philosopher once asked, 'Where is God?' The Christian answered, 'Let me first ask you, where is He not?'"
JOHN
ARROWSMITH

Most folks think of the Psalms as a book of praises to God, and that's true, but the praise hits a new high in the last of the five "books" of the Psalms, beginning at Psalm 107.

Here are a few selected verses on praise from Psalm 107–150:

◆ *Psalm 107:2*
Has the LORD redeemed you? Then speak out.

◆ *Psalm 111:9*
He has paid a full ransom for his people.
 He has guaranteed his covenant with them forever.

◆ *Psalm 113:3*
Everywhere—from east to west— praise the name of the LORD.

◆ *Psalm 116:1*
I love the LORD because he hears and answers my prayers.

◆ *Psalm 126:3*
Yes, the LORD has done amazing things for us!
 What joy!

◆ *Psalm 136:16*
Give thanks to him who led his people through the wilderness.

◆ *Psalm 139:14*
Thank you for making me so wonderfully complex!
 Your workmanship is marvelous—and how well I know it.

◆ *Psalm 149:5*
Let the faithful rejoice in this honor.
 Let them sing for joy as they lie on their beds.

◆ *Psalm 150:6*
Let everything that lives sing praises to the LORD!
 Praise the LORD!

We praise everything we enjoy—athletic victories, restful vacations, fascinating books, or good movies. C. S. Lewis said, "We delight to praise what we enjoy because the praise not only expresses but completes the enjoyment." That's also true of our praise to God.

These final forty-four psalms fall into three sections: 107–117, 118–135, and 136–150. Each of these sections begins with the same verse: "Give thanks to the Lord, for he is good! His faithful love endures forever." And each section is concluded with a psalm that begins and ends with *hallelujah*, or "praise the Lord."

In the earlier psalms (especially 1–72) there are many laments and cries to God for help. "Why have you forsaken me?" is typical of many. But in the latter psalms, there is a buildup of praise to God until the final psalms erupt with hallelujahs like a fireworks display. All creation joins in the mighty chorus. When F. B. Meyer paraphrased a verse in Psalm 148 to read: "Let the gnat make music with the stirring of her wings," he wasn't exaggerating.

At sunset, pious Swiss herdsmen used to take their alpine horns and shout loudly through them, "Praise the Lord!" On a distant mountain, another herdsman would hear him and take up the echo, "Praise the Lord!" Soon the Alps would be reverberating with praises and echoes of praises to the Lord.

In some medieval monasteries the chanting of praise to God was never allowed to cease. As soon as one choir of monks stopped sing-ing, another choir would begin. Maybe our life can be something like that as we take our cue from these psalms of exaltation. There is so much to praise God for—can we ever finish the task? As the apostle Paul put it, "No matter what happens, always be thankful" (1 Thessalonians 5:18).

∞

Praise to God, eternal praise
For the love that crowns our days;
Gracious source of every joy,
May your praise our tongues employ;
And when every blessing's flown,
I'll love you for yourself alone.
C. D. BARBOULD

∞

The closing chapters of the Psalms have something in common with the last chapters of the New Testament. Turn to Revelation 19:1-10, and see how often *hallelujah* ("praise the Lord") is repeated there.

Selah

PSALM 139:13-18

[13] You made all the delicate, inner parts of my body
and knit me together in my mother's womb.
[14] Thank you for making me so wonderfully complex!
Your workmanship is marvelous—and how well I
know it.
[15] You watched me as I was being formed in utter
seclusion,
as I was woven together in the dark of the womb.
[16] You saw me before I was born.
Every day of my life was recorded in your book.
Every moment was laid out
before a single day had passed.

[17] How precious are your thoughts about me, O God!
They are innumerable!
[18] I can't even count them;
they outnumber the grains of sand!
And when I wake up in the morning,
you are still with me!

*H*enry Ward Beecher, the famous nineteenth-century preacher, once said that an astronomer who didn't believe in God must be crazy, but a physiologist who didn't believe in God would be crazier yet. Why? Because the human body is the "most exquisite and wonderful organization which has come to us from the divine hand."

Shakespeare's Hamlet would agree. "What a piece of work is man!" he said. "How noble in reason! how infinite in faculty! in form and moving how express and admirable!"

But to the psalmist the wonder of it all was that this God—who superintended the psalmist's formation when he was still in his mother's womb—cared for him and was with him.

This was also the thought of Saint Patrick, the great Irish missionary of the fifth century. He loved the Bible, and after his death, it was required of Irish schoolchildren that they memorize the Psalms. The "Hymn of Saint Patrick," or "The Breastplate" as it is sometimes known, illustrates this same idea that our Lord knows us through and through. Its words are as follows:

> Christ be with me, Christ within me, Christ behind me, Christ before me,
> Christ beside me, Christ to win me, Christ to comfort and restore me,
> Christ beneath me, Christ above me, Christ in quiet, Christ in danger,
> Christ in hearts of all that love me, Christ in mouth of friend and stranger.

SAINT PATRICK, translated by Cecil Francis Alexander

PSALM 139:19-24

¹⁹ O God, if only you would destroy the wicked!
  Get out of my life, you murderers!
²⁰ They blaspheme you;
  your enemies take your name in vain.
²¹ O LORD, shouldn't I hate those who hate you?
  Shouldn't I despise those who resist you?
²² Yes, I hate them with complete hatred,
  for your enemies are my enemies.

²³ Search me, O God, and know my heart;
  test me and know my thoughts.
²⁴ Point out anything in me that offends you,
  and lead me along the path of everlasting life.

C arolus Linnaeus was an organized man. He believed that everything had its place, and that was where it should be put. He did his work so well that he is now regarded as "the father of systematic botany." Some have termed him the greatest botanist that ever lived.

Born in Sweden in the eighteenth century, he almost went into the ministry but chose medical studies instead. One of his first jobs, however, was working for a professor of theology who was compiling a treatise on plants in the Bible.

Soon Linnaeus was organizing plants and animals into groups and subgroups. Every known plant and animal was identified by a genus and a species. Today scientists date his *Species Plantarum* and *Systema Naturae* as the works that started the modern plant and animal classification system.

Linnaeus was awarded honors, medals, and titles, but he always remembered that God was the Creator and that he was God's creation. Everyone who came to hear Linnaeus (and many came from all over the world) saw an inscription over the door of his lecture hall. It was in Latin, just as all his botanical terms were, and it said: Live with Purity; God Is Here.

That is what David said, too, in Psalm 139. And even if you're not as organized as Carolus Linnaeus, it's a pretty good way to approach each day.

> Lord, we thy presence seek;
> May ours this blessing be;
> Give us a pure and lowly heart,
> A temple meet for thee.
> JOHN KEBLE

Bible Networking
Read Matthew 5:38-48 and Romans 12:17-21. What did Jesus and Paul say our attitude should be to our enemies?

Notable Quotable
"We may be grieving our blessed Lord more than we know; substituting an ideal religious standard or absorption in his work for that direct personal fellowship with Himself."
F. B. MEYER

PSALM 140:1-8
For the choir director: A psalm of David.

¹ O LORD, rescue me from evil people.
  Preserve me from those who are violent,
² those who plot evil in their hearts
  and stir up trouble all day long.
³ Their tongues sting like a snake;
  the poison of a viper drips from their lips.   *Interlude*

⁴ O LORD, keep me out of the hands of the wicked.
  Preserve me from those who are violent,
  for they are plotting against me.
⁵ The proud have set a trap to catch me;
  they have stretched out a net;
  they have placed traps all along the way.   *Interlude*

⁶ I said to the LORD, "You are my God!"
  Listen, O LORD, to my cries for mercy!
⁷ O Sovereign LORD, my strong savior,
  you protected me on the day of battle.
⁸ LORD, do not give in to their evil desires.
  Do not let their evil schemes succeed, O God.

                                        Interlude

*A*ccording to one of his fables, Aesop was a servant for a philosopher named Xanthus. The master had invited some honored guests to a feast, and so the whole household prepared for the occasion. Aesop was sent to the market with orders to bring home the best meat money could buy.

What did he buy? Tongue. The meal consisted of nothing but tongue, course after course of tongue.

As might be expected, Xanthus became angry. "Didn't I tell you to get the best you could buy?"

"I did," replied Aesop. "The tongue is truly a wonderful thing, the bond of society, the organ of reason, the instrument of praise and of worship."

The next day the frustrated employer, determined not to repeat his mistake, sent Aesop to buy the worst thing in the market. What did he buy this time? Tongue, again.

When Xanthus pressed him to explain, Aesop responded, "The tongue was surely the worst thing in the market. It is the instrument of strife and contention, the organ of lying and deceit, and the vehicle by which Deity is defamed and denied."

We see this duality even in Psalm 140, where the psalmist uses his tongue to cry out to God for relief from the persecution he faces from the tongues of others. How will your tongue be used today? What can you do to make sure it is used to bless and benefit instead of inflicting pain and distress?

> *Through all the changing scenes of life,*
> *In trouble and in joy,*
> *The praise of my God shall still*
> *My heart and tongue employ.*
> NAHUM TATE

Fascinating Fact
In ancient times a man was being interrogated and refused to give answers. "Are you holding your tongue because you don't know what to say or because you're a fool?" his questioners demanded.

"A fool cannot hold his tongue," he replied.

Bible Networking
For another picture of human depravity read Romans 3:10-18 (especially compare Psalm 140:3 with Romans 3:13).

PSALM 140:9-13

⁹ Let my enemies be destroyed
by the very evil they have planned for me.
¹⁰ Let burning coals fall down on their heads,
or throw them into the fire,
or into deep pits from which they can't escape.
¹¹ Don't let liars prosper here in our land.
Cause disaster to fall with great force on the violent.

¹² But I know the LORD will surely help those they
persecute;
he will maintain the rights of the poor.
¹³ Surely the godly are praising your name,
for they will live in your presence.

Sometimes it's hard to believe verse 12, that God "will surely help" the persecuted and "maintain the rights of the poor."

Young Charles Simeon had reason to question that verse, too. A recent graduate of Cambridge, he had been installed as rector of the Church of the Holy Trinity in that college town, much to the dismay of his liberal-thinking parishioners, who couldn't abide the evangelical preaching of this Bible-loving cleric. When the old-time members locked their pew doors to keep out other worshipers, Simeon put seats in the aisles. Then members came early and threw out the aisle seats.

Nicknamed Sims, Simeon was hooted at when he walked in the town. "I was the object of much contempt and derision," he admits. One day he took a walk, asking God to guide him to "some text which should sustain me." Opening his New Testament, he read about Simon of Cyrene, who bore the cross for Jesus. Simeon found this to be great encouragement indeed, partly because he thought they might have given Simon of Cyrene the nickname of Sims, too. "To have the cross laid upon me that I might bear it after Jesus. What a privilege! Now I would leap and sing for joy, as one whom Jesus was honoring with a participation in his sufferings."

If you're facing times of persecution and feel that you're misunderstood, learn a lesson from Sims—or from verse 13 of this psalm—and start praising God.

Nearer, my God, to thee, nearer to thee!
E'en though it be a cross that raiseth me;
Still all my song shalt be,
Nearer, my God, to thee, nearer to thee.
SARAH F. ADAMS

Psalm at a Glance
Previously in this psalm (verse 3) the tongue of the wicked was spoken of as an instrument of poison, but in verse 13 the psalmist speaks of the tongue as an instrument of praise.

Bible Networking
God will restore his own (verse 12) and deal harshly with those who persecute his loved ones. Read Zephaniah 3:19.

PSALM 141:1-5
A psalm of David.

1 O LORD, I am calling to you. Please hurry!
    Listen when I cry to you for help!
2 Accept my prayer as incense offered to you,
    and my upraised hands as an evening offering.

3 Take control of what I say, O LORD,
    and keep my lips sealed.
4 Don't let me lust for evil things;
    don't let me participate in acts of wickedness.
  Don't let me share in the delicacies
    of those who do evil.

5 Let the godly strike me!
    It will be a kindness!
  If they reprove me, it is soothing medicine.
    Don't let me refuse it.

  But I am in constant prayer
    against the wicked and their deeds.

The year was 1623. The Pilgrims had been in the New World for two and a half years. The first Thanksgiving of 1621 was only a memory by this time because this summer's drought was jeopardizing everything. Not even the Indians could remember anything like it. The settlers had planted more corn than before, but without any rainfall, there would be no harvest. Daily they had prayed that God would send rain, but he hadn't answered. As the psalmist did in Psalm 141:1, they were begging God to hurry.

Finally, the settlers set aside an entire day for prayer and worship. As they went for worship, the "heavens were as clear and the drought as like to continue as it ever was," yet when they left their meeting, "the weather was overcast, the clouds gathered on all sides." For the next fourteen days there were "moderate showers of rain," according to Edward Winslow, one of the pilgrims.

The Indians watched and were amazed at how the God of the new settlers had answered their prayers, and that year, after the harvest, a second Thanksgiving was celebrated with the Indians joining in as well.

"Hurry up, Lord," we often prod, wondering why the Almighty doesn't seem to be in as much of a rush as we are. Sometimes we need to set our watches to his clock.

> Not so in haste, my heart! Have faith in God and
>   wait;
> Although He linger long, He never comes too late.
> He never comes too late; He knoweth what is best;
> Vex not thyself in vain; until He cometh, rest.
> BRADFORD TORREY

Bible Networking
The psalmist says he is "in constant prayer" (verse 5). Read Philippians 4:6-7 to learn of the peace that comes through such prayer.

Notable Quotable
"True prayer is putting oneself under God's influence."
H. E. FOSDICK

PSALM 141:6-10

⁶ When their leaders are thrown down from a cliff,
  they will listen to my words and find them pleasing.
⁷ Even as a farmer breaks up the soil and brings up rocks,
  so the bones of the wicked will be scattered without
    a decent burial.

⁸ I look to you for help, O Sovereign LORD.
  You are my refuge; don't let them kill me.
⁹ Keep me out of the traps they have set for me,
  out of the snares of those who do evil.
¹⁰ Let the wicked fall into their own snares,
  but let me escape.

*T*he world that surrounds us is sometimes a sorry mess, sometimes a fearsome place, sometimes a glorious opportunity.

In his fascinating allegory *The Pilgrim's Progress*, John Bunyan traces the journey of a typical Christian through the world with all its pitfalls and allurements.

During the journey, Christian comes to the top of the Hill Difficulty, and he sees two lions, one on each side of his path. Bunyan writes:

> *Difficulty is behind, Fear is before;*
> *Though he's got on the Hill, the Lions roar;*
> *A Christian saint is never long at ease,*
> *When one fright's gone, another doth him seize.*

Then the porter of a nearby gate speaks: "Fear not the lions, for they are chained. . . . Keep in the middle of the path, and no hurt shall come unto you."

The way of God's people is not around difficulty but through. The psalmist knew this as well, and that's why he prayed, "Keep me out of the traps" (verse 9), rather than "Let me never encounter trouble." And our Good Shepherd can be trusted as a faithful guide no matter how fearsome our lions may be.

> *Take the world, but give me Jesus,*
> *All its joys are but a name.*
> *But His love abides forever*
> *Through eternal years the same.*
> FANNY J. CROSBY

Bible Networking
In Proverbs 3:25-26 we read some wonderful verses about how God "keeps" his own (see verse 9 of this psalm).

Notable Quotable
"It is marvelous how the feet are kept from snares and pitfalls, when the eyes, instead of being fixed upon the ground, are lifted upwards to the throne."
F. B. MEYER

PSALM 142

A psalm of David, regarding his experience in the cave. A prayer.

¹ I cry out to the LORD;

    I plead for the LORD's mercy.

² I pour out my complaints before him

    and tell him all my troubles.

³ For I am overwhelmed,

    and you alone know the way I should turn.

Wherever I go,

    my enemies have set traps for me.

⁴ I look for someone to come and help me,

    but no one gives me a passing thought!

No one will help me;

    no one cares a bit what happens to me.

⁵ Then I pray to you, O LORD.

    I say, "You are my place of refuge.

    You are all I really want in life.

⁶ Hear my cry,

    for I am very low.

Rescue me from my persecutors,

    for they are too strong for me.

⁷ Bring me out of prison

    so I can thank you.

The godly will crowd around me,

    for you treat me kindly."

*S*ome people enjoy spelunking—that is, exploring caves—as a hobby. For David, however, it was no hobby. It was a matter of life and death.

As David was trying to stay a step ahead of King Saul's goon squad, he fled to caves in the canyons of the Judean desert (1 Samuel 22:1; 24:1-3).

Imagine what it would be like living in the dark of a desert cave, not knowing if or when your pursuers would find you. Talk about stress! You would have to be on edge all the time, not to mention the anxiety involved in finding food for each day. On top of all this, you would be cut off from many of the people who mean the most to you. True, David had a band of loyal soldiers with him, but he was isolated from his family and friends. Besides that, he wouldn't be able to worship God in the Tabernacle. At times the physical darkness of the cave must have seemed like spiritual darkness as well.

Now read Psalm 142 again, and consider how David must have felt.

Have you ever felt that way—trapped in darkness, hoping for light to fall upon a particular situation in your life but finding no light at all?

David prayed, "You alone know the way I should turn." God knows what we don't know. In the darkness of the cave we can't see a thing, but God can. He could see everything even before he said, "Let there be light." In times of darkness, let him be your light.

> *There may be days of darkness and distress,*
> *When sin has power to tempt, and care to press;*
> *Yet in the darkest day I will not fear,*
> *For 'mid the shadows, Thou wilt still be near.*
> HENRY LEIGH

Bible Networking
Compare verse 6 with our Lord's words in John 12:27. Also check out John 11:33 and 13:21.

Notable Quotable
"Soul-emancipation is the noblest form of liberation and calls for the loudest praise. He who is delivered from the dungeon of despair is sure to magnify the name of the Lord."
CHARLES HADDON SPURGEON

The Psalms are packed with more blessings than a shopping mall is packed with gifts before Christmas—and you don't need a credit card to take advantage of them.

But the Psalms also remind us repeatedly to bless God. How do we do that? By praising him and acknowledging him as the source of all we have. Here are a few verses in the Psalms about blessing, both from God to us and from us to God.

GOD'S BLESSINGS TO US

◆ *Psalm 8:5*
You crowned us with glory and
    honor.

◆ *Psalm 29:11*
The LORD blesses [his people] with
    peace.

◆ *Psalm 91:11*
For he orders his angels
    to protect you wherever you go.

◆ *Psalm 103:3*
He forgives all my sins
    and heals all my diseases.

◆ *Psalm 104:14*
You cause plants to grow for people to use.

◆ *Psalm 136:25*
He gives food to every living thing.

◆ *Psalm 138:2*
Your promises are backed
    by all the honor of your name.

OUR BLESSINGS TO GOD

◆ *Psalm 16:7*
I will bless the LORD who guides
    me.

◆ *Psalm 26:12*
I have taken a stand,
    and I will publicly praise the
    LORD.

◆ *Psalm 66:8*
Let the whole world bless our God
    and sing aloud his praises.

◆ *Psalm 100:4*
Give thanks to [the LORD] and
    bless his name.

◆ *Psalm 103:2*
Praise the LORD, I tell myself,
and never forget the good things
he does for me.

◆ *Psalm 134:2*
Lift your hands in holiness,
and bless the LORD.

◆ *Psalm 145:1*
I will praise you, my God and
King,
and bless your name forever and
ever.

The Hebrew root word for "bless," "blessed," or "blessings" is *barak*, and it isn't easy to translate. It may be translated "oh, the joys" (Psalm 1:1) or "happy" (Psalm 119:1) or "oh, what joy" (Psalm 32:1). When the queen of Sheba saw Solomon's riches, the same word is translated "what a privilege" (1 Kings 10:8). It carries the idea of being supremely happy and fulfilled in life. The *barak* person is one who is right with God and who is enjoying the spiritual peace and joy that comes with that relationship.

When Psalm 1 begins with *barak*, it means that this psalm—and this book of Psalms—is going to tell you how to live a happy and fulfilling life. When Psalm 119 begins with the same Hebrew word, it is saying that God's Word is the key to this sort of life.

But *barak* isn't simply a word connoting absorption. That is, blessing is not something simply to be soaked up like a sponge. Instead, we are also commanded to bless God as well. But how in the world can we mere mortals bless God? By praising him, thereby mirroring God's blessings toward us. And this is exactly how *barak* is translated in Psalm 103:1: "Praise the LORD." By radiating his blessings toward us, we are telling him, as the queen of Sheba told Solomon, "What a privilege!"

God's blessings are like bonuses on TV quiz shows: You win a prize for coming up with the correct answer, but then suddenly you are unexpectedly showered with other good things.

But make sure you pass it on. Pray for God's blessing on your children, your church, and your neighbors, but don't stop there. The apostle Paul writes: "If people persecute you because you are a Christian, don't curse them; pray that God will bless them" (Romans 12:14). But Old Testament blessings were not merely prayers; they were hands-on actions that passed along God's blessings to others (see Psalm 106:3).

So how can you be a blessing to someone today?

∾

For we must share if would keep
That blessing from above;
Ceasing to give, we cease to have;
Such is the law of love.
R. C. TRENCH

PSALM 143:1-6
A psalm of David.

1 Hear my prayer, O LORD;
> listen to my plea!
> Answer me because you are faithful and righteous.
2 Don't bring your servant to trial!
> Compared to you, no one is perfect.
3 My enemy has chased me.
> He has knocked me to the ground.
> He forces me to live in darkness like those in the
> grave.
4 I am losing all hope;
> I am paralyzed with fear.
5 I remember the days of old.
> I ponder all your great works.
> I think about what you have done.
6 I reach out for you.
> I thirst for you as parched land thirsts for rain.

Interlude

You may find Hugh Latimer's name listed among England's religious reformers, but you probably won't find the name of Thomas Bilney, or "Little Bilney" as they called him. And that's a pity.

As a fellow at Cambridge, Bilney became a Christian. At that time Hugh Latimer was the most eloquent orator at the university, and Bilney prayed, "O God, I am but Little Bilney and shall never do any great thing for you; but give me the soul of that man Hugh Latimer, and what wonders he will do for you."

At a private meeting with Latimer, Bilney shared how he had received God's forgiveness and peace. To Bilney's astonishment, Latimer bowed before him and confessed that this was what he, too, had been seeking. Soon they were preaching the gospel together, with Latimer in the lead and Little Bilney following.

During the reign of Henry VIII, however, Bilney was arrested and sentenced to death for his beliefs. At first he feared that he wouldn't be courageous enough to die for his faith. But as the fire was lit beneath him, Bilney bravely recited Psalm 143:1-2, repeating the phrase "compared to you, no one is perfect" three times. Little Bilney knew he was a sinner, saved by a great Savior.

You may be a Little Bilney, too, but God isn't relying on your greatness. He wants you to rely on his. And he has great plans for you.

> Still to the lowly soul
> He doth Himself impart,
> And for His dwelling and His throne,
> Chooseth the pure in heart.
> JOHN KEBLE

Bible Networking
Verses 3 and 4 are heavy with distress. These emotions are similar to those of our Lord in Matthew 26:37 and Hebrews 5:7-8.

Notable Quotable
"Delight yourself in all your heavenly Father's handwork, and make it to be a ladder by which you climb to Himself."
CHARLES HADDON SPURGEON

PSALM 143:7-12

⁷ Come quickly, LORD, and answer me,
　for my depression deepens.
Don't turn away from me,
　or I will die.
⁸ Let me hear of your unfailing love to me in the
　　morning,
　for I am trusting you.
Show me where to walk,
　for I have come to you in prayer.
⁹ Save me from my enemies, LORD;
　I run to you to hide me.
¹⁰ Teach me to do your will,
　for you are my God.
May your gracious Spirit lead me forward
　on a firm footing.
¹¹ For the glory of your name, O LORD, save me.
　In your righteousness, bring me out of this distress.
¹² In your unfailing love, cut off all my enemies
　and destroy all my foes,
　for I am your servant.

Late in 1891 a friend suggested to twenty-five-year-old Wilfred Grenfell that he might like to take a trip from England to Newfoundland to visit the fisheries there. Always fascinated by deep-sea fishing, Grenfell was intrigued by the prospective journey.

But Grenfell had other matters to consider as well. For one thing, he had just finished his medical studies at Oxford. For another, he had recently committed his life to Christ after hearing the preaching of evangelist Dwight L. Moody.

So the invitation excited Grenfell and troubled him at the same time. Was this just a frivolous excursion when he should be getting on with the rest of his life?

When the young man asked his mother for advice, she responded, "I would use daily the words of Psalm 143:10."

Grenfell went to Newfoundland—but it was not merely a pleasure trip. His vacation became his vocation. For the next forty-two years Grenfell served as a medical missionary in Labrador and Newfoundland, setting up hospitals and nursing stations, and equipping them by using dog teams and motorboats.

Whatever you do today, ask God to teach you to do his will.

> When doubts and fears arise,
> Teach me thy way!
> When storm clouds fill the skies,
> Teach me thy way!
> Shine through the wind and rain,
> Through sorrow, grief and pain;
> Make now my pathway plain,
> Teach me thy way!
> B. MANSELL RAMSEY

Bible Networking

We need to be careful not to be hard of hearing when it comes to God's unfailing love and guidance (verses 8 and 10). Read Job 33:14-16; 36:10; and Isaiah 50:5.

Notable Quotable

"Knowledge without obedience is lame. Obedience without knowledge is blind; and we must never hope for acceptance if we offer the blind and the lame to God."
VINCENT ALSOP

PSALM 144:1-8
A psalm of David.

¹ Bless the LORD, who is my rock.
  He gives me strength for war
  and skill for battle.
² He is my loving ally and my fortress,
  my tower of safety, my deliverer.
  He stands before me as a shield, and I take refuge in
    him.
  He subdues the nations under me.

³ O LORD, what are mortals that you should notice us,
  mere humans that you should care for us?
⁴ For we are like a breath of air;
  our days are like a passing shadow.

⁵ Bend down the heavens, LORD, and come down.
  Touch the mountains so they billow smoke.
⁶ Release your lightning bolts and scatter your enemies!
  Release your arrows and confuse them!
⁷ Reach down from heaven and rescue me;
  deliver me from deep waters,
  from the power of my enemies.
⁸ Their mouths are full of lies;
  they swear to tell the truth, but they lie.

*A*t first we might think of these verses as a scrapbook. The compiler seemed to cut verses from other psalms and paste them together in this one. Verse 2 reminds us of Psalm 18:2; verse 3 reminds us of Psalm 8:4; verse 4 is like Psalm 39:5; and verses 5-8 are like Psalm 18:9-17.

But even scrapbooks are put together for a reason. So let's open the scrapbook. As we open it, we see nine pictures of God. He is a rock, a giver of strength, a loving ally, a fortress, a tower of safety, a deliverer, a shield, a refuge, and a subduer. Before you turn the page, notice the pronouns: nine references to *I, me,* or *my,* one for each divine portrayal.

On the next pages in the scrapbook, we see ourself. Often in a photo album that is where we look first. We want to see what we look like, and perhaps if we hadn't seen nine pictures of God first, we might look a little better. But having seen God, we marvel "that [he] should notice us."

Then come the action scenes. The verbs create excitement: *"Bend down," "come down," "touch the mountains," "release your lightning bolts,"* etc. Our mouths drop open in amazement. This mighty God not only takes notice of us but goes into action for us!

Why not ask God to go into action for you today? Maybe then you could add another page to the scrapbook.

> *I hunger and I thirst; Jesus, my manna be;*
> *Ye living waters, burst out of the rock for me.*
> *Thou true life-giving Vine, let me Thy sweetness prove;*
> *Renew my life with Thine, refresh my soul with love.*
> JOHN MONSELL

A Word on Words

The words loving ally in verse 2 are sometimes translated "my steadfast love." This a bold and striking term for God. See the same word used for "God's mercies" in Jonah 2:8.

Notable Quotable

"How is it that the Eternal should make so much of mortal man, who begins to die as soon as he begins to live?" CHARLES HADDON SPURGEON

PSALM 144:9-15

9 I will sing a new song to you, O God!

    I will sing your praises with a ten-stringed harp.

10 For you grant victory to kings!

    You are the one who rescued your servant David.

11 Save me from the fatal sword!

    Rescue me from the power of my enemies.

Their mouths are full of lies;

    they swear to tell the truth, but they lie.

12 May our sons flourish in their youth

    like well-nurtured plants.

May our daughters be like graceful pillars,

    carved to beautify a palace.

13 May our farms be filled

    with crops of every kind.

May the flocks in our fields multiply by the thousands,

    even tens of thousands,

14   and may our oxen be loaded down with produce.

May there be no breached walls, no forced exile,

    no cries of distress in our squares.

15 Yes, happy are those who have it like this!

    Happy indeed are those whose God is the LORD.

*M*atthias Claudius had started out to become a minister like his father when he was infected with the rationalism of his day. A disciple and friend of the German philosopher-poet Johann Wolfgang von Goethe, he believed that people must believe not in God but in themselves. After getting a degree in law, Claudius became a newspaper editor.

But he became seriously ill when he was thirty-seven, and he realized that he had to believe in someone besides himself. That "someone" was Jesus Christ. Claudius became a sweet-spirited Christian, and he began writing religious poetry for his newspaper.

When a friend, Paul Erdmans, invited Claudius to his house for a special dinner, he was asked to bring a poem with him. So Claudius wrote the poem "We Plow the Fields and Scatter." He originally wrote seventeen stanzas for it, thanking Erdmans and thanking God for friendship and for the abundant harvest.

Claudius had much to be thankful for, and his poem seems to echo the words of Psalm 144. But most of all, he was thankful because the Lord was his God.

> We plow the fields and scatter the good seed on
>   the land,
> But it is fed and watered by God's almighty hand;
> He sends the snow in winter, the warmth to swell
>   the grain,
> The breezes and the sunshine, and soft refreshing
>   rain.
> All good gifts around us are sent from heaven
>   above;
> Then thank the Lord, O thank the Lord for all his
>   love.

MATTHIAS CLAUDIUS

A Word on Words

The term "new song" can mean a song that is composed for a particular occasion, such as a victory. It could also mean a song that is sung at the time of renewal of a relationship. In the age to come people will sing a "new song." See Revelation 5:9 and 14:3.

Notable Quotable

"New songs are demanded by new mercies. Let us give God freshly broken loaves for his table."
F. B. MEYER

PSALM 145:1-7
A psalm of praise of David.

¹ I will praise you, my God and King,
and bless your name forever and ever.
² I will bless you every day,
and I will praise you forever.
³ Great is the LORD! He is most worthy of praise!
His greatness is beyond discovery!

⁴ Let each generation tell its children
of your mighty acts.
⁵ I will meditate on your majestic, glorious splendor
and your wonderful miracles.
⁶ Your awe-inspiring deeds will be on every tongue;
I will proclaim your greatness.
⁷ Everyone will share the story of your wonderful
goodness;
they will sing with joy of your righteousness.

*T*he Chinese called him Mr. Glory Face. Since his given name was Archibald Orr-Ewing, you can't blame the Chinese for finding a nickname. But how Archibald became Mr. Glory Face is an interesting story.

He came from a wealthy Scottish family that had one castle in Scotland and another on the Isle of Wight, which they occupied during the yachting season. When Archibald turned twenty-one, an uncle offered him a partnership in the family business. But Archibald wasn't Glory Face yet.

Trusting Christ through the ministry of evangelist Dwight L. Moody, Archibald went to China as a missionary. He walked sixty miles a day to preach the gospel. (After his marriage, his wife talked him into cutting his treks back to fifty miles a day!) And he did this in spite of very difficult circumstances. He lived a spartan life and gave what money he had to build buildings for the China Inland Mission.

So when the Chinese called him Mr. Glory Face, it wasn't simply because they couldn't pronounce his name. The joy of this psalm was exemplified in his life. He felt that if he spent time meditating on the Lord's glorious splendor (145:5), some of that glorious splendor should spill off onto him. And it did.

Has any of that glorious splendor spilled off onto you yet? Would anyone ever think of nicknaming you "Glory Face"?

> Our souls, we know, when He appears,
> Shall bear His image bright;
> For all His glory full disclosed
> Shall open to our sight.
> ISAAC WATTS

Fascinating Fact
Jewish rabbis taught that if you pray this psalm from the heart three times a day, you will prepare yourself for the world to come.

Notable Quotable
"These qualities of God's character and deeds should not merely be talked about and extolled in song but be deeply pondered and laid close upon our heart, so that the impression may be wrought into our very soul and may mold our whole spirit and character into God's own image."
HENRY COWLES

Thought to Ponder
Too many witnesses of God's goodness are silent witnesses.

COME, THOU LONG-EXPECTED JESUS

Come, thou long-expected Jesus,
Born to set thy people free;
From our fears and sins release us;
Let us find our rest in thee.
Israel's strength and consolation,
Hope of all the earth thou art;
Dear Desire of every nation,
Joy of every longing heart.

Born, thy people to deliver,
Born a child and yet a king,
Born to reign in us forever,
Now thy gracious kingdom bring.
By thine own eternal Spirit
Rule in all our hearts alone;
By thine all sufficient merit
Raise us to thy glorious throne.
CHARLES WESLEY

Psalm Link
PSALM 62:5-6

5 I wait quietly before God,
   for my hope is in him.
6 He alone is my rock and my salvation,
   my fortress where I will not be shaken.

Y ou may have fond memories of when you were a little child pressing your nose against the windowpane, eagerly awaiting the arrival of your grandparents at Christmastime. Of course, they would be bringing presents. The excitement was almost more than you could stand.

Do you ever remember taking a long trip with your parents and asking, after you had traveled about ten miles, "Are we there yet?"

Everything seems long for children, whether it's ten minutes or ten miles. But the truth is, waiting never comes easily for anyone. And after pressing your nose to the window for an hour or asking, "Are we there yet?" for the umpteenth time, you may have begun to lose hope.

Biblically speaking, however, hope is the expectant awaiting of that which is sure to come. It is not a wild stab at uncertainty, like "I hope I win the lottery." It is a sure thing.

When the psalmist said, "My hope is in him" (verse 5), he was saying what the songwriter was saying: "Come, thou long-expected Jesus." And when Charles Wesley wrote about Israel's strength and consolation, it was something like saying, "My rock and my salvation," because the word often translated "consolation" is the word for "advocate," "intercessor," or "comforter."

As you approach the Christmas season, what are you waiting for? The deepest need of your heart is met in the one whose name is Immanuel, God is with us, the "Dear Desire of every nation."

Bible Networking
Simeon the priest knew that the infant Jesus was Israel's long-expected consolation. See Luke 2:25-32.

PSALM 145:8-13

[8] The LORD is kind and merciful,
   slow to get angry, full of unfailing love.

[9] The LORD is good to everyone.
   He showers compassion on all his creation.

[10] All of your works will thank you, LORD,
   and your faithful followers will bless you.

[11] They will talk together about the glory of your
      kingdom;
   they will celebrate examples of your power.

[12] They will tell about your mighty deeds
   and about the majesty and glory of your reign.

[13] For your kingdom is an everlasting kingdom.
   You rule generation after generation.

The LORD is faithful in all he says;
   he is gracious in all he does.

*W*illiam Carey, often called the father of foreign missions, loved this psalm. A remarkable man, Carey taught himself the languages of India and translated the Bible into thirty-four Indian languages.

Carey was also an enthusiastic gardener and a scientific botanist, with 427 species of plants in his garden, carefully identified by their Latin names. When he published an edition of a classic botanical book, he prefixed it with the tenth verse of this psalm.

Although Carey suffered many hardships, perhaps the hardest came when his entire mission complex, which contained manuscripts on which he had worked for years, burned to the ground. "In one short evening," he said with tears in his eyes, "the labors of years are consumed. How unsearchable are the ways of God! The Lord has laid me low that I may look more simply to him." Then turning to a fellow missionary he said, "Return to your books, and let God be exalted in all your plans, purposes, and labors."

So Carey and his team continued translating God's Word, and God continued to work, too. The devastating fire made all of England aware of Carey's work, and donations more than covered Carey's losses. As the missionaries doubled their efforts, a more efficient printing operation was built on the ashes of the old one.

God is "faithful in all he says . . . gracious in all he does"—even when we are tested by fire.

And so through all the length of days
Thy goodness faileth never:
Good Shepherd, may I sing thy praise
Within thy house forever.
HENRY W. BAKER

Bible Networking
In this psalm verses 8 and 9 repeat God's self-revelation to Moses at Sinai. Read Exodus 34:6.

Notable Quotable
"It is a marvel that people are not always praising, since everything around us is continually inviting praise."
GREGORY THE GREAT

PSALM 145:14-21

¹⁴ The LORD helps the fallen
    and lifts up those bent beneath their loads.
¹⁵ All eyes look to you for help;
    you give them their food as they need it.
¹⁶ When you open your hand,
    you satisfy the hunger and thirst of every living thing.

¹⁷ The LORD is righteous in everything he does;
    he is filled with kindness.
¹⁸ The LORD is close to all who call on him,
    yes, to all who call on him sincerely.
¹⁹ He fulfills the desires of those who fear him;
    he hears their cries for help and rescues them.
²⁰ The LORD protects all those who love him,
    but he destroys the wicked.

²¹ I will praise the LORD,
    and everyone on earth will bless his holy name
    forever and forever.

This section of Psalm 145 speaks of the Lord's care for those in difficult circumstances and calls for God's people to praise him. It is easy to praise the Lord when our needs are miraculously met, but do we praise God when we don't see immediate answers to our prayers?

Consider Martin Rinckart in Eilenberg, Germany. He had arrived there just as the Thirty Years' War began in 1618, perhaps the most devastating war in history. Germany's population was decimated, falling from 16 million to 6 million.

Because Eilenberg was walled, refugees from the entire country came there seeking safety. Many brought disease into the crowded city. When the plague of 1637 ravaged the town, Rinckart was the only minister left in town. During that year alone, he conducted funerals for five thousand residents, including his wife.

During this dreadful thirty-year scourge, Rinckart wrote a hymn of thanksgiving: "Now Thank We All Our God." In the hymn he praises God for the "wondrous things" he has done and talks of joyful hearts and blessed peace.

Most of us find it hard to be thankful in the midst of short-term woes, but Martin Rinckart praised the Lord throughout a thirty-year ordeal. Let us all follow Rinckart's example of praise.

> Now thank we all our God with heart and hands
>   and voices,
> Who wondrous things hath done, in whom his
>   world rejoices;
> Who, from our mother's arms, hath blessed us on
>   our way
> With countless gifts of love, and still is ours today.
> MARTIN RINCKART

Fascinating Fact
Verses 14-19 each contain a royal virtue, something the ancient world expected of its kings. Of course, the Lord is the supreme ruler, and in him these virtues shine supremely.

Notable Quotable
"It is a kingly thing to help the fallen."
OVID

PSALM 146

¹ Praise the LORD!

Praise the LORD, I tell myself.

² I will praise the LORD as long as I live.
  I will sing praises to my God even with my dying
    breath.

³ Don't put your confidence in powerful people;
    there is no help for you there.
⁴ When their breathing stops, they return to the earth,
    and in a moment all their plans come to an end.
⁵ But happy are those who have the God of Israel as their
    helper,
    whose hope is in the LORD their God.
⁶ He is the one who made heaven and earth,
    the sea, and everything in them.

He is the one who keeps every promise forever,
⁷   who gives justice to the oppressed
    and food to the hungry.

The LORD frees the prisoners.
⁸   The LORD opens the eyes of the blind.

The LORD lifts the burdens of those bent beneath their
    loads.

The LORD loves the righteous.
⁹ The LORD protects the foreigners among us.
    He cares for the orphans and widows,
    but he frustrates the plans of the wicked.

¹⁰ The LORD will reign forever.
    O Jerusalem, your God is King in every generation!

Praise the LORD!

rederick Baedeker enjoyed going to prison. In 1877 he traveled to Russia to preach and give out Bibles. While there, he was allowed to visit the prisons, and for eighteen years he was the only person who had the right to visit any prison in Russia. And visit he did, from Poland to the Pacific. Wherever he went, he was watched by secret police, but he continued traveling, becoming one of the greatest distributors of Scripture of all time.

"Few people have any idea," he said, "of how many people in many lands are kept behind iron bars like wild animals." Though he was threatened, and his life was often in danger, Baedeker said, "These people need the gospel terribly, and I am going to give it to them."

When he met Count Lev Tolstoy, the Russian writer told him that if the Russian people had better education, there would be no need of prisons.

Baedeker disagreed and said, "The Evil One is stronger than we, and against him we are helpless." Then he paused before adding, "But my message to the prisoners of Russia is that there is a Stronger One still who is able to free the prisoners and slaves of Satan and to change them into holy and beloved children of God."

People today often make their own prisons. The message of Psalm 146:7 is that the Stronger One is still in the business of freeing prisoners.

Bible Networking
It is no coincidence that verse 7 mentions freeing prisoners and feeding the hungry in one breath. They are also mentioned together in Isaiah 58:6-7.

> *Now are we free—there's no condemnation,*
> *Jesus provides a perfect salvation;*
> *"Come unto me"—O hear His sweet call,*
> *Come, and He saves us once for all.*
> PHILIP P. BLISS

O COME, O COME, EMMANUEL

O come, O come, Emmanuel,
And ransom captive Israel,
That mourns in lonely exile here
Until the Son of God appear.

O come, O come, Thou Lord of might,
Who to Thy tribes, on Sinai's height,
In ancient times didst give the law
In cloud and majesty and awe.

O come, Thou Rod of Jesse, free
Thine own from Satan's tyranny;
From depths of hell Thy people save
And give them victory o'er the grave.

O come, Thou Dayspring, come and cheer
Our spirits by Thine advent here;
And drive away the shades of night,
And pierce the clouds and bring us light!

O come, Thou Key of David, come,
And open wide our heavenly home;
Make safe the way that leads on high,
And close the path to misery.

Rejoice! Rejoice! Emmanuel shall come to thee, O Israel.

TWELFTH-CENTURY LATIN HYMN, translated by John M. Neale

Psalm Link
PSALM 118:19

Open for me the gates where the righteous enter,
   and I will go in and thank the LORD.

ach stanza in this twelfth-century Christmas carol begins with a different reference to the Messiah. The initial mention of Emmanuel (or Immanuel) comes from Isaiah 7:14, as the name of the child that will be born of a virgin. Matthew quotes this verse in his account of Jesus' birth.

It would be worthwhile to trace the other references as well—Rod of Jesse, Dayspring, etc.—but one of the more interesting terms is in the last verse, "Key of David." What's that all about?

Isaiah 22 tells the story of a palace administrator in Jerusalem named Shebna. Isaiah spotted Shebna buying an impressive tombstone for himself on a prominent hill overlooking Jerusalem. At the time Shebna was involved in high-level negotiations with the enemy, and he may have been using his position to pad his own bank account, or at least to ensure his own legacy.

Isaiah said that God was going to pull Shebna down from his position and strip him of the key to David's house. The key would be given to another, who would "open doors, and no one will be able to shut them; he will close doors, and no one will be able to open them" (Isaiah 22:22).

The New Testament identifies Jesus as the one who has the key of David (Revelation 3:7). He is also the door to eternal life. "No one," he said, "can come to the Father except through me" (John 14:6).

Bible Networking
For the sources of some of the titles for Jesus in this hymn, read Isaiah 7:14; 8:8; 11:1; Matthew 1:23; and Luke 1:78.

PSALM 147:1-11

¹ Praise the LORD!

How good it is to sing praises to our God!
How delightful and how right!
² The LORD is rebuilding Jerusalem
and bringing the exiles back to Israel.
³ He heals the brokenhearted,
binding up their wounds.
⁴ He counts the stars
and calls them all by name.
⁵ How great is our Lord! His power is absolute!
His understanding is beyond comprehension!
⁶ The LORD supports the humble,
but he brings the wicked down into the dust.

⁷ Sing out your thanks to the LORD;
sing praises to our God, accompanied by harps.
⁸ He covers the heavens with clouds,
provides rain for the earth,
and makes the green grass grow in mountain
pastures.
⁹ He feeds the wild animals,
and the young ravens cry to him for food.
¹⁰ The strength of a horse does not impress him;
how puny in his sight is the strength of a man.
¹¹ Rather, the LORD's delight is in those who honor him,
those who put their hope in his unfailing love.

*T*hey called him "Hot Steam Schmidt." As a boy, Wilhelm Schmidt had trouble in school, but he enjoyed machines of all kinds. Locomotives fascinated him, and he frequented railroad stations, trying to find engineers who would answer his questions. Schmidt eventually focused his interests on high-compressed steam machines and received patents for twelve hundred inventions.

Every invention Schmidt perfected was a gift from God, as he saw it. Over and over again on his drawings or in his diaries was scribbled, "I thank you, O God, I thank you."

Though Schmidt often lived on the brink of bankruptcy, he opened his home to the needy. Because of his genius and his ability to harness power, Schmidt often received visits from military and political leaders, and they found themselves seated alongside the poor at Schmidt's table. He was never overawed by human abilities. "The decisive things of life," he said, "come not through our powers of intelligence but through God, the highest power."

The psalmist knew that the power of horses or humans could not compare with the power of God (verse 10). So whatever power you are battling today, know that God is even greater.

> I sing the mighty power of God
> That made the mountains rise,
> That spread the flowing seas abroad
> And built the lofty skies.
> I sing the wisdom that ordained
> The sun to rule the day;
> The moon shines full at his command
> ISAAC WATTS

Bible Networking
What a marvelous contrast there is in verses 3 and 4! He is the God of all the stars, yet he heals the brokenhearted. Read Isaiah 57:15 and 66:2.

Thought to Ponder
The power of God described in this psalm should dispel all worry. Someone once said, "Worry is a cycle of ineffective thoughts and emotions whirling around a thick center of fear." After you have read this psalm, what is there to fear?

PSALM 147:12-20

¹² Praise the LORD, O Jerusalem!
　　Praise your God, O Zion!
¹³ For he has fortified the bars of your gates
　　and blessed your children within you.
¹⁴ He sends peace across your nation
　　and satisfies you with plenty of the finest wheat.
¹⁵ He sends his orders to the world—
　　how swiftly his word flies!
¹⁶ He sends the snow like white wool;
　　he scatters frost upon the ground like ashes.
¹⁷ He hurls the hail like stones.
　　Who can stand against his freezing cold?
¹⁸ Then, at his command, it all melts.
　　He sends his winds, and the ice thaws.

¹⁹ He has revealed his words to Jacob,
　　his principles and laws to Israel.
²⁰ He has not done this with any other nation;
　　they do not know his laws.

Praise the LORD!

*W*hat did people in Bible lands know about ice, snow, and cold (see verses 16-18)?

We tend to think of Palestine as a semitropical land, but Mount Hermon is snowcapped much of the year. And the cold and snow were not confined only to Mount Hermon. In 2 Samuel 23:20 we read of one of David's mighty men killing a lion in a pit "despite the snow and slippery ground," and in Joshua 10 we read of a hailstorm that helped Joshua defeat the Amorites. During the winter months, worshipers in the Temple courts might have their faces pelted with icy drops, and even in April on the eve of Christ's crucifixion, Peter warmed himself at a fire in the Temple courtyard.

To the psalmist, snow was an amazing creation of God—as it is today. In the book of Job, when God boasts about all he has made, he includes snow (Job 38:22). Many of us marvel that no two snowflakes are made exactly alike, and we should, but snow is not just decorative. God also uses snow to purify the air, to insulate the ground, and to provide a slow supply of water to percolate to underground water reserves.

But even more remarkable is the fact that God can make us "as clean as freshly fallen snow" (Isaiah 1:18). Impurities fill our world and even our own heart, but God blankets us with his grace, covering us with a blanket of white wool donated by the Lamb of God.

> Lord Jesus, for this I most humbly entreat,
> I wait, blessed Lord, at thy crucified feet;
> By faith, for my cleansing, I see thy blood flow,
> Now wash me, and I shall be whiter than snow.
> JAMES NICHOLSON

Bible Networking
Snow and wool (verse 16) are used together elsewhere as images of a heart cleansed by God. See Isaiah 1:18.

Notable Quotable
"So it was on the day of Pentecost. The winter of spiritual captivity was thawed and dissolved by the soft breath of the Holy Ghost."
F. B. MEYER

NEHEMIAH 12:27-31, 45-47 (Song of Nehemiah)

²⁷During the dedication of the new wall of Jerusalem, the Levites throughout the land were asked to come to Jerusalem to assist in the ceremonies. They were to take part in the joyous occasion with their songs of thanksgiving and with the music of cymbals, lyres, and harps. ²⁸The singers were brought together from Jerusalem and its surrounding villages and from the villages of the Netophathites. ²⁹They also came from Beth-gilgal and the area of Geba and Azmaveth, for the singers had built their own villages around Jerusalem. ³⁰The priests and Levites first dedicated themselves, then the people, the gates, and the wall.

³¹I led the leaders of Judah to the top of the wall and organized two large choirs to give thanks. One of the choirs proceeded southward along the top of the wall to the Dung Gate. . . .

⁴⁵They performed the service of their God and the service of purification, as required by the laws of David and his son Solomon, and so did the singers and the gatekeepers. ⁴⁶The custom of having choir directors to lead the choirs in hymns of praise and thanks to God began long ago in the days of David and Asaph. ⁴⁷So now, in the days of Zerubbabel and of Nehemiah, the people brought a daily supply of food for the singers, the gatekeepers, and the Levites. The Levites, in turn, gave a portion of what they received to the priests, the descendants of Aaron.

Psalm Link
PSALM 147:1
Praise the LORD!

How good it is to sing praises to our God!
  How delightful and how right!

The years had been very hard and discouraging for the Israelites. Jerusalem had been destroyed a century and a half earlier. Now they were back in their homeland trying to rebuild. Disillusionment had set in. The job seemed bigger than they were.

Then came Nehemiah, a man with a plan. Somehow he made them believe that the job could be done after all. They still encountered plenty of problems, but under Nehemiah's leadership Jerusalem's walls were rebuilt in fifty-two days! The people hadn't been able to finish that job in the previous eighty years! And then came Ezra, with a back-to-the-Bible movement, and spiritual revival broke out.

At the time of Ezra's revival, there was much repentance and sorrow for sin, but Nehemiah told the people, "Don't be dejected and sad, for the joy of the Lord is your strength!" (Nehemiah 8:10).

No wonder Nehemiah 12 is a chapter about celebration! The people had a lot to sing about, and Nehemiah and Ezra led them in a festive walk along the top of the wall. You can be sure that the singers and instrumentalists were singing one psalm after another.

God's people today have a lot to sing about as well, and this is reflected in the great variety of Christian music we hear at Christmastime. In this season of celebration, let the joy of the Lord be your strength.

> Yes, on through life's long path still chanting as
>   you go;
> From youth to age, by night and day, in gladness
>   and in woe.
> Rejoice, rejoice, rejoice, give thanks and sing.
> EDWARD H. PLUMPTRE

Notable Quotable
"One of the most exuberant expressions of a happy heart is a singing mouth. . . . People are starved for happiness. When it is expressed in any authentic manner, they are encouraged."
CHARLES SWINDOLL

PSALM 148:1-6

¹ Praise the LORD!

Praise the LORD from the heavens!
  Praise him from the skies!
² Praise him, all his angels!
  Praise him, all the armies of heaven!
³ Praise him, sun and moon!
  Praise him, all you twinkling stars!
⁴ Praise him, skies above!
  Praise him, vapors high above the clouds!
⁵ Let every created thing give praise to the LORD,
    for he issued his command, and they came into
      being.
⁶ He established them forever and forever.
    His orders will never be revoked.

*A*ccording to legend, when Francis of Assisi preached, even the birds and animals enjoyed his sermons. Whether that's true or not, we know this: Saint Francis enjoyed all of God's creation.

A soldier in his early life, Francis was converted by a vision of Christ. Afterward, he took literally Jesus' words "Give as freely as you have received!" (Matthew 10:8), much to the displeasure of his father, a wealthy Italian cloth merchant. Wearing a ragged cloak and a rope belt taken from a scarecrow, Francis wandered through the countryside, begging from the rich in order to give to the poor. A group of people soon followed his lead, becoming the Franciscan Order of Friars.

One writer said of him, "With smiles he met the friendless, fed the poor, freed a trapped bird, led home a child." He wrote sixty hymns of praise and worship, but the one that is best remembered today is his "Canticle to the Sun," translated as "All Creatures of Our God and King" and based on Psalm 148.

It would seem that if the rest of creation is praising God, maybe we should join creation's choir today and make it unanimous.

> All creatures of our God and King,
> Lift up your voice and with us sing,
>   Alleluia, Alleluia!
> Thou burning sun with golden beam,
> Thou silver moon with softer gleam,
>   O praise him, O praise him!
>   Alleluia, Alleluia, Alleluia!

FRANCIS OF ASSISI, translated by William Henry Draper

Bible Networking
The Bible has much to say about celestial beings praising God. Read Job 38:7; Isaiah 6:2-3; Luke 2:13-14; and Revelation 5:11-12.

Notable Quotable
"This is a Hallelujah chorus, and is something to be listened to and felt. This is a blaze of glory that should be contemplated as a sublime sunrise or sunset, not subjected scientifically to prismatic analysis."
W. GRAHAM SCROGGIE

PSALM 148:7-14

[7] Praise the LORD from the earth,
   you creatures of the ocean depths,

[8] fire and hail, snow and storm,
   wind and weather that obey him,

[9] mountains and all hills,
   fruit trees and all cedars,

[10] wild animals and all livestock,
   reptiles and birds,

[11] kings of the earth and all people,
   rulers and judges of the earth,

[12] young men and maidens,
   old men and children.

[13] Let them all praise the name of the LORD.
   For his name is very great;
   his glory towers over the earth and heaven!

[14] He has made his people strong,
   honoring his godly ones—
   the people of Israel who are close to him.

Praise the LORD!

It's easy to think of birds and other lovely creatures praising God, but it's harder to think of crocodiles and pesky mosquitoes doing it. And how do "snow and storm . . . mountains and all hills" praise him?

Anyone and any thing can praise God by fulfilling the purpose for which it was created. In this way nonhuman creations glorify God by their daily existence. But we have a higher privilege, for part of the purpose for which we have been created involves knowing, loving, and obeying God.

The closing verses of this psalm reveal some additional secrets about our relationship with God. God is very great, and his glory towers over the heaven and earth. That's awesome. But the final words of the psalm (preceding "Praise the Lord") speak of those who are "close to him."

You get the picture of a mighty king or president with a three- or four-year-old son. The king may be conducting official business, while the young child is clinging to his father's pant leg. It is the closeness to the King that makes our praise more meaningful.

When you think of all that has gone on in this psalm, it may seem strange to conclude with "close to him." But that's the wonder of our great God and King. Although the entire created universe is in awe of him, he gives us the privilege of intimacy with him, and of calling him "Dear Father" (see Galatians 4:6).

Psalm at a Glance

In the first six verses of Psalm 148, all of heaven carried the melody in this mighty anthem. Now in the remaining verses, the melody is passed down to the earth and her inhabitants, so that we all might have our turn in singing God's praise.

Bible Networking

In verse 14 we have an amazing climax to an amazing psalm! This God, who deserves the acclaim of every created being, honors his own people by being close to them. This resembles what will happen at the coming of the new Jerusalem (Revelation 21:3).

> *Praise ye the Savior! great is his compassion,*
> *Tenderly cares he for his chosen people;*
> *Young men and maidens, ye old men and children,*
> *Praise ye the Savior!*
> SOURCE UNKNOWN

JOB 38:1-11 (Song of the Morning Stars)

Then the LORD answered Job from the whirlwind:

²"Who is this that questions my wisdom with such ignorant words? ³Brace yourself, because I have some questions for you, and you must answer them.

⁴"Where were you when I laid the foundations of the earth? Tell me, if you know so much. ⁵Do you know how its dimensions were determined and who did the surveying? ⁶What supports its foundations, and who laid its cornerstone ⁷as the morning stars sang together and all the angels shouted for joy?

⁸"Who defined the boundaries of the sea as it burst from the womb, ⁹and as I clothed it with clouds and thick darkness? ¹⁰For I locked it behind barred gates, limiting its shores. ¹¹I said, 'Thus far and no farther will you come. Here your proud waves must stop!' "

Psalm Link
PSALM 148:2-3

² Praise him, all his angels!

Praise him, all the armies of heaven!

³ Praise him, sun and moon!

Praise him, all you twinkling stars!

You missed that concert. Too bad! But so did the rest of us. It must have been unforgettable.

We're talking about the concert of the morning stars and the angelic hosts at the time of God's creation. We don't know the words they sang. We know only that they shouted for joy. Can you imagine the sound? We don't know how many angels there are, but Jesus spoke of ten thousand of them. That's quite a choir.

Angels do much more than sing. They are God's messengers and our guardians. They worship God and do his will. They get involved in the affairs of nations; they help churches; they punish God's enemies. All of these angelic activities are mentioned in Scripture (see Nehemiah 9:6; Psalm 34:7; 103:20; Revelation 1:1; 2:1; 16:1).

But what are they known for more than anything else? Music.

At the dawn of Creation, angels were singing along with the stars. And when God announced a new creation, the coming of the Christ child, angels were singing again. Angels apparently get excited about new creations.

Jesus mentions another time that angels sing. He puts it this way, "There is joy in the presence of God's angels when even one sinner repents" (Luke 15:10). Another new creation!

Have you made the angels start singing?

> Angels from the realms of glory,
> Wing your flight o'er all the earth;
> Ye who sang creation's story,
> Now proclaim Messiah's birth:
> Come and worship, come and worship,
> Worship Christ, the newborn King.
>
> JAMES MONTGOMERY

Bible Networking
Did David know the answers to the questions God was putting to Job? See Psalm 65.

Notable Quotable
"God created the world for reasons that are sufficient unto himself. It is not necessary that we be told these reasons. As long as we know God loves us, we have a base for hope."
EDWARD JOHN CARNELL

PSALM 149:1-4

¹ Praise the LORD!

Sing to the LORD a new song.
    Sing his praises in the assembly of the faithful.
² O Israel, rejoice in your Maker.
    O people of Jerusalem, exult in your King.
³ Praise his name with dancing,
    accompanied by tambourine and harp.
⁴ For the LORD delights in his people;
    he crowns the humble with salvation.

*T*he last five psalms all begin and end with the same word in Hebrew: *Halle-lujah!* In English, of course, it means, "Praise the Lord!"

In December the glorious strains of Handel's *Messiah* will ring forth, with its "Hallelujah Chorus" as the thrilling high point. Over fifty times the word *Hallelujah* is sung.

When the "Hallelujah Chorus" was developing in George Frideric Handel's mind, he said, "I did think I saw all heaven before me and the great God himself!" But Handel's circumstances looked quite dismal. Though he had been a successful musician earlier in his life, he had gone bankrupt, and by the time he was in his fifties, his career seemed behind him. He began writing biblical oratorios, composing his *Messiah* when he was fifty-six.

Can you imagine how he must have felt when the king of England attended the performance of his new oratorio and rose to his feet at the singing of the "Hallelujah Chorus"? All the audience stood as well, starting a custom that is still followed today.

In Psalm 149 the psalmist begins by praising God and then finds, in verse 4, blessing coming back upon him. That's what Handel discovered, too, and you'll discover it as well. Always start by taking time to praise God, and don't worry if your "Hallelujah Chorus" does not sound like Handel's. With a chorus of angels behind you, it will sound great.

> *Though high above all praise,*
> *Above all blessing high,*
> *Who would not fear his holy name,*
> *And praise and magnify.*
> JAMES MONTGOMERY

Bible Networking
In the Old Testament, people often expressed religious joy through dancing. See Exodus 15:20 and 2 Samuel 6:16.

Notable Quotable
"When the Lord saves a soul, its holy joy overflows; and it cannot find channels enough for its exceeding gratitude."
CHARLES HADDON SPURGEON

PSALM 149:5-9

[5] Let the faithful rejoice in this honor.
  Let them sing for joy as they lie on their beds.
[6] Let the praises of God be in their mouths,
  and a sharp sword in their hands—
[7] to execute vengeance on the nations
  and punishment on the peoples,
[8] to bind their kings with shackles
  and their leaders with iron chains,
[9] to execute the judgment written against them.
  This is the glory of his faithful ones.

Praise the LORD!

People sing in strange places. Some sing in the shower, others when driving their cars.

Sometimes worry keeps us from sleeping. The longer we stay in bed, the more we fret about tomorrow's problems, and the more upset we become. Finally, we get up and do things to get our mind off of negative thoughts.

But the psalmist calls us to sing for joy as we lie on our bed, and other psalms mention singing songs in the night.

Perhaps this is a skill we can learn from one of the many great hymn writers who have suffered from a long-term illness or physical limitation.

Songwriter Fanny Crosby went blind when she was only six weeks old. As a girl she heard someone sing the hymn "Alas and Did My Savior Bleed." When the line "Here, Lord, I give myself away" was sung, Fanny Crosby stood up and shouted, "Hallelujah." After that, joy characterized her life, and this shows through in many of her eight thousand hymns. She once said, "Darkness may throw a shadow over my outer vision, but there is no cloud that can keep the sunlight of hope from a trustful soul."

Whether you are bedridden or not, use one of Fanny Crosby's hymns to drive the clouds away.

> Praise Him! praise Him! Jesus, our blessed Redeemer!
> Sing, O Earth, His wonderful love proclaim!
> Hail Him! hail Him! Highest archangels in glory;
> Strength and honor give to His holy name!
> Like a shepherd, Jesus will guard His children,
> In His arms He carries them all day long:
> Praise Him! praise Him! tell of His excellent greatness;
> Praise Him! praise Him! ever in joyful song!
> FANNY J. CROSBY

Bible Networking

A time is coming when the Lord will assert his superiority over all other earthly authorities. Compare verse 8 with 1 Corinthians 15:24 and Philippians 2:9-11.

Notable Quotable

"Joy and judgment are wedded. Praise and power go hand in hand."
W. GRAHAM
SCROGGIE

PSALM 150

¹ Praise the LORD!

Praise God in his heavenly dwelling;
    praise him in his mighty heaven!
² Praise him for his mighty works;
    praise his unequaled greatness!
³ Praise him with a blast of the trumpet;
    praise him with the lyre and harp!
⁴ Praise him with the tambourine and dancing;
    praise him with stringed instruments and flutes!
⁵ Praise him with a clash of cymbals;
    praise him with loud clanging cymbals.
⁶ Let everything that lives sing praises to the LORD!

Praise the LORD!

*F*W. Boreham once wrote: "God said, 'Let there be light!' And there was light. He had no need to say, 'Let there be song!' because He was; and since He was, the morning stars sang together. Whenever and wherever created things have stood face-to-face with their Creator, they have burst into song."

In the Reformation of the early 1500s, when Martin Luther showed people that they could come before their Creator without fear, there was music. Luther later wrote more than thirty hymns and once said, "The Devil is the originator of sorrowful anxieties and restless troubles; he flees before the sound of music."

In the Methodist Revival of the early 1700s, when John and Charles Wesley urged people to honor their Creator with their life and heart, there was music. Charles Wesley wrote more than five thousand hymns.

At the dawn of creation the morning stars sang together (Job 38:7). And when we all get to heaven and see our Lord face-to-face, there will be songs of victory there: "Hallelujah! For the Lord our God, the Almighty, reigns. Let us be glad and rejoice and honor him" (Revelation 19:6-7).

Why don't you join the choir now and start practicing? Not necessarily your church choir, but the heavenly choir. Use all the instruments—your smile, your encouraging words, your obedient life—to make music for your Creator.

> Blessing and honor and glory and power
> Be unto him that sitteth upon the throne
> And unto the Lamb
> Forever and ever. Hallelujah! Amen.
>
> GEORGE F. HANDEL, taken from Revelation 5:13

Notable Quotable

"Each of our emotions and faculties may be a musical instrument in the best sense. Praise Him with the sound of your love! Praise Him with hope and faith! Praise Him with meekness and patience! Praise Him with courage and strength! Praise Him in work! Praise Him when tied by pain and weariness in a sick-bed."

F. B. MEYER

COLOSSIANS 1:15-20
(Hymn to Christ's Preeminence)

[15] Christ is the visible image of the invisible God.
    He existed before God made anything at all
    and is supreme over all creation.

[16] Christ is the one through whom God created everything
    in heaven and earth.
He made the things we can see and the things we can't
    see—
kings, kingdoms, rulers, and authorities.
Everything has been created through him and for him.

[17] He existed before everything else began,
    and he holds all creation together.

[18] Christ is the head of the church, which is his body.
    He is the first of all who will rise from the dead,
    so he is first in everything.

[19] For God in all his fullness was pleased to live in Christ,
[20]   and by him God reconciled everything to himself.
    He made peace with everything in heaven and on
        earth
    by means of his blood on the cross.

Psalm Link
PSALM 89:11

The heavens are yours, and the earth is yours;
    everything in the world is yours—you created it all.

*A*t Christmas we are constantly presented with the image of the cute little Christ child in the manger. Not good enough, says Paul.

At Easter we are presented with the image of the dying Jesus, hanging on the cross. Not good enough, says Paul.

Paul says, "Christ is the visible image of the invisible God." Commentator William Barclay tells of a letter written by a Greek soldier to his father. At the end of the papyrus letter, he writes: "I send you a little portrait of myself painted by Euctemon." The word translated as "portrait" in that letter is the same word translated as "image" in Colossians 1:15. The word is also used in the context of Greek legal documents.

The contracting parties were required to list their personal characteristics and distinguishing marks (their "image") so there would be no question about who signed the document.

Jesus is the portrait sent to us by the Father, and in him are all the personal characteristics of God. "God in all his fullness" was in Christ.

This Christmas, when you read the traditional Christmas story in Luke 2, read again this untraditional Christmas story in Colossians 1 to get the complete picture or, shall we say, the full portrait.

> Infant holy, infant lowly, for his bed a cattle stall;
> Oxen lowing, little knowing, Christ the Babe is
>   Lord of all.
> Swift are winging, angels singing, noels ringing,
>   tidings bringing,
> Christ the Babe is Lord of all; Christ the Babe is
>   Lord of all.

POLISH CAROL, Translated by Edith Reed

Bible Networking
Compare this passage with John 1:1-18. Both give a glorious portrayal of Jesus, the Son of God.

Notable Quotable
"Can we read this passage and not feel that it glows and moves with a personal joy in believing? Paul is not only discussing; he is worshiping."
H. C. G. MOULE

PHILIPPIANS 2:4-8
(Hymn on Christ's Humiliation)

⁴'Don't think only about your own affairs, but be interested in others, too, and what they are doing.

⁵Your attitude should be the same that Christ Jesus had.

⁶ Though he was God,
he did not demand
and cling to his rights as God.

⁷ He made himself nothing;
he took the humble position of a slave
and appeared in human form.

⁸ And in human form
he obediently humbled himself even further
by dying a criminal's death on a cross.

Psalm Link
PSALM 130:7

O Israel, hope in the LORD;
for with the LORD there is unfailing love
and an overflowing supply of salvation.

*D*evil's Island is really a cluster of islands ten miles off the South American coast. A hundred years ago it was notorious for its penal colony, where six thousand prisoners were confined. One visitor commented, "Hell is the only appropriate name for it, with its eternal fire of lust and remorse and impenitence."

But volunteers from the French Salvation Army went and lived there. They cleared some land and then gathered some prisoners to renovate an old house. Soon the word went out that these Salvationists not only worked alongside the convicts but slept on cots in the same rooms.

As a result, many prisoners turned to Christ. One convict was converted without attending a meeting. He said, "I don't need to go to the meetings. I have only to think that they left all to come here. That's enough."

Jesus left far more to come here, and he did far more after he came here. This hymn in Paul's letter to the Philippians tells the whole story in a few lines. God himself leaves heaven's glories and condescends to become a baby in a smelly manger. Even the angels on the hillside must have been amazed at what was happening. The Son of God came to Devil's Island, not only sleeping on a cot next to us, but taking our death penalty upon himself. And because the Son of God became the Son of Man, we are freed from Devil's Island and become children of God. Positively amazing!

> *You who were God beyond all praising,*
> *Because you loved me became a man*
> *Stooping so low, but sinners raising*
> *Heavenwards by your eternal plan.*
> FRENCH CAROL

Bible Networking
Check out 2 Corinthians 8:9 to see one reason why Christ became so poor.

Notable Quotable
"So poor was he that he was constantly borrowing: a place for his birth, a boat to preach from, a room for the Lord's supper, a tomb to be buried in. Moreover, he took upon himself a debt (Isaiah 53:6—'the guilt and sins of us all')."
WILLIAM HENDRICKSEN

PHILIPPIANS 2:9-11
(Hymn on Christ's Exaltation)

⁹ Because of [Jesus' humble obedience to the point of
     death],
    God raised him up to the heights of heaven
    and gave him a name that is above every other name,
¹⁰ so that at the name of Jesus every knee will bow,
    in heaven and on earth and under the earth,
¹¹ and every tongue will confess that Jesus Christ is Lord,
    to the glory of God the Father.

Psalm Link
PSALM 24:9-10

⁹ Open up, ancient gates!
    Open up, ancient doors,
    and let the King of glory enter.
¹⁰ Who is the King of glory?
    The LORD Almighty—
    he is the King of glory.

*W*e say the three names—Lord Jesus Christ—very casually, almost as if we were talking about someone named John Henry Doe or Mary Ann Smith. But if you were living in the first century, you would realize that there was nothing at all casual about the name.

Jesus was his given name. Although it means "Savior," it was not an unusual name in first-century Israel.

But to call Jesus "Christ" meant that you were naming him as God's anointed Messiah. This is what Peter affirmed when he said, "You are the Messiah, the Son of the living God" (Matthew 16:16). This was hard for Jews to accept.

And to call Jesus "Lord" would get you into trouble with the Gentiles as well as the Jews. "Lord" was an imperial title by which Roman citizens acknowledged the divinity of Caesar.

Besides that, "Lord" was a sacred title among Jews as well. Since Jews refrained from pronouncing the sacred name of Yahweh, they commonly used "Lord" instead. So when Christians spoke of Jesus as Lord, meaning he was Deity himself, this was risky business.

What is Jesus to you? Is he the Messiah, God's promised Redeemer? And is he also Lord, the divine Son of God? One day all of creation will bow before him and acknowledge, with full meaning, that threefold name.

> One day all creation shall bow to our Lord,
> Even now, among angels his name is adored.
> May we at his coming, with the glorified throng,
> Stand singing his praises in heaven's great song:
> Jesus, Jesus, Savior adored
> Of all men and angels, forever our Lord.
> DUTCH HYMN, translated by W. Kuipers

Bible Networking

To Paul and the other apostles, it was of tremendous significance that Jesus had the title "Lord." See Acts 2:36; Romans 10:9; and Revelation 17:14.

Notable Quotable

"It still remains true that if anyone can say, 'For me Jesus Christ is Lord,' he is a Christian. He is prepared to give to Jesus a love, a loyalty, an allegiance, that he will give to none other in all the universe."
WILLIAM BARCLAY

December 18

---

1 TIMOTHY 3:14-16
(Hymn on Christ's Adoration)

[14]I am writing these things to you now, even though I hope to be with you soon, [15]so that if I can't come for a while, you will know how people must conduct themselves in the household of God. This is the church of the living God, which is the pillar and support of the truth.

[16]Without question, this is the great mystery of our faith:

Christ appeared in the flesh
and was shown to be righteous by the Spirit.
He was seen by angels
and was announced to the nations.
He was believed on in the world
and was taken up into heaven.

Psalm Link
PSALM 72:19
Bless his glorious name forever!
Let the whole earth be filled with his glory.
Amen and amen!

*A*t Christmas do you ever try to guess what's in the packages under the tree? Surely you've learned by now that the size of the package can be very misleading. A diamond ring doesn't require a big box.

This early Christian hymn depicts Jesus as a surprise package, the "mystery of our faith." He came as a humble babe in a poor manger—not a very impressive package on the outside. He lived 90 percent of his life in Nazareth in the home of a carpenter. His ministry was among humble folk; his first disciples were fishermen.

Then the package opens, or rather, explodes with surprises. The Holy Spirit witnesses to Jesus' righteousness at his baptism. Filled with the Spirit's power, Jesus performs great miracles. After his crucifixion, he is raised by the Spirit, and angels witness his resurrection.

But there's more. Jesus' small band of frightened followers carries the gospel to the ends of the world, and people of every tribe and nation begin to worship him. One day all of creation will give him glory.

Don't make the mistake of misjudging that little surprise package in the manger!

> *Who is he in yonder stall, at whose feet the shepherd's fall?*
> *Who is he in deep distress, fasting in the wilderness?*
> *Who is he on yonder tree dies in grief and agony?*
> *Who is he that from his throne rules through all the world alone?*
> *'Tis the Lord! O wondrous story! 'Tis the Lord! the King of glory!*
> *At his feet we humbly fall, crown him, crown him Lord of all!*
> BENJAMIN HANBY

Bible Networking
For more on the angels' involvement in what was happening, see Matthew 28:2-7; Luke 2:9-15; and Acts 1:10-11.

Notable Quotable
"After Jesus died, the number of his followers was one hundred and twenty. All that his followers had to offer was the story of a Galilean carpenter. And yet before seventy years had passed, that story had gone out to the ends of the earth, and men of every nation accepted Jesus as Lord."
WILLIAM BARCLAY

2 TIMOTHY 2:8-9, 11-13
(Hymn of Christian Commitment)

[8]Never forget that Jesus Christ was a man born into King David's family and that he was raised from the dead. This is the Good News I preach. [9]And because I preach this Good News, I am suffering and have been chained like a criminal. But the word of God cannot be chained. . . .

[11]This is a true saying:

If we die with him,
  we will also live with him.
[12] If we endure hardship,
  we will reign with him.
If we deny him,
  he will deny us.
[13] If we are unfaithful,
  he remains faithful,
  for he cannot deny himself.

Psalm Link
PSALM 44:22
For your sake we are killed every day;
  we are being slaughtered like sheep.

*I*n 1838 newlywed James Calvert sailed from England to the Fiji Islands, but this was no tropical honeymoon. At that time those islands were peopled with fierce cannibals, and Calvert was taking a missionary team with him to share the good news of Christ.

When the ship captain learned of Calvert's plans, he tried to talk sense into him. "You will lose your life and the lives of those with you if you go among such savages!"

Calvert responded, "We died before we came here."

The Christmas season is no time to talk about death, is it? It's a celebration of birth, of new beginnings, of joy and peace. But when you think about it, the baby in the manger was born to die on a cross. The "peace on earth" the angels sang about would only come through his sacrificial death.

And Christians are asked to die with him. Jesus called his followers to "shoulder [their] cross" (Matthew 16:24). Certainly this occurs in a spiritual sense. Baptism, Paul said, symbolizes our dying with Christ (Romans 6:3-4). And dead people have nothing to lose, as James Calvert and his team realized. We can take enormous risks for God if he calls us to because the worst that could happen is that we would die and, as this hymn reminds us, live with Christ.

So this hymn shows us that Christianity is about death *and* life. We serve a risen Savior. And after we die with him, he raises us up.

> "Take up thy cross," the Savior said,
> "If thou wouldst my disciple be;
> Take up thy cross with willing heart,
> And humbly follow after me."
> CHARLES W. EVEREST

A Word on Words

The phrase "This is a true saying" is found four times, with minor variations, in Paul's pastoral epistles: here and in 1 Timothy 3:1; 4:9; and Titus 3:8. It seems to be Paul's way of emphasizing certain points.

Notable Quotable

"I go out to preach with two propositions in mind. First, every person ought to give his life to Christ. Second, whether or not anyone else gives him his life, I will give him mine."
JONATHAN EDWARDS

JOY TO THE WORLD

Joy to the world! the Lord is come;
Let earth receive her King;
Let every heart prepare him room,
And heaven and nature sing.

Joy to the earth! the Savior reigns;
Let men their songs employ;
While fields and floods, rocks, hills, and plains
Repeat the sounding joy.

No more let sins and sorrows grow,
Nor thorns infest the ground;
He comes to make his blessings flow,
Far as the curse is found.

He rules the world with truth and grace,
And makes the nations prove
The glories of his righteousness,
And wonders of his love.

ISAAC WATTS, taken from Psalm 98

Psalm Link
PSALM 98:4, 9

4 Shout to the LORD, all the earth;
    break out in praise and sing for joy! . . .
9 before the LORD.
For the LORD is coming to judge the earth.
    He will judge the world with justice,
    and the nations with fairness.

Often God doesn't blend things together the way we would. He gets praise when unlikely combinations are melded to honor him. Take Isaac Watts and George Frideric Handel, for instance. You certainly wouldn't have picked them to write what is probably our most joyful Christmas carol.

Watts had written his first hymn in his teenage years as a protest to his father, a minister. Watts had complained about singing from the old psalter that had been around for over a hundred years, and his father told him, "If you don't like these hymns, write better ones." So he did.

Watts, a small, unattractive man, was later jilted by the woman he loved. His health broke shortly after that, and he lived the rest of his life as a semi-invalid. He wrote metrical versions of all the Psalms. "Joy to the World" is a paraphrase of the last half of Psalm 98.

The music of "Joy to the World" is adapted from the *Messiah* by George Frideric Handel, a London contemporary of Watts. Handel, also unmarried, fell into bankruptcy after several musical failures. Partially paralyzed, he tried putting his life back together again, devoting himself to composing oratorios. Four years after his bankruptcy, he produced the *Messiah*.

Both Watts and Handel discovered independently that God "comes to make his blessings flow far as the curse is found." Out of sorrow God can produce great joy. Have you discovered that, too?

Bible Networking
For more on the curse that Christ has overcome (third stanza), read Genesis 3:17-19.

LUKE 1:39-45 (The Praise of Elizabeth)

[39]A few days later Mary hurried to the hill country of Judea, to the town [40]where Zechariah lived. She entered the house and greeted Elizabeth. [41]At the sound of Mary's greeting, Elizabeth's child leaped within her, and Elizabeth was filled with the Holy Spirit.

[42]Elizabeth gave a glad cry and exclaimed to Mary, "You are blessed by God above all other women, and your child is blessed. [43]What an honor this is, that the mother of my Lord should visit me! [44]When you came in and greeted me, my baby jumped for joy the instant I heard your voice! [45]You are blessed, because you believed that the Lord would do what he said."

Psalm Link
PSALM 68:3

Let the godly rejoice.

Let them be glad in God's presence.

Let them be filled with joy.

It's not unusual to see two expectant mothers talking to each other. But it is unusual if one of them is in her midteens, and the other is in her fifties or older.

Yet that's the scene we find in Luke 1 as teenage Mary meets with her older cousin Elizabeth. These two women had more in common than their pregnancies. Both Elizabeth's husband, Zechariah, and Mary had been visited by the angel Gabriel, announcing miraculous births. Both were stunned. Zechariah was incredulous because Elizabeth was well past her childbearing years; Mary couldn't understand how she, a virgin, could bear a child.

But the miracle went on, and both women found themselves pregnant, pondering the angel's strange messages. Elizabeth, treasuring the thought that her son would be the herald for the Messiah, must have wondered who the Messiah would be and if she would ever meet him. Elizabeth was joyfully expectant in more ways than one.

Then her cousin Mary showed up on her doorstep, and Elizabeth's baby "leaped within her." The Holy Spirit gave Elizabeth the insight to say, "You are blessed by God above all other women."

Unlike Mary, Elizabeth had waited a lifetime to bear a child. She was blessed by God and, in an unusual way, became the first to greet the Messiah. In this Christmas season, consider how God has blessed you, and take the opportunity to greet the Messiah yourself.

> How sweet the name of Jesus sounds
> In a believer's ear!
> It soothes his sorrows, heals his wounds,
> And drives away his fear.
> JOHN NEWTON

Notable Quotable

"It was the last poetic voice of the Old, and it greeted the New; the voice of a daughter of the priestly line, singing of him for whom the Old looked and sighed and sobbed and waited."
G. CAMPBELL MORGAN

LUKE 1:46-55
(The Magnificat: The Song of Mary)

⁴⁶ "Oh, how I praise the Lord.

⁴⁷   How I rejoice in God my Savior!

⁴⁸ For he took notice of his lowly servant girl,
        and now generation after generation
            will call me blessed.

⁴⁹ For he, the Mighty One, is holy,
        and he has done great things for me.

⁵⁰ His mercy goes on from generation to generation,
        to all who fear him.

⁵¹ His mighty arm does tremendous things!
        How he scatters the proud and haughty ones!

⁵² He has taken princes from their thrones
        and exalted the lowly.

⁵³ He has satisfied the hungry with good things
        and sent the rich away with empty hands.

⁵⁴ And how he has helped his servant Israel!
        He has not forgotten his promise to be merciful.

⁵⁵ For he promised our ancestors—Abraham and his
        children—
            to be merciful to them forever."

Psalm Link
PSALM 35:3

Lift up your spear and javelin
    and block the way of my enemies.
Let me hear you say,
    "I am your salvation!"

*S*cared stiff. Don't you think that would have been a suitable reaction of a teenager who had just met an angel? And what's more—an angel who had told her she would become the virgin mother of the Son of God?

Not Mary.

Of course, she may have had uncertainties, but her first reaction was to praise God. And what majestic praise! In her ten-verse Magnificat she quotes or alludes to at least nine psalms as well as a few other Old Testament texts. Despite the fact that most Jewish girls were not taught the Scriptures in the synagogue, Mary knew the Old Testament—and the God of the Old Testament—very well.

Mary knew that God is holy and mighty, a merciful God who does wonderful things for his people, a God who keeps his promises and answers prayer. And she was thrilled—ecstatic—that God would bring the Messiah to Israel through her.

When God asks you to do something, how do you respond? Are you scared stiff, or do you follow Mary's example, praising God that he has chosen to use you to accomplish his will. He has chosen some unlikely people in the past to do his bidding, so don't be too surprised if he chooses you.

> Hear the glad sound, the Savior comes, the Savior promised long!
> Let every heart prepare a throne, and every voice a song.
> He comes the broken heart to bind, the bleeding soul to cure,
> And with the treasures of his grace to raise the humble poor.

PHILIP DODDRIDGE

Fascinating Fact
This hymn of praise is known as the "Magnificat" because in the Latin Vulgate translation, the first word is magnificat, which means "praise" or "magnify."

Notable Quotable
"Mary sings of a God who is not bound by what men do. He turns human attitudes and orders of society upside down."
R. V. G. TASKER

LUKE 1:67-71, 76-79
(The Benedictus: The Song of Zechariah)

[67]Then his father, Zechariah, was filled with the Holy Spirit and gave this prophecy:

[68] "Praise the Lord, the God of Israel, because
      he has visited his people and redeemed them.
[69] He has sent us a mighty Savior
      from the royal line of his servant David,
[70] just as he promised
      through his holy prophets long ago.
[71] Now we will be saved from our enemies
      and from all who hate us.

[76] "And you, my little son,
      will be called the prophet of the Most High,
      because you will prepare the way for the Lord.
[77] You will tell his people how to find salvation
      through forgiveness of their sins.
[78] Because of God's tender mercy,
      the light from heaven is about to break upon us,
[79] to give light to those who sit in darkness and in the
        shadow of death,
      and to guide us to the path of peace."

Psalm Link
PSALM 71:23
I will shout for joy and sing your praises,
      for you have redeemed me.

Zechariah was over the hill; he had to know that. Besides that, there were too many priests, maybe about twenty thousand of them. What good was he anyway? He and his wife didn't even have any children with whom to celebrate special occasions. It must have seemed like no one would miss him if he were gone.

But God had a different perspective. When it came to be Zechariah's week to serve in the Temple (priests only served twice a year), his routine priestly chores were interrupted by an angelic visitor. The angel Gabriel announced that Zechariah and his wife would have a son, who would be the forerunner of the Messiah.

God delights in using people who seem to be over the hill. Abraham and Moses were certainly beyond retirement age when God called them into action. And this elderly couple, Zechariah and Elizabeth, now had a key role in God's redemptive drama.

No wonder Zechariah sang at his son's birth! And what prophetic insights God gave him! He quoted from Isaiah, Jeremiah, and particularly Malachi, the last of the Old Testament prophets.

"Praise the Lord," said teenage Mary in her Magnificat. "Yes, praise the Lord," said senior citizen Zechariah in his Benedictus. No matter your age, God wants to use you to bring him praise.

> This is he whom seers in old time
> Chanted of with one accord,
> Whom the voices of the prophets
> Promised in their faithful word;
> Now he shines, the long-expected;
> Let all people praise the Lord.
> AURELIUS CLEMENS PRUDENTIUS

Fascinating Fact
This song is called the "Benedictus," which is Latin for "blessed" or "praised," the first word in Zechariah's song. Although both are poetry, Mary's Magnificat reads more like a psalm, while Zechariah's Benedictus reads more like a prophecy.

Notable Quotable
"Forgiveness is not so much the remission of penalty as the restoration of a relationship."
WILLIAM BARCLAY

December 24

LUKE 2:8-14 (The Angel Chorus)

⁸That night some shepherds were in the fields outside the village, guarding their flocks of sheep. ⁹Suddenly, an angel of the Lord appeared among them, and the radiance of the Lord's glory surrounded them. They were terribly frightened, ¹⁰but the angel reassured them. "Don't be afraid!" he said. "I bring you good news of great joy for everyone! ¹¹The Savior—yes, the Messiah, the Lord—has been born tonight in Bethlehem, the city of David! ¹²And this is how you will recognize him: You will find a baby lying in a manger, wrapped snugly in strips of cloth!"

¹³Suddenly, the angel was joined by a vast host of others—the armies of heaven—praising God:

¹⁴ "Glory to God in the highest heaven,
   and peace on earth to all whom God favors."

Psalm Link
PSALM 148:1-2

¹ Praise the LORD!

Praise the LORD from the heavens!
   Praise him from the skies!
² Praise him, all his angels!
   Praise him, all the armies of heaven!

G ood news," said the angel. It was a breaking news story, and God's angelic network was well equipped to bring the story to remote areas like shepherds in a remote field.

Journalism professors teach that the best news stories have five characteristics: The news should be unusual ("man bites dog" better than "dog bites man"), vital (who cares about whether you jogged yesterday?), prominent (if the president breaks a leg, it's news), personal (if a new tax law affects most everyone, it's big news), and timely (yesterday's newspaper is only good for wrapping up fish).

The news the angels brought had all the characteristics of a sensational story. Was it unusual? Was it vital? Did it concern a prominent individual? Was it personal in that its impact affected most people? Was it timely? This was obviously front-page material. No wonder the shepherds ran to Bethlehem!

But notice one difference between most news stories today and this greatest of all news stories: It was good news. Today's headlines tell of crime and war, of heartache and suffering. This news story tells of salvation, peace on earth, joy to all people.

> On Christmas night all Christians sing to hear
> the news the angels bring,
> News of great joy, news of great mirth, news of a
> merciful Savior's birth.
> Then why should men on earth be sad, since our Re-
> deemer made us glad,
> When from our sin he set us free, all for to gain
> our liberty.
> TRADITIONAL ENGLISH CAROL

Bible Networking
Christ promised peace to his disciples (John 14:27), but he also brought conflict (Matthew 10:34-36). See also James 4:4.

Notable Quotable
"Peace between man and God is an essential prerequisite to peace between man and his fellowman."
CHARLES L. CHILDERS

HARK! THE HERALD ANGELS SING

Hark! the herald angels sing, "Glory to the newborn King:
Peace on earth, and mercy mild, God and sinners reconciled!"
Joyful, all ye nations, rise, join the triumph of the skies;
With th' angelic host proclaim, "Christ is born in
Bethlehem!"

Christ, by highest heaven adored, Christ, the everlasting
Lord,
Late in time behold him come, offspring of the Virgin's womb:
Veiled in flesh the Godhead see; Hail, th' incarnate Deity,
Pleased as man with men to dwell, Jesus, our Emmanuel.

Hail, the heaven-born Prince of Peace! Hail the Sun of
Righteousness!
Light and life to all he brings, risen with healing in his wings.
Mild he lays his glory by, born that man no more may die,
Born to raise the sons of earth, born to give them second
birth.

Hark! the herald angels sing, "Glory to the newborn King."
CHARLES WESLEY

Psalm Link
PSALM 103:20-21

[20] Praise the LORD, you angels of his,
   you mighty creatures who carry out his plans,
   listening for each of his commands.

[21] Yes, praise the LORD, you armies of angels
   who serve him and do his will!

Charles Wesley, the seventeenth of nineteen children born to Samuel and Susanna Wesley, wrote about sixty-five hundred hymns. Most of them are now forgotten—but not "Hark! the Herald Angels Sing."

He began writing hymns shortly after he committed his heart to Christ in 1738. Within a year he had written several of his greatest hymns. Among his earliest are "Jesus Lover of My Soul," "And Can It Be," "Christ the Lord Is Risen Today," and "Hark! the Herald Angels Sing."

Sometimes he is overshadowed by his brother John, the founder of the Methodist movement. But Charles was quite an evangelist himself, preaching despite violent opposition and threats of violence. He did his best preaching, though, through his hymns, packing them with rich scriptural teaching.

In the third stanza of "Hark! the Herald Angels Sing," for instance, Charles writes of Jesus as the Sun of Righteousness, "risen with healing in his wings." Where did he get that idea? From the prophet Malachi, who prophesied, "But for you who fear my name, the Sun of Righteousness will rise with healing in his wings. And you will go free, leaping with joy like calves let out to pasture" (Malachi 4:2). So Jesus is not only the Son but also the Sun. The Sun of Righteousness brings not only light but life.

Today, as we celebrate his birth, bask in the rays of the Sun of Righteousness.

Bible Networking
The second stanza of this hymn speaks of Jesus as the Godhead "veiled in flesh" and as "th' incarnate Deity." Paul spoke of Jesus in a similar way. See Colossians 1:15-20.

LUKE 2:25-35
(Nunc Dimittis: The Song of Simeon)

²⁵Now there was a man named Simeon who lived in Jerusalem. He was a righteous man and very devout. He was filled with the Holy Spirit, and he eagerly expected the Messiah to come and rescue Israel. ²⁶The Holy Spirit had revealed to him that he would not die until he had seen the Lord's Messiah. ²⁷That day the Spirit led him to the Temple. So when Mary and Joseph came to present the baby Jesus to the Lord as the law required, ²⁸Simeon was there. He took the child in his arms and praised God, saying,

²⁹ "Lord, now I can die in peace!
      As you promised me,
³⁰ I have seen the Savior
³¹   you have given to all people.
³² He is a light to reveal God to the nations,
      and he is the glory of your people Israel!"

³³Joseph and Mary were amazed at what was being said about Jesus. ³⁴Then Simeon blessed them, and he said to Mary, "This child will be rejected by many in Israel, and it will be their undoing. But he will be the greatest joy to many others. ³⁵Thus, the deepest thoughts of many hearts will be revealed. And a sword will pierce your very soul."

Psalm Link
PSALM 62:5
I wait quietly before God,
      for my hope is in him.

*A*ccording to an old story, a traveler walked into a country store in the hills of Kentucky one wintry day in 1809 and asked, "Anything new happen around here lately?" The proprietor almost laughed. "Around here, stranger? Nothing happens around here. A baby was born in the Lincoln cabin last night; that's all."

Who knows the eventual impact of a life? Simeon knew.

Mary and Joseph brought the baby Jesus to the Temple when he was eight days old, fulfilling the requirements of the law of Moses. Simeon was there with a prophecy of good news and bad news from the Lord. The good news was that this baby Messiah would save not just the Jews; he would be a light for all people. The bad news was that many of his own people would reject him, and Mary would experience great sorrow as a result.

Simeon's words could serve as an outline for the rest of the New Testament. Jesus' ministry glorified God within Israel at first. He was accepted by some and rejected by others. The message of his death and resurrection spread like lightning throughout the world. So Simeon was standing at the turning point of all history, and he knew it.

Don't let the significance of Jesus' birth pass you by. Celebrate this season of his entry into the world, and remember the day you first met him. Because of Jesus, nothing else will ever be the same.

> Thou didst leave thy throne and thy kingly crown
> When thou camest to earth for me;
> But in Bethlehem's home there was found no room
> For thy holy nativity:
> O come to my heart, Lord Jesus,
> There is room in my heart for thee.
> EMILY E. S. ELLIOTT

Bible Networking
To hear more of what would pierce Mary's heart, read the messianic Psalm 22.

Notable Quotable
"[For Simeon] to hold that baby in his arms was to have death revealed to him, not as dissolution, but as emancipation. The great and glorious fact that would emerge was that Christ has abolished death."
G. CAMPBELL MORGAN

REVELATION 5:9-14
(Heaven's Song of Redemption)

⁹ "You are worthy to take the scroll
  and break its seals and open it.
For you were killed, and your blood has ransomed
      people for God
    from every tribe and language and people and
      nation.
¹⁰ And you have caused them to become God's Kingdom
      and his priests.
    And they will reign on the earth."

¹¹Then I looked again, and I heard the singing of thousands and millions of angels around the throne and the living beings and the elders. ¹²And they sang in a mighty chorus:

"The Lamb is worthy—the Lamb who was killed.
  He is worthy to receive power and riches
  and wisdom and strength
  and honor and glory and blessing."

¹³And then I heard every creature in heaven and on earth and under the earth and in the sea. They also sang:

"Blessing and honor and glory and power
  belong to the one sitting on the throne
  and to the Lamb forever and ever."

¹⁴And the four living beings said, "Amen!" And the twenty-four elders fell down and worshiped God and the Lamb.

Psalm Link
PSALM 40:3
He has given me a new song to sing,
  a hymn of praise to our God.

Many will see what he has done and be
astounded.
They will put their trust in the LORD.

*M*ost of us are awed by the book of Revelation with its visions, its symbolism, and all the arguing about its interpretation. But just for today, see if you can put aside all the theological wrangling and just enjoy the music.

The music is coming from chapter 5. The song is a "new" one, yet some of the words are familiar. The scene is heaven. There's a throne, and the one sitting on it has a scroll in his hand. No one is worthy to open the scroll except the Lion of the tribe of Judah, who looks like a lamb that has been killed. As he takes the scroll, the first of three "new" songs is sung, all songs of praise to the Lion-Lamb.

Revelation, which is often associated with the end of things, also speaks of new beginnings—a new name (2:17); a new Jerusalem (3:12); a new heaven and a new earth (21:1); and all things new (21:5). It reads like a description of New Year's Eve. Ring out the old; ring in the new!

The music of the Psalms was based on the Old Covenant; the music of Revelation is based on the New Covenant. The Old Covenant spoke much about slain lambs, but the New Covenant's song is about the Lamb who was slain to redeem us. He alone is worthy to help us face the future.

> *"Worthy the Lamb that died," they cry,*
> *"To be exalted thus."*
> *"Worthy the Lamb," our lips reply,*
> *"For he was slain for us."*
> ISAAC WATTS

Bible Networking
The book of Psalms says much about singing "new songs." See Psalms 33:3; 40:3; 96:1; 98:1; 144:9; and 149:1.

Notable Quotable
"God has wrought redemption for the world, and those who behold the Lamb never get over it."
ROBERT E. COLEMAN

REVELATION 7:9-17 (Praise of the Great Multitude)

⁹After this I saw a vast crowd, too great to count, from every nation and tribe and people and language, standing in front of the throne and before the Lamb. They were clothed in white and held palm branches in their hands. ¹⁰And they were shouting with a mighty shout, "Salvation comes from our God on the throne and from the Lamb!"

¹¹And all the angels were standing around the throne and around the elders and the four living beings. And they fell face down before the throne and worshiped God. ¹²They said,

"Amen! Blessing and glory and wisdom
    and thanksgiving and honor and power and strength
    belong to our God forever and forever. Amen!"

¹³Then one of the twenty-four elders asked me, "Who are these who are clothed in white? Where do they come from?"

¹⁴And I said to him, "Sir, you are the one who knows."

Then he said to me, "These are the ones coming out of the great tribulation. They washed their robes in the blood of the Lamb and made them white. ¹⁵That is why they are standing in front of the throne of God, serving him day and night in his Temple. And he who sits on the throne will live among them and shelter them. ¹⁶They will never again be hungry or thirsty, and they will be fully protected from the scorching noontime heat. ¹⁷For the Lamb who stands in front of the throne will be their Shepherd. He will lead them to the springs of life-giving water. And God will wipe away all their tears."

Psalm Link
PSALM 3:8

Victory comes from you, O LORD.
    May your blessings rest on your people.

*I*n the Civil War a soldier was captured and taken to Libby Prison in Richmond, Virginia, for confinement. He feared what awaited him behind the foreboding, heavy gates.

Then he heard a deep bass voice singing out from an upper window in the prison: "Praise God from whom all blessings flow." When the singer reached the second line, more voices chimed in. Still more joined on the next line, until finally the entire prison was singing, "Praise Father, Son, and Holy Ghost."

The Doxology made a difference. Oh, the iron gates were still there, strong as ever. But the prisoner was no longer bound by fear.

In Revelation we read of a vast crowd that has endured suffering. Some are homeless, many are famished, others have been tortured. But what a glorious Hallelujah they sing together!

Then the Lion-Lamb becomes their Shepherd. He dries their tears and leads them beside the still waters.

What are you afraid of? Death? Pain? Loss? Join the crowd. Seriously, join the crowd of those through the ages who sing praises to the Lamb who has suffered for us. We find comfort, guidance, and eternal rest in him.

> Ten thousand times ten thousand in sparkling raiment bright,
> The armies of the ransomed saints throng up the steeps of light:
> 'Tis finished, all is finished, their fight with death and sin:
> Fling open wide the golden gates, and let the victors in.
>
> HENRY ALFORD

Bible Networking
For other pictures of the Good Shepherd in action, see Psalm 23; Psalm 36:8-9; Isaiah 40:11; Ezekiel 34:22-23; John 10:1-30.

Notable Quotable
"If there is joy before the angels of God over one sinner who repents, how unbelievably great will be the joyful adoration when all the redeemed stand before their God!"
ROBERT H. MOUNCE

REVELATION 11:15-19 (The Kingdom Carol)

[15]Then the seventh angel blew his trumpet, and there were loud voices shouting in heaven: "The whole world has now become the Kingdom of our Lord and of his Christ, and he will reign forever and ever."

[16]And the twenty-four elders sitting on their thrones before God fell on their faces and worshiped him. [17]And they said,

"We give thanks to you, Lord God Almighty,
　　the one who is and who always was,
for now you have assumed your great power
　　and have begun to reign.
[18] The nations were angry with you,
　　but now the time of your wrath has come.
It is time to judge the dead and reward your servants.
You will reward your prophets and your holy people,
　　all who fear your name, from the least to the greatest.
And you will destroy all who have caused destruction
　　　　on the earth."

[19]Then, in heaven, the Temple of God was opened and the Ark of his covenant could be seen inside the Temple. Lightning flashed, thunder crashed and roared; there was a great hailstorm, and the world was shaken by a mighty earthquake.

Psalm Links
PSALM 2:1
Why do the nations rage?
　　Why do the people waste their time with futile plans?

PSALM 10:16
The LORD is king forever and ever!
　　Let those who worship other gods be swept from the
　　　　land.

When the Carthaginian general Hannibal was leading his troops over the Alps into Italy, he pointed to the valleys of Piemonte below. "Look," he said. "See those vineyards? See those fields of grain? A few more struggles, and they all belong to you." As far as the general was concerned, his troops had already won. It was all over but the shouting.

Hannibal was right. But his men didn't win by confidence alone. They had to bring an entire army across the Alps, along with their pack-elephants. It wasn't easy, but they did it, and their superior power enabled them to defeat the Romans.

As Christians, we're on a winning team. Admittedly, that's hard to believe sometimes. It may seem that we're losing 30-0 in the last minute of the Super Bowl. But Christ has promised a victory, and he has the power to pull it off. It's all over but the shouting.

And what shouting that will be! Revelation 11:15 gives us an earful. "The whole world has now become the Kingdom of our Lord and of his Christ." The honking of New Year's Eve will be tame compared with the din of that ultimate victory party.

So don't face today, and don't face the New Year, acting as if the battle is lost. Christ is victor. Live with that confidence in your heart. As Hannibal said, "Only a few more struggles."

> His kingdom cannot fail, He rules o'er earth and
>   heaven;
> The keys of death and hell are to our Jesus given:
> Lift up your heart, lift up your voice!
> Rejoice, again I say rejoice!
> CHARLES WESLEY

REVELATION 15:1-4 (Song of Moses and the Lamb)

Then I saw in heaven another significant event, and it was great and marvelous. Seven angels were holding the seven last plagues, which would bring God's wrath to completion. ²I saw before me what seemed to be a crystal sea mixed with fire. And on it stood all the people who had been victorious over the beast and his statue and the number representing his name. They were all holding harps that God had given them. ³And they were singing the song of Moses, the servant of God, and the song of the Lamb:

"Great and marvelous are your actions,
    Lord God Almighty.
Just and true are your ways,
    O King of the nations.
⁴ Who will not fear, O Lord, and glorify your name?
    For you alone are holy.
All nations will come and worship before you,
    for your righteous deeds have been revealed."

Psalm Link
PSALM 98:2-3
² The LORD has announced his victory
    and has revealed his righteousness to every nation!
³ He has remembered his promise to love and be faithful
        to Israel.
    The whole earth has seen the salvation of our God.

*I*n North Africa in the dawn of the third century, some Christian women were put on trial for their faith. The officials tried to convince them to offer a sacrifice to the emperor and save their lives, but the women refused. After they were martyred, a contemporary wrote of the women: "The day of their victory dawned, and they walked from prison to the amphitheater as if they were walking to heaven, happy and serene in countenance."

People like that are singing in heaven, according to Revelation 15. They have won a victory over the enemies of Christ. How? By staying true to him despite enormous pressures. They are singing "the song of Moses . . . and of the Lamb," made up almost entirely of verses from the Psalms. The first song of Moses was composed when the Israelites emerged victorious from certain death in the Red Sea. And the Lamb of God, slain for us, arose victorious from death. So this song in Revelation 15 is the martyrs' victory song.

There are Christians in the world today who risk death to worship Christ, while many of us enjoy religious freedom. Have you been afraid this past year to let your allegiance to Christ be known? Are you swayed by the other gods of our age? Are you trying to practice dual citizenship, in this world and God's Kingdom?

The Lamb promises you ultimate victory if you take a stand for him. In the long run, you have nothing to lose.

> *Onward then, ye people, join our happy throng;*
> *Blend with ours your voices in the triumph song;*
> *Glory, laud, and honor unto Christ the King;*
> *This through countless ages, men and angels sing.*
> SABINE BARING-GOULD

Bible Networking
Notice all the similarities to the Psalms in this short song. See Psalms 92:5; 145:17; 86:9; 111:9; and 98:2.

REVELATION 19:1-8 (A Chorus of Hallelujahs)

After this, I heard the sound of a vast crowd in heaven shouting, "Hallelujah! Salvation is from our God. Glory and power belong to him alone. ²His judgments are just and true. He has punished the great prostitute who corrupted the earth with her immorality, and he has avenged the murder of his servants." ³Again and again their voices rang, "Hallelujah! The smoke from that city ascends forever and forever!"

⁴Then the twenty-four elders and the four living beings fell down and worshiped God, who was sitting on the throne. They cried out, "Amen! Hallelujah!"

⁵And from the throne came a voice that said, "Praise our God, all his servants, from the least to the greatest, all who fear him."

⁶Then I heard again what sounded like the shout of a huge crowd, or the roar of mighty ocean waves, or the crash of loud thunder: "Hallelujah! For the Lord our God, the Almighty, reigns. ⁷Let us be glad and rejoice and honor him. For the time has come for the wedding feast of the Lamb, and his bride has prepared herself. ⁸She is permitted to wear the finest white linen."

Psalm Link
PSALM 106:48

Blessed be the LORD, the God of Israel,
from everlasting to everlasting!
Let all the people say, "Amen!"

Praise the LORD!

No one remembers Charles Jenners, but it was his biblical excerpts that inspired George Frideric Handel to compose the *Messiah*. At points Handel became so excited at Charles's excerpts that he would jump up, wave his arms in the air, and shout, "Hallelujah! Hallelujah! Hallelujah!" He later recalled, "I did think I saw all heaven before me and the great God himself."

Handel's majestic "Hallelujah Chorus" is certainly inspiring, giving us a taste of the heavenly scene of Revelation 19. But just imagine what the real thing will be like!

Do you remember that Jesus and his disciples sang a hymn after the Last Supper? That hymn was undoubtedly the traditional Jewish Hallel (Psalms 113–118), which was sung at Passover to commemorate the Exodus. Now in Revelation 19 we have a new Hallel at another feast, the Marriage Supper of the Lamb. And this commemorates another deliverance—our escape from sin and death.

You may soon be celebrating the start of a new year, ringing out the old, ringing in the new. As you do, keep one word in mind: *Hallelujah!* Sometime in our future there's a party to end all parties. The Lamb of God will invite us to a bash that rings out the old life forever and rings in a new unity with him. Hatred, fear, and pride will go suddenly stale, as we feast on love, joy, and praise. What a day that will be! Hallelujah!

> *Alleluia! sing to Jesus! His the scepter, His the throne;*
> *Alleluia! His the triumph, His the victory alone;*
> *Hark! the songs of peaceful Zion thunder like a*
> *mighty flood;*
> *"Jesus, out of every nation has redeemed us by His*
> *blood."*
> WILLIAM CHATTERTON DIX

Fascinating Fact
The word hallelujah *occurs frequently in the Psalms, where it's translated "Praise the Lord," but Revelation 19 is the only appearance of the word in the New Testament.*

Notable Quotable
"There is something elevating about the praise of God. When we magnify His name and celebrate His glory, our own souls partake of greatness."
ROBERT E. COLEMAN

INDEX TO THE PSALMS

INDEX TO NON-PSALM PASSAGES

INDEX TO INTERLUDES

INDEX TO HYMN AUTHORS

INDEX TO NOTABLE QUOTABLES